The Testing of Vocation

The Testing of Vocation

Robert Reiss

CHURCH HOUSE PUBLISHING

Church House Publishing
Church House
Great Smith Street
London SW1P 3AZ

ISBN 978 0 7151 4332 2

Published 2013 for the Ministry Division of the Archbishops' Council
by Church House Publishing
in association with The Society of the Faith

The opinions expressed in this book are those of the author and do not necessarily reflect the official policy of the General Synod or the Archbishops' Council of the Church of England.

Typeset by Refine Catch Limited
Printed in England by
CPI Group (UK) Ltd, Croydon

Dedication

To the memory of Bishop Leslie Owen,
Chairman of CACTM when selection
conferences were established

Contents

Contents

The following illustrations are on pages 94 to 97

F. C. N. Hicks, General Secretary of CACTM 1913-24.

Bishop Llewellyn Gwynne, Deputy Chaplain-General to the British Expeditionary Forces 1915-18.

Students at Knutsford Test School c. 1920.

F. R. Barry, Principal of Knutsford Test School 1919-23.

Bishop Guy Warman, member of CACTM from 1913, Chairman 1928-43.

Meeting of the Church Assembly before the building of the present Church House, Westminster, c. 1930.

Bishop Leslie Owen, full-time Chairman of CACTM 1944-6.

Bishop Alwyn Williams, Chairman of the Archbishops' Commission on Training 1937-44.

Bishop Kenneth Riches, Director of Service Ordination Candidates 1943-5, Chairman of CACTM 1960-6.

Foreword

The Right Reverend Christopher Lowson

It can come as a surprise to learn that the concept of formal selection and theological education for ordained clergy in the Church of England is a relatively new one. As recently as the beginning of the twentieth century none of the diocesan bishops had gone to theological college prior to ordination; by the early 1920s the number had risen to four – some may argue that the greater entrepreneurial gifts of the bishops of those generations reflect that! Also, in 1901 there was little or no selection for training leading to ordination; neither was there any consistency in how men were selected for ordination.

As we approach the centenary of the Church of England's establishment of a central body to oversee the process of selection and training of candidates for the ordained ministry, I welcome this timely book which attempts to chart the development of the concept of vocation in the Church, alongside an account of the evolution of that central body into the Ministry Division of today.

Vocation has two aspects: an inner call and an external summons. These two aspects of vocation are not new: the are typified on the one hand by the calling of Isaiah in Chapter 6 – 'Here am I; send me!' – and by God's call to Jeremiah in Chapter 1 – '"Before I formed you in the womb I knew you, and before you were born I consecrated you; I appointed you a prophet to the nations".' (We might note in passing that although Jeremiah initially resisted the call, in the end he accepted it and became a prophet of the Lord.) Daring the course of the last century the Church of England wrestled with the question of whether to give one of these aspects priority over the other, and it continues to do so today.

While the Church was debating the nature of vocation, society in England was changing rapidly and radically. The main catalysts were the two world wars. After the Great War, society understood itself very differently, notably with the erosion of the class system and the struggle for women's suffrage, and then again after 1945 with the emergence of women in the workplace after their crucial role in factories and fields during World War Two, and the formation of the National Health Service and the Welfare State. In the latter half of the twentieth century social change and mobility continued at an ever more rapid rate. Throughout the centuries the Church has adapted in the light of social change so that it can react and respond to the society within and to which it is called to serve. The last century is no different, and Reiss charts the development of ministry from the model of an ordained priest in every parish in England, essentially unaltered since Saxon times, to the hugely diverse pattern we see today.

These recent changes in patterns of ministry have necessarily led to a need for the Church to reassess its understanding of vocation and service. Ordained ministry may still mean serving God and God's people as a parish priest, but in the twenty-first century it may also mean being a chaplain in a prison or a hospice, being a priest in secular employment, a chaplain to the armed forcer, a pastor on the streets of many of our towns and cities. Such diversity requires different models for selection and training. In the light of this emergent diversity, Reiss concludes that the external summons which comes from the Church should be given priority over any inner calling, and notes that, in Acts 6, the first deacons to be called to public ministry were chosen by the wider church community.

As the Church grapples with these issues, the Diocese of Lincoln has been an interesting and fertile test-bed in the search for effective and authentic expression of ordained ministry and continues to be so. Throughout the twentieth century the Diocese of Lincoln was at the forefront of the developing thinking about the nature of ordained ministry, whether at Lincoln Theological College, or now, as it re-imagines initial ministerial education and continuing ministerial development, or by its imaginative re-shaping of the deployment of ordained ministers in response to the changing needs of society and the places in which we minister.

Reiss, himself a former Team Rector of Grantham, notes that during this period, bishops of Lincoln have been regularly associated with the Church's oversight of selection and training for ministry. Edward King, Bishop at the beginning of the century, had previously been Principal of Cuddesdon; in the 1930s and 1940s, Leslie Owen was instrumental in setting up the first central body with oversight of selection and training; Kenneth Riches chaired this body through a time of significant change in the 1960s. Prior to my taking up office as Bishop of Lincoln, I was Director of the current central body for selection: the Ministry Division of the Archbishops' Council.

The rigorous testing of vocation and training for ministry are vital components of any living and dynamic church. This book chronicles the story of the Church of England's desire to equip itself with effective men and women to minister in an ever-changing world, that together we may fulfil our calling to proclaim the faith afresh in each generation.

+Christopher Lincoln:

List of Abbreviations

ABM	Advisory Board for Ministry
ACCM	Advisory Council for the Church's Ministry
APM	Auxiliary Parochial Ministry, but later Auxiliary Pastoral Ministry
ASB	Alternative Service Book 1980
BLA	British Land Armies
CACTM	Central Advisory Council of Training for the Ministry. From 1959 to 1966 Central Advisory Council for the Ministry
CA	Church Assembly
CBF	Central Board of Finance
CEE	Central Entrance Examination
CNAA	Council for National Academic Awards
DBF	Diocesan Board of Finance
DCG	Deputy Chaplain General
DDO	Diocesan Director of Ordinands
DLMA	Diocesan Lay Ministry Adviser
DSO	Distinguished Service Order
DSOC	Director of Service Ordination Candidates
GME	General Ministerial Examination
GOE	General Ordination Examination
GS	General Synod
LEA	Local Education Authority
LNSM	Local Non-Stipendiary Ministry
MC	Military Cross
MECCA	Missionary and Ecumenical Council of the Church Assembly
NSM	Non-Stipendiary Ministry
OCC	Ordination Candidates Committee
OCTU	Officer Cadet Training Unit
OIR	Officer Intelligence Ratings
OLM	Ordained Local Ministry

SM	Stipendiary Ministry
SPG	Society for the Propagation of the Gospel
SSM	Society of the Sacred Mission
UPE	Universities Preliminary Examination
VC	Victoria Cross
WOSB	War Office Selection Board

Some Key Dates

1901   The Upper House of the Convocation of Canterbury rejects a proposal from the Lower House to establish a Central Advisory Council to deal with matters for clergy training.

1908   The Archbishops' Commission publishes *The Report on the Supply and Training for Candidates for Holy Orders* which makes a number of recommendations, including the establishing of a Central Council.

      The Lambeth Conference includes a resolution that all candidates for ordination should eventually have a degree, which the Upper House of Canterbury thought should be brought into effect from 1917.

1912   The Bishops' Meeting agrees the constitution of the Central Advisory Council for the Training of the Ministry.

1913   CACTM meets for the first time under the chairmanship of Archibald Robertson, Bishop of Exeter. The Council agrees at its first meeting to delay until 1920 the implementation of the Lambeth Resolution regarding graduate status. It also agrees to press that graduate candidates for ministry should spend some period in a theological college.

1915   The Universities' Preliminary Examination changes its title to the General Ordination Examination.

1916   The Bishop of Exeter retires on grounds of ill health and is succeeded as Chairman by Winfrid Burrows, Bishop of Truro (translated to Chichester in 1919). In that year the Council agrees to postpone the implementation of the graduate status resolution until after the war.

The Archbishops of Canterbury and York (Davidson and Lang) issue a document to all serving military staff entitled 'Ordination After the War' which gave a clear commitment to returning servicemen that the Church would meet the cost of their training for ordination and would be flexible about the requirements for ancient languages.

1917   The creation of the Service Candidates Committee charged with the sifting of candidates for ordination from the services.

1918   What was to become the Knutsford Test School for returning servicemen to prepare them for ordination training starts in two centres in France and it moves to Knutsford Gaol in Cheshire in 1919 under F. R. Barry as Principal.

1920   The first meeting of the National Assembly of the Church of England, later to be known as the Church Assembly. From its start to 1922 there is a series of debates on the future of Knutsford, culminating in a decision to close it in 1922. The school continues, but without grants from the Church Assembly, on a much smaller scale for several more years.

The bishops accept that there should be a central register of ordination candidates.

1922   An inspection regime for theological colleges, started in 1913 but delayed by World War One, is completed and 28 colleges received official recognition.

1924   The Council's recommendation to abandon the proposal for graduate status is in effect accepted at a united session of the Upper Houses of Convocation and later formally by the Upper House of the Convocation of Canterbury in 1926.

The Church Assembly also accepts that CACTM is answerable to the bishops except on the allocation of funds, where it is answerable to the Church Assembly.

1927   The launch of the sponsorship scheme through a letter to *The Times* by Earl Grey, Chairman of the Central Board of Finance. The scheme operates through appeals in *The Times* until 1931. By then other bodies, both Diocesan Boards of Finance and bodies linked to various churchmanship traditions have started to raise significant sums of money for grants for ordination candidates to train.

Winfrid Burrows resigns as Chairman of CACTM and is succeeded in the following year by Guy Warman, Bishop of Chelmsford (translated to Manchester in 1929).

1928   Randall Davidson retires as Archbishop of Canterbury and is succeeded by the Archbishop of York, Cosmo Gordon Lang. Lang is succeeded at York by William Temple.

1937–44   The Archbishops' Commission on Training.

1942   Lang starts the process of forming a Service Ordinands Committee to deal with servicemen who might be ordained after the war. Lang retires in 1942 and is succeeded by Temple, who completes the process of forming the Service Ordinands Committee. Temple is succeeded at York by Cyril Forster Garbett.

1943   A new constitution for CACTM is agreed by the Church Assembly. Guy Warman resigns as chairman and is succeeded in the following year by Leslie Owen, Bishop of Maidstone, Bishop to the Forces and full-time Chairman of CACTM.

1944   CACTM agrees to use the War Office selection board method of choosing officers as the system for selecting ordinands, initially for candidates from the services but very quickly for all candidates. An experimental selection centre is held at Camberwell in

October 1944. Thereafter selection centres are held both in England and in various military centres abroad.

William Temple dies suddenly in October and is succeeded the following year by Geoffrey Fisher, Bishop of London, whose support for the principle of selection centres establishes them firmly.

1945   Report of the Financial Commission recommends that providing for the training of ordinands should be at the top of the list of priorities for the Church after the war.

1947   Leslie Owen dies having the year before moved to be Bishop of Lincoln. He is succeeded as Chairman of CACTM by Clifford Woodward, Bishop of Gloucester.

1949   A debate in the Church Assembly on the future financing of training does not accept a proposal from the CBF supported by CACTM that the financial responsibility should be passed to the dioceses. On the basis of an amendment proposed by the Bishop of Rochester it was agreed to leave CACTM to arrange the finances in consultation with the dioceses.

1950   The Bishop of Bath and Wells (Bradfield) succeeds the Bishop of Gloucester (Woodward) as Chairman.

1952   A Church Assembly commission on the financing of training recommends an apportionment system, with each diocese producing a sum for CACTM to distribute as grants, and the Central Fund for Ordination Candidates comes into being.

1953   The Committee on Central Funds is established by the Church Assembly. Its first report was considered by the Church Assembly in November 1956 and its final report in June 1957.

1955   The Archbishops appoint the Turner Commission to consider the capital needs of the theological colleges.

Some Key Dates

1957   The final report of the Committee on Central Funds includes a proposal to establish a Board of Ministry. It is defeated in the June Church Assembly. It is agreed to ask a new Commission under Kenneth Riches, Bishop of Lincoln, to consider both the Turner Commission's Report and the appropriate structure for dealing with ministry matters.

1959   The Riches Commission recommends the creation of a new board of ministry, but the proposal is amended in the February Church Assembly to revise CACTM to give it new additional responsibilities. The Central Advisory Council of Training for the Ministry becomes the Central Advisory Council for the Ministry, with a brief to examine wider ministry issues in addition to selection and training.

1960   Following the death in office of the Bishop of Bath and Wells (Bradfield) the Bishop of Lincoln (Riches) succeeds him as chairman.

1961   Michael Ramsey succeeds Geoffrey Fisher as Archbishop of Canterbury. He invites CACTM to examine the issue of 'supplementary ministries' which developed into non-stipendiary ministry.

1964   The Paul Report on *The Deployment and Payment of the Clergy* is published.

1965   Numbers of candidates drop dramatically and remain low for a number of years. A review of the constitution of CACTM after five years leads to the Advisory Council for the Church's Ministry coming into being. The Bishop of Warrington (Laurence Brown) succeeds the Bishop of Lincoln (Riches) and becomes the first Chairman of ACCM. Thereafter chairmen normally change every five to six years.

1968   *Theological Colleges for Tomorrow*, the report of the de Bunsen Commission, makes broad recommendations for the future of theological colleges, which lead to a process spread over the next seven years to reduce the number of theological colleges from 25 to 14.

1969   The General Synod debates 'A Supporting Ministry', which discussed the further development of non-stipendiary ministry.

1973   The Sheffield Scheme proposes a system for the fairer distribution of clergy between the dioceses and which is gradually implemented over the following years.

1975   *Alternative Patterns of Training* initiates a series of later reports dealing with non-residential training and in 1978 14 non-residential courses are recognized for training for both non-stipendiary and stipendiary ministry.

1978   The House of Bishops produces *The Future of the Ministry. A Report Containing Thirteen Resolutions of the House of Bishops*, which was endorsed by General Synod that year. This results in the establishment of the Ministry Co-ordinating Group.

A proposal from the Bishop of Birmingham to initiate the process of women being ordained is lost in General Synod, but the House of Bishops agrees to make the length of training the same for men and women candidates for all forms of ministry and introduces the General Ministerial Examination to replace the General Ordination Examination.

1980   *A Time of Review* begins a review of the selection methods leading to experiments with alternative patterns of conferences, including mixed conferences for men and women. The substantial changes become permanent from 1983.

The General Synod considers an ACCM report, *Local Ordained Ministry*, which allowed individual diocesan bishops to pursue that possibility within their dioceses.

Some Key Dates

1983   *A Strategy for the Church's Ministry* is published, written by Canon John Tiller, Chief Secretary of ACCM.

1987   *Education for the Church's Ministry*: the Report of the Working Party on Assessment (ACCM 22) recommends the abandonment of the General Ministerial Examination and its replacement by colleges and courses worked out locally with a validating institution and approved by ACCM.

               Women are ordained as deacons following the General Synod's vote in 1985.

1991   ACCM becomes the Advisory Board for Ministry (ABM), and produces the following year *Order and Diversity.*

1992   *Theological Training – A Way Ahead* is published, recommending among other things the closure of three theological colleges. The General Synod declines to 'take note' of the report, which results in a new group producing a further report the following year, which recommended the closure of two colleges and which was implemented.

1993   A new report on *Criteria for Selection* is produced by ABM.

1994   Women are ordained as priests following the General Synod vote in 1992.

1995   A review of the selection procedures results in further major changes to the selection system, brought into effect in 1997. From 1997 candidates are sponsored for either permanent non-stipendiary ministry or for a single category that includes both stipendiary and non-stipendiary clergy.

1998   *Stranger in the Wings* is published, a report on the 16 diocesan schemes for local non-stipendiary ministry which recommends the use of the title ordained local ministry.

1999   The Archbishops' Council comes into being replacing the role of the Standing Committee of the General Synod, and with all the bodies that were answerable to General Synod now being answerable to the Archbishops' Council. ABM becomes the Ministry Division under the new arrangements with additional responsibilities.

A Note on the Governance of the Church of England in the Twentieth Century

In 1900 the Church of England was essentially in the hands of the bishops and Parliament. Sir Andrew Lusk, the Liberal MP for Finsbury, said in 1878 'The Church is a department of the state for the management of which the House is responsible.'[1] However, pressure of parliamentary time meant that legislation relating to the Church often took a very long time to be dealt with.

From the middle of the nineteenth century the Convocations of the two Provinces of Canterbury and York became important contexts in which ecclesiastical issues could be discussed. The two Convocations were clerical bodies each with an Upper and Lower House, the Upper House being composed of the bishops of that Province and the Lower House of clergy from the Province. While the Lower Houses could make recommendations to the Upper Houses the final authority always lay with the bishops, who were of course also in the House of Lords. Meetings of the Houses of the two Convocations were fully reported in their published proceedings. There were also regular private meetings of the bishops from both Provinces which were not reported publicly. The bishops were always clear that responsibility for the selection and training of the clergy belonged to them.

There was pressure towards the end of the nineteenth century for laity to be represented in ways other than simply through those who were Members of Parliament, and by 1882 all but three dioceses had diocesan conferences. A lay house of the Convocation of Canterbury met for the first time in 1886, and there were some who argued for the clergy and the houses of laity to come together, but that did not happen until 1904, when the Representative Church Council, consisting of the two Convocations and the two houses of laity, met for the first time. These bodies had no legislative authority, and final authority for

---

1 Owen Chadwick, 1970, *The Victorian Church Part II*, London: SCM Press, p. 361. The nineteenth-century history is covered in pp. 359–65.

legislation still rested with the bishops and with Parliament, while the day-to-day management of the Church rested with the bishops who might consult the Convocations. The creation of the Central Advisory Council of Training for the Ministry in 1912 and the incorporation of the Central Board of Finance in 1914 were the first steps in the development of any form of central national bodies that had some administrative responsibility.

The 1919 Enabling Act created the National Assembly of the Church of England and is discussed in Chapter 5 and was later usually referred to as the Church Assembly. While the Convocations still met - and still do – more and more of the major discussions in the Church happened in the Church Assembly. It was replaced by the General Synod in 1970. The division of powers between the bishops and the Church Assembly and later the General Synod as it applied to the work of CACTM/ACCM/ABM is discussed throughout this book. The Archbishops' Council was created in 1999 and is discussed in Chapter 11.

1

Introduction: Vocation in the Twentieth Century

The ordained ministry in the Church of England changed dramatically during the twentieth century. In 1900 there were over 25,000 clergy serving a population of about 32 million in England and Wales.[1] By 2000 there were fewer than 12,000[2] within the diocesan structures of the Church of England, serving a population of just under 50 million in England. In 1900 the vast majority of the clergy were in stipendiary parochial ministry, but by 2000 a sixth of the serving clergy were non-stipendiary, a category created and developed in the second half of the century.

At the beginning of the century there was near universal agreement within the Church of England that it was responsible for providing a ministry of pastoral care based on the parochial system that would cover the whole of the nation. By the end of the century, while many still held to that ideal, there were other voices who stressed that the Church was by then in a missionary situation, with a far higher proportion of the population ignorant of the Christian faith, and which required a very different approach to ministry.

The social background from which the clergy came also broadened over the period, largely as a consequence of World War One and then the gradual development of a grants system that enabled ordinands to meet the cost of their training. Finance was, and remains, a critical issue.

The styles and manner of training also broadened. The hope of the bishops at the beginning of the century that all clergy would have a university degree was never realized, and in the first half of the century the ways of training expanded from university degrees only for some to an increasing use of residential theological colleges. In the second half of the century, however, there was also

---

1 Appendix N on statistics gives the details of where all the statistics in this book come from.

2 *Statistics of Licensed Ministers: Some Facts and Figures as of 31 December 2000* shows that there were 9,583 full-time stipendiary clergy, 148 part-time and 1,722 non-stipendiary ministers.

the development of non-residential part-time training that was available across the whole of England alongside the residential colleges.

While there were voices in the nineteenth century advocating better relations between different denominations, by the beginning of the twentieth century it very rarely translated into real ecumenical co-operation. Ecumenism developed throughout the twentieth century, and by the end much clergy training was done in ecumenical partnerships. But the nature of ordained ministry and the ways of reconciling the different understandings of it between different denominations remained a stumbling block. Within the Church of England, while most warmly welcomed the possibility, from 1994, of women being ordained, there remained a minority who were opposed, and handling the consequences of that was and remains a divisive issue in parts of the Church.

In 1912 the bishops agreed to the creation of a body to deal with many of the issues surrounding ordained ministry, although to start with it was largely concerned with training, as reflected in the first title of the body, the Central Advisory Council of Training for the Ministry (CACTM). Towards the end of World War Two it was also given oversight of selecting candidates for the ministry and then, in 1959, its title was changed to reflect yet wider responsibilities and it became the Central Advisory Council for the Ministry. In 1966 it was changed again to the Advisory Council for the Church's Ministry (ACCM); then, in 1991, to the Advisory Board of Ministry (ABM). Following the creation of the Archbishops' Council in 1999, it changed its name again to the Ministry Division.

Although the name changed and responsibilities were added in various ways and, after the creation of the Archbishops' Council in 1999, its accountability was slightly different, at each change the staff remained essentially the same and there was historical continuity. The core of this book is the history of that body told, wherever possible, in the words of some of those involved at each stage. While the Ministry Division continues to this day, and 2012 sees the 100th anniversary of the creation of its predecessor, CACTM, this book essentially ends at the end of the twentieth century as the changes that are going on now inevitably need the perspective of a few more years to judge what is finally significant.

Vocation

Throughout the period one word was regularly used about the ordained ministry: it was a vocation. Vocation as a concept is a multifaceted and, some might argue, even a muddled one.[3] At the most basic level there is the call to respond to Jesus' summary of the law, to love God and to love your neighbour. That is a call directed to the whole human race if they have the ears to hear. More specifically there is the call to respond to Jesus' request to follow him. That is directed to the Church as a whole and there is always a communal dimension to vocation in that sense; the call is to the Church to be the Church. That call is accepted implicitly by all who are baptized, and is the subject of some of the major writing about vocation in the twentieth century. Indeed it could be said that in thinking about its changing role in society the Church of England has been addressing the question of its corporate vocation, although the question has rarely been posed in that way. As this book will show, the Church of England is essentially a pragmatic body, responding to cultural and social changes less by detailed theological examination than by practical considerations of what might work. Those from other theological traditions might approach the matter differently.

Karl Barth included a substantial section on vocation in his *Church Dogmatics*,[4] although his concern there was far broader than any decision about what a person might do for his or her career, but more about all people receiving the divine call to become a Christian and to be faithful within that calling. Hans Urs von Balthasar's reaction to Barth[5] placed more emphasis on human response, but he did not address the issue of how the concept applied in terms of any personal career choice. Yet that is the third area where vocation is often used.[6] There has been surprisingly little by way of a thorough theological assessment of the concept of vocation as applied to individuals making a career choice written in the context of the Church of England in the twentieth century. As this book will show, from time to time it was addressed in books on other broader issues or in brief articles. F. R. Barry addressed it in *Vocation and Ministry*[7] published in 1958, as did Michael Ramsey, albeit briefly, in 1972, in *Christian Priesthood Today*[8] and Francis Dewar in 1991 *Called or Collared?: An Alternative*

---

3 A very helpful, if brief, guide to this is Gary Badcock, 1998, *The Way of Life: A Theology of Christian Vocation*, Grand Rapids: Eerdmans.

4 Karl Barth, *Church Dogmatics* Vol. IV/2. A useful brief series of extracts of Barth's writing on the subject can be found in William C. Platcher (ed.), 2005, *Callings*, Grand Rapids: Eerdmans.

5 Hans Urs von Balthasar, 1983, *The Christian State of Life*, San Fransisco: Ignatius Press.

6 This whole question is discussed in Badcock, pp. 54–70.

7 F. R. Barry, 1958, *Vocation and Ministry*, Welwyn: James Nisbet.

8 Michael Ramsey, 1972, *Christian Priesthood Today*, London: SPCK. Chapter 15 is 'The God who calls', pp. 100–5.

Approach to Vocation.[9] ACCM initiated a report on the subject entitled *Call to Order*, published in 1989, and there have been various articles in theological journals; and a lecture given by Mary Tanner to a conference of Diocesan Directors of Ordination and Lay Ministry Advisers in 1986 entitled *Towards a Theology of Vocation*[10] was often quoted, but otherwise there has been no careful and detailed theological examination of the notion in a Church of England context in the twentieth century. For the historian, that creates a problem, because much of what was said about vocation was probably said in private conversation, and subtle changes in the understanding of what was meant by the word may have happened over the century without it being made explicitly clear in the literature, or even clearly passed on from one generation to the next.

The word is also used in a wider sense than simply to holding a religious office, as in 'vocational training', which might apply to any preparation for a career. As early as 1785, when Samuel Johnson's *Dictionary of the English Language* was published, while vocation could certainly mean a calling by the will of God, it was already being used in the more general sense of a trade or employment. Partly this followed Martin Luther's discussion of vocation. Prior to the Reformation in medieval Europe, vocation would have been used almost exclusively in connection with a calling to a religious office, either as a priest or as a member of a religious community. Luther protested against such a narrow usage, especially if it were believed to be one that gave a person a privileged position with respect to God. He believed that the essential call of Christ to follow him was directed to all Christians and not just to those in some exclusive religious category, and the call was to love God and love one's neighbour. Also, in protest at the requirement of celibacy, Luther believed that someone could equally be called to marriage, which he also saw as a vocation. A person's vocation was the life they lived in terms of Christian service in whatever outward form that might be, which might well include a Christian man or woman having a vocation to marriage and pursuing a task that was not exclusively Christian as long as it was consistent with loving one's neighbour.

In Luther's time many people's occupation was determined by what he described as their station in life, so, for example, a person born into a farming

---

9 Francis Dewar, 1991, rev. 2000, *Called or Collared?: An Alternative Approach to Vocation,* London: SPCK.

10 A copy was lent by Mary Tanner to the author, but it has never been published.

community would almost certainly have had little choice but to work on the land, which Luther saw as their vocation. Those who had the opportunity of choosing a profession, which would have been only a fairly small proportion of the population, had to go through the process of application, passing whatever the examination requirements were for that profession and then being offered some sort of post; it is no accident that in German the word for profession (*Beruf*) means literally 'calling', but the 'calling' was done by those responsible for recruiting into the particular profession or career as well as by the inclinations given by God to the individual concerned.[11]

The wider application of vocational language was developed by Troeltsch in his *The Social Teaching of the Christian Churches* (1911). Troeltsch noted that in the first three centuries of the Christian Church it saw itself as a beleaguered minority in a society under the control of the devil, and so had no theological framework against which to develop a positive understanding of work. But in a post-Constantinian world, that began to change and society began to be seen as an organism established by the will of God. Any work that maintained or contributed towards the good ordering of society could be seen as fulfilling the will of God, and could be seen as the fulfilling of a vocation. Vocation in that wider sense raises large issues and has been the subject of extensive literature both from theological and sociological perspectives. It does, however, go well beyond the bounds of this particular book.

Vocation as a guide to a career choice

The narrower question of personal career choice obviously turns on one very fundamental question, the nature of God and the consequential issue of how God's relationship to the believer is seen. How specific is God's will? It is interesting to note that two clear but rather different views on that emerge from theological traditions that might have been expected to take opposite points of view.

One approach is in a booklet from a Roman Catholic perspective entitled *Vocation* written as recently as 1975. The author states:

The one who is calling is God. He has a specific plan for every man and woman who will ever exist and, in each plan, his own divine will and human

---

11 Luther's understanding of vocation is well described in Gustav Wingren, 1958, *The Christian's Calling,* trans. Carl C. Rasmussen, Edinburgh: Oliver and Boyd.

freedom of action are wonderfully bound up with one another ... Everything that happens to us is part of the plan, whether it seems to be just chance or the result of our own careful deliberation. We belittle the whole idea of divine vocation if we see it as nothing more than the religious equivalent of what we call vocation in the professional field or in society. God's call is not, when we really come down to it, something that arises from whatever aptitudes we happen to have, or whatever our natural inclinations suggest to us, nor is it a matter of being strongly drawn to some particular job. The call from God is something more than this. It is something quite objective, which arises from the eternal plan of God, and it cannot be reduced to a mere human choice.[12]

That is one approach, and no doubt there are Anglican clergy who would see their lives in that light, but apart from the difficulties of sustaining such a view of God's plan for every individual in the face of such events as the Holocaust or earthquakes or tsunamis, it is also difficult to see how it can easily be related to any notion a person may have of having some genuine freedom of choice. So at the other end of the spectrum there will be those who hold that God's will is far more general; it will include the wish that God's Church will be adequately led, and that a person's life should be fulfilling; but how that should be done, and by whom, God leaves to us human beings to decide for ourselves, and it is for human beings then to take responsibility for their own decisions.

With such reasons in mind a different point of view is presented by Gary D. Badcock, in his illuminating book *The Way of Life: A Theology of Christian Vocation*.[13] Writing from the perspective of an academic theologian who was also a lay minister in the Church of Scotland and knowledgeable therefore of the Calvinist tradition, he questions whether God has a specific plan for each person, indeed he holds that such a vision of Christian vocation is extremely unhelpful. Rather he believes that each Christian is free to examine him- or herself and their own gifts and to make decisions in the light of others' advice as to what to do with their lives. It is, he believes, quite possible for a Christian to ask themself what gifts God has given them, how those gifts might most

---

12 Jose Luis Soria, 1975, *Vocation*, London: Tamezin Publications.
13 Badcock, *Way of Life*.

constructively be used and so identify a number of career options from which he or she has to make a choice. If the personal decision is that the ordained ministry of the Church might be an appropriate way of using those gifts, then a person might reasonably apply, and it is then for the Church to decide. Following Luther, Badcock holds that the Christian vocation comes not in what a person does but how they do it. For example, he notes that it is quite possible for a theologian to be self-centred and faithless, as indeed it can be for a Church minister. God's call, he believes, lies not in the choice of career but in genuinely loving God and your neighbour in whatever career you pursue.

When it came to men offering to be ordained to the service of the Church, Luther believed that it was not essentially different from entering any other profession; it meant acquiring the academic qualifications required by the profession and being offered a post in a church. It was the congregation that called, which of course meant that the minister was its servant. It also meant that ministerial office could be temporary, and a man was a minister because a congregation had called him to that role, If for some reason the minister left that congregation and returned to a non-ministerial role, he ceased to be a minister, although he could always later be called to be a minister in another congregation. Later in the Lutheran tradition that was to be modified and today someone who has been ordained but is without a pastoral role is known as a minister *ausser Dienst*, without service.

Of the other Reformation leaders John Calvin had a different view from Luther's. He believed that the Church should certainly test and examine a call to ministry, but he believed that the call came ultimately from God, which clearly gave the minister authority over the congregation. The Church of England, if it followed any particular Protestant leader's view, tended more towards the Calvinist view at the time of the Reformation, but that was to change. It is therefore to the Church of England's experience of vocation in the last century that we must now turn.

Vocation in the Church of England

Throughout the twentieth century there were always some in the Church of England who spoke of the question of whether someone should be ordained as 'Has he (or later, also, she) got a vocation?' On the face of it that was a strange way of putting the question. It is difficult to imagine those responsible for selecting people for any other profession using such language. They may have asked why somebody wanted to work in that field in order to examine the nature of their commitment to the task, or whether a candidate had the intellectual ability, or the personality, or possibly even the leadership capacity to be a barrister, doctor, teacher, or nurse. Yet in common parlance any of those professions might have been described as a vocation.

At the beginning of the twentieth century there were no official Church of England documents on ministry other than the Canons, the Book of Common Prayer and the Thirty-Nine Articles. Various individuals had written on many aspects of the subject, and in the Church of England Year Books there was a certain amount about training, but there was nothing official other than what was contained in those documents. Yet the Thirty-Nine Articles and the Prayer Book were read against, and to some extent reflected, a rather confusing biblical picture of various models of vocation.

On the one hand there was the call to be a prophet, most notably given in the example of the call of Isaiah in chapter 6. One evangelical writer, W. H. Griffith Thomas, Principal of Wycliffe Hall from 1905 to 1910, writing in 1911, said of that call, 'This call and consciousness of God is essential to a man at the outset of his ministry. Unless he has it, he had better not start out. The ministry is a vocation, not a profession.'[14] He then examines the ministry of the Twelve, noting that the choice of them by Christ was a personal choice, and says, 'Selection for the ministry must come from Christ Himself, and must be due to His personal relation to the soul ... A divine call is imperative.'[15] He clearly put a great emphasis on the inward call to the individual by the Holy Spirit, 'all true ministry must commence here. It must be in some way the immediate appeal of God to the soul ... This call will not be primarily through the Church or the Bishop, but it is the internal work of the Holy Spirit.'[16]

That view lay behind much of the popular notion of vocation to the ordained ministry throughout the twentieth century.

But on Thomas' own evidence it was not universal. He comments, 'A friend of mine who has to interview candidates for the ministry once told me that many of the men who came before him were quite unable to adduce any definite proofs of a call from above. Indeed, they were without an idea on the subject,

---

14 W. H. Griffith Thomas, 1911, *The Work of the Ministry*, London: Hodder and Stoughton, p. 6.
15 Thomas, *Work*, p. 26.
16 Thomas, *Work*, p. 111f.

hopelessly confused about any such thing.'[17] At the beginning of the last century it is therefore evident that an inward strong sense of calling, while demanded by some principals of theological colleges, was far from universal.

Of the biblical patterns of calling, to be a prophet was not a calling to any recognized ministerial office, but to speak a truth that to the prophet concerned was overwhelming. That model by itself could not have constituted the grounds for becoming an Anglican clergyman, but others thought it should be added to the call of the disciples by Jesus. However, even within that model there is clearly a distinction to be made between a disciple who was personally called by Jesus during his earthly life and someone who offered for service in the Church after his death. The call by the historical Jesus in his lifetime was unambiguous and was very clearly directed by Jesus to the person concerned, but after Jesus' death, while someone might feel called by Christ, there was not the objectivity of receiving any call direct from the historical Jesus.

Neither being a prophet nor being a disciple was exactly like holding ministerial office under the authority of the Church, and if we come to the call to such offices in the New Testament after the death of Jesus we find different models. First there was the rather strange notion in the appointment of Matthias to fill the place left by Judas, where he was appointed by the drawing of lots. Then there were people appointed by the apostles as in the Council of Jerusalem in Acts 15 for a specific task, or by men such as St Paul to particular positions of leadership in local churches. Most notably, in chapter 6 of Acts, there was the appointment of men to serve as deacons in the emerging church.

And the twelve called together the whole community of the disciples and said, 'It is not right that we should neglect the word of God in order to wait at tables. Therefore, friends, select from among yourselves seven men of good standing, full of the Spirit and of wisdom, whom we may appoint to this task, while we, for our part, will devote ourselves to prayer and to serving the word.' What they said pleased the whole community, and they chose Stephen, a man full of faith and the Holy Spirit, together with Philip, Prochorus, Nicanor, Timon, Parmenas, and Nicolaus, a proselyte of Antioch. They had these men stand before the apostles, who prayed and laid their hands on them. (Acts 6:2–6)

---

17 Thomas, *Work*, p. 111.

Since all Anglican clergy must be appointed deacon before they are subsequently ordained as priests, it is not surprising that model was before Cranmer when he produced the Anglican Ordinal, which he did in consultation with Martin Bucer, the Protestant theologian who had been influential in the production of the rite used in Strasbourg. Candidates for the diaconate, priesthood and episcopal office were asked in a question that only slightly varied between each of the three orders of ministry, 'Do you think you are truly called, according to the will of our Lord Jesus Christ, to the Ministry of the Church?' to which the candidate replied, 'I think so.' However, Cranmer included an additional question for deacons: 'Do you trust that you are inwardly moved by the Holy Ghost to take upon you this Office and Ministration, to serve God for the promoting of His glory and the edifying of His people?' In his study of the Anglican Ordinal, Paul Bradshaw[18] believes that question is related to the passage from Acts dealing with the selection of the seven deacons, although of course the quotation says nothing about the men chosen being 'moved by the Holy Spirit' to offer; it simply says they were 'full of the Spirit', and neither does it say anything about the process of appointment. A more detailed comment on that is left to Article 23 of the Thirty-Nine Articles, which says of 'Ministering in the Congregation':

> It is not lawful for any man to take upon him the office of publick preaching, or ministering of the sacraments in the Congregation, before he be lawfully called and sent to execute the same. And those we ought to judge lawfully called and sent, which be chosen and called to this work by men who have publick authority given unto them in the Congregation, to call and send Ministers into the Lord's vineyard.

That is, of course, wholly consistent with the Acts 6 reading, where 'the Apostles direct the people to choose ...' That the Church had a vital role in choosing its clergy was clear even from the Thirty-Nine Articles.

Interestingly, Thomas makes no reference at all to Article 23 in his book on the work of the ministry although he quotes many of the other Articles. But that was not the stance of all evangelical writers; the Bishop of Liverpool, J. C. Ryle, a notable leader of the evangelical wing of the Church, quoted the Article with approval in his essay 'Thoughts on the Church' in *Principles for Churchmen*.[19]

---

18 Paul Bradshaw, 1971, *The Anglican Ordinal*, London: SPCK.

19 J. C. Ryle, 1884, *Principles for Churchmen*, London: W. Hunt and Co. p. 137.

It would be too simple to say that evangelicals supported the priority of the inward call and Anglo-Catholics favoured a call by the Church; the picture was far more varied than that.

However, it was a moderate Tractarian, Robert Moberly, Regius Professor of Pastoral Theology at Oxford from 1892 to 1903, who dwelt more on the role of the Church in his important work *Ministerial Priesthood*.[20] Moberly certainly thought that a divine commission was essential, but he examined three different ways in which that commission might be recognized by an individual.

First, there was the possibility of a divine calling manifesting itself purely in the conscience of the individual, which he considered was in some way the picture of prophetic Christian ministry given in the Didache, an early Church manual on morals and church practice. He was not convinced of that model, partly because of the possibility of self deception: 'It is certain that nothing is more apt to be manifestly self-deceiving than the fancies of a man's brain about himself or his own inspiration.' He thought that simply relying on a person's inward conviction, even if it were apparently supported by some allegedly miraculous sign, was no grounds for giving the decision credibility as 'it is at least an open question, on New Testament principles, whether the whole should not be treated far rather as an inscrutable delusion than a veritable sign from God.'[21] The view that an inward call to ministry was sufficient by itself was to him incredible.

Moberly believed that in the incarnation Jesus was seen to act through the things of nature, and that he describes as the principle of sacramental acts: 'The principle that inward acts through outward, grace through means of grace, Spirit through Body ... is a principle which in the great vital fact of the Incarnation seems to have received its full and final consecration.'[22] If Jesus acted through the things of nature, then that is how God still acts. If we are to talk about how Christ acts now, we cannot simply see him or the Holy Spirit as some sort of disembodied force flowing in people's minds; he acts through his body, the Church. And as the Church has that role, the Church must be involved in the process of appointing its clergy.

---

20 R. C. Moberly, *Ministerial Priesthood*, first published in 1897 by John Murray. Page numbers are taken from the edition reprinted by SPCK in 1969, with an Introduction by A. T. Hanson.

21 Moberly, *Priesthood*, p. 110.

22 Moberly, *Priesthood*, p. 105f.

If the principle of the consecration of the material and the outward has no place in the public authorisation of ministers to minister in spiritual things, the entire method which pervades the life of Christ's Church, the whole rationale of the sacramental system, is *pro tanto* invalidated.[23]

So Moberly believed that the Church must be involved in some way in the accepting of candidates for ministry, and that led him to the two other ways of looking at how the individual could receive Christ's commission. First, he thought there was a notion that the Church in every age could simply decide on how to organize its ministry according to the local needs. 'The Church is in no way bound. She can provide for herself ministers and instruments wherever, or however, she thinks fit.' That was, on the whole, the view of the more liberal members of the Church at the end of the nineteenth century, that the ministry of the Church was simply a convenient creation by the Church as a way of organizing its life.

In contrast to that, though, there was his third way which he describes as:

The familiar church view that none can be held divinely commissioned until he has received commission on earth from those who themselves have received authority to commission from such as held it in like manner before them; that is, when the matter is pressed home, that valid ministerial authority depends, upon its earthward side, upon continuous transmission from the Apostles of Jesus Christ.[24]

Here he was arguing for the doctrine of the apostolic succession; ministers have authority to minister in the Church because it was given them by those who could trace the line of authority back to Christ himself or, as he put it, 'Those only are duly commissioned who have received commission from such, before them, as were themselves commissioned to commission others.'

So, right at the beginning of the century there was a spectrum from those like Thomas, who essentially saw some sense of an inward call as the critical starting point of a true vocation, to those like Moberly, who put more emphasis on the role of the Church in choosing men, and at that stage it was just men, to enter the ministry.

---

23 Moberly, *Priesthood,* p. 106.
24 Moberly, *Priesthood,* p. 105f.

The Thomas view, however, was certainly widely held by many throughout much of the twentieth century, and after selection conferences started, many candidates would give evidence of some 'sign' they had been given to show that God wanted them to be ordained, and for some selectors that was of great importance. But also throughout the century there were some significant figures who raised questions about the emphasis put on 'the inward call'. Three examples will suffice at this stage, although more will be found in later chapters.

First, in the debate in the Upper House of Canterbury Convocation on a report from the Lower House on Supply and Training on 8 May 1901, the then recently appointed Bishop of London (Winnington-Ingram) noted a number of difficulties facing men considering ordination, and his first difficulty related to the nature of vocation. His language made a distinction between what he called 'the subjective call', by which he meant the type of inward call that Thomas was to write about, and 'the objective call', which was the call by the Church for ordained ministers.

> The objectiveness of the call is often left out when we speak about the subjective call. Time after time I have found that many of our best men have held back from a feeling of modesty. They have waited, as it were, for some voice from heaven. What they did not realise was the very great cry of the vast population for someone to come to help them. I have put before them that men have volunteered to go to South Africa [presumably those volunteering to fight in the Boer War] because of the great cry of the country's need, and I have put forward that the Church of England was asking for them, and that the cry was ringing through heaven and earth, and it was the answer that they had to give. I believe that time after time men have given themselves and said, 'here am I; send me', in a modest, self-sacrificing spirit when they have once understood that it is the will that is wanted rather than an over-exaggerated state of feeling.[25]

Second, in 1938, H. L. Goudge, Regius Professor of Divinity at Oxford, wrote a book entitled *The Church of England and Reunion*. In it he made the following statement:

---

25 Upper House of Canterbury Convocation on a report from the Lower House on Supply and Training, 8 May 1901, p. 137.

The first question put to those to be ordained to the Diaconate in the Anglican Ordinal – 'Do you trust that you are inwardly moved by the Holy Ghost to take upon you this office and ministration' ...? – is nothing less than a disaster. It has probably lost to the ministry hundreds of men who might have made admirable clergy; and it tends to cause painful searchings of heart in times of depression to many rightly ordained. A good meaning can be attached to the question, but what it suggests is the necessity for a strong sense of vocation, as in the case of an Old Testament prophet ... Our Reformers, misled by Martin Bucer, confused the regular with the prophetic ministry. The position of prophets does largely rest upon their inward call. The Church ... recognises their position and discriminates between true prophecy and false; but it does no more than this. But the position of the regular ministers, who may have no remarkable gifts, depends upon their ordination and commission by the Apostles, and it is for others to judge of their suitability rather than for themselves. They must believe that they are doing the will of God in what they do, and must keep back nothing which those who ordain them ought to know; but Scripture does not justify us in asking more than this, nor does any Church Ordinal earlier than the sixteenth century.[26]

Third, in April 1944 the issue came to the fore again through an article in *Theology* entitled 'Means and Ends' by A. G. Hebert SSM, himself much involved in the training of ordinands at Kelham and a member of the Archbishops' Commission on Training that started its work in 1937.

What constitutes vocation? There is first the fundamental principle of the essential sanctity of every honest way of life, and the relation of the priesthood to all those other vocations. With regard to this special vocation, there is the call of God, consisting in His purpose for a man's life; but how is that call known? A man's belief that he is called by God does not prove it, since various disturbing psychological factors come in, but needs to be checked by the judgment of others qualified to judge, especially those in charge of his training. Finally, there is the call, definite and irreversible,

---

26 H. L. Goudge, 1938, *The Church of England and Reunion*, London: SPCK, p. 181.

which the Church itself gives in the act of ordination. There is much here needing to be disentangled.[27]

Such disentangling as there was partly came about in the context of recruitment, and one of the men most involved in that was F. R. Barry. After being Principal of the Test School at Knutsford described in Chapters 4 and 5 he moved to be Professor of Theology at King's College, London, then became Vicar of the University Church in Oxford, and then a Canon of Westminster, where he combined his canonry with being Rector of St John's Smith Square. In all of those roles except perhaps the last he had much to do with the care of ordinands, and when, towards the end of World War Two, he was made Bishop of Southwell he was an obvious candidate for being chairman of what was then known as the recruitment committee of CACTM.

In 1958 he wrote *Vocation and Ministry*, which influential book discussed at some length the nature of vocation. He defended the notion of a divine calling: 'No one can take this Ministry upon him unless he be "inwardly moved by the Holy Ghost" and believes himself to be "truly called according to the will of our Lord Jesus Christ". These solemn phrases are guardians at the gate.'[28] But he goes on to argue for a far wider understanding of vocation than purely religious service. 'Vocation is not an officer's privilege which privates in the Church should not expect.'[29] In the case of those seeking ordination he thought one of the tests would be a desire to do it. 'On the whole the divine Artist works with the grain in the wood of character and inclination, rather than against it'[30] and 'a man's vocation is what he can do best.'[31]

On the critical question of how someone can know that ordination is the right way forward for them, while he acknowledged that a few people simply 'know' what they must do, most spend some time searching for their right role in life. In that decision he thought the advice of others was critical, as was a careful looking at the person's own constitutional make-up. 'The inward call must be taken in dead earnest. But it is, I think, true to say, in general, that its

---

27 A. G. Hebert, April 1944, *Theology*, p. 81.
28 Barry, *Vocation*, p. 7f.
29 Barry, *Vocation*, p. 9.
30 Barry, *Vocation*, p. 11.
31 Barry, *Vocation*, p. 22.

genuineness cannot be attested solely by inward and subjective proof.[32] He was therefore sceptical about those looking for special signs:

> To a few such visitations do come; but they certainly do not in the majority of cases; and they come very rarely to Anglo-Saxons. They ought not to be expected as normal, and in any case they are rather the accompaniments of the 'real thing' than the 'real thing' itself. We must not equate the reality of a call with its psychological or emotional temperature.[33]

He therefore believed the choice by the Church was critical but:

> One knows of Christians to whom it seems impious to suggest any idea of ordination where it is not being entertained already. The inner call (they think) is so sacred, so intimate, that no human being may rightly 'interfere' with its operation. We can respect their conscientious scruples, but they are theologically unsound. What kind of theology is it which suggests that God does not act through human agency, so that only those can be called 'acts of God' for which we can give no rational explanation? This may be the theology of insurance companies, but surely it is not that of the Christian Church. Christian experience on the whole refutes it. Nearly all the gifts of God's grace are mediated and conveyed to us directly or indirectly through the lives and influences of other men and women. That is surely implied in our membership in the Church and our community in the Holy Spirit.[34]

Some did not like the word 'recruitment' in that context, but he was very firmly in favour of it as he believed the Church had a duty to present the challenge of ministry to the most able in the land and invite them to consider whether that may not be for them. In his autobiography published in 1970 after his retirement, and freed from the constraints imposed by being a serving diocesan bishop, he wrote:

> Bishop Walter Frere said more than once that it had been a disastrous mistake when the Church had come to lay almost exclusive emphasis on the

---

32 Barry, *Vocation*, p. 24.
33 Barry, *Vocation*, p. 25.
34 Barry, *Vocation*, p. 28.

interior 'call' to Holy Orders. (It is a familiar fact that the weakest candidates, and by any rational standard the least fitted, are often invincibly certain of having been 'called'.) The call should come initially from the Church – meaning the Church, not merely its officials – and it has now to be publicly proclaimed. No committee, meeting in Westminster, could hope to supply the Church with the men it needed. All it could do was to get the facts presented and to try to stimulate local effort, in the dioceses and the parishes. If anything was to happen at all, the whole Church has got to be in on it.

On the basis of that, he believed that recruitment to the ministry was essential, and as we shall see he was quite effective in bringing that policy to bear, but he noted:

The word 'recruitment' came under criticism, as suggesting a kind of psychological press-gang. That was not in the least what we intended by it. What we meant was a resolute effort to secure that all concerned did hear the call, and hear it as something that might be addressed to themselves ... The Ministry had to be got back on the map again, and presented as something which could claim, and needed, the strongest and ablest men available, not the leavings of other professions. What was wanted now, on the widest possible scale, was a church-wide publicity campaign to put the claim of the ministry across ... I never ceased from insisting to my colleagues that the prime consideration was quality. If any profession seems to be in low water, put up the requirements – the Army learnt that long ago. When recruitment was flagging in the first war, the War Office raised the chest measurement. The more you ask for, the more you will get. If the Church gives the impression that it is prepared to accept men who could not make a living elsewhere, the more gifted will certainly look in another direction. To lower the standard in order to fill up the ranks is, for the Church, a policy of suicide. But for this I have found it hard to win more than lip service. I fear the Church has, on the whole, been too ready to think more of quantity than quality. I still believe that if we had been brave enough to require higher standards of qualification, we should have got more men as well as better men. And in the situation we are now in, a sub-standard Ministry may do positive harm.[35]

---

35 F. R. Barry, 1970, *Period of My Life*, London: Hodder and Stoughton, pp. 186–8.

But by quality he did not simply mean academic qualifications. He had written in *Vocation and Ministry,*

> Scholarship is not everything. First class men are not always men with first-classes. The pastoral work of Ministry demands many qualifications other than intellectual; understanding, sympathy, strength of character and those personal endowments that make for leadership. There are men endowed with these in full measure but lacking in scholastic ability.[36]

Barry's influence lasted for a long time, but by the 1980s other voices were heard within what by then was ACCM, and the Recruitment Committee was renamed the Vocations' Committee. It was a victory for a certain sort of spirituality, though there was little agreement on whether the new title was more effective. But disquiet was almost immediately being expressed not so much about the name of the Committee but about the emphasis on the 'inward call'. In 1985 ACCM published a series of essays entitled *Ministers of the Kingdom,*[37] which was an exploration of non-stipendiary ministry. In it Preb. Dr Kenneth Noakes quoted H. L. Goudge in the passage noted above and asserted the need for some element of the community calling people into ministry, which he thought might be developed in non-stipendiary ministry. That and other factors, including some concern about numbers, led to ACCM taking the initiative to set up a working party under the chairmanship of Peter Baelz, Dean of Durham, to examine the notion of vocation, which reported in 1989 with *Call to Order.*[38] The introduction included this comment on the practice of the Church:

> The approach has been one that is 'vocation-led' with a strong emphasis on the inner call of the individual to a particular role. When candidates have been in short supply this has led to a call to 'foster' vocations, and when numbers have increased the need for such vocations work, and the provision of resources for it, has been questioned. Increasingly however this approach has been seen to be both practically ineffective and theologically questionable.[39]

---

36 Barry, *Vocation,* p. 103.

37 P. Baelz and W. M. Jacob (eds), 1985, *Ministers of the Kingdom: Explorations in Non-Stipendiary Ministry,* London: CIO.

38 ACCM, 1989, *Call to Order. Vocation and Ministry in the Church of England.*

39 *Call to Order,* p. vii.

The report recommended a policy described as 'vigorous recruitment, rigorous selection, sustained support' and included the following statement on vocation:

> If our view of the theology of vocation is accepted, a view which we reached in conversation with scripture, tradition and experience, then it follows that the language of an inner call is neither the sole nor the most appropriate language to be used in connection with what is essentially a community office or role. In this context it is the community which, under God, calls, appoints and ordains. Consequently, instead of responding to a shortage of ordained ministers with a programme designed to 'foster vocations', the church would do far better to pursue a policy of vigorous and intelligent recruitment. It will need to identify those to whom God has given gifts that could and should be used for the work of ordained ministry, to ask them to consider seriously the possibility of devoting their lives to this work, and, indeed, to challenge them to suggest a good reason why they should not accept the responsibility which the community wishes them to assume.[40]

It is notable that, despite that report, in 2000 there was still within the Ministry Division a Vocations' Advisory Panel, although it was part of an overall body known as the Vocations, Recruitment and Selection Committee.

Later developments

Two other developments in ministry in the Church of England had their effect in the latter part of the twentieth century on thinking about vocation: the ordination of women and the development of ordained local ministry.

Arguments for the ordination of women came from at least two different routes. There were a number of women candidates, no doubt reflecting the views of parts of the Church from which they came, who suggested that because they personally felt a call to ordained ministry and that others thought they would be good potential priests, the Church should therefore accept their claim. Those who stressed that ordination was a matter of the Church's choosing rather than simply some form of a personal inner sense of calling were reluctant

---

40 *Call to Order,* p. 59f.

to accept such an argument by itself. But the other route for arguing for women to be ordained was from the perspective of what the Church needed. Here the argument was that if the priesthood was to represent humankind to God, a priesthood that included the feminine would be more representative of humanity and would therefore be a more complete priesthood.

The proposal to ordain women required a two-thirds majority in each house of General Synod, and in the vote in 1992 it only just obtained that in the House of Laity but it was accepted rather more comfortably in the House of Clergy and the House of Bishops. What the comparative strength of each of those ways of arguing for the ordination of women was on those who voted is impossible to measure, but on the basis of the arguments advanced by Moberly at the beginning of the twentieth century, the second of the two arguments would be the only one that could be satisfactorily measured by that yardstick.

The second development to affect reflection on vocation was the development of what finally came to be called ordained local ministry, described in Chapter 11. The Advisory Board for Ministry's Policy Paper 1, published in 1991, said, 'It is a mark of Local Non-Stipendiary Ministers that they should have been invited by the local church to set out on the path towards ordination.' In the Working Party's review of this style of ministry *Stranger in the Wings*,[41] the survey initiated by the working party asked OLMs, 'How did you come to recognize that God wanted you to be a priest?' and their answers were coded according to three themes, personal, vicar and congregation. The personal was the most significant theme for 30 of the respondents; the congregation was the most significant for 27; and the vicar most significant for five. The original desire of Policy Paper 1 was not therefore entirely fulfilled, but it does seem that just over half of those ordained did so because of initiatives of others rather than from any more personal inward calling.

Liturgical expressions of vocation

A further dimension to the question of vocation comes in the area of liturgy, and particularly by a change to the liturgy that came in with the Alternative Service Book published in 1980. Cranmer's question in the making of deacons was in the present tense, '*are* you inwardly moved by the Holy Ghost?' and the question

---

41 *Stranger in the Wings: A Report on Local Non-Stipendiary Ministry,* GS Misc. 532, 1998.

was asked in the context of the service when someone was just about to be made deacon. It was quite possible to interpret that as meaning that if that condition was met, the act of making that person a deacon gave them their vocation, even if at the time many who had been motivated by the notion of some sort of 'inward call' did not interpret it in that way. The first draft of the ASB replaced that for all three orders of ministry with the question, 'Do you trust that God has called you to the office and work of deacon in his Church?' to which the response was, 'I trust that I am called.' The significant change was that it moved the question into the past tense, 'that God *has* called you.' The effect, apparently unrecognized at the time, was to separate the receiving of a vocation from the act of ordination. The change gave a firmer liturgical basis than it had ever before to the notion of vocation as something that somehow started in the mind of God and which was conveyed by God into a person's heart. And that emotional element in it was further advanced when the Revision Committee accepted a proposal that their original wording lacked warmth, and so turned the first draft question into the one that finally appeared for all three orders of ministry, 'Do you believe, insofar as you know your own heart, that God has called you to the office of . . .'

Although it is slightly beyond the period of this book, it is worth recording the end of that process of liturgical revision culminating in the creation of *Common Worship.* The book of *Services and Prayers for the Church of England* was published in 2000, but work then continued on additional services, and a draft from the Liturgical Committee on a new Ordinal was produced for discussion in General Synod in 2004 which contained the same question as the one posed in the ASB. In the debate the representative of the Orthodox Churches, Archimandrite Ephrem Lash, expressed his concern about that question. He spoke of a former Anglican Bishop of Bombay and said:

> Some thirty years later, when I was in danger of becoming a liturgist, he was staying with me. He said 'I've got a question. When I was ordained they asked me a question: "Do you consider that God has called you to this office?"' He said to me 'What I wanted to say was "No, I want to stay in my asha, but I have been called by the Synod of the Church of Bombay and I obey their call."' He said 'Where did this come from? Was it in the pre-Reformation rites?' I said 'No, it was Martin Bucer', so he looked a bit dubious. [The Archimandrite continued] 'Many of us experience the sad case of people who are convinced that God has called them to be priests

but somehow no bishop seems to recognise it! They wander sadly from diocese to diocese, from church to church, and usually end up in a front room in Balham with an episcopus vagans, in order to get the ordination God has called them to.'[42]

The Archimandrite wanted to suggest that far greater emphasis should be placed on the choosing by the Church rather than some inward sense of call that may or may not be felt by the individual. The Archdeacon of Surrey supported him in the debate, drawing on his experience as a former Senior Selection Secretary of ACCM.

There was a range of attitudes towards vocation among those we interviewed. At one end, there were those who said, 'This is part of the discernment process. I have come to meet you, as representatives of the Church, bringing these particular gifts, these qualities, these feelings. Do you think it is right for me to go further towards ordination?' At the other end of the spectrum, there were those who came and said, 'I know God has called me to be a priest, and I want you, the selectors, to ratify that decision.' I have to say that I was not always convinced that it was the people at the latter end who were the best candidates.[43]

This resulted in subsequent correspondence with the Liturgical Committee's revision committee, and the suggestion that the question should ideally be modified to the form used by the Lutheran Church of America, where the question was, 'Will you take the Church's call as God's call . . .', or, if that was not acceptable, at least to place the question of service in the present tense.

The final decision which appears in the current ordinal opted for the latter, but preceded it with a question about the Church's call. At the presentation of the candidates both for the diaconate and for priesthood, the bishop asks those responsible in some way for the candidates' formation and training:

Have those whose duty it is to know these ordinands and examine them found them to be of godly life and sound learning?
They have.

---

42 General Synod Debate on the proposed Ordinal 2004, Report of Proceedings, p. 242.
43 Debate, p. 353.

Do they believe them to be duly called to serve God in this ministry?
They do.
The Bishop turns to the ordinands and says
Do you believe God is calling you to this ministry?
I do so believe.

It was a significant move from the language of the Alternative Service Book ordination service, for here first the representatives of the Church affirm that they believe the candidates are called and then the candidate affirms that for him- or herself in the present tense. That reflects the understanding of ministry contained in the Book of Common Prayer and Article 23, and gives liturgical expression to the developing understanding of vocation over the century. This was what A. G. Hebert in 1944 called 'the call, definite and irreversible, which the Church itself gives in the act of ordination'.

That liturgical development came against the background of the wider thinking about ordained ministry in the Church of England over the century. It is therefore to that historical development which we now turn.

2

The Establishment of the Central Advisory Council of Training for the Ministry from the Beginning of the Century to 1913

Randall Davidson became Archbishop of Canterbury in 1903 at the age of 55. He was to hold that post for a quarter of a century, the longest serving archbishop since the Reformation, and was to be the first archbishop to retire in post. He proved to be a great archbishop, guiding the Church through such complexities as World War One and the whole social transformation of which the war was the instigator. When he took over from Frederick Temple he was a part of the Victorian Church, of which Temple was an embodiment, but he was well able to respond cautiously but creatively to change, and the Church of England changed in dramatic ways under his leadership, albeit normally under the pressure of external factors of which the war was the most obvious. He inherited the leadership of a Church that had many problems, not least of all in its ministry.

From the perspective of the present day, at the beginning of the twentieth century the ordained ministry of the Church of England appeared to be in a strong position. In 1901 there were 25,363 clergy in the Provinces of Canterbury and York, Canterbury then including the four ancient Welsh Dioceses that were eventually to form the Church in Wales some 20 years later. They served a population of 32,678,000 in England and Wales, giving a ratio of one clergyman to every 1,288 of the population.[1]

They were not evenly distributed. Of the parochial clergy many were in country parishes, some with very small populations, but in the cities the ratio was very different. Earlier in the nineteenth century it was reported that in Liverpool there was one clergyman to every 4,000 of the population, and Archdeacon Charles Thorpe reported that in Newcastle it was one to every 7,000.[2] When

---

1 Alan Haig, 1984, *The Victorian Clergy*, London: Croom Helm, p. 3.
2 Brian Heeney, 1976, *A Different Kind of Gentleman*, Archon Books, p. 27.

Hensley Henson, later to be Bishop of Durham, was appointed Vicar of Barking in Essex in 1888, he served a population of 9,000 and was assisted by only two assistant clergy, although that rose to four after only a few months.[3]

Not all clergy were in parochial ministry. Some were academics, either ordained schoolmasters in both public and grammar schools or in universities such as Fellows of Oxford or Cambridge colleges. With the passing of the Universities Tests Acts in 1871, which ended the practice of all office holders at the Universities of Oxford, Cambridge and Durham having to be members of the Church of England, the universities had fewer ordained members than earlier in the nineteenth century. Also, fewer schoolmasters felt the need to be ordained for their career's sake even though many headmasters of the major public schools at the time were ordained. In 1908 the Headmaster of Westminster, James Gow, as chairman of the Headmasters' Conference, wrote to the bishops showing the change that had occurred over the previous 40 years in the ratio of clergy to laymen among the schoolmasters of ten of the leading public schools. In 1870 it had been 54 clergy to one layman. By 1889 that had moved to 27 to seven. By 1906 it was 13 to three.[4] But although numbers of clergy had declined in both the public schools and universities, numerically they were still significant.

Earlier in the nineteenth century the vast majority of clergy came from the upper and upper-middle classes. In the 1830s about 80 per cent of those ordained were graduates of Oxford or Cambridge, universities mainly open to the sons of professional or better-off parents, and who were described in the terminology of the day as 'the sons of the middling sort'. Many joined the ranks of the ordained clergy because it was seen as a reasonably financially secure life. H. Byerley Thomson devoted a chapter in his book *The Choice of a Profession* to a review of 'the Church as a Profession'.

> In a single respect, it does, or ought to differ from other professions, namely in the class of motives with which it is entered. These motives are supposed to be founded on an exalted piety, and anxiety for God's service, although it is an assured fact that the true motives which practically induce the youth of England to engage in the ministry of the establishment, are not one whit less time-serving, or selfish, than those which create the lawyer, or the civilian, and might often bend in shame before the patriotic

---

3 Owen Chadwick, 1983, *Hensley Henson*, Oxford: Clarendon Press, p. 52.
4 Davidson papers, Vol. 158, p. 257f.

motives that call the soldier to the field, or the noble love of art that guides the destiny of the struggling artist.[5]

After discussing the structure, educational requirements and patronage system of the Establishment, he considered the average income of a clergyman, and noted that it 'is higher than the average income of barristers, much higher than the average pay of the military officer, and not much inferior to the average profits of the medical man'.[6] He then listed what he conceived to be the practical advantages of the clerical profession: 'opportunities for early independence'; 'comparative security of position'; 'opportunities of leisure'; 'absence of any risk of total failure'; 'easy work compared to the struggles of other callings'; 'ready admission into society'; and, the closest he came to anything like vocational idealism, a 'satisfactory sphere of usefulness which is his daily life'.[7] By the end of the nineteenth century, however, the financial position of the clergy meant that was changing fast. In *An Entrance Guide to Professions and Business*, Henry Jones, Commercial Master at Liverpool College, wrote of the clergy: 'material prospects ... are undoubtedly poor', and although 'the social prospects are, of course, good, for clergymen are admitted into the best society', his last words reminded the reader that 'a social position without an adequate income is rather a drawback than an advantage'.[8]

At the end of the nineteenth century over half the clergy ordained at that time were graduates of Oxford or Cambridge, many of whom would have had only pass degrees rather than honours degrees, but of the other half there was a growing group of non-graduates, made more possible by the creation throughout the nineteenth century of many theological colleges. Some of the colleges were exclusively for non-graduates, but others were open to either graduates or non-graduates and some were exclusively for graduates. Entry into the ministry depended on being offered a title post in a parish by the incumbent and with the diocesan bishop being willing to ordain. Incumbents would, of course, have varied in what they were looking for in potential curates both in terms of social and educational background, to some extent depending on how desperate they were for assistance. Each bishop might set his own standards both of general educational background and through the examinations set

---

5 H. Byerley Thomson, 1857, *The Choice of a Profession*, London: Chapman and Hall, p. 69f.

6 Thomson, *Choice*, p. 74.

7 Thomson, *Choice*, p. 90.

8 Henry Jones, 1898, *An Entrance Guide to Professions and Business*, London: Methuen & Co, p. 30f.

through his examining chaplains. No doubt they would also have been influenced by the ease or otherwise of attracting clergy to their dioceses, with different bishops having different criteria in terms of educational and possibly social background. A number also had theological colleges attached mainly for ordinands from their dioceses, which may too have influenced the rigour of their examinations for their dioceses as a whole. Against that broad background there were some major concerns.

The number and supply of clergy

In 1886, 814 men were made deacons, the first time the number was over 800 in any year. But from that high point numbers declined, to 745 in 1891, 704 in 1896, and 569 in 1901, the first year it had dropped below 600. At the same time there was a steady increase in the population of just over a quarter of a million each year so that the ratio of clergy to the population at large was changing; in 1861 it was one clergyman to every 1,045, by 1881 that had changed to one to every 1,199 and by 1901 one to every 1,288.[9] The 1883 *Church of England Year Book* stated 'Presuming that no one clergyman can satisfactorily watch over the spiritual interests of more than 2,000 souls, at least 2,500 additional clergy are needed in order promptly and successfully to cope with the continually increasing claims upon the Church's service.'[10]

Concern about numbers was reflected in diocesan debates in 1899 and 1900 in ten dioceses (London, Chester, St Albans, Bath and Wells, Lichfield, Norwich, Oxford, Worcester, Winchester and Chichester), in the Convocation of York in 1899 and in the Convocation of Canterbury in 1900. In the Canterbury Convocation 12 resolutions on the supply of clergy were proposed by a committee of the Lower House that had produced a report on the matter, and the bishops were

> respectfully invited to commend to the attention of Churchmen the duty of providing an adequate supply of Ministers, and to press upon the parochial Clergy the importance both of bringing the subject prominently before their people, especially at the Ember seasons, and also of seeking

---

9 Haig, *Clergy*, p. 3.
10 *Church of England Year Book*, 1883, p. 1.

out suitable candidates for holy orders, with a view to encourage and direct them as to their preparation.[11]

In the committee's report, and in the debates in both the Lower and Upper House, four factors were identified as causing the problem.

First, there was the relative decline in the value of clergy stipends. Inflation was not officially measured in the nineteenth century and estimated historical inflation rates show that for much of the century it was relatively low or even negative. But there were substantial rises in the 1860s and 1870s, and the unofficial estimate of inflation for 1900 was 5.1 per cent.[12] But more significant was the decline in agricultural tithes from the 1870s, brought about by refrigeration in ships allowing cheap food to be imported into England. That decline in tithe income, coupled with the fact that incumbents' basic stipends were largely fixed, meant the relatively comfortable position described by Thomson in 1857 had become the relative poverty noted by Jones in 1898. That was perceived as a disincentive for men without private means to come forward and cumulatively had the effect of changing the respect in which clergy were held: a rich clergyman was respected in a different way from a poor one.

Second, closely related to that and in the view of many the most significant, was the cost of training. While other churches made appeals for funds for helping men to train, albeit not always very successfully,[13] and there were some modest funds in some dioceses to assist some candidates for training for ordination,[14] the Church of England had grown accustomed to wealthy members of society paying for the education of their sons to produce the Church's ministers. In that it was no different from most other professions in England at the time, but the lowered value of clerical stipends had weakened the enthusiasm of many parents and so lessened that source of supply. There were some charities offering grants to those training for Holy Orders, but the sums available to them were way below the actual cost. Various speakers in

---

11 Report of Convocation, 1900, p. 195.

12 Estimates of historic inflation rates are on a website: http://safalra.com/other/historical-uk-price-conversion/

13 Kenneth D. Brown, 1988, *A Social History of the Nonconformist Ministry in England and Wales 1800–1930*, Oxford: Clarendon Press. The financing of training is discussed in Chapter 3, particularly pp. 81f. and pp. 85–9.

14 The *Church of England Year Book* 1883 lists five national societies, some of which were specifically for candidates of a particular churchmanship, and four diocesan funds.

the Convocation noted that that prevented some otherwise excellent candidates from offering.

Third, there were a number of other opportunities for service in both the Home Civil Service and overseas Colonial Service that attracted some of the best men emerging from universities, a point particularly made in the Upper House by the Bishop of Winchester (Davidson) and the Bishop of London (Winnington-Ingram). Davidson noted that that had also an adverse effect on candidates for medical schools and the teaching profession.

Fourth, although few openly acknowledged that this was a major factor, there was considerable theological ferment during the later part of the nineteenth century, partly in response to such scientific challenges to perceived Christian orthodoxy as provided by biologists such as Charles Darwin and geologists such as Charles Lyell and partly by the work of biblical criticism on both the Old and New Testaments. Subscription to the Thirty-Nine Articles of Religion required of clergy at the time was perceived to be a barrier by some who were open to these challenges to a conservatively conceived Christian orthodoxy. There was also party strife within the Church of England over matters such as ritualism, which was also considered a reason why some would be unwilling to consider ordination.

The response of the Upper House of Canterbury to the resolutions of the Lower House in 1900 was led by the Bishop of Winchester (Davidson), soon to become Archbishop of Canterbury. He acknowledged the problem, but all were agreed that the lowering of the standard of ordination would be no solution. The Preface to the 1901 *Church of England Year Book* stated the case clearly:

> The foremost need of the church is a ministry adequate in numbers and efficiency for the wants of the day, but whilst the rapid growth of population has only intensified this necessity, there is on the other hand unhappily no sign of any corresponding response. The number of candidates for Holy Orders still falls sadly short of demand ... Fully admitting the seriousness of such a drawback, the Bishops have wisely determined that this evil of diminution in numbers must be met with patience, and not by any lowering of the standard of intellectual equipment. An uneducated Clergy could only bring fatal disaster.[15]

---

15 *Church of England Year Book,* 1901.

When Davidson became Archbishop of Canterbury in 1903 he put that patience into practice. It was not until May 1907 that he met at Lambeth to talk about the matter with Stuart Donaldson, Master of Magdalene College, Cambridge. Donaldson subsequently wrote to Davidson suggesting that a committee be established to investigate the supply and training of candidates for Holy Orders, and the bishops formally asked the Archbishop to set up such a body. It met under the chairmanship of the Dean of Winchester, W. M. Furneaux, with eight other members, two of whom were lay, of whom one (M. E. Sadler) was Professor of the History and Administration of Education at the University of Manchester. Of the other six clergy three were residentiary canons and one was Stuart Donaldson.

The establishment of the committee was not without controversy, reflecting the party spirit that was seen as a problem within the Church. Two of the leading High Churchmen of the day were Walter Frere, co-founder with Charles Gore of the Community of the Resurrection at Mirfield, and Herbert Kelly, founder of the Society of the Sacred Mission, which in 1903 had moved to Kelham in Nottinghamshire where there was a major theological college for non-graduates. Evidently they had spoken to the Bishop of Oxford, Francis Paget, expressing concern at the lack of High Churchmen on the committee and Paget had evidently spoken to Davidson about the matter. Davidson wrote to him:

> I confess to being somewhat sore at these constant suspicions that I am trying to do everything in a partisan way. You will not suppose that I think you believe this, but it is evident that others do. The true fact is that we simply tried to find half-a-dozen men who have adequate leisure and adequate capacity to put together existing facts upon a subject which needs intelligence to be brought to bear upon it. To try to form a Committee of investigation which should be a balance of different opinions was not my notion at all. I took a great deal of trouble about this and it is very disappointing to find the view held about it. Frere has I find been writing very strongly to criticise us, or rather me. He says that non-partisan people are always the worst partisans of all.[16]

Davidson subsequently wrote to two High Churchmen to join the committee. One agreed, the other declined.

---

16 Davidson papers, Vol. 158, p. 242f.

The report on the *Supply and Training of Candidates for Holy Orders* appeared in June 1908. Regarding the supply of candidates it saw the financial cost of training as the main barrier that needed to be overcome as they concluded there was no shortage of potential candidates. They noted the figures for a number of different institutions. Kelham, for example, which provided its education free to suitable candidates but which then expected them to pay the money back once they were ordained, had 300 enquirers each year, 80 to 90 suitable candidates, but places for only 12 each year; Mirfield had very similar figures. St Aidan's, Birkenhead, a college in a more evangelical tradition, reported that for the 18 years up to 1908 it had 2,770 enquirers, 920 of whom were ultimately ordained, so there were 1,850 candidates whom the report described as 'unused', and it says of them, 'Allowing one-third to be unsuitable candidates, there remain unused during eighteen years, 1,230.'[17]

The solution, the committee believed, lay in a better financial approach. They noted that 'there were then 21 Diocesan Councils or Funds to aid candidates in training, 14 of which had been put in place since 1900', and went on,

> These facts lead to the conviction that, were a large and comprehensive scheme to be inaugurated for adjusting and co-ordinating existing agencies so as to secure united action, and at the same time for augmenting their incomes, the result would be to call out a great body of recruits from whom the best might be selected for acceptance and ultimately for ordination.[18]

This led the authors also to commend a continued widening of the social class from which ordinands came.

The financial solution they recommended was the creation of a Central Board of Finance for each of the provinces and each diocese to establish a Diocesan Board of Finance. The boards would implement what they saw as a fundamental principle: the financial support of students qualifying for the Church's service has been, and is still, put before the Church as a commendable charity. It should be regarded as a serious and necessary obligation, and not be allowed to take its place and chance with a multitude of other charitable appeals.

---

17 *Supply and Training of Candidates for Holy Orders*, 1908, London: SPCK, Appendix II, p. 39.
18 *Candidates*, p. 13.

They believed that such bodies should not simply concern themselves with the financing of training, but also wider questions of the maintenance of the clergy and the provision of decent pensions. It was a far-seeing proposal, even though it took some years to implement.

The report and the debates that preceded it began to have some effect. In 1907, 587 clergy were ordained, the last time the number was below 600 until World War One. In 1908 it was 670 and stayed at that level, going over the 700 mark once in 1911 when 711 men were ordained, but remaining in the high 600s until the war intervened so disastrously.

Training and the episcopal suspicion of theological colleges

At the end of the Victorian period ordination training was provided by universities and theological colleges. The universities had made some attempt in the later part of the nineteenth century to institute a more ordered approach to those reading theology. In 1873–4 the Theological Tripos was introduced in Cambridge University and at Oxford an honours school in theology was created in 1869–70,[19] but not all those considering the possibility of ordination would have read theology, and of those who did, many obtained only a pass degree. In 1902 only 53 per cent of Cambridge degrees were honours.[20] There were also attempts to provide some religious teaching and regular morning and evening worship in the colleges of the university, but it was not always considered very effective. Dowland comments:

> The quality of chapel in colleges was often not admired. The services were seen as too formal and tending to discourage devotion. The amount of religious instruction in colleges seems to have been unimpressive, even at the beginning of the 1900s. Facilities for pastoral and devotional training remained scanty.[21]

Various attempts had been made to introduce some co-ordinated policy for the Church as a whole, particularly in the matter of examinations, some of which did

---

19 David, Dowland, 1997, *Nineteenth-Century Anglican Theological Training,* Oxford: Clarendon Press, p. 192f.

20 Dowland, *Training,* p. 197.

21 Dowland, *Training,* p. 196.

have some effect, but individual bishops were very reluctant to limit or hand over to anyone else their choice of who should be ordained, or what training they should have. This led to a wide variety of practice between the dioceses, and that fact, and the pattern of training as a whole, had led to various complaints.

The theological colleges had a more ordered approach to teaching the subjects required for ministry, but the criticism that was made of them by some bishops of the later nineteenth century, particularly of those for non-graduates, was that they were too narrow in their outlook and encouraged what was described as a class approach, by which was meant a class of occupation. Bickersteth, Bishop of Ripon, wrote in 1867:

> the education of a theological college is necessarily a class education. That is the last thing desired for the clergy of our Church. If they are really to mould or direct the current of ordinary life not less than in matters of religion, there should be a breadth and depth in their education which the contracted sphere of a Theological College does not permit. They should mingle freely during their intellectual training with students from other callings, if they are to escape the narrowness of view which generally characterises persons who associate exclusively with one class.

He thought this in part stemmed from the background from which such students came. In his diocesan charge of 1876 he wrote: 'A larger proportion of the students have been very imperfectly educated to begin with and they resort to Theological Colleges with a view of qualifying themselves in the cheapest and most expeditious manner to pass the ordination examination.'[22]

In 1891 a conference on the Training of Candidates for Holy Orders consisting of professors of theology at Oxford and Cambridge, some college principals and a large number of examining chaplains, laid resolutions before the archbishop and bishops asking that 'at least one year's Theological study and training under recognised supervision *after graduation* be as a rule required of University candidates for Ordination'. At the time if a candidate had been to university the college authorities had to produce a testimonial as to the man's moral character and piety, of which Thomson had commented, 'It is almost unnecessary to appraise anyone the least acquainted with college life that this last document is little better than waste paper, as regards it being any real test of character

---

22 Dowland, *Training*, p. 178f.

and piety.'[23] The conference implicitly recognized the force of that while maintaining the status quo.

> We are of the opinion (a) that the customary College testimonial as to moral character should still be required, and (b) that this testimonial should be supplemented by further evidence as to the candidate's life at the University, with especial reference to his fitness to be a candidate for Holy Orders, such evidence being obtained by the Bishop through private communications.[24]

In the same year a memorial on the Training of Candidates for Holy Orders was presented to the archbishops and bishops from 232 laymen of the Church of England, including seven peers, six Members of Parliament, nine members of the House of Laymen, 22 Justices of the Peace, 17 officers in the army or navy, 19 barristers and solicitors, 15 physicians and surgeons, etc. [25]

> We – the undersigned lay members of the Church of England – venture to approach your Lordships, with the expression of our profound conviction that the lack of more thorough, systematic and prolonged training of Candidates for Holy Orders, and newly ordained men, is seriously impeding the spiritual usefulness of the Church, especially in its influence over *men* of all classes.[26]

The Principal of Wells Theological College (Edgar Gibson) wrote on 4 January 1895 to Davidson while he was Bishop of Rochester:

> It is surely time to put an end to the burning shame that the Church of England is the only religious body which will admit men to the ministry without a course of definite theological training. And might not the bishops insist on some preparation over and above that which is implied by the possession of a university degree? So long as men are ordained on the strength of having secured a degree, and being able to satisfy the very moderate requirements of the ordination examination, we may be

---

23 Thomson, *Choice*, p. 5f.
24 Davidson papers, Vol. 31, p. 430.
25 Davidson papers, Vol. 31, p. 434.
26 Davidson papers, Vol. 31, p. 430.

quite sure that some will mistake their vocation, and either repudiate their orders in later life, or else content themselves with the perfunctory performance of a minimum of clerical duty, even this being regarded as an unwelcome task.[27]

In 1899 the Lower House of the York Convocation Committee's report on the Supply and Training of Candidates for Holy Orders said, 'There is no learned profession into which young men can enter with so little special training as the Ministry of the Church of England.' York Province was more dependent on the supply of non-graduates than Canterbury Province and their next comment reflected that.

> Your committee have evidence before them which shows that the need is felt by the men themselves, and that considerable numbers of valuable men are year by year lost to the Ministry, because they are unable to obtain that special training without which they rightly shrink from offering themselves for Holy Orders.[28]

The problems were therefore well recognized even by the turn of the century, but of the graduates who were ordained at that time only about half had received any further formal training.[29] Partly this was because bishops were prepared to ordain graduates who had received no further training, but there was also a suspicion of theological colleges, some of which were the creation of trusts from a particular form of churchmanship, Catholic or Evangelical, and were seen to be the chief agents of 'party spirit' in the Church, a view, as will be shown, shared by both Frederick Temple and Davidson.

However, formal training did not simply mean going to a theological college. Some clergy were willing to have groups of young men working with them involved in the pastoral work of the parish and pursuing a course of reading. Davidson, who was ordained in 1874, had never gone to a theological college. As a young Oxford graduate he had stayed with a clergyman, Dr Vaughan, a former headmaster of Harrow but then Master of the Temple, and had enjoyed

---

27 Davidson papers, Vol. 40, p. 403f.

28 *Report of the Committee to consider the training of Candidates for Holy Orders.* York Journal of Convocation, Session of February 9 and 10, 1899, p. xviii.

29 Haig, *Clergy,* p. 87.

the experience of having some supervised reading and being given some pastoral experience. Vaughan had offered this to various graduates both as Vicar of Doncaster and at the Temple; those who had studied under him were known as 'Vaughan's Doves'. Davidson wrote of the experience:

> Looking back at it now, I honestly think that it would have been difficult to find any other plan of preparation for Orders which would have suited me so well as Vaughan's arrangements did. I did not take kindly to the notion of a theological college, and I cannot honestly say that this was in my judgement due to any fault on my part. The three years which passed between my graduating and my Ordination were in a very real sense a time of development and thought.[30]

No doubt it was that formative experience that led him, as Bishop of Winchester, to establish the Bishop's Hostel in Farnham for a small number of graduates preparing for ministry under the Vicar of Farnham and with the help of a theological tutor, and which was certainly intended to be other than a normal theological college. His suspicion of theological colleges was no doubt reinforced by comments he received after the announcement of the Bishop's Hostel being formed. The Master of Merton College, Oxford, George Brodrick, wrote to the bishop on 17 November 1898 saying that he would give notice of the new plan for Farnham and added, 'I sympathise only too much with what you say – quite apart from the burning questions now agitating the Church, I dislike the spirit of clerical freemasonry engendered by Theological Colleges.'[31] Another Head of House (Thomas Fowler, Master of Corpus Christi College, Oxford) wrote:

> I believe that our present troubles in the Church of England are largely due to some of the existing Theological Colleges, and I can think of few steps which would have a more wholesome influence on the Church than the institution of Colleges or Houses which will give a sound Church of England training to candidates for Holy Orders, free from sectarian bias.[32]

Experience of a theological college as a student would have been unknown to the bishops at the time; none of the 35 diocesan bishops in post at the beginning

---

30 George Bell, 1952, *Randall Davidson*, 3rd edn, London: OUP, p. 29.
31 Davidson papers, Vol. 52, p. 236.
32 Davidson papers, Vol. 52, p. 241.

of 1901 had been at a theological college as a student, although Edward King of Lincoln had been Principal of Cuddesdon Theological College, and other bishops would have had diocesan theological colleges in their dioceses. But direct episcopal personal experience of a theological college as a student would have to wait for some time. Cosmo Gordon Lang, ordained in 1890 and successor to Davidson in 1928, was the first Archbishop of Canterbury to experience a year at a theological college (Cuddesdon) prior to ordination, but William Temple, Lang's successor as Archbishop of Canterbury, who was ordained in 1908, never went to a theological college, and Geoffrey Fisher, ordained in 1912 and Temple's successor at Canterbury, spent only a very short time at Wells Theological College prior to ordination while Headmaster of Repton School. Of the diocesan bishops in post in 1911 only two recorded themselves as having gone to a theological college in *Who's Who* and by 1921 that had gone up to only four.[33]

Attending a theological college was far more likely for a non-graduate wishing to be ordained, and many of the colleges were founded explicitly for such candidates. Davidson's suspicion of some of those institutions was expressed when he led the discussion of the Upper House of the Canterbury Convocation to the 1900 Report the Lower House while still Bishop of Winchester. He was unhappy about the proposed resolution from the Lower House (the seventh) regarding theological colleges, when they stated 'That this House cordially acknowledges the great advantages which candidates for holy orders derive, both from the special training and also from the spiritual atmosphere of Theological Colleges.' Davidson commented to the bishops:

> the wording of it, as it stands, [gives] our absolute *imprimatur* practically to every theological college that exists in England today ... I have drafted a different Resolution on the same subject, but not, I admit, to quite the same effect – that is to say it safeguards us very much more. I am bound in honesty to admit that I have met men whose attitude on ecclesiastical questions seemed to me due to some teaching which they had received

---

33 The two in 1911 were Wakefield at Birmingham, who had been at Cuddesdon, and Watts-Ditchfield at Chelmsford, who had been at the London College of Divinity. Both were still in post in 1921, by when Donaldson was at Salisbury and who had attended Wells, and Garbett at Southwark who had also been to Cuddesdon. Some caution is needed with this, however, as Lang did not mention in his *Who's Who* entry that he was at Cuddesdon, although that was the place to which he returned each year for refreshment.

at a theological college in which, as far as I can gather, the 'spiritual atmosphere' was precisely that which I did not wish specially to give my *imprimatur* to. I do not want to name colleges, and I am far from wishing to discredit to the smallest degree the teaching given in our ordinary theological colleges.[34]

His draft resolution said:

That this House desires gratefully to recognise the help which many ordination candidates have received from residence in theological colleges in which the teaching is sound and the devotional system is loyal to the spirit and character of the Church of England. To such colleges the Bishops are ready to give every assistance and encouragement in their power.

Other bishops, most notably the Bishop of Ely (Compton[35]), were against this. Compton said, 'I think it would be very mischievous indeed for us in this House to agree to a Resolution which does most strongly imply that there are colleges in this country which are unsound in their teaching.'[36] The Archbishop of Canterbury (Temple) who was to retire two years later and whose mindset was wholly Victorian, said as President in recommending an adjournment:

I think it well that I should just mention one thing that strikes me and would weigh with me in dealing with such a question as this – namely that over and above the question of the good that the theological colleges may do, there is always the question of what mischief may be done by altogether disregarding the due proportion of different matters in the working of the Church. I certainly think that the theological colleges have not in all cases quite considered the due proportion sufficiently, and I find the theological colleges tending very much indeed to encourage party views in a form which I think hurts the church very much. It would be impossible for me to concur in this seventh Resolution as it came up to us.[37]

---

34 *Report of the Upper House of Canterbury Convocation,* 1900, p. 390 (4 July 1900).

35 Rt Revd Lord Alwyn Compton was 76 years old at the time and had been Bishop of Ely since 1886, having previously been Prolocutor of the Lower House of Canterbury.

36 *Report of the Upper House of Canterbury Convocation,* p. 394.

37 *Report of the Upper House of Canterbury Convocation,* p. 396.

The debate was resumed in the Upper House on 18 February 1901. Davidson had changed the motion and it was finally passed as:

> That this House, cordially acknowledging the great advantages which theological colleges have conferred upon candidates for Holy Orders, affirms the importance of maintaining Episcopal direction over these colleges and of keeping them in close personal relations with the bishops of the dioceses in which they are situated.[38]

Despite this warning shot, which was well publicized, the pressure for making study either at a theological college or through some form of episcopally recognized preparation a formal requirement strengthened over the first decade of the century. By the 1908 report, the Bishop's Hostel at Farnham, instead of being seen as an alternative to a theological college as Davidson originally conceived it, was now fully acknowledged as one, and all the existing theological colleges were put into five categories with their year of foundation:

1. Ten colleges, admission to which was confined to graduates: Cambridge Clergy School (later renamed Westcott House) (1881); Ridley Hall (1881); Cuddesdon (1854); Ely (1876); Farnham (Bishop's Hostel) (1899); Leeds Clergy School (1876); Newcastle Bishop's Hostel (1901); Wycliffe Hall (Oxford) (1878); Ripon College (1899); Wells (1840).
2. Eleven colleges open to graduates and non-graduates or to non-graduates only: St Aidan's, Birkenhead (1846); Chichester (1839); Highbury (1863); Isle of Man (1889); Kelham (1891); Lichfield (1857); Lincoln (1874); Llandaff (1892); Manchester (1890); St Stephen's, Oxford (1876); Salisbury (1860).
3. Five colleges devoted to preparation for overseas service: St Paul's College, Burgh (1878); St Augustine's, Canterbury (1848); SS Peter and Paul, Dorchester (1825); CMS College, Islington (1825); Warminster St Boniface (1860).
4. King's College, London; St David's College, Lampeter; Durham University.
5. Two colleges of special character, St Chad's, Durham (1904) (with its preliminary course of one year at St Chad's Hostel, Hooton Pagnall) and

---

38 *Report of the Upper House of Canterbury Convocation*, 1901, p. 49.

Mirfield (1902). Kelham was included in 2 above but its special character was noted.

The report summarized the pressure that had been developing for some years and recommended that in the longer term two years should be the normal training for graduates after a three-year university course, and for non-graduates five years, the first three of which should be a literary or arts course followed by two years' special training.

> Meanwhile it may be possible to require that all graduate candidates should have one year's course of special training subsequent to their degree; and all non-graduates a four years' course, of which the first part should be devoted to Higher Education, and the latter part to Ministerial Training.[39]

The report was one of the documents used in the preparation for the Lambeth Conference, which met in the summer of 1908, and some aspects of the report were thereafter subsumed in the discussion about the Lambeth proposals.

Concern about examinations

In the mid-nineteenth century, apart from university degrees, examinations prior to ordination were in the hands of individual diocesan bishops, normally acting through their examining chaplains. There was a wide variety of practice and standards. The examinations were normally taken shortly before ordination, so there was little chance of any prayerful preparation for ordained life, and the fact that different bishops had different examinations made it difficult for those seeking to prepare candidates except those in the ancient universities, whose degrees were often accepted as substitutes for at least part of the bishops' examinations. There were various attempts around the turn of the century to change this.

In 1874 the Universities' Preliminary Examination was established. A council of management was formed by those divinity professors of the two ancient universities who were willing to serve, some elected representatives of the

---

39 *The Supply and Training of Candidates for Holy Orders.* Report of a committee appointed by the archbishop at the request of the bishops of the Provinces of Canterbury and York, June 1908, p. 25.

theological faculties and an examining chaplain from those bishops who chose to recognize this examination. It was open to graduates of English universities, to members of theological colleges who had entered on the last term of the complete course and were recommended by the principal, and to any other person who had been nominated by a bishop with a view to ordination in his own diocese. The examination was designed to test candidates in the more academic aspects of theology, the Old and New Testaments, some Ecclesiastical History, Latin and Greek, normally tested by knowledge of set books, and a voluntary paper on Hebrew. Graduates in theology were exempt from taking some of the papers. The UPE was recognized by many, but not all, diocesan bishops, but it was supplemented by examinations set by individual bishops working through their examining chaplains to test matters such as doctrine, the use of the Book of Common Prayer, and a more general knowledge of the Bible.

The UPE, which was normally set three times a year a few weeks before the normal dates for ordinations at Trinity, Michaelmas and Advent, could be taken at a number of venues throughout the country. It partly met the problem of men being preoccupied with academic examinations so that there was no opportunity for more thoughtful reflection immediately prior to ordination and it at least provided a common syllabus for those preparing men for ordination irrespective of which diocese they were going to. But there were concerns about it.

First, the bishops only recognized it, they did not control it, and attempts to exercise some sort of episcopal control met with some opposition from the Examining Board. The result was that different bishops recognized it in different ways, and whereas in one diocese it might be regarded as an adequate substitute for some part of the bishop's examination, that might not apply to another neighbouring diocese.

Second, there was a concern, expressed most forcibly by Arthur Headlam, Principal of King's College, London (and later Bishop of Gloucester) that it could be passed by what he considered the greatest of educational failures, 'cramming'. There were those who prepared men to pass examinations simply by learning parts of set texts, rather than developing any real understanding of the subject.

Third, there was concern about the ability of bishops to nominate anyone for the examination even if they had received no formal theological education in a university or theological college. In the Bishops' Meeting of October 1911 the Bishop of Exeter, Archibald Robertson, by then Chairman of the Episcopal Committee on the Training of Ordination Candidates, referred to a letter which had been written by Canon Stanton, Chairman of the Council of the Examination, to the Archbishop of Canterbury with regard to the nomination of candidates to sit for the examination by bishops. These nominations in Canon Stanton's opinion worked unsatisfactorily, and he would be glad to see bishops abandon their right. The Bishop of Exeter's committee had considered the letter, recommended that the bishops should abandon their right, and the Bishop of Exeter moved that they should adopt this resolution.

In the discussion that followed, attention was drawn to the difference between the case of men who had been students at a theological college and abandoned the course there or other courses from lack of means to complete it, and the case of other literates (the title used for non-graduates) whom the bishops might in exceptional conditions desire to nominate. Several bishops pressed for the retention of this liberty. The Bishop of Exeter's first motion was put to the meeting and lost by 12 votes to eight. He then moved a further motion, 'That it is expedient that the bishops should not nominate for the Universities' Preliminary Examination for candidates for Holy Orders, candidates who have been students of any theological college except at the request of the authorities of that College.' This was accepted. That still gave bishops the ability to put someone forward for the examination who had received no other formal training.[40]

This all formed part of the more general concern about the examination, expressed in the comment of the 1908 *Report on the Supply and Training*:

> There is a strong feeling amongst the Principals of Theological Colleges that these examinations are not satisfactory, and that some modification is desirable here as well as in the system of Bishops' examinations, the subjects of which are directly based on the Universities' Preliminary.

Individual institutions had also proposed additional ways of preparing men for ordination. The University of Cambridge, for example, had introduced the Cambridge Divinity Testimonium, which was designed for students who were pursuing degrees in other subjects but who were thinking of taking Holy Orders in the longer term. It was described in a paper dated May 1904 sent to Davidson:

> It is not their wish that the course prescribed by these regulations shall be regarded as a substitute for a year spent at a theological college, or

---

40 Minutes of the Bishops' Meeting of 1911, p. 237f.

in some form of systematic training after graduation. But they hope by this scheme to check the tendency which exists among certain undergraduates to defer the study of subjects which as ordained men they will have to teach, on the plea that they intend when graduates to enter a theological college.[41]

It required such students to attend six courses of lectures, three of which should be given by divinity professors. Of these courses at least one should be on the Old Testament, one on the New Testament, one on Early Church History, and one of a doctrinal character.

A Certificate for a course of lectures shall not be given to any student who has not, by regularity of attendance, and by papers or exercises done during the course, or by a paper at its termination, given satisfactory proof of diligence. Undergraduates shall not be allowed to obtain certificates for more than two courses in one term, nor graduates for more than three.

This was to apply to all members of the University who began their residence in or after the Michaelmas term of 1904.

Davidson welcomed this, but an attempt to persuade the University of Oxford to follow a similar path failed. It was not simply bishops who were independently minded, so too were the institutions preparing men for ordination.

The matter of the training of non-graduates was different. An attempt to control what was a somewhat disordered and varied approach to their ordination training was established by the bishops in 1892. The growth and development of non-graduate colleges had been a significant feature of the second half of the nineteenth century, and the bishops were concerned about the general education of those who attended those colleges. They therefore created the Central Entrance Examination, which any non-graduate was required to pass before embarking on the final two years of training at a theological college. It required knowledge of Latin and Greek, mainly tested through set books, as well as a more general education expressed in papers on British history and elementary logic and some preliminary study of the Bible.

This affected those theological colleges which were largely preparing non-graduates as it limited those whom the college could admit, sometimes to the

---

41 Davidson papers, Vol. 102, p. 190.

consternation of the principals, who found their freedom of action curtailed. It was possible for a student to start at the college if he was able to find the fees, but he would not be allowed to proceed to the final two years unless he passed this examination. The most vociferous opponent of the examination was Arthur Headlam, Principal of King's College, London. In a memorandum on the subject in 1910 he summarized a criticism he had been expressing for some years. As regards the training in Latin and Greek he wrote:

> the examination has been so conducted that many have been able to pass it without learning these languages, by learning the translation of their books by heart, and by committing to memory a minimum of Greek and Latin grammar without grasping the essential elements. We at one time tried to give certain exhibitions on the results of the examination which was courteously furnished to us by the Board, and we found that in one case we had given an exhibition to a candidate who gained 80% of the marks for Greek, but who knew nothing of the language.[42]

He also contended that the second purpose of the course, to give a broad education, failed even more and men simply passed it by 'cramming'. He argued for King's College to have the right to admit men for a three-year course and to have their own internal examination after the first year to test whether men should then go on to the second year. He had argued this for some years and was supported in that by those diocesan bishops who were on his Council, London, Southwark, St Albans and Rochester, who in effect had allowed him to proceed in that way for candidates for their dioceses. This had caused some resentment in the Council of the Examination, and the Bishop of Exeter as Chairman of that Council (and a former Principal of King's College, London) was asked to convene a meeting of four bishops to consider the question. The Bishop of Exeter wrote in despair to the archbishop after the meeting to report that they were completely divided on how to respond. The attempt to introduce some co-ordinated action by the bishops could not overcome the equal determination of some bishops to preserve their own independence, and revision of the Central Entrance Examination had to await the founding of the Central Advisory Council of the Training for the Ministry.

---

42 Memorandum on the course for preliminary year for candidates for orders at King's College, 12 September 1910.

Graduate status for the clergy

Some bishops had always been in favour of having only graduates as clergy in their dioceses, particularly with the creation of new civic universities during the latter part of the nineteenth century, although few were able to enforce that rule completely. Davidson, when he became Bishop of Rochester in 1891, preferred graduates but was prepared to consider exceptionally well-qualified non-graduates from colleges such as King's College, London and St John's, Highbury. This led to an extraordinary correspondence with the Principal of St John's, Highbury in March 1895, who asked that any candidate who had passed the Central Entrance Examination and the course at his college should be considered by Rochester Diocese. (An edited version of the correspondence is in Appendix A.) The correspondence reveals the wide diversity of practice between different dioceses, the attitudes of the time and the different perspectives of diocesan bishops on one hand and college principals on the other. Davidson's view that individual diocesan bishops had the right to decide policy for their own dioceses prevailed.

The variety of practice between bishops continued, but in 1906 Charles Gore, who had become bishop of the new Diocese of Birmingham the year before, brought a series of proposals before the Upper House of the Canterbury Convocation. They included the suggestion that 'this House is of the opinion that the time has come to secure a more uniform and adequate standard of qualification and training for the ministry of the Church of England' and that, 'We are of the opinion that a degree in Arts, or its equivalent, followed by at least one year's training in theology in a theological college, or at least under proper supervision, should as soon as practicable be generally required of candidates for Holy Orders.' Gore argued for this largely on the grounds that the Presbyterian Church of Scotland, a number of other Nonconformist churches in England and the Episcopal Church in the United States required this and he could see no reason why, in principle, the Church of England should not do the same. In response to a question from the Bishop of London, it was noted that 'generally' would cover the Associateship of King's College, London. Gore and the other bishops recognized that the consequence of this would need to be the raising of funds for men training for ordination, but he believed that this would be forthcoming from the laity. He asked that the whole matter should come before the bishops of both Provinces.[43]

---

43 Chronicle of Convocation XXIII, 1906, pp. 258–67.

The debate, which was reported in the church press, became one more factor behind the 1908 *Report on Supply and Training*, although the authors of that report did not explicitly endorse the recommendation that all candidates for ordination should be graduates. That was left to the Lambeth Conference itself, which met in the summer of 1908 and where a report from a committee of 43 bishops under the chairmanship of the Bishop of London, Winnington-Ingram, considered the whole issue of candidates for Holy Orders. They noted the causes of decline in numbers coming forward for ordination, of which the financial cost of training was recognized as a major one. They recommended that every province should have an Ordination Candidates Council to make financial grants to enable men to train for the ministry. They also suggested that funds should be raised for this purpose.

> The example of other Christian bodies should be followed, in which almost invariably the supply, training, and support of the ministry is the first charge upon the offerings of the faithful; in the Anglican Communion it has up to now been to a great extent the last.[44]

It was their proposal on training that was then to cause some major difficulties. They stated:

> The time has now come when, in view of the development of education and of the increased opportunities afforded for University training, all candidates for Holy Orders should be graduates of some recognised University, as the increased facilities for obtaining degrees from the newer universities, with or without residence, bring a degree within the reach of those who are being trained at theological colleges.[45]

It appeared that the bishops believed this would not cause the closure of theological colleges training non-graduates, but that each college could establish a relationship with a university so that their courses could be adapted to enable a university to award a degree. It was obviously difficult for a

---

44 Lambeth Conference 1908, *Encyclical letter from the Bishops with the Resolutions and Reports*, SPCK, 1908, p. 85. As Kenneth Brown in *The Social History of Nonconformist Ministry in England and Wales 1800–1930* shows, the bishops somewhat exaggerated the generosity of other churches. See note 13 above.

45 Lambeth Conference 1908, *Encyclical letter*, p. 87.

worldwide collection of Anglican bishops to deal with the practical problems in the way of such a proposal, but it was on the practicalities as well as on the broad principle that the future debate was to take place.

That Lambeth Resolution came back to the Upper House of Canterbury in February 1909, and they were confronted with the issue of the date from which this should become applicable. They decided that it should be from 1917, giving the theological colleges eight years to adjust to the new situation. They also resolved that all candidates, in addition to being graduates, should 'be required also to have received at least one year's theological, practical, and devotional training at a recognised theological college, or under some other authorised supervision'. and 'that in order to promote uniformity of action and standard, any bishop making an exception to these requirements, whether as touching individuals or as touching special classes of men, should be requested to report the same to the Archbishop of Canterbury'. The fact that exceptions were to be allowed was considered vital, the Standing Committee of the Lower House stressing that fact, particularly in the case of men over the age of 30.[46] They also stressed that each diocese would need to establish an Ordination Candidates' Council with funds to meet this requirement.

The requirement of graduate status alarmed some in the theological colleges. The Conference of Principals met in Lincoln in January 1910.

> We admit of course that a degree is the usually accepted test of a general education, and that it is very desirable as a general rule that all candidates for Holy Orders should be Graduates. But the experience of training non-graduates for ordination has proved that there are a number of men who since their ordination have done work of the highest value for the church, but who, whether through lack of early education, or through age, of for other reasons – could never have profited from a university course. For such men we respectfully venture to suggest that some other adequate course of general education should be recognised, under proper guarantees for its width and thoroughness.[47]

The matter first came before the Upper House of York in 1910. Cosmo Lang had become the Archbishop of York the year before and he was reported as saying:

---

46 Chronicle of Convocation XXVII, 1910, No. 436, 24 February 1910, p. 72.
47 Davidson papers, Vol. 162, p. 128.

It was with some disappointment, and, indeed, he thought he might go further and say with some annoyance that they had found that their brethren in the Upper House of the Canterbury Convocation had not only discussed but also published a series of very far-reaching resolutions without giving the Upper House of the Northern province an opportunity of consulting with them on the matter. [He added] conscious although they might be of the inconvenience of one House in a matter of this kind taking public action without consulting the other House in the other Province, what they said in the matter must not be in the least regarded as implying in the minds of all of them any want of sympathy with the object the Upper House of Canterbury had in view.[48]

The matter was more difficult for the Northern Province as many more of their clergy were non-graduates, and they did not finally vote on the proposition until 1912. In the debate then there was continuing concern about the proposal. The Bishop of Carlisle was reported as saying:

He thought a good, broad, enlightened university training would tend to mitigate the vices of professionalism and to make them not only better men but better clergymen. At the same time, as the Bishops of Durham and Ripon had so well pointed out, to make this rule obligatory and universal would be to shut out from the ranks of the ministry of the Church of England some of the very best men in the ministry now.[49]

The Archbishop of York, commenting on Kelham, which was in the Northern Province, reported:

He thought that had embodied a most original and most fruitful theory of education which he did not think had received the attention it deserved, but he could only hope that in some way or another means might be found to enable students educated on the most interesting Kelham intellectual system to obtain some kind of degree.[50]

---

48 York Convocation, 25 May 1910, p. 80.
49 York Convocation, 15 February 1912, p. 21.
50 York Convocation, 15 February 1912, p. 26.

In the end, pressure from the Archbishop of York to accept the thrust of the Canterbury proposals won the day, but there was some clear unease. In fact, as described in the next chapter, the proposal for graduate status for all clergy was never implemented.

A central council?

With the divergent practice of bishops and the debate about training, examinations and graduate status, some had thought there needed to be a central council to advise the bishops on how theological education should be organized. There were various centres of influence: the principals of the theological colleges who met every other year in conference, the professors of divinity at the ancient universities, conferences for all engaged in theological education, the Councils for the Universities' Preliminary Examination and the Central Entrance Examination, together with the two Upper Houses of Convocation, the Bishops' Meetings, which were for bishops from both Provinces and which were private, unreported meetings, and the Episcopal Committee on the Training of Ordination Candidates.

At the beginning of the decade the 1900 Lower House of Canterbury Convocation's Report on the Supply of Clergy recommended that there should be a central advisory council, but it was a proposal squashed in the Upper House. The Bishop of Winchester (Davidson) thought that they had enough bodies dealing with aspects of training without creating a new one. The President, the Archbishop of Canterbury (Temple), reflecting no doubt his generation's view of such matters, said, 'I confess that as far as I am concerned I have not the smallest desire for a board of this kind. I do not think it will help us at all. I think that this House is a better board than any that could be formed for all purposes of this kind.'[51]

At the time the Convocations of Canterbury and York were the only official bodies that gave any opportunities for collective discussion and agreement, although informal and private bishops meetings for all bishops happened for many years, with official written records of meetings kept from 1871.[52] Dioceses had developed their corporate life in the nineteenth century, not least of all with the creation by the end of the century in all but three dioceses of diocesan

---

51 Chronicle of Convocation, 18 February 1901, p. 76.
52 From information supplied by Lambeth Palace Library.

conferences of both clergy and laity chaired by the diocesan bishop,[53] but little had happened nationally. The Church congresses, which started in 1861 and which did draw people from many parts of the country, were chaired by the diocesan bishop of the place where they met and were essentially informal meetings with no official status. By the end of the nineteenth century they were considered to have had their day.[54] The Church Reform League, largely led by Gore, had argued as early as 1874 for the principle of a national assembly that should be able to legislate for the Church by sending measures to the Crown for Royal Assent, but there were still many at the time who regarded Crown, Lords and Commons as the lay voice of the Church of England. Gore's proposal finally resulted in the creation of the Representative Church Council, consisting of the two Convocations and the two Houses of Laity, and it first met in July 1904,[55] but its powers were severely limited; it was essentially consultative rather than executive. Other gatherings that drew clergy and laity together were normally around particular issues and were never official bodies. Against such a background it is easy to understand why there was a reluctance to create any new, semi-official central Church body in 1901.

Four things changed that over the next 12 years apart from the creation of the Representative Church Council. First, the 1908 *Report on the Supply and Training of Candidates for Holy Orders* made the same recommendation.

> As a means of carrying out the suggestions and considerations here brought forward, we desire to recommend that a permanent Central Council be created by authority, especially trusted with the supervision of the supply and training of Candidates for the sacred Ministry. The creation of such a Board has already been recommended in the report of the Committee of Convocation of Canterbury, referred to above. Although it may be urged that such a Board would experience considerable difficulty in exercising even a general supervision over Theological Colleges already in existence, it is probable that in the course of a very few years it would accumulate a mass of experience, both as regards curriculum and training, which would ensure increasing influence.[56]

---

53 Owen Chadwick, 1970, *The Victorian Church Part II*, London: SCM Press, p. 359f., and Arthur Burns, 1999, *The Diocesan Revival in the Church of England*, Oxford: Clarendon Press.

54 Chadwick, *Victorian Church*, p. 362f.

55 Chadwick, *Victorian Church*, p. 365.

56 *The Supply and Training of Candidates for Holy Orders*, 1908, p. 27.

As this was the report of a committee appointed by the archbishop at the request of the bishops of the Provinces of Canterbury and York, such a proposal had to be taken more seriously.

Second, the Episcopal Committee on the Training of Ordination candidates was deeply divided. The final presenting problem was the argument about examinations. The chairman at the time, the Bishop of Manchester (Edmund Knox[57]) wrote to Davidson on 17 May 1910 on the subject. 'Our committee met this afternoon and found itself unable to agree even on the principle of a common examination for Ordination candidates other than such as is now provided by the U.P.E. or may hereafter be provided by the requirement of a university degree.' The bishop therefore asked if the committee could be discharged from its labours. Davidson asked that it should continue to see if the matter could be resolved.[58] The Bishop of Manchester wrote again on 2 July 1910:

Of course I am anxious to obey your Grace on the matter of the Ordination Candidates Committee, but I confess that our discussion on the final day of our last meeting filled me with dismay. The line taken by the Bishops of London, St Albans, Southwark & Newcastle[59] seemed to make all rules and regulations on the subject of ordinands useless, and the more so when after the meeting I heard what is really the meaning of residence at King's College. Further there is opposition on the part of bishops such as the Bishop of Ely[60] to any common examination for graduates, and this opposition divided our commission into two halves, so that we could only bring up two reports, if any. I am profoundly disappointed such matters should stand thus, and the two facts together, reluctance to conform to any rules, and cleavage of opinion seems to throw us back into a position

---

57 Edmund Arbuthnott Knox was born in 1847, had been at Corpus Christi College, Oxford, where he had obtained a First and won the Boden Sanskrit Scholarship in 1867. He then became Dean of Merton College, Oxford, where he was known as a strong disciplinarian, with the nickname Hard Knox. After various appointments, in the Church he became Bishop of Manchester in 1903, and was seen as one of the leading Evangelical bishops and a determined opponent of the Enabling Act, to the embarrassment of his successor at Manchester, William Temple. He was the father of Wilfred Knox, an Anglo-Catholic priest; Ronald Knox, who after a period as an Anglican priest became a Roman Catholic priest; and E. V. Knox, a future editor of *Punch*. He wrote an autobiography, *Reminiscences of an Octogenarian 1847–1934*, but made no reference to the Episcopal Committee on the Training of Ordination Candidates.

58 Davidson papers, Vol. 162, p. 134.

59 London was A. F. Winnington-Ingram; Southwark, E. S. Talbot; St Albans, Edgar Jacob; and Newcastle, Norman Stratton.

60 Ely was F. H. Chase.

almost worst than that in which we were when the committee was first appointed.[61]

Davidson accepted the Bishop of Manchester's resignation and appointed the Bishop of Exeter (Archibald Robertson[62]) as Chairman of the Committee.

A third possible factor, the influence of which is more difficult to assess, lay in the other matters that would have occupied bishops' minds at the time. There was significant debate happening nationally about constitutional change following the rejection by the House of Lords of Lloyd George's People's Budget of 1908. It led to proposals for the whole reform of the House of Lords culminating in the 1911 Parliament Act, described as 'the most decisive step in British constitutional development since the franchise extension of 1867'.[63] The bishops in the House of Lords were key players in the process, 13 of the 15 bishops voting in the House of Lords for the Bill. If they had voted otherwise the Bill would have been defeated in the House of Lords and the Liberal Party may well have carried out their threat to appoint a whole host of new Liberal Peers to ensure the Bill was then passed. Compared to such major constitutional matters, voting for the creation of a new body to oversee theological college training may have seemed a minor matter.

A fourth factor was that most bishops probably still thought it would not undermine episcopal independence. So used were the bishops to being the masters in their own dioceses that they may not have realized that the new body with the word 'Advisory' in its title would acquire the authority that it subsequently did.

It was therefore a combination of an official report, a recognition of the bishops' inability to handle the issues alone, other pragmatic considerations including pressure from below and, possibly, a lack of awareness of what they were creating rather than any great ideological principle that led to creating such a central body. When the Principal of Cuddesdon, Canon J. O. Johnston,

---

61 Davidson papers, Vol. 163, p. 392f.

62 Archibald Robertson was born in 1853 and obtained First Class Honours at Trinity College, Oxford. He was Fellow and Dean, and then became Principal of Bishop Hatfield's Hall, Durham University, and then Principal of King's College, London from 1897. He moved to be Bishop of Exeter in 1903. His charge of 1905 summarized his approach to the C. of E. '*English Churchmanship, an invitation to brotherly union on the basis of the Book of Common Prayer*.' He is most remembered as a contributor to patristic and historical studies, particularly to St Athenasius.

63 Sir Robert Ensor, 1936, *The Oxford History of England 1870–1914*, Oxford: Clarendon Press, p. 430.

wrote to the archbishop in 1912 on behalf of the Principals' Conference asking that the recommendation of the 1908 Committee should be accepted, he found he was pushing at an open door. Davidson acknowledged it on 17 January saying he would refer it to a committee meeting under the Bishop of Exeter. 'I may add, though this is not a formal statement, that the bishop appeared to think that there ought to be no practical difficulty in giving effect to your wishes.'[64] In fact the Bishop of Exeter must have breathed a sigh of relief, for no longer would he have to mediate between different groups within the bishops and the various other centres of influence. The Bishops' Meeting of 22 and 23 October 1912 approved the Constitution, and so the Central Advisory Council of Training for the Ministry came into being, with the Bishop of Exeter appointed the first Chairman. At least from then onwards the key people in most decisions about training would all be in the same room at the same time.

---

64 Davidson papers, Vol. 247, p. 6.

3

The New Council Starts Work from 1913

The new Council made an immediate start on the issues that it had been bequeathed, some of which it could more easily resolve than others; the graduate status question, for example, rumbled on for 30 years. Initially the declaration of war in October 1914 and its consequences, which are discussed in Chapter 4, had relatively little effect on the work of the Council, and it was not until 1916 that the war began to become the dominant issue it would eventually be. So the new Council embarked on some difficult questions, many of which could be finally resolved only after the war ended.

But this happened only after an initial embarrassment. The Central Advisory Council of Training for the Ministry (CACTM) held its first provisional meeting on 19 February 1913, an inauspicious choice of date as evidently no one had bothered to check that it clashed with a meeting of the York Convocation. Not surprisingly, strong protests were made and an apology given at the April meeting of the York Convocation.

> The prolocutor intimated that his Grace the President had communicated with the Convenor of the Advisory Council of Training for the Ministry in regard to the oversight which had led him to call the first meeting of that Council at a time when the Houses of the Northern Convocation were sitting, and had received an expression of regret on the part of the Convenor that such a thing had happened, together with a promise that greater care would be taken in the future.[1]

Given the differences in emphasis on the approach to graduate status for all clergy between the two Provinces, the impression of slighting the York

---

1 York Convocation Chronicle, April 1913, p. 121.

Convocation was potentially damaging, but the apology appears to have been accepted.

Membership and functions

At the beginning, the full Council consisted of eight bishops, six from the Southern Province and two from the Northern, as applied to the previous Episcopal Committee on the Training of Ordination Candidates, but it was agreed from the outset that, when the opportunity occurred, that should be reduced to seven, five elected from Canterbury and two elected from York. The Chairman, Archibald Robertson, Bishop of Exeter, was 57 at the start of the Council's life. He brought the extensive educational experience he had as a College Principal in Durham and King's College, London before becoming Bishop of Exeter in 1903, and the two years experience of chairing the Episcopal Committee on the Training of Ordination Candidates following the resignation of Bishop Knox in 1910. (Biographical details of all the Chairmen of CACTM and its successor bodies are in Appendix B.) Of the other bishops Charles Gore had recently been moved to Oxford from Birmingham and was seen as a leading figure of the Anglo-Catholics. Handley Moule had been Bishop of Durham since 1901 and his evangelicalism was a balance to Gore's Anglo-Catholicism. Winfrid Burrows was Bishop of Truro having earlier been Principal of Leeds Clergy School and was to succeed Robertson as Chairman when ill-health forced Robertson to resign in 1916. In 1919 Burrows moved to Chichester but remained Chairman until 1927.

There was one representative from each of the theological faculties of Oxford, Cambridge, Durham, King's College, London and St David's College, Lampeter, with the stipulation that from those bodies that included non-Anglicans on their faculties (Oxford, Cambridge and Durham) only members of the Church of England should be elected.

The principals of recognized theological colleges elected seven members, although at first the notion of a 'recognized theological college' was a complex one as part of the task of the new Council was to inspect theological colleges and decide which should be recognized. For the beginning of the Council it was agreed that those principals who were represented at the Ninth Conference on the Training of Candidates for Holy Orders in 1909 should be the qualified electors for the process of the first appointments. Of the seven principals appointed at the outset three were to be particularly significant figures for the new Council.

Canon J. O. Johnson was Principal of Cuddesdon, a graduate-only college, and was elected Vice-Chairman of the Council, a role he continued to hold when shortly after he moved to be Chancellor of Lincoln Cathedral.

F. C. N. Hicks was Principal of Bishops' College, Cheshunt, a theological college formed in 1908, and was 40 when elected Secretary of the Council, a role he held while being Principal of Cheshunt until 1920 when he became full-time Secretary of the Council until he was appointed Vicar of Brighton in 1924. In 1927 he became Bishop of Gibraltar and then in 1933 Bishop of Lincoln.

Guy Warman, who was also 40 when CACTM started, was Principal of St Aidan's College, Birkenhead, a broadly Evangelical college that trained both graduates and non-graduates, from where he was to be appointed Vicar of Bradford in 1916. He then became Bishop of Truro in 1919, succeeding Winfrid Burrows, and in 1923 became Bishop of Chelmsford, moving to Manchester, where he succeeded William Temple in 1929. In 1928, when Burrows resigned as Chairman of the Council, Warman succeeded him and remained chairman until 1944.

Four members of the Lower House of Canterbury and three from the Lower House of York were to be elected as well as seven representatives of the Houses of Laymen. The Council was free to co-opt no more than seven other members, and among those co-opted were Canon Bullock-Webster, Secretary of the 1908 Archbishops' Committee on the Supply and Training of Candidates for Holy Orders, and the Headmaster of Repton, William Temple, who was to remain a member of the Council for eight years until he became Bishop of Manchester. It made for a large body of 41 members if all attended.

The Council's functions were provided by its constitution which had been produced by the Standing Committee of the Bishops' Meeting but which incorporated some of the suggestions from the 1901 Lower House of Canterbury Report on Supply. (Appendix C contains full details of the recommendation of the 1901 Report, the Constitution of CACTM, the various later modifications, and the constitution of its successor bodies.) The functions identified in 1913 were:

1. To watch the supply of candidates for Holy Orders, and its sources.
2. To consider the best methods of training and testing candidates.
3. To draw up, and from time to time to review the list of theological colleges the recognition of which by the bishops the Council advises.

4. To provide for the inspection of existing theological colleges; and to advise as to the formation and supply of new theological colleges.
5. Generally to promote unity of action between all those concerned in the training of candidates for Holy Orders, and to collect information and make suggestions for the guidance of bishops.

With such aims and with such a body of strong and independently minded individuals representing a variety of interests and schools of thought, it would be almost impossible for any one person or group to dominate the Council. To discover what happened in any Council meeting in assessing the cut and thrust of debate is quite difficult to discern. The minutes had a wide circulation, so the pressure to hide conflict and suppress dissent was strong. Who proposed or seconded a motion was recorded but no actual vote was recorded until 1917, when it was noted that the decision to recommend to the bishops that for service candidates Greek should be allowed to replace Latin, was passed by 15 votes to two, the bishops not voting. The following year a vote was also recorded on a proposal that, for candidates wounded in the war, 'total loss of sight should be an absolute disqualification' was lost by eight votes to seven. Otherwise it was simply noted that a resolution was carried, or, if amended, the amendment was then carried or lost, or a resolution was referred back to the body from where the recommendation was made, presumably for amendment and reconsideration. Where the conclusion of opinion lay was recorded by the final resolution, but what arguments lay behind that discussion are normally lost in the mists of history. The prevailing impression from the decisions recorded is that while the Council certainly made firm decisions even on matters where the bishops had been divided before, it would be very unlikely that any foolish decision would be passed but equally that any really adventurous and far-sighted resolution would be passed either. It is only possible to speculate on the grounds of opinions expressed elsewhere how individuals voted or voiced their opinions in Council meetings, but it seems highly likely that the composition and constitution of the Council ensured that it was essentially pragmatic, consensual and cautious in its final resolutions.

Graduate status 1913–44

The first and most pressing issue was the question of graduate status for the clergy in the future. There were at least two good reasons for some of the bishops to press for this. First, there was a fear of what was to be described as the 'seminarist approach', which separated ordinands from those training for other professions; some bishops thought training for ordination should take place in the context of a university alongside others as that provided a more rounded education. Second, with the creation of the new universities, there were opportunities for the Church to establish creative links with those bodies and to use their resources. How far that was also accompanied by a third factor that can only be described as social snobbishness is impossible to judge. On the other hand the colleges training non-graduates had produced what other bishops considered to be excellent clergy, and there was reluctance on the part of bishops, particularly those in the Northern Province, who had always had more non-graduate clergy than the Southern Province, to close that route to such candidates in the future. There was also a concern about the financial implications of requiring a degree at a time when the resources for grants from the Church were very limited.

At the Council's first full meeting in April 1913 it recommended that the proposed rule requiring that candidates for Holy Orders should have a university degree should not apply to men who entered upon a three-year course of preparation for Holy Orders after they were 26. It also said that:

> in view of the fact that the Bishops of the Northern Province only accepted the first resolution requiring a degree from all Candidates for Holy Orders nearly three years after it was agreed to by the Bishops of the Southern Province, and of the fact that there has been more delay than was anticipated in meeting the financial difficulties involved in carrying it out, the Council recommends that the operation of the resolution be postponed for three years viz: till 1920.[2]

There was clearly a division on the underlying issue between different members of the Council; Gore had proposed in the Upper House of Canterbury in 1906 that candidates for Holy Orders should be graduates, but Warman as principal of a college that trained non-graduates as well as graduates and who was one of the principals who had written to Davidson from the Lincoln Conference of Principals in 1910 questioning the policy, would have taken a different view, as would Temple, who despite his own great learning was

---

2 CACTM minutes for 2/3 April 1913, in CERC.CACTM/COU/M/1.

very much in favour of widening the social base of those coming forward for ordination.

The Upper Houses of the Convocations accepted the resolutions, although the Bishop of Winchester (Talbot) obtained from the Archbishop of Canterbury an acknowledgement 'that any Resolution which we pass here should be worded in such a way as not in any degree to impair the recognition of the independence and freedom of individual Bishops in this matter'. Gore, then Bishop of Oxford, said that:

> the Bishop of Winchester might be reminded that this matter was carefully guarded, and that the House thought that the utmost that they could do was what was embodied in the Resolutions, namely, that every Bishop who proposed to ordain a man who was not a graduate should signify that fact to the Archbishop ... He thought that the feeling was very widespread that this was a matter with regard to which concordant action among the Bishops was very much to be desired.[3]

The decision certainly gave some breathing space to consider the implications of the proposed changes, both financially but also in terms of the possible effect on some of the existing non-graduate colleges. In 1915 it was agreed to form a committee to examine the position of King's College, London and other similar institutions, to see whether 'exemption from the resolution of the Bishops arranged to come into force in 1920 may be granted, not to particular colleges, but under proper safeguards to approved schemes of education in recognised colleges'.[4] It was further resolved 'that the committee number among its members the representatives of Durham University and of King's College, London, and at least one representative of the non-graduate colleges'.

The realities of World War One then intervened and by May 1916, when the numbers ordained were only just over half those ordained in 1914, the date for implementing the Lambeth Resolution on graduate status was effectively abandoned, with the war providing both a reason and an excuse. The Council said it was 'as firmly convinced as ever of the grave importance and great advantages of the requirements for Ordination announced by the Bishops to take effect from 1920', but it had 'unwillingly come to the conclusion that it

---

3 Chronicle of Convocation 1913, p. 212f.
4 CACTM minutes, 4 February 1915.

may be necessary to postpone the requirement of graduation for a definite period after the war to be settled by the Bishops.'[5] How universal among the members of the Council that unwillingness was is not known; it could be that many were grateful that the opportunity was presented to delay any final decision.

There the matter rested until some bishops raised the matter again in the Upper House of Canterbury in May 1924, provoking a tortuous discussion both within that House and between them and the Upper House of York that lasted two years.

CACTM through its Chairman, the Bishop of Chichester (Burrows), presented a proposal regarding training:

> That in future a normal candidate should be required, in addition to the passing of the General Ordination Examination, or one of its equivalents, to take a three years' theological course after passing an examination of matriculation standard, if he is not a graduate, or a two years' course if he is a graduate who has not taken a First or Second Class Honours in Theology.[6]

Over two days the debate was broadened to the wider question of having an all-graduate ministry. The Chairman noted that in 1909 the Canterbury bishops had passed a resolution about all candidates requiring a degree but he did not think his resolution affected that point; it was purely concerned about the length of training in the current circumstances. The Bishop of London (Winnington-Ingram), who had led the group in the Lambeth Conference that produced the first resolution about an all-graduate ministry, questioned that. 'The resolutions now before the House indirectly cancelled a Resolution passed with great solemnity in 1909, and he wanted to know where they were.'[7] In the debate a number of bishops, including London, Bristol (Nickson[8]) and St Albans

---

5 CACTM Minutes, 23 May 1916.

6 Chronicle of Convocation, 6 May 1924, p. 119. The whole debate is reported on pp. 113–35 for the debate on 6 May, and pp. 195–209 for the debate on 7 May.

7 Chronicle, p. 124.

8 George Nickson (1864–1949) became Bishop of Bristol in 1914 having previously been Bishop of Jarrow from 1906. He had been tutor at Ridley Hall in Cambridge as a young man and had developed firm evangelical principles, but he was to be an exponent of a broad-minded evangelicalism. He retired from Bristol in 1933.

(Furse[9]), spoke in favour of reviving the 1909 request for graduate status for all. Nickson said that 'for the last three years he had maintained that he would ordain nobody who was not a graduate'[10] so he thought a resolution that could be interpreted as treating non-graduates as acceptable would put him in a difficult position. Exeter (Gascoyne-Cecil[11]), on the other hand, said that 'the debate had filled him with a feeling of despair. He quite agreed with every word of it, but he thought that there was no possible chance of carrying through what was proposed. At present there were hundreds of vacancies.'[12] In response St Albans (Furse) thought that raising the standard would be a way of raising the number of candidates who would come forward. 'If the bishops were bold and were strong enough to demand a higher standard, in five or ten years' time the corner would have been turned, and it would be seen that by raising the standard a permanent contribution had been made towards improving the ministry of the Church of England.'[13] Davidson described the issue as 'a very, very difficult one', and quoted Barry, who as Principal of Knutsford (see the following chapters) had certainly wanted high standards but was opposed to lengthening training.[14] Warman, by now Bishop of Chelmsford but reflecting on his experience as principal of a theological college for non-graduates, commented that 'some very good men indeed came from non-graduate colleges, and he would be very sorry to see the rule about graduation put into force until there was a larger opportunity of helping men take degrees.'[15] He thought that insisting on a three-year course would deal with the bishops' concerns.

The Bishop of Chichester as Chairman of CACTM accepted a proposal that sought to make 1930 the date from which there would be a formal requirement for all future clergy to be graduates, while allowing up to then non-graduates who had passed an examination of matriculation standard to do a three-year course at a recognized theological college.[16] The following day the Bishop of

---

9 Michael Furse (1870–1955) was Bishop of Pretoria from 1909 to 1920 and was Bishop of St Albans from 1920 to 1944. He was from a High Church Tractarian background.

10 Chronicle of Convocation, 6 May 1924, p. 125.

11 Lord William Gascoyne-Cecil (1863–1936), second son of the 3rd Marquis of Salisbury. He spent 28 years as Rector of Hatfield, the family seat of the Cecil family, but in 1916 was appointed to succeed Robertson as Bishop of Exeter, where he was to remain for 20 years until he died in office.

12 Chronicle, p. 201.

13 Chronicle, p. 202.

14 Chronicle, p. 125f.

15 Chronicle, p. 124f.

16 Upper House of Canterbury, 7 May 1924.

Chichester said that the resolutions would not affect candidates from King's College, London, or Kelham, and the Upper House of Canterbury accepted the resolution, which was:

> That in future it shall be required of ordinary candidates that they be graduates who either (a) have taken Honours in Theology, or First Class Honours in some other subject and have subsequently had a year's theological, devotional and practical training at a recognised theological college or under some other authorised supervision, or (b) have had two years of such training after qualifying for their degree. This second condition is not to come into full force until 1927; meanwhile one year's training will be required.
>
> In continuation of the Resolutions of the Upper House of July 1909, and July 5th 1916, non-graduates shall not generally be admissible after December 31st, 1930. Meanwhile they shall be required, in addition to the passing of the General Ordination Examination (or one of its equivalents), to have taken a three years' theological course subsequent to passing an examination of matriculation standard.[17]

The Upper House of York Convocation, meeting at the same time but not knowing what was happening in the other Upper House, simply agreed the CACTM recommendation on the level of training for non-graduates, and did not pass any additional amendment suggesting a date when only graduates would be admitted.[18]

To solve the conflict between the two Upper Houses a CACTM committee under the chairmanship of Warman was appointed to look at the implementation of these recommendations. They noted that, in the Province of Canterbury, exceptions were allowed in the case of those trained at Kelham and King's College, London, and the committee recommended that either there should be no exceptions, because once you had allowed an exception in the case of one particular college, other colleges would come asking for the same freedom, or that the resolution of the Upper House of York should be accepted, and that the Canterbury resolution left in abeyance. The latter was their preferred option. They also noted that requiring a university degree of every candidate would add considerably to the cost.[19]

---

17 Chronicle, p. 209.
18 Upper House of York, 7 May 1924.
19 CACTM paper 169, 1924, in CERC.CACTM/COU/D1.

In July 1924 there was what the Archbishop of Canterbury described as 'a united Session of the Upper House of Canterbury and the Upper House of York sitting together but not as a joint body in the technical sense of the word'.[20] They were primarily meeting to discuss the ordination of deaconesses but it also provided an opportunity to resolve the conflict between the two Upper Houses. Each passed the resolution 'in ordinary cases non-graduate Candidates for Holy Orders shall be expected, in addition to passing the General Ordination Examination (or one of its equivalents) to have taken a three year theological course after passing an examination of matriculation standard' with the addition in the case of Canterbury, 'and that the requirements as to graduation and the theological training of graduate candidates be reconsidered'. In the case of York the same addition omitted the reference to 'as to graduation'.[21] CACTM had effectively brokered an agreement between the two Provinces, and it was finally resolved when the Upper House of Canterbury, meeting in 1926 and essentially using words provided for it by CACTM,[22] stated:

> while reaffirming its conviction that a graduate Ministry is desirable, and that the difficulties in the way of securing it are not such as cannot be overcome in the course of time, is of the opinion that it would be impracticable to make this rule absolute on the date mentioned. Before a date is finally fixed, fresh consideration should be given to the possibility of adjusting the existing methods of training to the situation which the resolutions of the Upper House of Canterbury would create.[23]

In fact the joint meeting paved the way for the Canterbury Convocation in February 1926 to give consideration to having joint meetings of the two Upper Houses. Davidson noted that it was in the power of the Archbishops to call such meetings and that the Lower House of Canterbury had encouraged the appointment of a Joint Committee:

> to consider further (in consultation with the authorities of the Northern Convocation) ... the most convenient method or methods ... whereby the

---

20 Chronicle of Convocation, 1924, p. 269.
21 Chronicle, p. 296.
22 CACTM minutes, 28 January 1925 in CERC.CACTM/COU/M/3.
23 Chronicle of Convocation Upper House of Canterbury, 19 February 1926, p. 95.

two Convocations of Canterbury and York, while preserving their full liberty of independent action, may henceforth be enabled to deliberate together and reach joint decisions in all matters affecting not merely the two Provinces but the entire Church of England.[24]

Davidson thought it might be useful to happen more frequently. Other bishops supported this on the grounds that they already had to attend too many meetings and some simplification of the processes would help.

No further resolutions on graduate status were passed by either of the Upper Houses, but an attempt was made in October 1928 to reintroduce it in the Council, which was resolved by the chairman (by then Warman) successfully proposing that the Council 'should move to next business'.[25] This did not prevent individual bishops ordaining only graduates in their dioceses, which caused some problems for those theological colleges that trained non-graduates, and the Warden of Kelham drew this to the attention of the Council in March 1934. He was advised to consult with other principals and the matter was referred to the Conference of Principals of Theological Colleges. The Conference passed a resolution:

> this conference, being of the opinion that the categories 'graduate' and 'non-graduate', as applied to candidates for ordination, no longer bear the significance that once belonged to them, requests CACTM to appoint a commission to reconsider what courses of training for the Ministry should be required and recognised by the Church.[26]

This CACTM agreed to do, but it was then overtaken by the establishment of the Archbishops' Commission on Training for the Ministry which had a far wider remit than that, but which also concluded in its 1942 Interim Report and again in the 1944 Final Report:

> While we think that a University Course, followed by a Degree, is a very great advantage, and that as many candidates as possible should possess such a qualification, it is not practicable under present conditions to insist

24 Chronicle, p. 73.

25 CACTM minutes, 25 October 1927.

26 CACTM minutes, 22 March 1935 in CERC.CACTM/COU/M/4.

upon it in all cases, and the fine service rendered by many non-graduate clergy forbids us to do so.[27]

The resolutions taken by the Lambeth bishops in 1908, by Canterbury in 1909 and York in 1911, were therefore never implemented.

The training of graduates (1913–26)

The training of non-graduates, as opposed to their acceptance in principle as candidates for ordination, was never really an issue; all agreed, even though it was not then universally the case, that ideally training should be for three years after completing successfully the Central Entrance Examination or what became its equivalent, matriculation. The training of graduates, however, was more complex. The first full meeting of the new Council in April 1913 strongly recommended that the bishops' requirement that graduate candidates should have some formal training at a theological college or other recognized training should come into operation at the date originally suggested (1917), but the bishops were urged to press this requirement without any delay at all on graduates who applied to them for ordination, as they believed that comparatively little pressure was required to make this effective immediately. In February and April 1914 the case for at least a year's training for graduates continued to be pressed by the vice-chairman, J. O. Johnston, who by then had moved from Cuddesdon to Lincoln, and the Council also accepted his proposal that the bishops should give 'some special encouragement and mark of approval' to those graduates who followed a two-year course.

By April 1914 that was further developed to suggest that candidates beginning their university course at the normal age of 18 should aim primarily at taking a full degree course in arts, science, or some other (preferably non-theological) subject, followed by two years given to theological study, so that, as far as finance allowed, the normal course should be at least five years. When two years' theological work could be arranged after an arts degree it was recommended that the first of the two might well be spent at a university and the second at a theological college.[28]

---

27 *Archbishops' Commission on Training for the Ministry.* Interim report (as presented to the Archbishops, January 1942) p. 9. Final report p. 50.

28 CACTM minutes, 21 April 1914.

The war delayed that proposal, but by May 1919 the requirement of two years' training following graduation was formally agreed by the Council, but was never formally implemented. Individual bishops might well have been reluctant to impose on otherwise good candidates new conditions that might encourage them to go to other dioceses that were more accommodating. As late as January 1926 a Council minute says of its reaction to the proposal of two years' further training for graduates:

> in view of the fact that a change of this nature cannot be effected generally for some time to come, [the Council] suggests respectfully (1) that this longer course be encouraged by counsel and the giving of grants rather than enforced by regulation; and (2) that, for the present, a special training of not less than 18 months be required of all graduates, except that in the case of those who have obtained first or second-class honours in theology one year only should be compulsory.[29]

That was accepted by the Convocation of Canterbury in February 1926 and it continued to be the recommendation and the practice until the Archbishops' Commission on Training reported in the 1940s.

A new examination

The complexities about examinations noted in Chapter 2 were partly resolved at the second meeting of the Council in July 1913, when it was noted that the Council of the Universities' Preliminary Examination was willing to hand over that examination to CACTM. A committee was formed to put that change into effect. When, in October 1915, it was reported that the Central Entrance Examination was also handed over to CACTM, it meant that the two major national examinations relating to ordination were in the hands of CACTM, and a permanent committee was established by the Council to deal with training and examination questions. It would be the duty of the committee:

> to select, arrange and announce the subjects of the examinations, to appoint examiners, to choose convenient centres at which the

---

29 CACTM minutes, 29 January 1926.

examinations may be held; to consider what examinations may be accepted as equivalent for either of these examinations, and to make recommendations on the subject for the Central Advisory Council; to make provision for furnishing certificates to the candidates who have passed the examinations, or the equivalents for either of them; through the Secretary of the Council, to inform newly consecrated Bishops of the Church of England of the regulations in respect of the examinations which have been recommended by the Advisory Council to the bishops and approved by the latter collectively, and in case of changes in the regulations similarly to inform all Bishops ... to recommend to the Advisory Council such changes in the regulations for the examinations as may from time to time seem to them expedient.[30]

In the case of the UPE in 1915 the name of the examination was changed to the General Ordination Examination, which title was to last for well over half a century. To start with, the content essentially remained the same as the UPE but in 1919 a new examination was established for service candidates known as the Central Service Candidates' Examination which is considered in Chapter 4. The two examinations were combined into one in the early 1920s.

In the case of the Central Entrance Examination there was a different problem. When it was handed over to the Council the CACTM Report on Examinations of 1915 noted that, because the prospectus for the CEE required those who had not passed the examination to spend a preliminary year in a recognized theological college, not necessarily residentially, many students had been encouraged to pursue alternative examinations to the CEE, which could be taken in less than a year. The committee recommended that the solution lay in requiring all non-graduate candidates to spend three years in a theological college, but to allow them to take the CEE at various times in the first year of their course. This had not significantly increased the numbers taking the CEE and in 1921 the Examinations Committee recommended to the Council that the CEE should be abolished.[31] The Council's recommendation was accepted by the bishops and reported back to the Council in the same year.[32] In the future it was agreed that no one could start at a theological college unless they had passed

---

30 CACTM minutes, 25/26 October 1915.
31 CACTM minutes, 26 January 1921.
32 CACTM minutes, 24 May 1921.

'an examination of matriculation standard',[33] which was then the requirement for entry into a university. It therefore meant that any candidate wishing to enter a theological college had to get up to the standard of matriculation before formally starting at a college, which did not prevent some colleges from providing informal help prior to a candidate officially starting at the college, using the alternatives to the CEE that they had long used. By 1921 many candidates were also being raised to the level of matriculation by the Test School at Knutsford, discussed in Chapters 4 and 5, so the abolition of the CEE may not have been seen as causing huge disruption to the less academic candidate.

The financing of training

A fundamental issue for the future was the financing of training. At the very first meeting of the Council in April 1913 it called upon the bishops to note 'the establishment of diocesan Ordination Candidates' Funds (where they do not exist) and their greatly increased support (where they do exist) are urgently necessary'. They did, however, a year later recommend that 'funds collected under the Church Finance Schemes should be used to assist individuals rather than to subsidise institutions'.[34]

The importance of the role of finance was recognized even more after the war started when, in October 1916, the Convocations were requested to increase the numbers on the Council to allow the Central Board of Finance to appoint not more than three members to sit on the Council, and at the following meeting, no doubt anticipating what they knew would happen in dealing with returning servicemen seeking ordination after the war, they asked the archbishops to send a circular letter 'pointing out to the secretaries of Diocesan Boards of Finance and other Ordination Candidates' Funds, that there will undoubtedly be a considerable accumulation of ordination candidates after the war and urging the necessity of accumulating funds, before the close of the war, for the assistance of these candidates'. They also asked the archbishops to 'issue an appeal for an emergency fund to be received by the Central Board of Finance,

---

33 Both Upper Houses of the two Convocations had passed resolutions with this form of words in May 1924.
34 CACTM minutes, 13/14 February 1914.

and to be administered by the Central Advisory Council, the powers of the Council to be enlarged for that purpose'.[35]

In the event these suggestions were caught up in the financial proposals discussed in Chapter 4, but the need to act to provide financial support for those in training as recommended by the 1908 Commission was recognized from the very outset by the new Council.

The new universities

From its beginning the Council was also concerned in establishing a church presence in the new universities. It appointed a committee to consider hostels at them and noted that there were three sorts of hostels: those that were for ordinands alone, those that were for any churchman and those that were secular in character. The Committee was concerned with the first two. It noted that Durham University was well provided for (with St Chad's and St John's Colleges), and that progress was being made in a number of other universities with hostels or forming links with theological colleges (for example, Lichfield with Birmingham University, and Mirfield with Leeds University), but that in some there was little or no provision or even plans for halls where ordinands could reside. It recommended the development of the hostels' system in London, Manchester, Liverpool, Leeds, Sheffield and Wales and the establishing of new hostels in Birmingham and Bristol, and they drew the attention of the Council to the possibility of such a hostel system encouraging ordinands from the new universities.[36] In the event the proposal was overtaken by World War One and its consequences, but using the resources of the new universities, and particularly those with theological faculties, was recognized from an early stage.

The only hostel that appears to have been established as a result of this initiative was Brassey Hall which provided accommodation for those attending Victoria University in Manchester. Its constitution was reported in 1920 to CACTM where it was stated:

> Before the beginning of each financial year the Council [of the Hall] shall send to the Central Advisory Council for Training for the Ministry an

---

35 CACTM minutes, 13 February 1917.

36 The early papers of CACTM are available in CERC.CACTM/COU/D/1 and the very earliest were not numbered. The second and more substantial report on this question is CACTM paper 6 of 1913.

estimate of the sum required for the ensuing year, specifying the proposed expenditure in detail, and the Central Advisory Council of Training for the Ministry after consultation with the Council shall recommend to the Central Board of Finance the sum to be provided.[37]

It was a hall vested in the Central Board of Finance, and it housed some 30 service candidates taking their university courses. The financial pressures under which the Church was operating at the time make it the more remarkable that even one such hall was established rather than the many that were envisaged in the report of 1913.

An inspection regime

The Council's Terms of Reference required it to provide for the inspections of theological colleges, and at the Council's second meeting in July 1913 a committee was set up to establish the arrangements. The committee was chaired by Johnson, the Principal of Cuddesdon; and it included Warman, then Principal of St Aidan's, Birkenhead. It reported at the following meeting in November, when the Council passed a resolution that 'all colleges desiring recognition to apply at once for inspection and that the work be begun as soon as possible; but that no list of colleges recommended by the Council should be drawn up till the work of inspection be far advanced'.[38] The scope of the inspections was outlined in the first report of the committee to the Council.[39] There were four areas identified.

The first was the theological training offered by the college. Inspectors would examine the curriculum and observe lectures and examination scripts with a view to ensuring that the range of subjects was appropriate and what it described as 'its proportion, its definiteness and its tone' was acceptable, by which was presumably meant that it was broad enough to reflect the Church of England in which the students would be subsequently ministering.

The second matter was practical training, in which were included voice production, composing and delivering sermons, teaching, the principles and practice

---

37 The Constitution of the Manchester hostel was reported in CACTM paper 117a in 1920 and the numbers there reported in the 1921 Summary of Proceedings of CACTM (paper 129) in CERC.CACTM/COU/D2.

38 CACTM minutes, 19/20 November 1913.

39 CACTM paper 5, 1913.

of parish work including sick visiting, charitable relief and some understanding of social questions and what was described as 'the right attitude towards them' – presumably it was for the inspectors to judge what the 'right attitude' was. The report also included in this area some knowledge of the missionary work of the Church and the place of foreign missions in Christian life and thought.

The third area was considered to be the most difficult and delicate part of any inspection – devotional training – but the Committee stated that it believed this could be investigated by a few days' residence in the college and being present at services and having entry to all parts of college life.

Finally, there were the practical business arrangements of the college, including the state of the premises and finances, including its sources and payment of staff. 'It is certain that a collection of information in this respect would be invaluable for those who have to establish new Colleges.'

The report recommended that there should be at least two inspectors for each inspection, one of whom should be experienced in the inspection of educational establishments, where it was recognized that 'for this post a layman would be as efficient as one in Holy Orders'. The other should be an experienced clergyman.

In April 1915 it was agreed that the inspection committee would send to each college that it would recommend to the Council for recognition a copy of the inspectors' report to the principal, the chairman of the governing body and the bishop in whose diocese the college was situated.

In May 1917 some resolutions were considered regarding the publishing of any list of officially recognized colleges before the inspection process was completed. It was finally agreed that it should be said that no list was yet available but 'pending the issue of such a list, the following information is extracted from the handbook of theological colleges' (Longmans 1915).

There is no evidence that bishops were unhappy with these proposals, or saw them as a limitation of their power, indeed many would probably have welcomed an external judgement of the institutions for which they were responsible, but in October of the same year the inspection committee's report raised the question of episcopal visitorship of colleges and agreed that no college be recommended for recognition by the bishops which had not an English or Welsh diocesan bishop as visitor. However, it was also agreed that where there was already a visitor who was not a diocesan bishop this requirement should not be pressed until there was a vacancy in the office.

Inevitably the war had delayed the process and it was not until January 1921 that the chairman of the inspections committee (Warman, by then Bishop of

Truro) reported that the work of the inspection of theological colleges had been resumed. Just over a year later the process was complete and in May 1922 Warman moved on behalf of the inspections committee that 28 colleges be recommended to the bishops for recognition.[40]

There was, however, an interesting footnote to the report. The Conference of Modern Churchmen had been recently held at Girton College, Cambridge, where some traditional expressions of belief found in many other parts of the Church were called into question. One of the acknowledged leaders of English Modernism was the Principal of Ripon Hall, Oxford, Dr H. D. A. Major. The footnote said:

> Ripon Hall, Oxford is included in the list. It was inspected by the Bishop of Edinburgh and the Dean of Lincoln, whose report dated June 11, 1921, was entirely favourable, only minor matters being the subject of criticism; but at the same time we cannot ignore the prominent position taken by the Principal in connection with the Conference of Modern Churchmen held at Girton College, Cambridge, which took place after the visit of the inspectors. The Committee declined, as outside its competence, to express an opinion on the subject, nor does it recommend the Council to do so. It seems to us that it is for the Bishops and not for the Council to decide what steps, if any, should be taken, but we do not feel justified in passing over the matter in silence.

The bishops remained silent and Ripon Hall continued to be recognized.

---

40 The colleges recommended to the bishops for recognition were listed in an unnumbered paper accepted by the Council on 16 May 1922:

St Aidan's Birkenhead	Bishop Wilson's, Isle of Man	Lichfield	Ridley Hall, Cambridge
Westcott House, Cambridge	Lincoln	Ely	Wells
Llandaff	King's College, London	Cuddesdon	Dorchester
St John's Highbury	Leeds Clergy School	St Paul's, Burgh	Mirfield
Bishops' College, Cheshunt	St Stephen's House, Oxford	Chichester	Egerton Hall, Manchester
Ripon Hall, Oxford	Wycliffe Hall, Oxford	Warminster	St Augustine's, Canterbury
St John's College, Durham	Coates Hall, Edinburgh	Salisbury	Kelham

Quite aside from the specific question about Ripon Hall it is not clear how rigorous or demanding the inspection regime was. There is certainly no evidence that any college was closed as a result of any critical inspection, and neither is there any evidence from the inspection committee's reports to the Council that colleges were rebelling against the demands of the scheme. Nonetheless the fact that any inspection at all of colleges was taking place was a new departure for the theological colleges and that might have brought some comfort to the bishops ultimately responsible for them. The inspection process started then continued, with modifications, throughout the century and continues to the present day.

Widening the social base

The 1908 Commission's report recommended that the social base from which candidates for ordination came should be broadened, and this was a matter close to the heart of Temple. In May 1915 he pressed the case for working-class candidates and successfully proposed a resolution, seconded by Warman:

> Whereas it appears that the difficulty of obtaining in great numbers satisfactory candidates from the working classes is partly due to the fact that candidates have to offer themselves, and the best working men shrink from doing this – that it is desirable in every diocese to form some organisation for discovering those who ought to consider the claims of the ministry, and for putting those claims before them. That all grown-up men so 'called' to the Ministry, if of working class origin, should be required to attend a three years tutorial class, while still pursuing their secular trade, as part of the test of fitness.[41]

A committee was established under the chairmanship of the Bishop of Exeter to examine the matter and a conference was called in May 1915 with representatives from the Diocesan Ordination Candidates Committee, with bishops' nominees, and a number of interested people including members of the Council. The committee report (Appendix D) essentially encouraged the careful recruitment

---

41 CACTM minutes, 4 February 1915.

of suitable candidates described as 'vigorous, intelligent and earnest lads, between fourteen and eighteen years of age, at work in dockyards, factories, collieries, and other industrial works'. It went on to suggest careful selection and then careful training, the abundant provision of funds through the Central Board of Finance, and the establishment of a central committee rather than leaving it to diocesan committees.

The report, dated October 1915, was presented to CACTM that month and received. It was clearly a very far-seeing recommendation which, had it been put into practice as suggested, might have had far-reaching consequences. However, it would have represented the creating of a centrally sponsored programme in the context when decision-making was largely in the hands of dioceses and the forces of pragmatism and caution in the Council prevailed. At the suggestion of the Bishop of Oxford (Gore) the report was referred back to the committee to reconsider the recommendation. The matter came back to the Council at their February 1916 meeting. They moved the burden on providing this to the dioceses rather than the Central Board and concluded that a separate body was not needed either nationally or diocesan, but that this should be part of the responsibility of any Diocesan Ordination Candidates Committee. They recommended:

1. That the Central Advisory Council hold it to be of the greatest possible importance that in every diocese an Ordination Candidates Committee should be established and made effective and adequately supplied with funds by the Diocesan Board of Finance and from other sources and that the members of the Upper House of Canterbury and the Upper House of York be respectfully requested to give effect of this resolution wherever such Committees are not already established and provided.
2. That a memorandum on the scope and duties and functions of Diocesan Ordination Candidates Committees be drawn up with as little delay as possible, and when approved by the Council be sent to every Diocesan Bishop for the assistance and information of Ordination Candidates Committees.

It would have been remarkable if any other conclusion had been reached in 1916 as by then the consequences of the devastation of the war was evident to all, to say nothing of the forthcoming debate between the relative power of the dioceses and the central church bodies and on the overall financial position of the Central Board of Finance.

How far individual Diocesan Ordination Candidates Committees sought to implement the proposals for candidates who had little early education is not known and probably impossible to discover, but the work done by CACTM was widely reported. The CACTM decision effectively prevented Temple's scheme from being given any national basis, but his desire to broaden the social base of the Church's ministers was achieved by something else which he must have detested, World War One.

Within the first few years of its life the Council had therefore embarked on some critical issues. It acquired responsibility for the major examinations regarding ordination; it started the process of establishing an inspection regime for theological colleges; encouraged although not enforced graduate candidates to attend theological colleges; presented the issue of the financing of training as a challenge to the Church; started some engagement with the new universities; and had at least debated the widening of the backgrounds from which clergy came. It was an impressive beginning.

4

World War One

The war was a traumatic event for the whole of Europe, and its consequences profound. The sheer level of human misery it engendered presented a huge challenge for the Church of England in seeking to minister to the people left at home, many of whom were bereaved, to say nothing of the difficulties facing the chaplains ministering to servicemen; nearly three-quarters of a million from the United Kingdom alone were killed and one and a half million men were permanently weakened by wounds or the effect of gas.[1] Clergy who served as chaplains to the forces were brought face-to-face with suffering on an unimaginable scale: 20,000 soldiers killed and 40,000 injured on the first day of the Battle of the Somme in 1916. At the beginning of the war 97 Anglican chaplains were available to the Chaplain-General. By the Armistice the total number had risen to 1,985 out of the total of 3,475 chaplains of all denominations. Temporary chaplains were appointed for a year and not all renewed when their tour ended, some 668 resigning their commissions during the war. Speaking at the Convocation of Canterbury in February 1918, Archbishop Davidson stated that 2,472 Anglican chaplains had held commissions since the start of the war.[2] The war and the suffering they encountered had a profound effect on their theological understanding and their empathy with ordinary Englishmen facing extraordinary circumstances. The human and religious challenges were enormous.

The effectiveness of the chaplains is a debated issue. Alan Wilkinson quotes a number of authors who served in the war including Robert Graves, C. E. Montague, Siegfried Sassoon and Wilfrid Owen, who were critical of the chaplains they encountered, in some cases for being lazy, normally being well behind the lines, and often engaged purely on social activities. Owen offered a deeper critique of the failure of Christianity itself to engage with the real horrors

---

1 A. J. P. Taylor, 1965, *English History 1914–1945*, Oxford: Clarendon Press, p. 120 (Book Club Associates edition 1977).

2 Michael Snape, 2008, *The Royal Army Chaplains' Department, 1796–1953*, Woodbridge: Boydell Press, p. 183f. In *The Church of England and the First World War*, Alan Wilkinson gives slightly different figures for the start of the war but the general picture remains the same.

of war. Wilkinson also commented on the role of class: 'whereas many ordinary soldiers came from working-class backgrounds, and knew what hardship and privation were, the clergy of the C of E were almost wholly from a professional background and most had no experience of an ordinary job before ordination.'[3] Roman Catholic chaplains did not suffer from the same problem. He concluded:

> It is precisely the Church of England's pride in its 'national and cultural herit-age' which has prevented it from evolving a genuinely working-class priest-hood or churchmanship. So, both Anglican chaplains and soldiers arrived at the front with virtually no commonly accepted sacramental shorthand with which to communicate, either with God or with one another.[4]

He quoted B. K. Cunningham, who was warden of the chaplains' training school in St Omar:

> My own opinion is that the pre-war theological college system, as judged by the padres it produced, did not come well out of the experiences of war; the devotional training had been along too narrow lines and depended too much on favourable environment, and when that was no longer given the padre was apt to lose his bearings.[5]

Wilkinson's criticism is, however, balanced by his recognition that some of the chaplains were outstanding in their bravery and their ability to relate to the troops, and he notes with approval the role of men such as Geoffrey Studdert Kennedy,[6] F. R. Barry,[7] Charles Raven,[8] Neville Talbot[9] and 'Tubby' Clayton.[10]

---

3 Wilkinson, *War*, p. 131.

4 Wilkinson, *War*, p. 134.

5 Wilkinson, *War*, p. 152.

6 Geoffrey Studdert-Kennedy (1883–1929) volunteered to be an army chaplain in 1914 and won the MC in 1917 for helping wounded men in no-man's land. He was known to the troops as Woodbine Willie because he always carried a pack of Woodbine cigarettes to offer to wounded and dying men. He wrote a series of poems, some in dialect form, which were later published as *The Unutterable Beauty*.

7 Frank Russell Barry (1890–1976) was to be Principal of Knutsford Test School discussed later in this chapter.

8 Charles Raven (1885–1964) was later to be Regius Professor of Divinity in Cambridge, Master of Christ's College and a member of the Archbishops' Commission on Training from 1937.

9 Neville Talbot (1879–1943) was involved with Tubby Clayton in establishing Talbot House. In 1920 he was appointed Bishop of Pretoria in South Africa, serving there until 1933, when he retired to England to be Vicar of St Mary's, Nottingham.

10 P. B. Clayton (1885–1972) was known to all as 'Tubby' Clayton. With Neville Talbot he founded Talbot House and subsequently TocH. For 40 years from 1922 he was the Vicar of All Hallows, by the Tower of London.

Michael Snape, who has written the official history of the Royal Army Chaplains' Department, gives a slightly different picture. He questions whether the social background of the chaplains was quite as limiting in enabling them to relate to the men[11] and he notes that of the chaplains three received the Victoria Cross for bravery, all for rescuing or caring for the wounded; 37 DSOs; and 205 MCs and bars.[12] He also says 'a recent estimate put the number of chaplains who were killed as a result of enemy action in the First World War at 102'.[13] It scarcely reveals a group of men hiding well in the rear of battle.

While the debate between Wilkinson and Snape is wider than merely the effectiveness of World War One Anglican army chaplains it is, of course, possible that on that specific issue both Wilkinson and Snape are partly right. Measuring ministerial effectiveness is not an exact science, expectations of clergy might vary hugely, and a chaplain who may have been very effective to one group of people might be seen as a failure to another. Also, it would be remarkable if, out of the nearly 2,500 men who served for periods as chaplains there were not some who revealed weaknesses of temperament, intellect, imagination, human sensitivity, character or sheer bravery. Some, too, might have found it impossible to shake off their class background to relate to ordinary soldiers. What is clear, as both Wilkinson and Snape acknowledge, is that some of the chaplains were outstanding and effective in relating to ordinary men. Exactly what proportion they were of the whole and what the numerical division was between the good, the bad and the indifferent is probably now impossible to judge.

At the beginning of the war few if any realized what the full consequences would be, indeed in October 1914 many spoke of the 'men being home by Christmas'. The first meeting of the Council after war started appears to have been primarily concerned with the possible loss of ordination candidates to war service. In the atmosphere of the time the Council's recommendations may have seemed measured:

> In view of the desire which many candidates for ordination feel to offer themselves as combatants in this war, and in view of the pressure which is being put upon them from many quarters to do so, this Council considers

---

11 Snape, *Chaplains*, p. 11.

12 Snape, *Chaplains*, p. 224.

13 Snape, *Chaplains*, p. 226.

that it is acting in accordance with the constant sentiment of the Church if it encourages those who have a clear sense of vocation to the ministry and are preparing for it to resist the inclination and pressure which we have referred to, and to go straight forward in their preparation for Holy Orders.[14]

That was not a policy universally observed. Several ordinands offered immediately for war service, perhaps influenced by some of the more jingoistic bishops, but also no doubt by the wider public atmosphere of the time. Three of the eleven men in training at Bishops' Hostel, Farnham, enlisted as combatants at the outset of the war, and similar proportions applied to those in training at Mirfield.[15] Out of 32 theological colleges 362 men withdrew for war service.[16] At a conference of theological college principals it was agreed that they should give no central guidance, it was a matter for each man's individual conscience.[17] Many were subsequently killed in the fighting, and certainly many believed that it was quite right that the Church of England should identify with the nation and suffer its losses among the nation's youth as a whole. Others completed their training but then offered for war service as chaplains. Some felt that the demands of ministering to those left behind in England was sufficient justification for them to pursue their calling as suggested by the Council's recommendation. On one matter, however, Davidson was clear. 'By every line of thought which I have pursued I am led to the conclusion that I have been right in maintaining from the first that the position of an actual combatant in our Army is incompatible with the position of one who has sought and received Holy Orders.' Neville Talbot, an army chaplain later to become Bishop of Pretoria, wrote to the men at Farnham: 'Authority has been loyal to the true Christian instinct and tradition. Those that minister about holy things, and hold their Lord's commission, must not have blood upon their hands, however justly shed.'[18]

One issue that came to the fore quite quickly in the bishops' minds was the effect of the war on the colleges, and a special meeting of the Council

---

14 CACTM minutes, 19 October 1914.

15 F. W. B. Bullock, 1976, *A History of Training for the Ministry*, London: Home Words Printing and Publishing, p. 58.

16 John Moorman, 1947, *B. K. Cunningham*, London: SCM, p. 69. The figure of 32 theological colleges does not tally with the number of colleges recorded either before or after the war in official Church of England publications, but Moorman may have included some non-Anglican colleges.

17 Moorman, *Cunningham*, p. 69.

18 Moorman, *Cunningham*, p. 70.

was called at Lambeth Palace on 13 July 1915. The Archbishop of Canterbury addressed the Council seeking advice on whether amalgamations of colleges should be sought, although without any suggestion that they should be forced to do so. No resolution was proposed, and the general opinion seemed to be that the colleges were able to continue without a central and public appeal for help, such as had been supposed to be necessary, and that transference or amalgamation would not be desirable. In 1912 the Church of England Year Book listed 29 theological colleges or hostels, and in 1922, 28 were recommended by the inspections committee, so it seems the bishops' fears were unrealized in any great measure.

The effect of the war on recruitment for the ministry can be seen in the numbers ordained over that period. In 1911, 711 men had been ordained, the first time the annual figure had exceeded 700 since 1895. In 1912 that declined slightly to 686, in 1913 to 670, but in 1914 went up to 685. But thereafter the decline following so many men serving in the Forces was rapid; in 1915 it was down to 526, in 1916 to 387, in 1917 to 210, and in 1918 to 119. Urgent action was clearly necessary.

It was realized that the serving forces might well provide a number of candidates when the war ended. In 1915 two chaplains, Neville Talbot and P. B. (Tubby) Clayton, instituted Talbot House (named after Neville Talbot's brother who had been killed nearby) in Poperinge, near Ypres in Flanders. Talbot House became a place of peace and quiet from where chaplaincy could be exercised to the troops in a Belgian town that had become a garrison town for the British Army. Although Clayton was himself very well connected socially he put up a sign 'Abandon rank all ye who enter here', but he also put up a notice asking for signatures to the statement 'If God decides to bring me through this War, I vow to take this as a hint from him that I shall serve and help the church in future throughout the life he gives back to me.' All who signed it were asked to pray with Clayton, with the recognition that many would remain as laymen.[19]

Other chaplains were also finding cases of men who wished to offer for some service if they survived the war and on 11 October 1916 Bishop Llewellyn Gwynne, Deputy Chaplain General to the Forces (DCG),[20] wrote to

19 R. V. H. Burne, 1960, *Knutsford: The Story of the Ordination Test School*, London: SPCK.

20 Llewellyn Henry Gwynne trained at St John's, Highbury, where he was a contemporary of the Chaplain-General, Bishop Taylor Smith. Gwynne then ministered in the East Midlands before he moved

Davidson suggesting that the recruitment of suitable candidates should be carefully considered.[21] This was sent by the archbishop to the bishops, in the first instance for private consideration. Gwynne wrote:

The purpose of this Memorandum, written at the request of the Archbishop of Canterbury, is –

To state for the information of the Archbishops of Canterbury and York and the Bishops at home such facts as have come to the knowledge of the Chaplains serving with the British Expeditionary Forces as to the existence of a supply of Ordination candidates, actual and prospective, among officers, non-commissioned officers, and men of the Army; and further:

To put on paper what is felt by many of the Chaplains as to the opportunities which there are for discovering and fostering vocations to the Ministry among both officers and men, and as to the response which would be forthcoming in answer to any well-thought-out scheme put forward by the Church to deal with the situation.

And it is hoped that two definite things may follow:

That the Archbishops and Bishops will be able to assure the Deputy Chaplain-General and other Chaplains in France that the means of training and financial assistance are being prepared by the Church at home to meet the arrival of such candidates after the war, and

That they will be able to give to the Chaplains by some such means as will be suggested in this Memorandum authoritative encouragement and direction in dealing with this task of the discovery and fostering of vocation, which in the providence of God has come to them at this crisis in the history of our Church.

---

to the Sudan as a CMS missionary in 1899. He was consecrated suffragan Bishop of Khartoum in 1908 and was on leave in London when war broke out. He volunteered as a temporary chaplain and was accepted even though he was over the age of 50, which Taylor Smith normally considered the upper limit. Gwynne was appointed Deputy Chaplain-General after pressure from Lord Halifax, a leading Anglo-Catholic layman, to find someone more sympathetic to non-evangelicals than Bishop Taylor Smith. In fact Gwynne was himself, if anything, an evangelical, but he was clearly a warm and friendly man who inspired great loyalty from Anglican chaplains. Michael Snape points out that his appointment had the effect of dividing the Chaplains Department as Gwynne was asked primarily to relate to Anglicans, while the Department included Church of Scotland and Roman Catholic Chaplains. It was a problem that would be repeated in a slightly different way in World War Two.

21 Davidson papers, Vol. 346, pp. 17–30.

The memorandum went on to note the urgency of the need for more candidates and of the fact of deaths of theological college students. The rolls of honour of theological colleges at the end of September 1916 gave the figures:

Killed – 75

Missing – 11

Permanently Disabled – 7

Total – 93

Gwynne also pointed out that most candidates for ordination would come from those in military service. 'The advent of compulsory service[22] has really settled the matter. It is here, and with the other forces at home and abroad, that the ordination candidates of the future now are.'[23]

Gwynne thought the future hopeful as there were many potential candidates for ordination in the services. He had already sent an enquiry and had a number of names of officers and men whose training for ordination had been interrupted by their war service and others who had already expressed their feeling that they had a vocation if they survived the war. By 1 October 1916, 100 names had been sent in, almost equally divided between those two groups, and by then only one-eighth of the divisions had made returns. Gwynne therefore estimated that there could be around 1,000 men in those two categories. This did not include those who were 'thinking towards' ordination, which could substantially increase the numbers. But some assurance was needed that provision would be available to help those who offered.

He was anxious that the thought should be put in men's minds earlier rather than later, not least of all because he believed a situation of stress could provide the context for someone thinking of the possibility of ordination. 'No instinct among the wounded or among thoughtful survivors, after some stern ordeal, is more natural or more sacred than a deep spirit of thankfulness. And it is the task of religion to transmute the thanks-giving into thanks-living.'[24] He therefore proposed that the army chaplains should produce a central register to be kept in England of possible candidates. It would be a varied group and he fully understood the implications for the traditional picture of Church of England

---

22 Introduced in January 1916 for unmarried men between the ages of 18 and 41. Taylor, *History*, p. 53.

23 Memorandum, p. 3; Davidson papers, Vol. 346, p. 19.

24 Memorandum, p. 5.

clergymen. Of the list he said that while some would have been men thinking of ordination before the war the majority would be non-university men from both officers and men of the new armies. He recognized that many of them might initially think that ordination was beyond them; however good their intellectual energies in other directions, they 'do not belong to the Levitical tribe'.[25]

Gwynne was more than prepared to see that challenged. He was not arguing for the introduction of ignorant men into the ministry, but he wanted to widen the ministry to those whose education had been other than the normal experience of pre-war clergy, and he saw that as a clear gain. 'As education other than classical becomes more and more general, there is a danger of the Church having a clergy ignorant of much that forms the outlook, intellectual as well as social, of other men'.[26]

Not only should the cultural challenge be made, but so too should the financial consequences be faced. He believed that the need for ordained men should be put frankly to those serving in the forces and argued for a pastoral letter from the archbishops in the name of the bishops saying that the door was open without financial or university qualifications, and that the Church would provide both financial and educational opportunities. He then hoped that this would encourage potential candidates to approach their chaplain.

He also was wise and far-seeing enough to note that not every chaplain could be entrusted with the final responsibility of accepting men onto the register. That would have to be the work of picked men, and he noted that the Deputy Chaplain-General was already taking steps to find the names of chaplains to whom could be given the all-important task.

The memorandum went on to suggest some conditions of acceptance, including that candidates should normally be under 35 and unmarried, but Gwynne also importantly suggested that funds should be made available to train candidates and that the training should be appropriately adapted to the needs of returning servicemen.[27] On the latter point there had been some debate already in CACTM. In February 1916 the Bishop of Oxford, Gore, had proposed:

> that the Council, anticipating a perhaps considerable number of candidates for Holy Orders from the ranks of those who are at present combatants,

---

25 Memorandum, p. 8.
26 Memorandum, p. 12.
27 Memorandum, p. 9.

desires to represent to the Bishops its earnest hope that, in the case of those who are of normal and of abnormal age, their course of special theological training – viz. in the case of graduates one year and in the case of non-graduates two years – shall not be shortened.

A rider was added by the Bishop of Ely, seconded by Temple and carried:

The Council would, however, strongly urge that the course of training for such men be specially constructed, the aim being to concentrate entirely upon the systematic study of the Bible and of the principles of theology; in particular, Greek should for such men be an optional subject. [28]

The requirement of ancient languages was not solved so easily; in October 1917 the chairman reported that the conditions of acceptance of service candidates had been accepted by the bishops, but 'with a modification as regards the requirement of Latin'. The bishops had insisted that Latin should still be required, but Dr Walter Frere, at the time Superior of Mirfield, moved 'that the Council very respectfully approach the Bishops begging them to reconsider their decision as to the necessity of requiring knowledge of Latin from Service candidates, and to allow them to offer Greek as an alternative'.[29] His motion was passed by 15 votes to two, the bishops present not voting. The bishops in Convocation subsequently accepted the advice.

Meanwhile the archbishops (Davidson and Lang) wrote to all soldiers, dated Advent 1916 and entitled 'Ordination after the War'. It was a remarkable document in the range of men to whom it was distributed, the change to traditional attitudes towards the social background of those who might enter the ordained ministry it implied, in a modification in the rules required of those to be ordained in terms of their knowledge of ancient languages, and the clear commitment it gave to fund training for ordained ministry. It ended:

The Church of the future will need recruits for its Ministry from men of all kinds of upbringing, circumstances and education. Christ is calling labourers into a harvest field, ready, as perhaps never before, for labourers of the right kind. It is our duty, as it is our privilege, to point out that the

---

28 CACTM minutes, 1/2 February 1916.
29 CACTM minutes, 25 October 1917.

door is open not to those only who have had certain previous advantages of upbringing and education, but to all who have the requisite character, fitness and mental equipment. They must realise what lies before them in the preparation years, but, given the necessary self-sacrifice on their part, we have no doubt of being able to find such money as will be needed, and to adapt to an unusual kind of demand our requirements as to training and examination. They may, for example, be instances in which even the elementary knowledge of Greek which is usually required might be dispensed with. But there ought not to be, and there need be, no lowering of our standard. For let us be quite clear. The last thing we could promise and the last thing true-hearted men would seek would be an easy entrance to an easy life. The entrance will have real difficulties, real but surmountable. The life work, just in proportion to its joy of service and its noble range of opportunity, will be exacting in its demands, but a man may pass with courage from the venture of War to the venture, at home and across the sea, of winning men to the Kingdom of Christ. It is to that enterprise that we invite you when the war is won. To a Christian man it is the noblest calling in the world.[30]

Gwynne also wrote assuring suitable men of financial support, and advising them to contact the newly planned Service Candidates' Committee, the details of which were finally recommended by CACTM in 1917. It was independent of CACTM but closely connected with it and it was charged with the work of interviewing and sifting service candidates. It contained a representative of every Diocesan Ordination Candidates Council, representatives of navy and army chaplains, some of the existing members of CACTM and other appointed members. It was chaired by the Dean of York. Meanwhile, as mentioned in the previous chapter, CACTM had asked the archbishops and bishops to write to all Diocesan Boards of Finance asking them to make provision for financing the training of service ordinands, and to launch an appeal for funds to be given to the Central Board of Finance to receive money that would be administered by CACTM. A letter was received from the CBF saying that 'Chaplains of the Forces may without hesitation encourage really suitable men to offer themselves for ordination, in the anticipation that bursaries will be forthcoming for the

---

30 Davidson papers, Vol. 346, p. 45f.

college expenses of those who may be acceptable.'[31] It was a brave commitment by the CBF.

A register was established by the Chaplains' Department of those who wished to be considered as candidates for ordination, although it was recognized that any such register would be provisional as decisions on who should be ordained rested ultimately with the ordaining bishop. It was resolved to ask the bishops to appoint from CACTM a board or boards for the testing of candidates and the chaplains were told 'that it is of the utmost importance that only names should be sent in of men with such mental capacity and general education as will render them capable of profiting by their Theological College course, and will give them a reasonable chance of passing the required examination.'[32] Testing would be done by the methods adopted at the time, evidence from examinations (if taken) and personal interview.

One delicate question that confronted the Service Candidates Committee and CACTM was how to deal with those who had suffered physically and psychologically as a result of war service. A CACTM committee was established to investigate the issue and it tried to combine sympathy for the men involved with the needs of the Church for effective ministry, not least of all in the practical consequences of administering the sacraments. Its 1917 conclusions bear repeating, if only for revealing the harrowing nature of the matters they had to consider. It concluded with:

the following suggestions as regards the chief defects:

Hand. – The loss of both hands must be an absolute disqualification. If the candidate has lost one hand, he must be able to hold the paten firm by the aid of some device, either of the nature of an artificial hand or by the use of some special kind of paten, or both, so as to have the uninjured hand free for administrating the consecrated bread.

Leg. – The candidate must be able to move in such a way as to have both hands available (as defined above) for administering the paten. The bishop should assure himself of the candidate's capacity to carry out pastoral

---

31 CACTM minutes, 25 October 1917.
32 CACTM minutes, 13 February 1917.

visitation effectively. Attention is drawn to the difficulty of narrow, steep or winding stairs.

Eye. – In the case of blinded men the Bishop should assure himself of the candidate's celebrating and administering without real risk of accident, and that he will be able to read or repeat the service in a way that is edifying. It is most desirable that he will be able to have learnt to read Braille.

Hearing. – Total deafness should be an absolute disqualification. Short of that the very greatest care should be taken before accepting a deaf man; but quickness of perception may in part make up for the defect. The real difficulty is at the sick bed. Enquiry should be made as to the danger of the deafness increasing.

Defective speech. – This is a question of degree. In any serious case a strict view should be taken.

Nerves and General Health. – These require very careful enquiry. In severe cases reference should be made to an expert medical adviser, both with regard to the present state of the candidate and to what is likely to be anticipated in the more distant future.[33]

By 1919 agreement had been reached in the Examinations Committee and by the Council about the examination of service candidates, which would be by means of a specially created examination known as the Service Candidates Examination, for which successful candidates would not be divided into classes (unlike for the UPE). There would be nine papers in all: two on the Old Testament; two on the New Testament; one on the nature of religious truth, its evidence and authority, the Doctrine of God, of Christ, of Man; one on the Person and Work – in the Church and in the individual – of the Holy Spirit, the Ministry and the Sacraments, the Doctrine of the Last Things. In these two papers questions would also be set on the three Creeds, medieval developments, later formularies (Anglican and non-Anglican), and the historical background of these doctrinal

---

33 Davidson papers, Vol. 247, p. 210.

statements and divergences. A seventh paper would be on the continuity of the life of the Church from the beginning, with special reference to the History and Position of the Church of England. There would then be a paper on Christian Worship and one on Christian Morals. Candidates could ask for exemption from either Latin or Greek. It was recognized by the Committee that produced the paper that each bishop would desire before ordination to test his own candidates in Bible, Prayer Book and Doctrine.

> They believe that such an arrangement would enable the Bishop to establish complete individual contact between himself and the candidate through his Chaplains, and to satisfy himself as to the candidate's doctrinal position and aptitude for ministerial work, while leaving the Bishop complete freedom to reject a candidate on these grounds as well as those of intellectual fitness.[34]

With the end of the war it was proposed that the Service Candidates Committee should be integrated into CACTM as a Committee of the Council and it was agreed to appoint Canon Hicks as the first full-time Secretary of the Council and Secretary of the Service Candidates Committee. The assistant secretary was Revd Leslie Owen, a man who was to hold a critical position in CACTM in future years.

Knutsford Test School

One of the most remarkable developments from the war for the Church of England was the creation of the Test School at Knutsford. Dealing with those who came forward for ordination after the war presented only a small part of the challenge that faced the services in demobilizing men, and the British Army virtually turned itself into a university, with various 'schools' established by the military to prepare men for the occupations of civilian life. At the time of the Armistice over 3,000 candidates for ordination were on the register and Bishop Gwynne was given enthusiastic backing by General Headquarters to gather some of the service candidates who needed preliminary training. Officers went to Radingham under Talbot, and the Lewis Gun School at Le Touquet was given

---

34 CACTM paper 102, 1919, Examination of Service Candidates.

to Gwynne for other ranks. The Chaplains' Department was entrusted with full and absolute discretion for the carrying out of the experiment with non-commissioned candidates. A start was made at Le Touquet in December 1918 with the first draft of 70 candidates, increased almost immediately to 150.

F. R. Barry was appointed by Gwynne as the first principal at Le Touquet and he proved an inspired choice. The son of a country clergyman, he had won a scholarship to Bradfield School and then to Oriel College, Oxford, where he obtained a first in Greats. He stayed on for a fifth year to read theology, and in 1913 was elected fellow and chaplain and appointed tutor in theology. The Bishop of Oxford (Gore) required him to spend a term at Wells Theological College, after which he was ordained by Gore in Cuddesdon Parish Church in June 1914. After ordination as a priest he was commissioned as an army chaplain, going first to Egypt, then to France and the Somme. He was transferred to the 20th division and was with them for Passchendale, and also at the battle of Cambrai, when tanks were first used. In 1918 he was promoted to Deputy Assistant Chaplain-General, having won the DSO for ministering to wounded men in no-man's land. According to one of his biographers his men were angry that he was not awarded the VC. He was very slightly wounded, and then nearly succumbed to influenza, which killed 150,000 English people in the winter of 1918–19,[35] but he survived to be principal of the new Ordination Test School, appointed at the age of 28.

In January 1919 Archbishop Davidson visited the camp and agreed that the whole venture, together with the school for officers at Radingham, should be transferred to England. While there, Davidson also told the men of the pledge of financial support for those seeking ordination; Barry subsequently maintained that the first CACTM grants were issued at Le Touquet. Clayton was sent home to find somewhere and over lunch with a friend in the Home Office was told the only possibility of finding accommodation for the numbers required was a prison. 'Lead me to one,' replied Clayton, and he was taken to see the prison at Knutsford in Cheshire, then occupied by German prisoners of war. R. V. H. Burne was the historian of Knutsford and wrote:

It required vision and imagination to see in that grim, dirty and out-of-date building a possible home for ordination candidates. Fortunately those

---

35 Taylor, *History*, p. 112.

qualities were not lacking; and Clayton returned to Le Touquet with the news. When the school was finally established there some wag had pinned to the notice board a temperance leaflet warning of the dangers of alcohol containing a picture of a convict in a cell and the legend 'What has brought him to this?' Beneath it was written 'The Church of England!'[36]

The first group arrived from Flanders in March 1919, and the school prepared men for the Oxford Local Examinations, which allowed entrance to the universities. A candidate normally stayed there for six to nine months before passing to higher training either at a university or a theological college as soon as he was ready, and provided he was recommended for further training by Barry. It was known as the Ordination Test School because it did test candidates, not only academically but also more personally for their suitability for ministry.

Of the first 194 who passed through, 30 went to Oxford, 30 to Cambridge, 15 to Durham, 35 to Manchester, where a special hostel was started, seven to King's College, London and a few to the Welsh universities. A democratic structure, supported no doubt by years of army discipline, prevailed; the men wore shorts and no hats. Under Barry the staff included Clayton, soon to found TocH, R. V. H. Burne, who was to succeed Barry as principal and who became Archdeacon of Chester, and E. G. S. Wickham, who in turn succeeded Burne as principal in 1938. Mervyn Haigh, who was three years older than Barry, met Barry at Knutsford station to talk about working at the school having himself served as an army chaplain. Barry was subsequently to write a biography of Haigh, where he quotes Haigh's own private memoire. 'Before we had crossed the station bridge I began to feel that I had met a man with whom I should be more one in mind and spirit than I had ever been with any man before.' The principal certainly had the same feeling. 'Within a few hours it had been decided that Mervyn should join us as lecturer in Reformation and Renaissance history.'[37] Haigh was later to become chaplain to Cosmo Lang, Bishop of Coventry, later Bishop of Winchester.

At the end of the summer term 1920, 155 men left for further education, 111 for universities and 44 for theological colleges. By the Lent term of 1921, 690 men had passed through the school, only a small number of whom were civilians.

---

36 R. V. H. Burne, 1960, *Knutsford: The Story of the Ordination Test School*, London: SPCK, p. 3.
37 Frank Russell Barry, 1964, *Mervyn Haigh*, London: SPCK, p. 61.

In its critical years while at the gaol a total of 675 ex-servicemen were prepared for full-time ordination training of whom 435 were eventually ordained.[38]

Not all service candidates needed to go to Knutsford; some were suitably qualified to go straight to university or to theological colleges. Some universities, Oxford, Cambridge, Durham and King's College, London made special provision for war degrees which did not involve three years' residence as war service would count towards the degree. In the Council minutes of 24 October 1918 the committee charged with looking at the proposals from both Oxford and Cambridge to prepare men for the ministry reported. The final resolution was:

> That the Council welcomes heartily the proposal to provide fuller preparation for Ordination at Oxford and Cambridge. As far as those who avail themselves of it reside in halls or hostels inspected by the Council and recognised by the Bishops, they satisfy the Bishops' requirements; but the Council feels bound to point out the great difficulty of adequate supervision over the spiritual training and discipline of habits of life of those who live in College, or in lodgings, or in private houses, and would be glad to have further information from the Committees as to the method by which they propose that such supervision should be exercised.

In practice in Cambridge and Oxford candidates resided in one of the theological colleges and so a system of supervision was provided. As was noted at Manchester University, Brassey Hall was opened in 1920 for nearly 30 service candidates taking their university course, and Durham and King's College, London continued to take service candidates.

In January 1923 the Council responded to a request from the CBF to the archbishops about the final date from which grants to new service candidates should be made, and the Council agreed that it should be from 30 September 1923.[39]

According to the CACTM 1924 Summary of Proceedings, which was published in 1925, a total of 3,584 men had been on the Register of Service Candidates, which would have included all those who had gone to Knutsford. Of that 3,584 some had died, some were rejected, some had withdrawn or there was no information about them since 1919, but of the rest, of those who were not

---

38 Wilkinson, *War*, p. 278.
39 CACTM minutes, 24 January 1923.

assisted financially 635 had been ordained and 159 were still in training, and of those who had been assisted financially 777 had been ordained and 99 were still in training.[40] If all those who were still in training were ordained it meant that 1,670 service candidates[41] joined the ministry of the Church of England.

In terms of the life of the Church of England and its ministry the war brought about a remarkable change in atmosphere. At the most fundamental level it was a theological challenge, to make sense of the notion of God in such circumstances, but more prosaically, it brought about major changes for the ministry itself. Through the archbishops' letter it vastly extended the range of the sort of candidates who might come into the ministry, it made the educational requirements more flexible, it created a body that had the power to oversee individual candidates for ordination, and it brought about the principle of full financial support for those in training. World War One brought many major social changes to England; the Church of England was not exempt from that process.

---

40 CACTM Summary of Proceedings 1924, No. 161.

41 This contrasts with the figures given by Roger Lloyd, 1966, *The Church of England 1900–65*, London: SCM, where Lloyd speaks of the archbishop's promise raising £378,000 to pay for the training of 1,039 service candidates. He gives no reference in his book to where those figures came from. His figures for those service candidates who went to Knutsford tally exactly with the figures given in this chapter, but his claim that of the ex-servicemen who were trained at the time 'the vast majority had much of their training at Knutsford' even by his own figures seems an exaggeration. 435 is not 'the vast majority' of 1,039, still less of 1,670. But Knutsford clearly was a very significant institution.

5

The Inter-War Years 1919–39

World War One had brought about great change to the Church of England's ministry, but was this change to be made permanent? Much of the debate within the Church of England after the war was whether the grants system that had made ordained ministry an option to those from a broader social class than had been the case before the war should continue and, if so, how. That was to be the dominant issue for CACTM for most of the period, yet it had to face it against the background of a new style of Church government.

The first meeting of the Church Assembly (then known as the National Assembly of the Church of England) was in June 1920. It had been brought about by the Enabling Act of 1919, which was seen by Davidson as a way of dealing with the problem of legislation required for the better management of the Church being squeezed out by pressure on parliamentary time. The Act provided for the Church itself to prepare and bring to Parliament its own legislation, although Davidson believed it would not be possible to get its creation through Parliament in wartime. The Life and Liberty Movement developed to challenge that delay and to bring pressure both on the Church and Parliament to expedite the change. William Temple in particular led the movement, but others including 'Dick' Sheppard, Vicar of St Martin's-in-the-Fields and F. A. Ironmonger, later Dean of Lichfield (and Temple's biographer) worked indefatigably for it. Temple in particular had toured the country eliciting support and the passing of the Act was a great personal triumph for him. The new Assembly replaced the Representative Church Council, established in 1903, which was essentially a consultative not an executive body. The Assembly had a legislative committee that was able to draw up draft legislation which could be presented to Parliament to bring about some long-standing requests for change for the Church. Without that essentially pragmatic pressure to produce a better system for dealing with Church legislation it is unlikely that the Enabling Act would have gone through.

2.64 Bishop of Gibraltar.
(F.C.N.Hicks)

F. C. N. Hicks
General Secretary of CACTM
1913–24
Bishop of Gibraltar 1927–33
Bishop of Lincoln 1933–42

Bishop Llewellyn Gwynne
Bishop of Khartoum 1908–20.
Voluntary Chaplain to the
Expeditionary Force in France from
1914, Deputy Chaplain-General
from 1915. After World War One he
returned to Khartoum, and from
1920 to 1945 was Bishop of Egypt
and the Sudan. Died in 1957

180.

BISHOP IN KHARTOUM. (LL.H.GWYNNE.)

Students at Knutsford Test School c. 1920

F. R. Barry
Principal of Knutsford Test School
1919–23
Bishop of Southwell 1941–63

Guy Warman
Member of CACTM from its instigation
in 1913
Chairman 1928–43
Bishop of Manchester 1929–47

Meeting of the Church Assembly before the building of the present Church House, Westminster c. 1930

Leslie Owen
Secretary of the Candidates Committee
1922–4
Member of the Archbishops' Commission on
Training 1937–44
Chairman of CACTM 1944–6
Bishop of Lincoln 1946–7

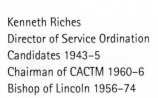

Alwyn T P Williams
Chairman of the Archbishops'
Commission on Training
1937–44
Dean of Christ Church, Oxford
1934–9
Bishop of Durham 1939–52
Bishop of Winchester 1952–61

Kenneth Riches
Director of Service Ordination
Candidates 1943–5
Chairman of CACTM 1960–6
Bishop of Lincoln 1956–74

But the role of the new Assembly was more than simply a drafting body for parliamentary legislation; it was a forum for debate on many issues affecting the Church, and its resolutions had at the very least a strong democratic force. It was hoped it would be a body that would revitalize the whole Church and, as such, was greeted, at least by some, with great enthusiasm. Others viewed it with foreboding and disquiet, most notably Hensley Henson, Bishop of Hereford, who had written of his opposition to the whole move. He believed that creating a new body which in some way spoke for the Church and which could draft legislation for itself represented the Church moving in a clearly sectarian direction. Between the two extremes represented by Henson and Temple was Davidson, by now after the war an immensely influential archbishop. At its initial meeting Davidson welcomed the new Assembly, 'It is a great hour in the history of the Church and the people of England', but he was cautious in his hopes for it.[1] But whatever Henson's fears, the Assembly now existed and Henson was not afraid to use the power of his rhetoric within it. CACTM was to discover just how significant the Church Assembly was, not least of all in its financial control over its budget.

Numbers of ordinations had dropped dramatically during World War One. Before the war, at its peak 711 men were ordained in 1911 and numbers remained in the high 600s. Thereafter they dropped rapidly, to 210 in 1917 and 119 in 1918. Recruitment, primarily from the military, was the key and numbers gradually rose, although never to the levels of before the war. By 1922 the annual figure of ordinations had risen to 458 and stayed above 400 until 1925, by which time the Church in Wales was disestablished and its ordinations were not included in the national figures. Numbers remained in the 300s a year for the rest of that decade until 1929, when they rose to 439, and then passed the 500 mark in 1930 and for most of the 1930s stayed above 500, often well above.

The debate about Knutsford 1919–37

For the early part of the period Knutsford was considered a great success by CACTM. Not only had it made a significant contribution to the numbers of

---

1 The story of the creation of the new Assembly is well told by Roger Lloyd, 1966, *The Church of England 1900–1965*, London: SCM, pp. 232–8 (where he seems to have got the date for the Life and Liberty's meeting in the Queen's Hall wrong; according to Henson it was on 16 July 1917, not the 26th as stated by Lloyd), pp. 243–5. Hensley Henson's opposition is best told by himself in *Retrospect of an Unimportant Life 1863–1939*, London: OUP, 1942, pp. 206–10, 301–10. Davidson's view of the whole development is well recorded in his life by G. K. A. Bell.

men who had been ordained, but it had also greatly increased the range of backgrounds from which men came for ordination. Men for whom university would have seemed a hopeless dream before the war were, through Knutsford, able to get the qualifications to go to university or theological college. In 1920 Barry wrote in *Ducdame*, the school's magazine, 'For the first time since the Reformation the Church in her corporate capacity has given an opportunity for boys of every section of society, regardless of their economic status, to realise a vocation to the Ministry.'[2]

It had also done one other very significant thing; it had enabled some candidates to be tested. No longer were some men to be allowed into a theological college simply on the basis of an interview with a principal, they were observed by the staff at Knutsford over a long period, their capacity to absorb education was noticed and no doubt their interaction with their fellow students was also observed. By the time they were recommended for a university or theological college the staff knew them well – and some were not recommended to continue. Canon Hicks, Secretary of CACTM and the Service Candidates Committee, reported in March 1920 that 177 service candidates had passed through Knutsford and been sent on for further training, but 77 had been rejected.[3] Major Birchall MP, a key supporter of Knutsford in the Church Assembly and on the Central Board of Finance, said in a critical debate in 1922, 'The one thing wanted was some place of the character of Knutsford to which a man could be sent and be tested as to his vocation. The essential point about Knutsford was not so much the men who got there as the men who did not. It was the men who were turned down, as much as the men who were turned out, that proved the value of Knutsford.'[4] That did, of course, apply only to those candidates who needed to go to Knutsford, many other candidates who had the academic qualifications were admitted to university or theological college courses as in the traditional pre-war days. But Knutsford did represent an initial start in a serious approach to selecting ordinands.

The question therefore was whether Knutsford should be enabled to continue and to provide both the training and the selection for civilian candidates after the service candidates had completed their initial training. CACTM wanted to do that and had been used to asking the bishops whether it could do something. If they agreed, then CACTM did it. In 1920 CACTM had established a new Central

---

2 *Ducdame*, the Test School magazine, July 1920, p. 67.
3 Minutes of Executive Committee of the Service Candidates Committee, 20 March 1920.
4 CA Report of Proceedings, Spring 1922, p. 111.

Candidates Committee with the approval of the bishops that would be concerned with all candidates for ordination and in a published report it explained the role of the new Central Candidates Committee including a section on the Ordination Test School, for which the new Candidates Committee would be the management committee. It noted that what was required in the first place was an efficient method of finding the right man. In the past that had been done by the efforts of individuals and societies, and though their work had been admirable, it had been necessarily incomplete and sporadic. The appeal for candidates should come from the Church, and there should be an organization which could guarantee a thorough and preliminary sifting of the material produced. The report noted that the experience of societies which looked for such candidates in the past had been consistently that there were many more suitable men than could be dealt with by the existing agencies; and it was clear that if the whole of the available material could be discovered, a far higher standard could be secured in the selection of those who were accepted.

> In the preliminary training of the new type of candidate, a double process is required. Any method, however efficient, of searching for the candidates cannot do more than produce men – or boys – of whose spiritual and intellectual fitness some doubt will still remain. When this has been cleared up they will need to be fitted educationally for the University stage of their training.

It was that which CACTM proposed to provide 'through the thorough central system of testing and preliminary training which is required by continuing the Ordination Test School, now at Knutsford, for civilian candidates'. The report said CACTM contemplated that the age of candidates would be between 16 and 19, and that only in exceptional cases would candidates above 19 be admitted.

> The School in its new form would act as a central clearing house, drawing on all the dioceses, and in turn feeding the Universities and Theological Colleges. Its functions would be to test vocation, character and intellectual ability, and to prepare candidates up to matriculation standard for the University or College to which they are to go. The success of the present School proves the possibilities of such a scheme.[5]

---

5 CACTM Report on the Central Candidates Committee 1920, No. 114.

This provoked a major debate in the Church at large, including in the new Church Assembly. The concerns centred on four matters, finance, centralizing tendencies, the appropriate style of training for Anglican clergy and the effect of any such proposal on other institutions. Financially the Central Board of Finance had been the agent of change in the grant-making situation. It had honoured its commitment to the archbishops to meet the cost of training those ordinands from the services who needed grants (according to the Chairman of CACTM just over half of the service candidates[6]) and produced major sums of money, only some of which was needed for Knutsford students as other ordinands were already qualified to go straight to university or theological college. In 1919 it paid just over £53,000 in grants; in 1920 that went up to just under £71,000, and in the following year reached its highest figure in the inter-war period of just over £83,000. In that same year diocesan grants amounted to just under £18,000, producing a total of over £100,000 (which in 2010 terms would be the equivalent of £3.6 million[7]). The Church Pastoral Aid Society grants for 1921 totalled £447, which seemed very modest by comparison (although in 2010 figures that would be the equivalent of £16,000).

The economic background in England was, however, very difficult. An immediate post-war boom broke abruptly in the winter of 1920–1, government spending was slashed, taxation increased and unemployment more than doubled between December 1920 and March 1921. *The Economist* called 1921 'one of the worst years of depression since the industrial revolution'.[8] Death duties and supertax (later called surtax) remained at what A. J. P. Taylor described as 'punitive levels'.[9] Many of the wealthy families who were the natural supporters of the Church had lost not only sons but also land and wealth during the war. This made for a financially difficult period for the Church. Committing the Church centrally to continue to find such sums for the long-term future was obviously financially problematical, a problem made the more acute by the failure of many diocesan Boards of Finance to find the money requested by the Central Board of Finance. In a Church Assembly debate in November 1921

6 Chronicle of Convocation 1921, Part 1, p. 162.

7 The Retail Prices Index (RPI) inflation measure is used – the historical inflation data comes from the 2004 paper 'Consumer Price Inflation Since 1750' (ISSN 0013-0400, Economic Trends No. 604, pp. 38–46) by Jim O'Donoghue, Louise Goulding and Grahame Allen, which estimates historic British inflation back to 1750. The calculator is available on the website www.safalra.com/other/historical-uk-inflation-price-conversion/

8 A. J. P. Taylor, 1965, *English History 1914–1945*, Oxford: Clarendon Press, pp. 144–5.

9 Taylor, *History*, pp. 40f, 124, 163, 237.

the Earl of Selborne on behalf of the CBF proposed that no more civilian candidates should be taken and that the Knutsford Test School should be closed. The report on the debate says:

> He made the motion with the greatest possible regret, and also with a sense of shame, because he thought it was a terrible thing that the Church of England, through its central organisation, should not be able to assist its poorer sons to seek the training necessary for ordination.[10]

He went on to say that it was the diocesan Boards of Finance who had placed the National Assembly in this impossible position as the DBFs had not voted the money that was requested for the 1922 budget. 'The financial returns for the CBF showed that the average percentage of receipts to apportionment in the various dioceses, down to October 26th, 1921, was less than 22 per cent.'[11]

Centralizing tendencies in the Church were also a source of concern. In the experience of most worshippers in the Church of England the most significant expression of the church was the local one, the parish first, and for some maybe then the diocese, which had certainly become a more significant focus during the Victorian period. A relatively new powerful central national organization like CACTM, and particularly one with financial power, would have seemed suspect to many. Individual parishioners might support diocesan grants (although in practice the level of support was fairly modest), but there was concern about financing a central body. A member of the Church Assembly, L. H. Booth, was opposed to the continuation of Knutsford on those grounds in a Church Assembly debate in 1922.

> The first fact to realise was that there was a strong and sincere opposition to a centralising policy, and to the policy of training civilian candidates from a central source. This opposition was growing. The proper business of the Assembly was to develop and encourage the growth of strong diocesan bodies ... It was the common experience that money could be obtained for Church purposes far more easily when it was to be administered and controlled entirely locally, than when it was sent to what had been called an 'ultramontane institution in the south-east of England' ... It must not

---

10 CA Report of Proceedings, Autumn 1921, p. 57.
11 Report of Proceedings, p. 58, footnote.

be forgotten that central finance had suffered a shock. Public confidence had been shaken, and the only way to restore it was to convince the public that an honest attempt was being made to balance the accounts, to abandon the centralising policy, and to reduce necessary expenditure to manageable limits.[12]

A third area of unease was the long-standing concern of some bishops about the encouragement of any form of seminary training. Henson, who in 1920 became Bishop of Durham, spoke against establishing what he described as 'seminarist clergy', by which he meant:

first, men who had been prematurely committed to lifelong obligations. Vocations ought not to be sought and stereotyped in adolescence. Next, by the seminarist method he meant the method not only of recruiting too early, but of bringing prematurely recruited men into a clericalist atmosphere at a time when the atmosphere, perhaps more than anything else, coloured and shaped the whole type of character. The third thing that he meant was a system so organised that it tended to turn out artificial and uniform type of clergymen.[13]

The Bishop of Southwark, Cyril Garbett,[14] while agreeing that the seminarist method was undesirable, challenged whether that was actually the effect of Knutsford.[15] In fact, while Knutsford was taking service candidates who came there from wartime experience and who stayed for a maximum of nine months, it probably was not what Henson feared, but taking civilian candidates, some of whom might be as young as 16, might well have changed the balance of the argument, even if they were then to be dispersed to universities and theological colleges.

The fourth area of concern was what the establishment of Knutsford on a more permanent basis might do to other training institutions. This was most

---

12 Report of Proceedings, pp. 107f.

13 Church Assembly Report of Proceedings, Summer Session 1921, p. 51.

14 Cyril Garbett became Bishop of Southwark in 1919 having previously been curate and then Vicar of St Mary's, Portsea, where he had the reputation of being a strong disciplinarian who pushed himself even harder than he pushed his curates. He was at Southwark until 1932, then moved to Winchester from 1932 to 1942, and then to be Archbishop of York from 1942 to 1955. He decided to resign his post at the age of 80, but died before he formally left the diocese.

15 Report of Proceedings, p. 52.

strongly expressed at a Council meeting of CACTM on 1 February 1922. Arthur Headlam, by then Regius Professor of Divinity at Oxford but no doubt remembering his time as Principal of King's College, London, proposed that no central church funds should be made available to Knutsford; he spoke of a 'serious difference of opinion' on the continuation of Knutsford and his area of concern included what it might do to other training institutions. His proposal was lost by ten votes to seven, but instead a resolution, carefully worded to show that the money could be used for places other than Knutsford, was proposed:

> that the Council hopes that the National Assembly will adopt the modified scheme of civilian training set forth in the memorandum submitted to the Central Board of Finance, provided that in the case of candidates in their pre-matriculation period the Central Advisory Council of Training for the Ministry recommends that central funds raised for their support should be as soon as possible available for their support at theological colleges which have approved preparatory classes, as well as at a Test School of the limited size mentioned in the Memorandum.[16]

This was passed by ten votes to seven. A majority of the Council clearly still wanted Knutsford to continue and for it to be available for civilian candidates.

The matter came to a head at a series of Church Assembly debates in the early 1920s. A difficult debate in the Church Assembly in 1920 finally agreed that the school should continue for another year, and the principle was asserted that there should be an open door policy for candidates to enter training including civilian candidates, in other words that money should be forthcoming to enable those who did not have the financial basis to pay for their own training to receive Church grants. In July 1921 majorities in each House supported the financial implications of continuing the Test School, but with significant minorities opposed.

In November 1921 the Earl of Selborne on behalf of the CBF and on the financial grounds outlined earlier proposed that no more civilian candidates should be taken and that the Knutsford Test School should be closed. Major J. D. Birchall MP, who was a member of the CBF, moved as an amendment that the element in the motion on the closure of Knutsford should be omitted and that a conference should happen between the CBF and CACTM 'as to the best

---

16 CACTM minutes, 1 February 1922.

methods of carrying out the considered policy of the National Assembly' (that is, of an 'open door' for civilian candidates). The debate lasted two days. Canon F. C. N. Hicks said in a personal capacity rather than as Secretary of CACTM that he was sure the money could be raised. He had 'issued a letter to his friends and to his friends' friends and put to them the seriousness of the situation ... The sum obtained at the moment was £8,730 ... he therefore pleaded for the Assembly to accept Major Birchall's amendment.'[17] This would have the effect of giving the Church time to consider. The CBF effectively accepted the amendment, but said it would accept no further responsibility for civilian candidates until the conference with CACTM was concluded.

The joint conference between representatives of the CBF and of CACTM took place in January 1922. Major Birchall presided and Canon Partridge, Secretary of CBF, was present with three other members of the board. The CACTM representation was led by the Chairman, the Bishop of Chichester, and included among its seven other members Canon Hicks, the Secretary of CACTM and F. R. Barry, the Principal of Knutsford. The conference concluded that there would be little or no savings in moving Knutsford from its present buildings, and that the Church should resolve to keep a school of 75 students, on the grounds that larger numbers would be too financially demanding but that lower numbers would not meet the need. They also noted that the money obtained by Canon Hicks from private sources would meet the cost in 1922, so the concern was from 1923 onwards. They estimated the annual cost in the longer term as being £55,000 to £60,000 a year, which would meet not only the cost of the Test School but also provide grants for final training which should produce 100 clergy per annum.[18]

When the Assembly returned to the issue on 9 February 1922, it began with a debate on the financial difficulties facing the CBF, which stemmed from the low level of support it had received from dioceses in their requests for funding. The debate on Knutsford the following day was against that background. Earl Grey on behalf of the CBF moved 'that the Knutsford Test School be closed as soon as may be consistent with the equitable treatment of all who are concerned'. He acknowledged that there had been a division of opinion on the matter in the CBF. The Bishop of Chichester, Winfrid Burrows, Chairman of CACTM, moved as an amendment that 'the Assembly directs the Central Board of Finance to adopt

---

17 CA Report of Proceedings, Summer 1921, p. 64f.
18 The report is NAF 11, from Central Board of Finance.

the modified scheme of civilian training set out in the report', that is, the report on the Joint Conference. The Bishop pointed out that the decision had been taken that training for the ministry was in the future to be, in the main, an affair of central finance, whereas the maintenance of the clergy was to be, in the main, a parochial and diocesan affair. He therefore 'begged the Assembly not to foreclose the issue by breaking up the Test School, which they could never reconstruct, in a moment of panic today'.[19]

Sir Lewis Dibden from the CBF presented the alternative view.

They had to face the fact that there was a very great conflict of opinion in the country with regard to the whole question of Knutsford, and whether it ought to exist or not. The finance committee of the Central Board had from the beginning – not only this year or last year, but throughout – advised the Board strongly not to embark on this expenditure for civilian candidates. The Board in its wisdom, by small majorities, had not followed its finance committee. Throughout the North of England the policy of assisting civilian candidates was exceedingly unpopular. And everywhere, in diocesan conferences and on diocesan boards of finance, one of the great difficulties had been this question of civilian candidates.[20]

Major Birchall continued to support Knutsford.

It had been subjected to attacks from two or three opposite directions, which should have been mutually destructive, but apparently were going to succeed. The net liability next year would be something like £14,000, and it would rise to a total liability of rather more than £50,000. What was £50,000? £50,000 was 6d. a year for every communicant. Was the Assembly going to scrap what a great many people thought was the finest, the boldest and the best thing they had done, for the sake of £50,000, which, at its ultimate and largest liability, would not arrive for five years?[21]

He then made his comment about Knutsford's importance as a place of testing candidates.

---

19 CA Report of Proceedings, Spring 1922, pp. 104–6.
20 Report of Proceedings, p. 106.
21 Report of Proceedings, p. 111.

The majority view, however, was that the financial crisis meant that the school should close and the bishop's amendment was rejected. The argument about growing financial centralization had a wider context. One of the consequences of World War One nationally was that the central instruments of government had become more powerful, both financially and in the control they exercised over the population. No doubt in some places that caused satisfaction, but in others resentment. The arguments raised against CACTM in the National Assembly could have had their parallels in the discussions about growing government power in the post-war nation. In the case of the Church the National Assembly had provided the platform for opposition and the power to stop a development that, up to then, had received the broad support of the bishops.

Despite that decision taken by the Assembly the school did not close, but it never again became the force it was in ordination training. A Knutsford resident offered a house, Kilrie, standing on the edge of the common in Knutsford, as a new home for the school and the Principal of Mirfield said he would send his candidates there for pre-matriculation training. Thus it reopened in October 1922 with 36 students, 20 of whom came from the gaol. In January 1923 Barry announced he would be leaving to become Archdeacon of Egypt at the invitation of Gwynne, the former Deputy Chaplain General and by then Bishop of Egypt[22] and R. V. H. Burne was appointed the new principal. Apart from the candidates who had started in the gaol and who were paid for from central funds, no funds were forthcoming for the other students, so bursaries had to be arranged for the civilian candidates from generous supporters. Henry Gladstone, later Lord Gladstone, gave the school a new home in the Old Rectory at Hawarden in North Wales where they moved in 1927. Burne continued as principal in the new home, but left in 1937 having been appointed Archdeacon of Chester, and Revd E. S. G. Wickham, who had been on the staff in the gaol days, was appointed as the new principal. He and the school hoped that the Archbishops' Commission on Training would encourage the future of Knutsford, but in fact the Commission made no mention of it. Each student spent three terms there until war forced the school to close in 1940, when it was commandeered as a home for blind and infirm patients. From when the school moved from the gaol to 1937, 365 men trained there, 180 of whom went on to universities and 136 to theological

---

22 Gwynne had moved back to being Bishop of Khartoum after the war but was then appointed Bishop of Egypt. Barry stayed there only for a short time until, in 1923, he became Professor of Theology at King's College, London.

colleges.[23] It was estimated that the school contributed 245 men to the ordained ministry after it moved from the gaol.

The answerability of CACTM

During the course of all these debates and with the Church Assembly wanting to flex its muscles it was not surprising that the Assembly sought to make CACTM a body answerable to it. It was not to be the last time that an attempt was made to wrest control of CACTM from the bishops. The Council responded at a meeting in February 1922, saying that it was ready to fall in with the proposals from the National Assembly 'except that there are important parts of its work on which it can only report to the Bishops; but that it wishes to draw attention to the fact that it was appointed by the Convocations, and that therefore alterations in its constitution do not appear to be within the competence of the National Assembly'.[24]

At the following meeting the Chairman reported that the Convocations had agreed that representatives of the laity on CACTM should be elected by the House of Laity of the National Assembly instead of by the Canterbury and York Houses of Laymen sitting separately; a very modest reform. But by January 1923 the National Assembly had suggested that:

in future CACTM should be a Committee of the National Assembly, with 21 ordinary members appointed by the Assembly, 7 Bishops, 7 clergy and 7 laity, and then with a number of others, 5 representing Faculties of Theology, and 7 the Principals of theological colleges with a further 7 co-opted members but that all questions involving expenditure of funds by the National Assembly shall be decided by the votes of the ordinary members.[25]

The Council pointed out again that it was a body appointed by the bishops and advisory to them, so the Assembly's proposals should be forwarded to the bishops. The Upper Houses' response was reported to the Council in January 1924. They had referred the constitution back to the Convocations but had recorded:

---

23 T. W. Pritchard, *2002, A History of the Old Parish of Hawarden,* Wrexham: Bridge Books, p. 132.

24 CACTM minutes, 1 February 1922.

25 CACTM minutes, 24 January 1923.

CACTM is an Advisory Council to the bishops, and deals with many matters concerning ordination, on which the decision must rest with the bishops. It should not be asked to report to the Church Assembly, except on matters that concern the administration of the funds entrusted to it by that Assembly.[26]

That was accepted by the Convocations and remained the basic constitutional position for many years (see Appendix C). The Council membership was largely brought into line with what the National Assembly had proposed, which did not represent a huge change from what already existed, but the Assembly's scope for holding CACTM accountable was more limited than some on the Assembly may have wished. The bishops may have become accustomed to receiving advice from CACTM, and they had to accept the power of the Assembly over strategic financial issues, but they were not prepared to hand over authority for matters that they had always believed belonged especially to the episcopal role.[27]

A central register

Constitutional issues did not merely relate to CACTM's relationship to the Assembly; there was one very significant internal change within CACTM's way of working in the aftermath of the war that was to make a profound change in the longer term for dealing with candidates for ordination.

In October 1919 it was noted that there were cases of men who had been rejected by Knutsford subsequently being accepted at theological colleges, and a resolution was passed 'that each Principal of a Theological College be asked to refer to the Service Candidates' Committee before accepting any candidate for admission to his college'.[28] At the following Council meeting it was agreed that a Central Candidates Committee should be constituted, which would incorporate the work of the Service Candidates Committee, and

that all candidates applying to be accepted for training for Holy Orders should be registered with the Central Candidates Committee and that

---

26 CACTM minutes, 30 January 1924.

27 In his introduction to F. W. B. Bullock's *A History of Training for the Ministry of the Church of England 1875–1974*, Revd T. Elliot says, 'In 1924 CACTM was integrated into the Church Assembly as an executive committee.' The decision reported here shows that it was not quite as straightforward as that.

28 CACTM minutes, 23 October 1919.

Bishops, Diocesan Training Committees, Principals of Theological Colleges, and those responsible for University Ordination Courses should be asked to refer to the register before accepting a candidate for training, and to inform the Committee whether he had been accepted or rejected.[29]

It was also agreed that this register should be kept confidential to those four groups, 'or other persons authorised to supervise the training of candidates'. The record would say whether a candidate was accepted or rejected, but no reason would be recorded.[30]

It is noteworthy that the bishops accepted the notion of a central register, but when the matter was put before a Bishops' Meeting, the record of which was confidential and not in the public sphere, a different gloss was put on the reasons for introducing it. It was presented by the Bishop of Chichester, as Chairman of CACTM, and the minutes record that

he called attention to certain cases in which candidates who had been rejected on moral grounds by a particular Bishop or College or Diocesan Committee had been accepted by another Bishop in ignorance of that fact, and he moved accordingly that there should be a Central Register of Candidates.

The motion was carried and there is no record of any discussion.[31] Establishing a central register of candidates was a remarkable development in a centralizing direction for the bishops, and it is interesting to note that while it was publicly introduced as a pragmatic solution to the problem of candidates touting themselves around college principals trying to find a place, more privately it was shown that there was a moral dimension to the whole issue. How far all bishops observed the new policy in practice for all their candidates is less clear.

The supply of candidates 1922–39

Collectively the bishops were more than willing to seek advice, and in July 1922 the Upper House of Canterbury requested that CACTM should report on the

---

29 CACTM minutes, 28 January 1920.
30 CACTM minutes, 28 October 1920.
31 From the minutes of the Bishops' Meeting, May 1920.

general question of the supply of candidates for Holy Orders and to formulate any recommendations for the consideration of the bishops. Numbers being ordained explains the reason for their concern. After the very low point of 119 ordained in 1918, reflecting the conditions in the last year of the war, numbers had increased but not sufficient to meet the numbers dying or retiring each year. Ordinations for the following three years were 192 in 1919, 280 in 1920 and 379 in 1921, but the increases were almost entirely as a result of the facilities offered for training under the service candidates scheme. There had also been the whole controversy surrounding grants for civilian candidates, and those two facts caused the bishops to think that some careful attention should be paid to the issue.

A committee of 27 members met under the Chairman of CACTM, the Bishop of Chichester. Their report appeared in 1925.[32] It spelled out the problem clearly, noting in particular the diminution in the proportion of graduates offering for ministry, the average for the past ten years being 15 per cent less than for the previous ten years. They were also concerned about the shortage of younger men in the ranks of the ministry, calculating that the average age of clergy on the active list was 'no less than 52', and that fewer than 12 per cent were under 36. They were also frank about the weaknesses in the Church that might have inhibited men from offering, including what they termed 'intellectual difficulties'.

Part of that difficulty was in giving assent to formularies, and they stated that the Thirty-Nine Articles 'are no longer a satisfactory statement for the purpose of assent', but another part was wider intellectual uncertainty. They did not believe that an attempt should be made to rewrite the creeds (a suggestion that had been made), but they commended a statement from the bishops in 1922:

> This House recognises the gain which arises from enquiry, at once fearless and reverent, into the meaning and expressions of the Faith, and welcomes every aid which the thoughtful student finds in the results of sound historical and literary criticism, and of modern scientific investigation of the problems of human psychology.[33]

---

32 *The Supply of Candidates for Holy Orders.* Report of a committee appointed by the Archbishops of Canterbury and York, 1925, London: SPCK.

33 Chronicles of Convocation 1922, p. 326.

They suggested that statement could be followed up by 'a statement from the Episcopate as a whole to the effect that recognising the intellectual difficulties which arise out of some of the clauses in the Creeds, they would not look upon perplexity or uncertainty on such points as in all cases a necessary barrier to Ordination'. And they concluded that section:

> The evidence before the Committee seems to show that many men of the right character and temperament who might in former times have come forward as candidates do not contemplate Ordination because of a belief, often vague and indefinite, that the doctrines of the Church are incompatible with the developments of modern thought, or with the discoveries of modern science. The Christian Faith appears to involve an artificial scheme of the universe, which is not in harmony with the general body of knowledge. We think it is essential that there should be some more widely known, and more accessible, expression of the attitude of the Church towards modern thought and discovery. We hope that in this respect the findings of the Commission on Doctrine may prove to be of great service.[34]

On the financial barriers they repeated the comment that the cost of training remained a major difficulty: 'It should be regarded not as a charity, but as a fundamental part of church finance, and as a serious and necessary obligation on the Church as a whole.' The practice of the Church of England was contrasted unfavourably with that of other denominations: 'The Roman Catholics, the Wesleyans, the Congregationalists and the Baptists are in a better position than ourselves.'[35] But they were also clear that only those of real potential should receive grants.

> We desire to emphasise the fact that though the need for an increase in numbers is urgent, the quality and efficiency of the clergy is of the first importance, and will ultimately affect the quantity. We are of the opinion that much harm may be done by giving help from the Church's funds to men of inferior quality. We therefore urge very strongly that grants out of central or diocesan funds should be given only to men of real ability and

---

34 *The Supply of Candidates for Holy Orders*, p. 15.

35 Whether they really were is a moot point, given the evidence in Kenneth Brown, 1988, *A Social History of the Nonconformist Ministry in England and Wales 1800–1930*, Oxford: Clarendon.

character. It is highly important that the men so sent to the Universities and parishes should be such as to commend the Ministry to others.

What that meant in practice was that in future any selection other than that by a principal of a theological college only occurred in the case of those who applied for grants, and was carried out by whatever the grant-awarding body was.

Of the other financial matter, clerical poverty, they felt that was less of a deterrent, but they sympathized with a 'genial cynic' who wrote to *The Times*, 'the laity are determined on two points – that the clergy should be married, and that they should be paid as though they were not'.[36]

The report made a few general recommendations on recruiting, and commended the possibility of some non-residential training.

A clergyman might be invited by the diocesan authorities to undertake the direction of a little group of men who are thinking seriously of the Ministry, but, owing to domestic ties or commitments, are unable to surrender their secular occupations. A course of study, general and theological, extending, say, over a course of four years, would be arranged for them. Each candidate would be tested periodically, and if at the end of four years he was still of the same mind, and had proved his ability and fitness for the Ministry, he would be sent to a theological college for a period of special training, the expense of which, together with the cost of maintaining his dependants, would be borne by the diocese.[37]

It took over half a century for that recommendation, in a modified form, to become part of the regular practice of the Church of England.

Appendix V of the report also dealt with the 'Signs of Vocation' and it is an important statement of how the matter was conceived at least by some of the more thoughtful members of the Church at that time. It bears repeating in full.

Signs of Vocation

We think it is not foreign to our task to add a few words on a question which is sometimes to be asked: 'How are we to detect vocation?' It is a

---

36 *The Times*, 11 April 1925.
37 *The Supply of Candidates for Holy Orders*, p. 32.

question which is not easy to answer, especially in the case of boys who are still at school, or have only recently left it. It is important, however, to remember that there is a distinction between a strong desire to be ordained and a fitness of Ordination. The desire is, of course, one of the signs of vocation, but it should be combined with other qualifications. The same is true of perseverance, though here is a danger of mistaking obstinacy for perseverance. Generally speaking, in dealing with boys it would be wiser to pay attention to the presence of those natural qualifications which are most valuable to the Ministry, and to show reverence and reserve in the matter of spiritual signs of vocation. The best type of candidate will not be willing to parade his spiritual experience, nor can we rely on such tests as being a regular server or Sunday School teacher. Nor, again, is mere goodness a reliable test, for goodness is no more the mark of a priest than of a layman, and it may go with mental thickness which would be a hindrance in the exercise of the teaching office.

What we should look for is a certain promise, however fitful, of spiritual life, together with signs of the development of that kind of character which is wanted in the Ministry. Such signs would be application to study in view of the task to which the boy thinks himself to be called, independence, moral courage, leadership that is not priggish, and a sympathy and a sense of responsibility in his dealing with other boys.

At the university it ought to be less difficult to detect signs of vocation. What is looked for at school will be looked for here in a higher degree. If the man of 20 or 21 has not yet seen for himself the intimate connection between his thoughts of Ordination and application to study, self-discipline, and the life of prayer, he cannot be regarded as a satisfactory candidate, or at least he is not as mature as he ought to be. Something of a definite spiritual experience ought also to be taking place. Though it is good that men should take part in evangelistic and missionary campaigns, stress need not be laid at this stage on lack of activity in religious enterprises, for the impulse to pastoral work may as yet not be strongly felt, or it may be deliberately and rightly suppressed in favour of the more pressing and immediate duty of reading and thinking; but signs of it may often be seen in private friendships and in the fellowship of college life.

It is interesting to compare that statement, which obviously saw the bulk of candidates as young men, with the criteria for selection advanced many years later.

Five years after that report was published a further report relating more to the need for clergy rather than to their supply appeared. The 1930 report on *Staffing of Parishes*[38] was produced in response to a request from Church Assembly in 1929 by a group of which Cyril Garbett, Bishop of Southwark, was chairman; it was not a CACTM document. Among its 13 resolutions it stated that the Church should aim at an ordination list of 630 per annum (which would have meant an increase of about 100 a year over those being ordained at that time), but that the increase in ordinands should not be obtained by lowering the standards of qualifications. It also believed that the decline in the number of ordinands was due to 'the secularisation of our time, to difficulties in the formularies of our faith, to understanding about the life and work of a clergyman, to financial barriers'. Accordingly they believed that assent to the Thirty-Nine Articles should no longer be required as part of the doctrinal test necessary for admission to Holy Orders and that renewed efforts should be made to place the stipends of the clergy on a satisfactory footing.[39]

The comment on the Thirty-Nine Articles no doubt added to the general theological ferment of the 1930s, but from the point of view of candidates for ministry the new target figure of 630 a year was significant. In fact numbers started to increase shortly after the publication of the report. In 1930, 503 men were ordained, the first year the number had been over 500 since 1915. By 1932 585 were ordained and the numbers remained over 550 a year until World War Two intervened, so the new target was certainly in sight, although never actually achieved until 1962, when 633 men were ordained.

Finance again and the sponsorship scheme

However, financial questions remained among the most critical ones for the inter-war years, and they occupied a large amount of CACTM's (and the CBF's) time thereafter.

One relatively trivial financial matter occurred early in the period. It appears that relationships between the Council and the CBF were generally good despite when Knutsford was brought to an end. In the case of CACTM a majority were in favour of continuing Knutsford while in the CBF a majority concluded it should be closed, but each body had members on both sides of the debate.

---

38 *Report of the Commission on Staffing of Parishes*, CA 334 Church Assembly and SPCK.
39 Bullock, *History*, p. 89 and pp. 56–61, 65–8 of CA 334.

But then there was a strange conflict over the details of the awarding of grants and the wording attached to them. The level of grant awarded depended on the financial circumstances of the man requesting help, and a Council meeting in January 1923 agreed that candidates requesting grants should be asked to make a declaration: 'I hereby declare that my financial position has not in any way changed for the better, except as stated below, since my last declaration to the Service or Central Candidates Committee.' The Central Board of Finance had requested that the words 'upon honour' should be added after 'I hereby declare' and that the forms should be returned to the CBF. The Council did not wish the additional words to be added, since they were not included in declarations made regarding Board of Education grants nor to County Council Scholarships. A motion was also carried that forms should be returned to the Central Candidates Committee, which in 1920 had fully incorporated the old Service Candidates Committee into CACTM's structures. The CBF had wanted grants to be paid direct to college bursars rather than to the candidates, but CACTM wanted to follow the practice of Rhodes Scholarships which were paid direct to the students concerned.[40]

A joint committee was established to deal with the issue and a compromise agreed. CACTM agreed to accept the addition of the words 'upon honour', and the CBF agreed that application forms should be returned to the CACTM Candidates Committee and that grants should be paid direct to the students. No doubt the conflict needed to be seen in the wider context of the constitution of CACTM and its relationship to the National Assembly as well as in the debate over Knutsford.[41] The compromise solution seemed acceptable to everyone.

On the more general issue of financing training, the central Church authorities, both CACTM and the CBF, had a major problem. The 1921 *Church of England Year Book*, following the passing of the budget in that year, stated that the budget meant the Assembly had given its sanction to continuing for civilian candidates for ordination the offer of help and guidance that was made during the war to service candidates. 'There is now, therefore, an open door to all really qualified boys and young men, whatever their previous training and occupation may have been.' It therefore promised to help parents who could not afford the whole expense of a university course and the subsequent special training and even offered to help keep candidates at school until they were old enough for

40 CACTM minutes, 24 January 1923.
41 CACTM minutes, 14 May 1923.

university. It also promised that candidates between 18 and 25 could have their vocation tested at Knutsford.

That desire and policy had been blocked by the unwillingness of the diocesan Boards of Finance to vote the necessary funds for the Central Board of Finance. However, not only CACTM but leading figures in the CBF wanted as a matter of urgency to enable the sons of poorer families to get the necessary training for ordination, so the question was from where else they might get the money if the dioceses would not produce it. There was a very limited figure in CACTM's budget for bursaries, and an attempt by the Council in January 1927 to increase that budget from £30,000 to £40,000 was foiled by the Church Assembly in July 1927, who retained the £30,000 limit, but the Assembly did approve a scheme put forward by the CBF for obtaining 'sponsors'.

The sponsorship scheme was launched by a letter in *The Times* on 4 June 1927 from Earl Grey, Chairman of the CBF. Grey pointed out that there was a shortage of candidates coming forward for ordination, mainly because of financial difficulties meeting the cost of training, and giving anonymous but real examples of men in need. In the same edition a leader gave support for the scheme and encouraged its readers to be generous. (Grey's letter and parts of the leader are in Appendix E.)

Two days later, on 6 June 1927, a letter from the Warden of Keble College, Oxford (B. J. Kidd) said that at least a third of the men who had come to his college had come with the intention of ordination. He argued that this showed there was no dearth of candidates, but that the problem was the cost of training them. He commended the sponsorship scheme.

Grey wrote again to *The Times* on 14 June reporting that, among others, Queen Mary had agreed to become a sponsor. Grey ended, 'A great deal remains to be done, but with such a splendid lead surely no single one of the 150 will lack the help he needs.'

In April 1928 Grey reported in a further letter to *The Times* that the Keeper of His Majesty's Privy Purse had granted £100 for the 1928 appeal. (The equivalent of just under £5,000 in 2010 terms.[42])

The sponsorship scheme was to prove effective, and the generosity of *Times* readers enabled many to train. According to the Minutes of the Council, by October 1927 it had raised £31,280, and in subsequent years Earl Grey repeated the appeal in *The Times,* until 1931. By June 1930 it was reported that

---

42 From www.safalra.com/other/historical-uk-inflation-price-conversion/

451 candidates had been trained at the cost of £78,674.[43] Appeals continued in 1931, and thereafter there was no further public appeal, but generous individuals were approached privately. In July 1932 it was reported that the CBF had resolved to expend a sum of £7,500 for the 1932 list, which would be used in such a way as to ensure the completion of the training of those supported but that, 'This guarantee entirely exhausted the resources of the Board present and prospective, and at the present time no monies of any kind appeared to be available for candidates on the 1933 list'[44] In all, the sponsorship scheme enabled 680 men to be ordained,[45] but the long-standing aim since the early days of CACTM that the financing of training should, in the words of the 1925 Report on the Supply of Candidates for Holy Orders 'be regarded not as a charity, but as a fundamental part of church finance, and as a serious and necessary obligation on the Church as a whole' was yet to be realized.

Earl Grey's example had, however, been followed elsewhere. Both Anglo-Catholic and Evangelical bodies recognized the need to assist in the training of candidates sympathetic to their traditions. The Anglo-Catholic Fund was established in 1927 and raised £13,479 in the first year. The Church Pastoral Aid Society had a candidates' fund for many years, but from 1927 onwards it raised substantially more money each year (£1,547 in 1927, £2,188 in 1928), while the Evangelical Churchman Fund was started in 1928 and raised £3,457 in its first year. There was also a fund known as the Ordination Candidates Exhibition Fund started in 1925, which raised over £2,000 for each of the first ten years of its life. Diocesan contributions to diocesan candidates also increased over these years (from £12,467 in 1920 to £38,847 in 1931), and by the end of 1937 a total of over £1.2 million had been raised over 20 years for grants. About half of that (£615,449) was provided through the Central Board of Finance, slightly under half by Diocesan Boards of Finance (£508,404), by the Anglo-Catholic Fund (£69,224), and about £29,000 each from the Church Pastoral Aid Society, the Evangelical Churchman Fund and the Ordination Candidates Exhibition Fund. (Full details are given in Appendix F, which is taken from the evidence given by the CBF to the Archbishops' Commission on Training in 1937.)

A joint conference involving CACTM, the Central Board of Finance and representatives of dioceses was held in December 1932, and a system was

---

43 CACTM minutes, 3 June 1930.
44 CACTM minutes, 27 July 1932.
45 Lloyd, Church of England, p. 339.

agreed for joint sponsorship between dioceses and central funds with the possibility of loans being made to students with no interest to be paid. (Details of the agreed scheme are in Appendix G.) Candidates were to be considered either diocesan ones or central ones and would be put into three grades, with the priority for grants being awarded on the basis of the grades of the candidates. It was also agreed that when a candidate was considered a 'central candidate' because he received a grant from central funds he should be interviewed by at least two people, one of whom should be a layman.[46] This, of course, only applied to those candidates who needed central grants, but it did appear to help towards an increase in candidates. In 1930 the numbers ordained passed the 500 mark for the first time since 1915.

Throughout the inter-war years, apart from the continuing debate about graduate status for all clergy described in Chapter 3, the cost of training was the recurring theme. Against the background of some concern about centralizing tendencies expressed in the debates about Knutsford it was not surprising that a variety of grant-awarding bodies emerged, some diocesan and central, but others based on churchmanship considerations. Candidates applying for grants from those bodies would have gone though some form of interview process, but apart from an interview with the principal of a theological college to gain admission that would not apply to those who had the finance to fund themselves through their training. The broader matter of selection by the Church and a more comprehensive solution to financing training would take another Archbishops' Commission, another war and a very different style of government to bring about a more ordered, universal and central system.

---

46 See Appendix G, para. 1.b.

6

The Archbishops' Commission on Training, 1937–44

By the 1930s numbers being ordained each year had started to increase. In 1930 there were 503, by 1932 that had increased to 585 and it was to continue between 550 and 590 (in 1938) each year until World War Two started to have its effect. But the 1930s were a time of considerable economic hardship in England through the Depression and there was a major problem, particularly in industrial areas, in finding the money to pay curates. A parish normally had to find additional money to supplement grants to provide a living wage for curates, and according to Roger Lloyd:

> The time came, in the middle thirties, when the bishops had to be very cautious in accepting even very suitable men who offered themselves for ordination, because they knew well it might happen that no parish could be found which could afford to employ them. In those years most of the dioceses which were worst hit by unemployment had three or four men who were in the cruel position of having exhausted their resources on their training, and who could not be ordained because no parish could be found which could afford to take them.[1]

That would have been difficult enough, but the bishops also found that they were not only being asked to accept suitable men. As was explained in the previous chapter, if a man applied for a grant he would have had to go through some sort of interview process, although how rigorous that interview was would have varied according to the body making the grant, but if he (or his family) was able to pay for his training it may well be that no bishop would encounter him until an incumbent in his diocese asked that the man concerned be ordained.

---

1 Roger Lloyd, 1966, *The Church of England 1900–1965,* London: SCM, p. 341.

There was considerable episcopal unease about the quality of some of the candidates presented to them.

At the same time the long-standing concern about graduate status, and the resolution of the Principals' Conference already noted, was reported to the Council.

> This conference, being of the opinion that the categories 'graduate' and 'non-graduate', as applied to candidates for ordination, no longer bear the significance that once belonged to them, requests CACTM to appoint a commission to reconsider what courses of training for the Ministry should be required and recognised by the Church.[2]

The Council proposed to set up a body to look again at that question, but the proposal was overtaken by a request to another body to look at wider issues, although it seems the CACTM bishops were behind it. It started with co-ordinated moves in the Upper Houses of the Convocations.

The establishing of the Commission

On 28 May 1936 the chairman of CACTM, Warman, Bishop of Manchester, proposed to the Upper House of York Convocation, 'That His Grace the President be respectfully requested to confer with the President of the Convocation of Canterbury with a view to the appointment of a Commission, in the light of the experience gained by the Central Advisory Council of Training for the Ministry and in other ways, during recent years, to consider the problems connected with the selection, testing and training, both before and after ordination to the diaconate, of those being called to serve in the sacred ministry of the Church.' The president, Temple, noted that the fact the proposal came from the Chairman of CACTM was itself important as otherwise this could have been seen as an attempt to take from CACTM part of its central responsibilities.

Warman was in a strong position to make the proposal. He had been chairman of CACTM since 1928, appointed while still Bishop of Chelmsford but in 1929 he had succeeded Temple as Bishop of Manchester, so had experience of both Provinces as a bishop. He had been a member of CACTM since its formation

---

2 CACTM minutes, 22 March 1935.

in 1913, when he was Principal of St Aidan's, Birkenhead, and one of the principals elected to serve on the Council. At the time of the Convocation meeting he was 63.

He noted that CACTM had achieved a good deal in its 24 years of existence, not least the establishing of an inspections regime for the theological colleges, and had gone some way in revising the examinations relating to ordination; but there remained three outstanding issues.

The first was the curriculum for theological colleges. He pointed out that the matter had been considered many times over the years of CACTM's existence, and every consideration had resulted in something being notionally added to the curriculum, but 'if all those additions during the last 24 years had been made, the curriculum of the theological college would be a book of several volumes', and the matter was further complicated by the fact that 'the theological colleges were either private venture arrangements, the result of some kindly benefactor, or diocesan arrangements, but that they were all independent bodies'.[3]

The second problem was the issue of post-ordination training, where there was huge variety across the dioceses but no coherent process.

The third was the matter of selection. Warman noted:

Those who were helped financially normally appealed either to the Council [i.e. CACTM] or to one of the dioceses. In either event they probably came into contact with a bishop. But those who were not helped selected themselves or offered themselves to principals of theological colleges, who selected them. He made no reflection upon the principals – he had been one himself – but he was not sure that they were quite the right body to select candidates for holy orders. It did seem to him that those who offered themselves should be refused or accepted in a rather different way.[4]

He was strongly supported by the Bishop of Bradford, Alfred Blunt,[5] who had earlier produced a memorandum which had been seen by some of the bishops

---

3 York Journal of Convocation, 28 May 1936, p. 51.

4 York Journal of Convocation, 28 May 1936, p. 54.

5 Alfred Walter Frank Blunt (1879–1957) became Bishop of Bradford in 1931 having been incumbent of St Werburgh's in Derby for 14 years, then a church in the broad central tradition. While at Bradford he became well known for a comment about the future King Edward VIII, which was interpreted as being critical of the king's intention to marry a divorcee, although it is not clear that was his original intention. He retired in 1955. (See Smallwood)

and which was a large part of the pressure to establish a commission. He was particularly concerned about selection.

> On the one hand, there was the fact that there seemed to be no universally recognised standard by which to act, and, on the other hand, the fact that a good many men offered themselves for ordination who seemed pretty obviously unqualified or not well qualified for ordination, and yet who were in the position of having committed themselves by their studies to such a line as could only lead to ordination. If these men were not ordained there was nothing else in prospect for them, and one had to make up one's mind whether to adhere rigidly to the high standard or give in to one's natural feeling of sympathy for the younger man in difficulty.[6]

The motion was carried in York, and the same motion was presented the following day in the Upper House of the Convocation of Canterbury by the Bishop of Bristol, Clifford Woodward. Woodward had been bishop since 1933, having previously been a canon of Westminster and Rector of St John's Smith Square. He was later to become Chairman of CACTM. Woodward identified the same three matters, starting with selection.

> It seemed to him that it was at the present time, and in fact always had been, a very haphazard business ... There was a certain percentage – he supposed 40 or 50 per cent – of the men who came forward who did come before Diocesan Boards of Finance or their Committees before they received grants, and that gave them a certain amount of official approval before they commenced; but, as they knew quite well, a considerable number of men simply applied for admission to the head of a theological college, who might or might not be a good judge of men, but who, at any rate, had no official standing in the matter. He would accept a man, and when that man had done his two or three years training and passed the necessary examination, it was very unlikely that he would not find some Bishop kind-hearted enough to ordain him, though in many cases he might know him quite well to be a most unsuitable man for the ministry. As he looked at some of the men with whom he had to deal, he could not

6 York Journal of Convocation, 28 May 1936, p. 56.

conceive how anybody could have thought they were ever likely to be effective and efficient priests.[7]

Secondly he thought the training was far too committed to understanding the past, but not to preparing men for the actual work they would do in the parishes. He looked at some of the questions in the General Ordination Examination 'What were the main types of liturgy in the East up to the seventh century?' ... 'Trace briefly the causes, course and effects of the rebellion of Jehu against the house of Omri' and suggested that men crammed to pass those examinations without being prepared for the difficult pastoral work they were likely to be facing.[8]

The president, Lang, said of the proposals about selection:

I confess I see some difficulties in regard to any body which could undertake such a very, very delicate task as that of deciding what we call, and I hope with some reality of language, vocation. The Board of the Admiralty has a much more limited and easy task, with regard to general intelligence, alertness and the like; it has not got to go into these deeper spiritual conditions.[9]

Given Lang's personal experience reported in his biography[10] as having a strong sense of calling on a walk to and from Cuddesdon, that was not surprising, but Lang's experience was not universal and the other statements about vocation made over the period certainly allowed and even required the prospect of careful selection. Despite Lang's comment the motion was passed, and the archbishops conferred on who should serve on the Commission.

The most critical choice was the chairman. Alwyn Williams had been a fellow of All Souls, Oxford, and then became Headmaster of Winchester College in 1924 when only 36. Ten years later he became Dean of Christ Church, Oxford, and he accepted the invitation from the archbishops to chair the Commission. He was an immensely assiduous chairman, not only chairing the main Commission but many of its sub-committees as well, even when, in 1939,

---

7 Chronicle of Convocation, 29 May 1936, p. 258.

8 Chronicle of Convocation, 29 May 1936, p. 259f.

9 Chronicle of Convocation, 29 May 1936, p. 266.

10 J. G. Lockhart, 1949, *Cosmo Gordon Lang*, London: Hodder and Stoughton.

he was appointed Bishop of Durham at the age of 51. The Commission's members were seven diocesan bishops (including Warman of Manchester and Woodward of Bristol), three archdeacons, one of whom, Leslie Owen, was to become Bishop of Jarrow during the Commission's lifetime and was to be a later full-time Chairman of CACTM, the masters of two Oxford Colleges and one Cambridge College (Canon Charles Raven), ten clergy many of whom were involved in teaching either in universities or theological colleges, and five laymen.

The first meeting of the Commission was held in Lambeth Palace in January 1937. The Archbishop of Canterbury opened the meeting with prayer and asked leave to address the Commission.

> He said that the Resolutions of the Convocations which established the Commission also defined its terms of reference, but he hoped the precise words of those Resolutions would not be regarded by the Commission as limiting its range of enquiry. The problem to which Churchmen had to set themselves was the eliciting of the quality of spiritual leadership in the future ministers of the Church of England. Something more was required than the mere fulfilling of a conscientious routine of ministerial duty.[11]

The Commission was to last for nearly eight years, a delay inevitably brought about by the war in 1939. Lang wrote to Williams in October 1939 that:

> You should try to get a first draft as complete as possible so that it may be ready when you are able to resume your work in happier conditions. I think it will be worthwhile to attempt this in spite of difficulties rather than to leave something which is so nearly finished unfinished. It will be a definite basis on which you can build the rest of your Report and which will be even more valuable if it takes into account the new circumstances that might arise after the war.
>
> As for the Commission itself, I certainly wish that it should continue in being because I cannot bring myself to the belief that the war will last indefinitely and I trust that most of you will be able and willing to carry on a work from which so much has been expected.[12]

---

11 Minutes of Archbishops' Commission on Training. First meeting January 1937.
12 Lang papers, Vol. 172, p. 240.

The Commission therefore continued, and issued an interim report in the spring of 1942, and the final report to the archbishops in February 1944.

Debates within the Commission

When the Commission started its work in 1937 there was already much public discussion about the nature of faith, so one matter that occupied a substantial part of the Commission's attention was the content of the faith required of a candidate. Requiring detailed assent to the Thirty-Nine Articles was questioned openly by some bishops, the possible conflict between the traditional Christian way of looking at the world and some scientific discoveries was before many people's minds, and Temple's chairmanship of the Commission on Doctrine meant that its results were eagerly awaited. When the Commission on Training requested a number of memoranda from both members of the Commission and from many others it was not surprising that some on the Commission were quick to respond to Lang's challenge to go beyond their immediate terms of reference. Charles Raven[13] produced two early submissions.

'The Alternatives before us'[14] invited the Commission to take a wide view of its task, to consider for what reasons the range of potential candidates was so limited, why so many were deterred by the training offered, why others benefited so little from it, and whether the normal clerical life of parish and diocese really met the spiritual (and material) conditions of life. He advocated specialist ministries for experts in education, psychology, apologetics and sociology.

> Men exist in considerable numbers who would seek ordination if they saw one of those specialities as their life's work. At present they associate the priesthood with routine functions and a jack-of-all-trades qualification, and do not consider it right to seek it.

He noted that subscription to the Thirty-Nine Articles, a failure to reform services and, in general, suspicions of intellectual honesty were also problems.

---

13 Charles Raven (1885–1964) was a chaplain to the forces in World War One, and after an incumbency and a period as a canon at Liverpool Cathedral was Regius Professor of Divinity at Cambridge from 1932 to 1950, and Master of Christ's College, Cambridge from 1939 to 1950.

14 CTM paper 4.

But his biggest broadside came in a later submission, 'On Attitudes Towards Ordination of Certain Outstanding Young Men.' Raven wrote about his own experience as a fellow of a Cambridge College (Christ's, of which he was soon to become Master), and also as a parent, having a son at Trinity College and a daughter at Girton. He suggested that able young people had very little respect for the Church, partly because of its dogmatism and a moral stance on many issues relating to property, sex and war which many found uncongenial, but was also concerned about the content of what was expected about belief. 'The Church's Creeds and formularies seem to them hardly compatible with common honesty.'

It is inconceivable that all the other members of the Commission would have agreed with Raven's onslaught, which must have produced considerable debate. But a later draft for the report dated December 1937 appeared over the initials of the more measured chairman, Alwyn Williams. He acknowledged the nature of the problem:

> Science and historical criticism have disproved so much of religious teaching of the past, and what still remains unchallenged is thereby placed under suspicion ... Thus it is asked whether the Virgin Birth, the Resurrection, the Ascension and other episodes in the Gospels are really credible, since as events in the physical sphere, in which in such matters uniformity seems to be unbroken, they would be absolutely unique.

He also noted the question of the historical accuracy of the Gospels, given they were written some years after the events they were describing.[15] After what must have been yet more robust conversation on the fundamentals of the Christian faith a much modified version appeared in the final report of the Commission.

> The church would appeal to many vigorous minds with more force if those minds were convinced that a real effort had been made by the Church to present its doctrinal basis authoritatively and intelligibly with due regard both to the essentials of the Faith and to the statement of it in language which should be as far as possible simple and unambiguous.

---

15 Folder AC/TM/10/1, Note in CTM 25, Draft C Note: p. 3.

(Raven's original paper, Williams' restatement of the issue and the final statement by the Commission on the subject are in Appendix H.) This opened up a theological debate that continues to this day, arguably not as robustly as it should.

Training and finance

One of the Commission's prime tasks was to consider the matter of the best training for ordination, and a critical issue was the relationship of theological colleges to university faculties of Theology. Should Theology be taught primarily within the believing community of the Church, or should it be taught in the more rigorous atmosphere of a modern university? The interim report was read as being hostile to colleges that were detached from universities, and the final report only slightly modified that view. It continued to recommend that most theological colleges should be in closer contact with universities with faculties of Theology. 'The universities in which theological faculties exist ... will ... concentrate in themselves ... the best theological knowledge ... It will be a great misfortune if these bodies of learning and teaching power cannot by one means or another be brought into closer relation with the training of ordinands.'[16] The report even encouraged the building of two new colleges and the moving of some existing ones to be closer to universities. They were prepared to allow some of the 'detached' colleges to remain.[17] Of the detached colleges they said, 'We believe some men will certainly profit from a period of training, which will generally be the final period, in such colleges and that there will certainly be opportunity for these colleges to give special attention to needs which can be best met in them.'[18]

The report also recommended a significant extension of the training that should be required. They suggested that a theology graduate should do two years' post-graduate training to prepare for ordination, that a non-theology graduate should do three years' and that non-graduates should have four years'. That the recommendation was eventually brought about probably owed as much to the availability of government and local authority grants after World War Two as to the fact of the recommendation.

---

16 Final Report, para. 85, p. 40f.
17 Final Report, para. 97, p. 48.
18 Final Report, para. 127, p. 62.

Inevitably the Commission considered financial issues and had received some guardedly supportive comments from the CBF. In a lengthy memorandum to the Commission dated 15 July 1938, the CBF cautiously advocated the possibility of grants to theological colleges rather than just to students, partly based on their good experience of financing the Church Training Colleges for teachers in such a way. That suggestion was not taken up by the Commission, but the CBF's final comment was significant.

> The cumulative result of these considerations would appear to be that larger sums of money are required for the training of priests in the Church of England than are now available. It would be the desire of the Central Board of Finance to ask the Commission on Training not to allow their recommendations for reform to be watered down by a sense of the impossibility of raising funds, or the probable continued inadequacy of resources. More than once in the last twenty years the Central Board has been able to elicit greatly increased support by an arresting statement to the country. Though the tide of effort thus stimulated may afterwards have ebbed, the low water mark has always remained higher than its previous level; it seems probable that financial effort will always show the same gradual increase.[19]

The later criticisms of the report's financial proposals as being vague and casual have to be read against the background of that paper from the CBF.

Selection

The biggest debate within the Commission appears to have surrounded the question of selection, starting with a memorandum on vocation from the Warden of Kelham (Stephen F. B. Bedale).[20]

> Christian tradition in general and the Anglican Ordinal in particular make it clear that priesthood is a matter of divine calling, given through the church, and not merely of the individual's choosing. To be 'called' involves not simply to choose, but rather to be chosen. To be chosen in any real

---

19 Archives folder AC/TM/6, p. 15 of CBF paper.
20 CTM paper 9.

sense involves at least the effective possibility of being rejected .... I do not know very exactly on what principles and by what methods Diocesan and other committees make their initial selection of candidates. I do know that the recognition of the marks of vocation is distinctly expert work, and I expect that existing practice calls for careful examination. But it certainly seems to be the case that, when once a man has been selected and given a grant, the present system makes it difficult for his personal suitability for Ordination ever again to be seriously questioned, unless he fails in some examination, or (patently) in the recognised standards of British respectability.

He went on to advocate Kelham's system of training, which he saw as being an alternative to what happened elsewhere and more rooted in developing a general theological interest rather than following rather specialized aspects of training.

In his memorandum 'The Process of Selection'[21] Revd A. G. Hebert SSM, also of Kelham, and a member of the Commission, wrote of references:

> We must eliminate the formal testimonial which amounts to no more than a certificate of respectability ... It must be recognised that testimonials at this stage are not of great value, as a rule, because the candidate is still, at least from the point of view of the Christian Ministry, quite immature, and so there is great difficulty in judging, at this stage, whether he has the makings of a good priest. It is much harder to judge the capacities of an outstanding young man in a parish, where he is the only candidate for Orders, than when he is seen side by side with other candidates. Hence the testimony of his schoolmaster is often worth more than that of his vicar.

The major recommendation on selection from the Commission emerged, however, not from any individual's memorandum. At an early stage a sub-committee, chaired by Williams and including Hebert, Owen and Raven, suggested setting up regional or inter-diocesan selection committees, each covering a group of dioceses and consisting of both clergy and laity. It suggested that the committees should interview the candidates and accept or reject them for consideration for admission to the theological hostels and colleges. The theological

---

21 CTM paper 74.

hostels and colleges should admit no one who had not been accepted by those committees, though they would be able to make their own selection from those accepted. It should be clearly understood that no one would have the right to be ordained even though accepted by the selection committee. They further urged that while the final responsibility for ordination must rest with the bishop, in his exercise of that responsibility he should not go outside the men accepted by the selection committee. They also suggested that when, in certain special cases because of age or for other reasons, candidates were not going through the ordinary course of training, the candidature of those men should also be controlled by the selection committee.[22]

At that stage Hebert, as a member of the sub-committee, agreed with that proposal. In examining the advantages and disadvantages of diocesan committees he noted the difficulty they had in rejecting some who had a strong recommendation by interested persons within a diocese. He also noted that finding the right place for a diocesan candidate could prove difficult, so he thought that a diocese, even if it had provided grants, should have no claim on its men. On regional committees and CACTM, at that stage he believed they were necessary, because the diocesan committees could not stand alone, because co-ordination between the dioceses was needed, and because there needed to be a central list kept by CACTM. Regarding selection during training, which was, of course, what happened at Kelham, he wrote:

> The Principals are undoubted the men who are experts at the job. Unlike Selection committees, they have afterwards to live with the men they select, and this provides the strongest inducement to select the right men. Perhaps the chief difficulty here is that they are in constant danger of accepting unsuitable men to keep the College full, and solvent.[23]

The last sentence was a very frank statement from someone involved in a theological college, but it was undoubtedly correct.

It was agreed by the full Commission that the notion of regional or inter-diocesan selection committees should be referred to a Bishops' Meeting in October 1937. The minutes of the Bishops' Meeting reported that many bishops took part in the discussion and 'revealed considerable divergence of opinion

---

22 CTM paper 27, modified in later versions CTM 27, B–E.
23 CTM paper 74.

with regard to the desirability of setting up Regional Committees on the lines suggested in the memorandum', but the Archbishop of Canterbury in summing up said that

> he thought that Bishops as a whole would welcome the assistance which such Regional Committees could give and would be unwilling to go outside the recommendations of those Committees save in quite exceptional cases. This was generally agreed on the understanding that the scheme would be referred back to the Bishops after further consideration by the Commission and by Principals of Theological Colleges.[24]

The Bishops of Manchester and Chester reported back to the Commission that 'the Bishops gave general approval to the suggestions, though somewhat reluctantly, and reserving their Episcopal rights in the matter, but would like to see the scheme worked out in more detail as there seemed to be sufficient in it to merit investigation.'[25]

Correspondence in the Lang papers shows that the Bishop of St Albans[26] (Furse), who was unable to attend the Bishops' Meeting because of illness, was concerned about the proposal. He wrote to Lang:

> I believe we are all agreed that it is desirable that there should be a more definite and efficient system of selection of those to be trained for the Ministry; but as I have read the memorandum – which I have done carefully several times – I confess it seems to me that as far as I can understand it, if these suggestions were carried out, the ultimate responsibility vested in the Bishop of the Diocese with regard to the ordination of Candidates for the Ministry might be seriously threatened ... I quite recognise that it is not suggested that any pressure would be brought upon Diocesan Bishops to ordain any particular men, but it does quite definitely attempt to restrict a Bishop from ordaining a man, or even have him tested at a Theological College. I do not know what Principals of Theological Colleges would say to the suggestion that they should only take men who had been passed by a Central Committee, but I am sure I should require a great deal of

---

24 Bishops' meetings 1932–8, p. 306f.
25 Minutes of the fourth meeting of the Commission, 26 November 1937.
26 For biographical information see footnote 9, p. 61.

persuasion before I agreed to such restrictions upon myself as a diocesan Bishop, as I can conceive cases arising where I should not be in agreement with the Committee's view that the man was necessarily undesirable.[27]

As what was being proposed was a major departure from the then current practice it seems unlikely that he was the only bishop who took that view, but the cautious support from the majority of the bishops encouraged the Commission to proceed with the proposal.

However, the debate on regional selection evidently continued within the Commission. The recommendation to refer all candidates to the regional selection committees was withdrawn at a revision of the committee's report presented in July 1938. They recommended that in the first instance diocesan committees should consider all candidates and only doubtful ones should be referred to the regional committees. In September of that year the Bishop of Bristol (Woodward), and a member of the Commission, wrote regretting that decision, 'because it would perpetuate the lack of a uniform standard and that it does nothing to deal with the valid and cogent criticisms brought forward by Father Hebert.' (This presumably referred to Hebert's concern that the sons of diocesan officials might have a particular advantage.) He therefore recommended that either a bishop or an area committee could accept someone, but not a diocesan committee. He thought most bishops would refer all cases to the area committees.

> Those should be quite small, consisting of four or five members at most. They should be appointed by CACTM after consultation with the bishops of the dioceses involved. Their ideal constitution would be a Bishop or an Archdeacon, the head of a theological college or a senior member of the staff, an experienced parish priest, and one or two laymen accustomed to dealing with men, either in business or one of the Services. Interviewers should be prepared to give the best part of one day a month to interviewing candidates. Ten such committees should be enough to cover the ground.[28]

The Commission broadly accepted the Bishop of Bristol's proposal at their seventh meeting in September 1938.

---

27 Lang papers, Vol. 154, p. 280f.
28 CTM paper 27f.

However, the following year Hebert produced a memorandum on 'The Dangers of Regional Committees',[29] which he saw as 'a symptom of the dangerous tendency towards centralisation in a bureaucratic age' and he suggested that diocesan committees should be entrusted with the task of selection, with the only exceptions being 'the sons of diocesan officials', who he thought should be considered by a selection committee at a university, at Oxford, Cambridge, Durham and perhaps London. 'Those Committees would deal as required with the cases I have alluded to, and also with the stray candidates who have no obvious diocesan connection. It seems then the need for regional Committees disappears. The Diocesan and University Committees between them would cover the whole ground.'

The Commission did not accept this argument, but if Hebert wished to pursue the matter 'a note of reservation' could be agreed with the chairman and published with the final report. It was a slightly strange view for Hebert to take then, given the statement in his earlier memorandum that 'Diocesan Committees cannot stand alone'; he clearly had a radical change of mind. Williams allowed that his objection could be a comment in the final report, which it was, but the recommendation of both the interim and the final reports was the creation of regional selection committees, which it saw as a way of overcoming the grave differences in standards between the dioceses, the overcoming of which might encourage more easily interchange of clergy between dioceses.

Reactions to the report

The Interim Report was issued in the spring of 1942. It was a relatively brief document given the years of work that preceded it, only 23 pages. Bishop Williams explained in introducing it to a joint meeting of the two Houses of the York Convocation that the Commission was further advanced on its work than the interim report suggested, particularly in the contacts it was having with the principals of theological colleges on possible groupings of them, and he hoped the Convocation would not wish to press him too much on those details, but the broad principles were available for comment. Its main proposals were to advocate the use of regional committees for selection, to provide stronger links

---

29 CTM paper 113.

between theological colleges and faculties of theology in universities even to the extent of encouraging some closures, amalgamations and moving of colleges, and to suggest that most courses of training should be lengthened.

In the ensuing discussion the Bishop of Warrington (Herbert Gresford Jones) supported a more ordered approach to selection. 'Both clergy and laity were gravely concerned at the quality of a certain number of men who were appearing in the ranks of the Anglican ministry, and that concern would not be diminished if they realised how haphazard and un-coordinated was the method [of selection] involved.'[30] The Archdeacon of Chester (Burne, the former principal and historian of Knutsford) thought there were two rocks on which the report might founder; the bishops, who might make exceptions to the regional committees as they so often had done to the advice of the advisory Council on the principles that should underlie selection, and finance.[31] In the Lower House discussion Revd E. K. Talbot (Superior of Mirfield until 1940) was not persuaded of the value of bringing all the detached colleges into a relationship with a university faculty of theology.

The *Church Times* was more critical. In a leader on 24 April 1942 it suggested that selection should be done by diocesan committees rather than by 'a remote Committee composed of well-disposed but not necessarily experienced representatives of the professions, and probably controlled by an all-powerful bureaucratic secretary'. After further correspondence in its columns it returned to the battle on the report in another leader on 24 July 1942:

> Its major suggestions – the establishment of regional committees ... and the replacement of seminaries by theological halls in University towns – have been riddled with unanswerable criticism. Moribund from the moment of publication, the report will serve its most useful purpose as a basis for constructive debate and planning.

Such comments were unlikely to deter the Commission, who continued with their work, and the final report, which was a much more substantial document of 77 pages with ten appendices, was presented by the chairman, by now Bishop of Durham, to the York Convocation and by the Bishop of Bristol (Woodward) to the Canterbury Convocation in May 1944. The report had also been published

---

30 *York Journal of Convocation*, 15 October 1942, p. 23.
31 *York Journal of Convocation*, 15 October 1942, p. 24.

prior to its considerations by the two Convocations and so was now available for broader comment.

The *Church Times* in a leader of 31 March 1944 said of the final report that it 'is a much more balanced, statesmanlike document than its interim predecessor of two years ago', but it continued in its opposition to regional selection, saying the best way of dealing with the problems was for the bishops to agree on a settled policy and then to carry it out through their diocesan committees. A fortnight later the Bishop of Bristol responded in the *Church Times* correspondence columns, pointing out that diocesan committees often only saw candidates towards the end of their time in training, and the whole point of the regional committees was to have a selection process before anyone could even start training. Canon H. Balmforth, Principal of Ely Theological College, reviewed the report in the *Guardian*, and wondered whether regional selection committees would necessarily do a better job than revamped diocesan committees, who should review every candidate before they started their training. He also noted, with agreement, that the *Church Times* had commented that the proposals on finance were 'casual'. Hebert published in *Theology* his reasons for dissenting from the proposal for regional committees. Ten leading evangelicals also sent a comment to the Archbishop of Canterbury (Temple) in which they too argued against the regional committees and in favour of selection by colleges:

The appointment and powers of the proposed Regional Committees give ground for real anxiety even though the proposals are tentative and subject to revision after ten years. The appointment of these committees and chairmen and secretaries by the Bishops concerned is unsatisfactory. In practice undue power would be exercised by the secretary as already happens in certain dioceses. Moreover it would tend to a dull uniformity and mediocrity and exclude from the ministry many of those who would be the most faithful instruments for the glory of God. Candidates of definite conviction not popular with local authority would be refused, or find their training uncongenial and not calculated to develop their fullest capacity. It is noted that the report recognises that a candidate may, in the first instance, have applied to a bishop or a theological college. In actual practice he is likely first of all to have consulted his vicar or his school or his college chaplain. Regional committees themselves might be more widely and consistently representative and more acceptable if they were nominated not exclusively by bishops of the Region but also by

Visitors and governing bodies of theological colleges or by the Councils of Ordination funds or by all of these in combination. Still better would be a Selection Committee for each theological college formed primarily from the governing body of the college, with agreed outside representation.[32]

There were also wider criticisms of the report. The Bishop of Oxford (Kirk) gave a university sermon in Oxford reported in the *Church Times* on 19 May 1944 criticizing the proposals on the broader front that its understanding of the nature of the ministry was too man-centred and not God-centred enough. In the Upper House of Canterbury discussion of the report, Kirk's article was referred to and the Bishop of Chichester (George Bell) said that ministry had to have a two-fold outlook – both to God and to man, and Kirk slightly modified his criticism to say that he thought the pattern of training suggested was too fragmented. But Bell, and Mervyn Haigh of Winchester (the former Vice-Principal of Knutsford) both expressed some reservations about the practical workings of the proposed regional committees.

In the Lower House of Canterbury's discussion perhaps the most telling comment came from W. R. Matthews, Dean of St Paul's and a former Dean of King's College, London, whose primary criticism was of the bishops.

> He was quite sure that everyone who had been in a similar position to that which he had occupied at King's College for fourteen years could remember numbers of cases in which he had said quite definitely of a candidate: 'This is not a man who ought to be ordained,' and had found a month or so afterwards (not so much to his astonishment as might be thought) that the man had been ordained, having perhaps written a few essays for one of the examining chaplains. It is really useless to discuss the training of candidates for ordination and it was vain to draw up reports and schemas for carrying out that training unless the bishops were prepared to exercise their undoubted right of selecting the men to be ordained with some sense of responsibility not only for the parish and the diocese but also for the church as a whole. That was the foundation of the whole problem of training for the ministry.[33]

---

32 Temple papers, Vol. 3, p. 88. The paper is undated but appears to come from 1944 and therefore refers to the Final Report.

33 Chronicle of Convocation, 15 May 1945, p. 39.

In the Upper House the Bishop of London (Fisher) had proposed that the report should be forwarded to CACTM for them to furnish the bishops with advice, and that proposal was accepted. No doubt Fisher took with him the memory of the comments of his dean, for when he became archbishop he was to take firm action to prevent such things happening in future.

The report was discussed in a variety of contexts including the Church press at various stages of its life and it certainly focused attention on a number of critical issues for the future of the ministry, not least of all for the members of the Commission, one of whom, Leslie Owen, was to be a key figure in subsequent developments. It was not, however, until 7 February 1945 that the report was formally considered in the Church Assembly, by which time the proposals on selection had been overtaken by CACTM's action in responding to the practical consequences of the war. The report's proposals did represent a huge change from the practice that had operated earlier, both in asking for longer training and in asking that every candidate irrespective of whether they needed financial support or not should go through a thorough selection procedure before starting training, which process would limit the power of both bishops and principals. In view of the criticism that was given of the proposals for regional selection it is interesting to speculate what might have happened had World War Two not intervened. As it turned out, it was the Church's experience towards the end of that war that proved the final and effective catalyst for change.

7

World War Two and the Establishing of Selection Conferences, 1939–45

The outbreak of war in September 1939 heralded a new type of warfare. The Zeppelin raids of World War One were now replaced by a more widespread bombing campaign of civilian targets, and many towns and cities of the nation experienced a new level of destruction. War was brought to the civilian population in a way that had never been known before, and that inevitably also meant the Church in those communities faced new and uncharted challenges.

William Temple became Archbishop of Canterbury in 1942, at about the time the tide of war was beginning to move in the Allies' favour, although none could be certain of the outcome at that stage. It is to his great credit that from his arrival at Lambeth, among all the other concerns an archbishop would have had in wartime conditions, he developed Lang's initial moves to plan for the Church after the war. In his brief period of just over two years as archbishop in Lambeth he was to create the conditions that were to transform the selection of ordinands for the future Church.

Even before World War Two began, conscription to the services for all able-bodied young men had been discussed as a possibility, although actual registration only happened from June 1940 onwards. Lang therefore realized, as Davidson had before him, that candidates from the services were likely to be critical for the ordained ministry of the future. Lang had therefore asked the Archbishops' Commission on Training to consider how best to deal with this matter and in February 1942, towards the end of Lang's tenure as archbishop, the Bishop of Bristol (Woodward) submitted to him the draft report on service candidates. The report suggested that service candidates should be the concern of a special services candidates committee and not go to the proposed regional committees, and it was suggested that the archbishop should appoint such a services candidates committee. It was that which Temple took over after his appointment to Canterbury in February 1942.

One of his first tasks was to sort out the immediate administrative structure. In March 1942 he met Revd Kenneth Riches, chaplain and librarian of Sidney Sussex College, Cambridge, who, at the age of 36, had been suggested by the Archbishops' Commission's group as the director of service ordinands, a post to be held in conjunction with a parish in Suffolk. Temple had already seen the senior chaplains of the three services who had all approved of the appointment, and of the appointment of a panel of bishops and experienced priests to visit the various commands to interview the chaplains and, where possible, to meet some of the men who were contemplating ordination.[1]

Temple also completed the process started under Lang of appointing a Services Ordinands Committee, the membership of which illustrated the extent to which those who had experience as army chaplains in World War One now held positions of influence within the Church. The chairman was Woodward, the Bishop of Bristol, who was later to describe the committee as 'the strongest and most competent committee of its kind I have ever sat on'. It included, apart from Woodward, four other diocesan bishops all of whom, like him, had been army chaplains: Christopher Chavasse, a former Deputy Assistant Chaplain General of the Forces (Rochester); John Victor Macmillan, who had been involved in the establishing of Knutsford (Guildford); Mervyn Haigh, former Vice-Principal of Knutsford (Winchester); F. Russell Barry, former Principal of Knutsford, (Southwell); and one Suffragan Bishop, Leslie Owen (Jarrow) who had experience of World War One's service candidates committee and who had also served on the Archbishops' Commission on Training. There were nine clergy, many of whom had extensive experience of training ordinands, including Canon Eric Abbott (Warden of Lincoln Theological College), J. S. Brewis (Principal of St Chad's College, Durham), S. F. B. Bedale (Warden of Kelham), W. D. Greer (Principal of Westcott House, later Bishop of Manchester), Cyril Eastaugh (Vicar of St John the Divine, Kennington, formerly Chaplain and Vice-Principal of Cuddesdon, later Bishop of Peterborough), and Kenneth Riches (Director of Service Ordination Candidates). Other members included the three Chaplains General; two headmasters, Robert Birley (Charterhouse) and R. W. Moore (Harrow); Sir Montague-Barlow (a barrister who was Chairman of the House of Laity of the Church Assembly); H. Willink (then a lawyer and Special

---

1 Temple papers, Vol. 3, p. 90.

Commissioner for the London Region, later to become Master of Magdalene College, Cambridge). The Chief Accountant of the Central Board of Finance (Sawden) was also a member to give financial advice.

A second task was to issue the challenge of considering ordination to those serving in the forces. The Service Ordinands Committee produced a memorandum to go from the archbishops, and it is interesting to note that, unlike in World War One, when the archbishops' letter was sent to all servicemen, in World War Two it went to forces' chaplains. The memorandum included some description of what was to be looked for in potential candidates, and they set their standards high in terms of intellectual ability, potential pastoral capacity and the quality of devotion. Although it used the language of vocation it talked of it more in terms of vocation being the end of the discernment process rather than it being a necessary feeling at the outset. (The full memorandum is Appendix I.)

In a letter to the archbishop dated 2 September 1942 Riches indicated that he already had 500 names of men hoping for ordination, and by June 1943 that had risen to 3,000.

A third, far more complex task was to resolve the future of CACTM, which had met only once (in January 1942) since the start of the war. At that meeting the Secretary of the Principals' Conference had reported that various reading lists had been drawn up for the possible service candidates, and it was reported that the plans for a Service Candidates Committee were being established. CACTM appears to have been excluded from many of the major discussions that were happening at the time.

The Bishop of Jarrow (Owen) wrote to the Chairman of the Service Candidates Committee (Woodward) saying that it was vital to get a new CACTM without delay, but a new CACTM would need a lot of thought and daring.

> You probably know its constitution and that it is only partly under the thumb of the Assembly. The result is that not only are the numbers far too big, but that with this democratic representation from the three Houses, it tends to get a lot of people who know little or nothing about the job itself, and worse still, have axes to grind, ecclesiastical or otherwise.

He thought what was needed was a body of men who 'know their stuff from their own particular angles and did not have to have everything explained to them'. He recognized that it would need diocesan bishops ('not those too angular or academic'), some from universities and theological colleges and even a few headmasters.

> But I do plead for a strong body of opinion in CACTM that has had pastoral experience in parishes. I do not care whether they are Bishops or Archdeacons or Examining Chaplains but we have suffered far too much from the purely academic overweight which thinks that it understands what is needed because it has heard, but never really experienced.

He realized that a handpicked CACTM would be best, but that was probably impossible.

Woodward forwarded the letter to Temple and said that he thought the question of the re-formation of CACTM was urgent. 'The life of the church for the next twenty or thirty years really depends on the men we recruit now and the training which we can give them. I do not feel that CACTM as it is at present constituted is really up to the job.' He wondered whether, if the Services Candidates Committee took on men in industry, as the Principals' Conference had suggested, that committee might, without any formal step being taken, really become the operative body. He concluded:

> I need hardly add that if the Services Candidates Committee is to assume this larger and far more important function, it would be necessary to appoint a Chairman who is far more competent for the job than I can claim to be. Either the Bishop of Winchester [Mervyn Haigh] or the Bishop of Jarrow [Leslie Owen], himself, would, I think, do it excellently. But you may feel that this is not a practical proposal.[2]

Temple clearly did think it was practical, and was no doubt also reflecting on the letters he was getting from bishops suggesting that the Chaplain-General, while an admirable man, lacked the imagination needed for the new and developing situation in the war in supporting the chaplains. He responded in two ways. First, on 20 November 1942 he wrote to the Bishop of Manchester (Warman) as chairman of CACTM, whose 70th birthday was earlier that month. He noted that over the next few years candidates for ordination would almost entirely come from those on war service, who were the responsibility of the Services Ordinands

---

2 Temple papers, Vol. 3, pp. 123–4.

Committee and he therefore wondered whether CACTM might consider going into suspense for the coming period. Second, two days later he wrote to Anthony Bevir, the prime minister's secretary, asking whether it might be possible to revive a provincial suffragan. 'He would be concerned with such matters as the recruiting and training of Service Ordination Candidates, and some parts of the dealings with the Anglican communion overseas. He could also meet Admirals and Generals – and other Bishops – so to speak "on a level" as no senior chaplain, however able, could.'[3]

The Bishop of Manchester replied saying that he foresaw a problem with the principals of the theological colleges who were on CACTM agreeing to the responsibility for GOE being given to a nominated body rather than to the existing CACTM. However, he thought it would be possible to reconstitute CACTM so that the Service Ordinands Committee could become part of CACTM and form a new CACTM candidates committee. He also thought this would be a help to the Bishop of Durham's Commission. The letter was copied to the Bishop of Bristol.

The Bishop of Bristol replied to the Bishop of Manchester on 30 November 1942 with a copy to Temple. He said he never thought of the Services Candidates Committee becoming CACTM, but he was in favour of a nominated rather than an elected CACTM, and he would be happy to hand over the work of the Services Candidates Committee to a reconstituted CACTM. He also did not think he was the man to chair a future CACTM and he doubted whether any diocesan bishop would have the time to do the role justice. 'CACTM will need a Chairman who can make this his primary, if not his only work.'[4] The Secretary of the Principals' Conference (J. O. Cobham) also wrote to Temple saying the principals thought that CACTM needed a more radical change, and thought that the chairman should be someone with ready access to the archbishops and bishops, but possibly not a diocesan bishop because he would not have the time to devote to it, and that the body itself should be hand-picked and not elected.

The way was therefore open for a constitution for a new CACTM to be proposed, and it was approved by the Church Assembly on 1 March 1943. Fifteen members were elected from the Church Assembly, 15 were appointed by the archbishops, six were appointed by the conference of theological college principals and one from each of seven faculties of theology (full details

3 Temple papers, Vol. 9, p. 255.
4 Temple papers, Vol. 9, p. 258.

are in Appendix C). A body of 43 people would still be quite unwieldy, but the archbishops' ability to appoint 15 of the members gave them sufficient control.

The fourth task therefore was to resolve three inter-related issues. First, he had to find a way of responding to the needs of Anglican forces' chaplains. He recognized that the Royal Army Chaplains' Department was an ecumenical body so that any proposal would need to be discussed with other churches. Second, he had to find the right person to be chairman of CACTM and to manage a body that some clearly thought was unwieldy. Third, if the new chairman was not a diocesan bishop he had to find a way of paying a full-time chairman.

His first thought involved reviving the role that Bishop Gwynne had in World War One as Deputy Chaplain General. Temple and the Archbishop of York (Garbett) arranged to see the Secretary of State for War (Sir James Grigg) on 10 February 1943. On 15 March Grigg wrote to Temple. He said that the most important suggestion the two archbishops had made was that 'a Bishop, e.g. the Bishop of Jarrow, should be appointed as an extra Deputy Chaplain General, for spiritual affairs only, to strengthen the Royal Army Chaplains' Department on its religious as distinct from its administrative side.[5] Grigg said there was no objection to the Bishop of Jarrow personally, but he feared for what it might do to the Chaplain General's position and what the other churches would feel. In view of the difficulties Gwynne's appointment as a bishop with a particular responsibility for Anglican chaplains had caused within the Army Chaplains' Department, that was not an entirely surprising response.[6] After consulting the Archbishop of York, Temple wrote again asking whether a new DCG who was not a bishop would be acceptable. Grigg replied that he would be. In further correspondence with York, Garbett suggested to Temple Eric Abbott,[7] then Warden of Lincoln Theological College and a member of the Service Candidates Committee.

Grigg consulted other churches on the proposal as he was obliged to do since the Army Chaplains' Department included clergy from other denominations, but meanwhile, on 19 May 1943 the Bishop of Durham as Chairman of the Archbishops' Commission on Training wrote to Temple about the constitution of CACTM.

---

5 Temple papers, Vol. 9, p. 278ff.

6 See footnote 20, p. 80.

7 Abbott was later to be Dean of King's College, London, Warden of Keble College, Oxford and then Dean of Westminster.

It was strongly urged that the Chairman of the reformed CACTM must be in a position to give the great part of his time and thought at all events for the next few years to this work. He will certainly need a full time secretary and probably two. If this view is right it seems to follow that no Diocesan Bishop can give the necessary time; yet everyone agreed that it is important the chairman should have direct and regular touch with the Bishops, and that is most easily secured by his attendance at Bishops' meetings for at least part of each session.[8]

One possible solution was to appoint a full-time chairman of CACTM and on 21 May Temple wrote to Garbett saying that he would like the Bishop of Jarrow to become the full-time chairman of CACTM, although he recognized that there might be problems about meeting the stipend.

Whether we shall need a whole-time Chairman after the ex-Service men are trained can be settled when the time comes – but of course a man of Leslie Owen's quality would always be easy to place and he need have no anxieties about his future, though he would not have a legal freehold.[9]

Meanwhile Grigg had raised the matter of other churches and Temple over some weeks received replies which were cautiously supportive but, eventually on 29 June 1943 he received a letter from the Convenor of the Church of Scotland Committee on Chaplains to His Majesty's Forces. He was against anyone being appointed as Deputy Chaplain General but suggested someone should be appointed at a more lowly rank in the Chaplains' Department.

Temple sent the letter on to Grigg with the final comment: 'May I express the very fervent hope that the period of discussions is now ended and a decision be reached? I am beginning to sympathise with Hitler when he begins to explain that his patience is failing!'[10] Grigg replied saying that, while he was personally very sympathetic to the appointment, because of the reactions of the other churches and the fact that in time the Church of Scotland and possibly the Methodists would want someone similar, he would have to say no. Temple

---

8 Temple papers, Vol. 9, p. 317.
9 Temple papers, Vol. 9, p. 320.
10 Temple papers, Vol. 9, p. 339.

replied saying that he accepted that and would come back with a fresh proposal, but that he and other bishops remained very concerned about meeting the real pastoral needs of military chaplains.

Having that door firmly closed, on 29 September Temple wrote to Leslie Owen on the possibility of becoming a full-time chairman of CACTM and Bishop to the Forces in the suffragan post he was proposing to revive as Bishop of Maidstone.[11] On 2 October the Bishop of Manchester as outgoing chairman of CACTM wrote to say that the appointment of the Bishop of Jarrow as chairman would be acceptable to CACTM.

Appointing Owen was to prove complex. On 4 October 1943 Owen wrote to Temple accepting the post but suggesting some conditions:

1. That the new Chairman of CACTM (if not a Diocesan Bishop) should be permitted to attend the Bishops meetings; that he should be responsible personally for reporting to them on CACTM policy, & be ready to answer questions, relevant to this, as well as to report, when required, on CACTM finance.

2. That he should be given facility to attend the sessions of the Church Assembly, as well as to report, when required, on CACTM finance. I think you said in our conversation that you would ask the bishops on the one hand, & the appropriate authority of the CA on the other, for such permission to be present as your Provincial Suffragan, & that you did not anticipate difficulty.

3. That in the capacity as Suffragan you would wish me to act as your representative to the Chaplains & to Ordination Candidates in the Forces, & that you would secure the approval of the Chaplains in Chief for this, & the Diocesan Bishops for Confirmations which might be required within their Dioceses in this connection. I hope I understood you rightly in believing that there would be no serious obstacle in such an arrangement.

---

11 Michael Snape suggests in *The Royal Army Chaplains' Department* that this represented an attempt to sideline the Chaplain-General and was part of a 'web of conspiracy'. While it is certainly true that Temple was concerned about many aspects of the Chaplains' Department under the Chaplain-General, Snape does not mention at all the equally important role that Owen was to have in CACTM. In fact in both wars bishops recognized the critical importance of the recruitment of new clergy for the Church of the future, Gwynne as Deputy Chaplain General in World War One and Owen as Bishop to the Forces in World War Two. Their work in that sphere was a wholly right and proper concern of an archbishop.

4. That both for interviews with Ordination Candidates & other C.A.C.T.M. work, a house or quarters should be found easily accessible to Westminster. . . .

5. That financially I should be ready to accept the equivalent of my present emoluments which are £1500 p.a. with house, rates and dilapidations free.

I am prepared therefore to act on the assurance you give me in your letter of September 29th.[12]

Temple was not able to give the assurances the Bishop of Jarrow sought, in particular the right to speak at the Church Assembly, and the financial arrangements. Temple did assure Owen that he would receive £1,500 and he hoped there would be a further £300 to enable the bishop to find his own house.

Owen replied on 9 October stressing that he thought the right to speak was essential and that he was unhappy about the proposed £1,800, partly on the grounds that it would be more than suffragan bishops received, but also because the extra £300 would not be enough to find a suitable house. He therefore wrote, 'It seems, therefore, that I can only decline the proposal which you and CACTM have so graciously made to me. I write this with deep reluctance of the disappointment it will bring on in which I share, but I am sure that, in the circumstances, I cannot do otherwise and that to delay will only cause further inconvenience.'[13]

Temple wrote on 12 October saying that he hoped Owen would not consider his letter as final and that he was on the track of some possibilities. Owen confirmed in a letter of 15 October that the purpose of his letter was certainly not to lock any door.[14] Meanwhile Temple continued to write to wealthy contacts seeking to raise the funds for this post.

The Archbishop of York wrote on 22 October to Temple after he had a long conversation with Owen, who was taking a clergy retreat in his diocese. Garbett said that Owen:

feels very strongly about having a recognised place at the Bishops' Meetings, and he would not be satisfied if he only came in when CACTM

---

12 Temple papers, Vol. 10, p. 5.
13 Temple papers, Vol. 10, p. 12.
14 Temple papers, Vol. 10, p. 19.

business was under discussion.... I showed him that personally I was doubtful about his claim to attend the whole of the Bishops' Meetings, and I felt that in some ways it might be even more difficult if the claim were made on the ground that he was a Provincial Suffragan. I hope however some way out of the difficulty can be found. He is I think certainly the best man we could obtain for this work, but he is inclined to be rather finicky.[15]

Temple replied on 25 October 1943:

I talked to the Bishop of London [Fisher] about bringing him to Bishops' Meetings. He took the view, to which I myself was inclined, namely, that I could quite well bring him in as a member of my own staff; instead of two Chaplains I should have one Suffragan and one Chaplain, and the former would take part in one section of our business. Geoffrey thought nobody would raise the smallest objection, especially if I did not ask them! That the Archbishop should bring his own staff might be generally accepted, but that the Chairman of any council should attend as such would arouse expectations in other Chairmen who might want the same privilege.[16]

On 10 November 1943 Temple wrote to the prime minister outlining the proposal. He explained that he wanted Owen to become full-time chairman of CACTM and was working on raising the necessary funds for his stipend, but he also wanted to recreate a suffragan post in Canterbury.

There is in connexion with the See of Canterbury a Suffragan See of Maidstone which has not been filled for a very long time, if indeed it was ever filled at all: but it has legal existence and my proposition is that I should be allowed to submit to the Crown as usual two names for the Suffragan See of Maidstone.[17]

He sent a similar letter to the king's private secretary.

On 17 November 1943 CACTM resolved unanimously:

---

15 Temple papers, Vol. 10, p. 23.
16 Temple papers, Vol. 10, p. 25.
17 Temple papers, Vol. 10, p. 43.

1. That Leslie Owen, now Bishop of Jarrow, be appointed Chairman.
2. That the Council approves of the payment to Bishop Owen as stipend such sum as the Archbishop of Canterbury shall arrange with him, provided that it shall not from the funds of the Council exceed £1000 per annum.

On 23 November Temple wrote to Owen telling him that both the prime minister and the king had approved his appointment.

> Further, I have got promises of over £1,500 a year in covenanted subscriptions though some of the payments will not begin to come in till about April. I may still get one or two more Covenants. But it is clear that you can count upon say £1,200 a year, and if need be £1,500 a year, from this source. What I hope you may be able to do is to arrange that CACTM shall supply you with an office and secretarial help and also with a house or flat or a large contribution towards it; and then your whole personal stipend, apart from these things, should come from my fund which will be held by the Central Board of Finance in a special account. I trust this news sets your mind still more at ease. Several of my friends have sent a favourable response since I last saw you.[18]

Owen was 57 when appointed as Bishop of Maidstone and the first (and so far only) full-time episcopal chairman of CACTM (or any of its successor bodies). Temple's commitment to the outcome and the extraordinary amount of time and trouble he took over the process including raising the money for Owen's stipend was remarkable for an archbishop in the midst of a war and with many other matters on his mind.

Finance yet again

During the course of 1942 and 1943 there had also been much discussion and correspondence about financing training for returning servicemen and practical arrangements for their return. The service ordination candidates committee had identified three types of candidates:

---

18 Temple papers, Vol. 10, p. 101.

1. Men already accepted who started training or will be ready to start after demobilisation.
2. Graduates and older men of the graduate type who found their vocation during the war.
3. Men with comparatively little educational background who have been moved during the war to offer themselves for Ordination. They will need very careful testing and must pass some examination of the Matriculation type before commencing their theological training. They form our chief problem.[19]

The committee suggested that categories 1 and 2 would graduate and then spend two years in theological college; or those not taking a degree, three years. For those in category 3 test or pre-training schools would be needed. The committee hoped that universities would establish a matriculation examination for all ex-servicemen who were proposing to enter one of the learned professions, the examination to be of a cultural kind. 'It will be necessary to set up at least two pre-Training Schools to take about 100 men each.' Probably they would only be needed to absorb the war intake, but maybe one would be left open.

Woodward wrote to Temple on the subject. Temple replied pointing out the need for finance for this. Woodward replied on 11 November 1942 saying that the CBF were very unwilling to launch a separate appeal as it might interfere with an appeal that might be required following the Financial Commission's proposals. He then wrote:

At the same time, we are losing an absolutely golden opportunity of raising money now. This is just the time when a great many people would respond to an appeal to help with the training of Ordinands who are now serving in the Forces. I can't help feeling that Grey, and those who advise him, are making a rather serious mistake. It may even be necessary for us to kick over the traces and go ahead on our own ... I believe that the Central Board would be willing for a fund to be opened, so long as no great publicity were given to an appeal. This is, of course, better than nothing, but only a little better![20]

---

19 Temple papers, Vol. 3, p. 141.
20 Temple papers, Vol. 3, p. 130.

Temple wrote to Earl Grey, Chairman of the Central Board of Finance, asking him to consider this, on 12 November. He also wrote to McCorquodale (Parliamentary Secretary to the Ministry of Labour) to ask about government money for the training of ordinands after the war, explaining what had happened after World War One.

Woodward sent Temple a letter he had received from Sir John Guillum Scott, joint secretary of the Church Assembly, dated 8 February 1943, saying that the Financial Commission of the Church Assembly had passed a resolution saying 'Unless the object of the appeal was one of prime urgency the Financial Commission would urge the Church Assembly to consider the desirability of not issuing any appeal for objects within the scope of the Commission's enquiry until such time as its report was available.'[21] Woodward responded to Temple in a letter of 9 February:

> If the Financial Commission or its representatives in the Assembly carry their point, I shall feel obliged to resign my position as Chairman of the Service Candidates' Committee. I could not make myself responsible for collecting the names of a considerable number of men with the assumption that money will be forthcoming for their training if no kind of provision is made for the raising of the necessary funds.[22]

Temple wrote to Sawden, Chief Accountant of the Church Assembly (and member of the Service Candidates Committee), basically supporting the Bishop of Bristol. Sawden sent a conciliatory letter, and in the event there was some support for the appeal. There was some correspondence with senior military figures about who should sign from the three services.

Meanwhile Grey had been pursuing the possibility of government grants for returning servicemen and wrote to Temple:

> You will be glad to get official confirmation of the fact that ex-Service ordinands come within the framework of the Government scheme for the further education of demobilised members of H. M. Forces. The Government grant will cover, where necessary, a four year course of education, with a possible fifth year for some selected candidates of particular promise. A beneficiary

---

21 Temple papers, Vol. 3, p. 150.
22 Temple papers, Vol. 3, p. 149.

under this Scheme will receive full tuition fees, and adequate maintenance grants to cover term time. In addition, married beneficiaries will receive marriage allowances and children's allowances. There will no doubt be a reasonable means test, but it is not at all likely to be of a harsh character.[23]

He went on to argue that this changed the argument for the need for the appeal.

Grey was right and the appeal did not go ahead. What seems extraordinary is that Grey did not explain to the Chairman of the Service Candidates Committee the possibilities he was pursuing. The difficulty in their relationship was revealed when Woodward also raised the question with Temple of the early release of ordination candidates. He wrote to Temple on 26 May 1943 suggesting that representation should be made to the Ministry of Labour for their release. In a postscript he also said: 'I am finding Grey almost intolerable. So far as I can judge from his letters he regards himself as the ultimate authority in the whole business. Perhaps I had better resign the Chairmanship of the Service Candidates Committee to him!'[24]

On the matter of the early release of service candidates Temple wrote to Ernest Bevin, Minister of Labour and National Service, on 9 June 1943, having got the agreement from the Archbishop of York that this should be a joint request. 'We should not think of asking for any early priority for all Ordination candidates, but there are some whose training had proceeded a long way but who did not take advantage of the reservation offered to them because of their eagerness to serve the national cause.'[25] He received a cautiously friendly letter from Bevin outlining the difficulties of getting a fair system for demobilization but assuring the archbishop that 'full account will be taken of the considerations which you advance in your letter or of any further statement which you might then be disposed to put forward'.[26]

Selection

Finding the right way of selecting men was clearly the next issue that had to be resolved. G. F. Woolley from the British North Africa forces headquarters

---

23 Temple papers, Vol. 3, p. 175.
24 Temple papers, Vol. 3, p. 183.
25 Temple papers, Vol. 3, p. 192.
26 Temple papers, Vol. 3, p. 197.

(of unrevealed rank) wrote to Temple on 24 November 1943. He was not impressed by some who had asked about ordination: 'the soldier who had not risen above the rank of private, who has no education, and is of the well-wishing server type who hopes to have a soft job'. He went on to suggest a proposal whereby:

> men be asked for of the officer or business manager type of experience, who have made good in their job and as keen Christians. Age should be at least 35 years. They should receive three-months training: biblical, philosophical, technical. They should be commissioned for lay-reader work at home and abroad. Those who obviously make good, and offer themselves for it, should receive subsequent training for Ordination. Such men could be attached, like Chaplains, to units and take services other than Holy Communion, teach, take discussions, and give personal help of a pastoral kind. It would be an excellent experience and test for Ordination Candidates and so help to solve future problems as well as meet a present emergency.[27]

Temple passed the letter on to Owen, who was not inclined to think that those who had expressed an interest in ordination in that context were necessarily typical. 'Probably there are many men, and perhaps more virile, who are thinking of ordination, but have been too engaged in fighting battles to send in their names to Riches.' He was sympathetic to Woolley's proposal, except that he saw some practical difficulties with the military and was concerned about considering readership as a gateway to ordination.[28]

On the broader issue of selection, Owen presented a report to the Bishops' Meeting in July 1944. A paper circulated to the bishops stated:

Methods of Selection

> Under this heading CACTM will be asked to consider the proposal to set up Regional Committees. This proposal has however met with criticism both in Convocation and elsewhere. It may be that the time is not ripe for a final decision on the matter.

---

27 Temple papers, Vol. 10, p. 108.
28 Temple papers, Vol. 10, p. 139.

An alternative policy might be to set up two or three pre-training centres where the majority of service candidates should go for testing for a shorter or longer period.

The experience of the Selection Board for Officers in the Services might be valuable in the setting up of such centres.[29]

It was agreed that 'the matters set out should be in the mind of CACTM and should first be considered by them.'

This paved the way for the more major development which happened following a residential meeting of the new CACTM from 11 to 15 September 1944 at Westcott House in Cambridge. By then Revd Kenneth M. Carey had been appointed General Secretary of the Council while Kenneth Riches was part-time secretary of the Service Candidates Committee, but at the meeting it was reported that Riches was to be Principal of Cuddesdon and that he would be succeeded by Revd W. L. S. Fleming, Fellow of Trinity Hall, Cambridge. The meeting was to consider the Archbishops' Commission on Training report, as proposed by Fisher at the Upper House of Convocation.

The Council reflected on the criticisms that had been offered of regional selection conferences but also on the experience many service chaplains had of the War Office selection boards, when men were brought to a centre for a residential conference for selection. These selection boards had been started in 1942 and were revolutionary in selection methods in that they did not rely merely on interviews and examination results, but also observed the interaction between candidates. (Appendix J gives further details.) The Council considered such boards an appropriate way forward to dealing with returning servicemen, and indeed considered it appropriate for all candidates. The Council acknowledged that the setting up of regional committees in the immediate future was not regarded as either possible or desirable, but also considered that the principles underlying the commission's recommendations, that there should be some authority to which bishops and principals of theological colleges should first refer, was an essential safeguard in the preliminary testing of candidates for the ministry. They therefore suggested for war service candidates that selection centres should be set up in different parts of this country and possibly in other centres overseas. All candidates should be required to attend these centres for a period of four days or more. Representatives of CACTM with assessors from

---

29 Bishops' meetings 1939–44, p. 371.

the area chosen and from diocesan committees, and other qualified persons would be present, with dossiers of candidates, for personal interviews to recommend them (or otherwise) for training. The purposes of such conferences would be to help men discover their particular vocation in the Church and not simply ordained ministry.

They also decided that there should be pre-training centres, one in each Province of Canterbury and York, for such war service candidates whose vocation to the ministry was doubtful, or who needed some further cultural and devotional training to fit them for university or theological college courses. Matriculation or its equivalent, for example the Services' Preliminary Academic and Professional Examination should be required of all candidates before entry to these pre-training centres. The Council hoped that selection centres attended by candidates before demobilization would be arranged by the service authorities, but for civilian and ex-service candidates after demobilization, the expenses would have to be met by the Church unless the candidates were in a position to pay for it themselves. It was agreed that men should be expected to pay where possible, but that the Church should be ready to help in cases of need. The hope was expressed that these plans, with such modification as experience proved necessary, might be applicable to all candidates later, and a recommendation was made that the appointment of the principals of the two pre-training centres should be in the hands of the archbishops. It was also agreed that the process of earmarking a man for a particular diocese if that diocese had helped with fees was undesirable, and that a strong recommendation should be made to the bishops that it should cease.

Owen wrote to Temple on 15 September 1944, having just returned from the Cambridge conference. He submitted a memorandum and hoped that since the bishops at their last meeting approved of the general principles which CACTM now officially recommended as the beginning of an interim policy there would be no need for a long discussion. He also added:

> I want to talk over with you two points. (1) The desirability of asking the Bishops to extend the operation of the Selection Boards to all candidates and not only war service candidates. I am sure that either sooner or later this ought to happen unless we allow theological colleges to have the freedom to admit men to training apart from any authority either of Bishops or CACTM. This is a very weak spot. (2) It is most urgent that if the Bishops do agree to CACTM's proposals they should observe them strictly.

I have discovered lately, from both the heads of theological colleges and groups of Chaplains that perhaps the strongest factor in 'distrust of Bishops' is that they vary so much in their requirements of Ordinands and so frequently break the published requirements which they themselves have made. I say this of course to you very privately and will elaborate it more fully sometime. I do it now because I am very eager that we bear this in mind in our future plans.[30]

The matter returned to the Bishops' Meeting on 9 and 10 October 1944, when it was agreed that '*all* candidates should be sent to Selection Centres and that the Centres themselves should be appointed by CACTM and any diocesan representative on them by the Bishop of the diocese concerned'.[31]

Meanwhile preparations must have been put in hand for what was reported at the following Council meeting in November 1944.

An experimental Selection Centre had been held at St. Gabriel's College, Camberwell, from October 13th–16th. A full report was given by the Secretary and discussed. It was agreed that any decisions taken by the Assessors at the Selection Centre must be regarded as final.

Temple died suddenly on 26 October 1944, which was obviously a huge shock to both Church and nation. He had, however, established a process that now had a life of its own. Temple was succeeded the following year as archbishop by the Bishop of London, Geoffrey Fisher, who was to bring a rather different style of leadership to the Church, but who was very sympathetic to the work that had been done on selection. When consulted about the possibility of the model being used for all candidates he was encouraging, and selection centres were established in the first instance at Cuddesdon Theological College near Oxford and, from January 1946 at Lichfield Theological College, both of which were regularly used as CACTM selection centres. Centres were also established in various places for forces candidates overseas. There appear to be no extant records of these centres, but conferences certainly took place in Germany,[32] in

---

30 Temple papers, Vol. 10, p. 185.

31 Bishops meetings 1939–44, p. 370f.

32 From information provided by Rt Revd Mark Green to the author about a year before he died in August 2009.

the Middle East,[33] in East Africa,[34] in India,[35] and probably in other theatres of war. The military had often provided temporary houses where forces chaplains could gather groups of servicemen, and such places were used for selection centres at no cost to the Church. Some explanation of the process was provided in the Church Assembly's discussion of the Archbishops' Commission's report on 7 February 1945 when Canon Cyril Eastaugh (Southwark), a member of the Service Candidates Committee, spoke of his experience as a selector at a conference.

It was not a question of acceptance for ordination, but of acceptance for training. It was thought desirable to take a leaf out of the War Office procedure, and to adopt some such scheme as the selection boards which had been organised under War Office auspices. In that arrangement a number of men were invited to spend some four days with a body of selectors, the proportion of selectors to candidates being about five to twenty-five. They lived together, and the candidates were observed both individually and corporately, each member of the selection board interviewing each candidate. The whole atmosphere of that corporate life was immensely valuable, whether for officership in the Army or for training for the ministry. Four of these selection conferences had been arranged for the Church, two in London and two in Cambridge. They were vocational in their outlook; those who proved not to be suitable for ordination were helped to see the entire vocation of the layman in the world today ... On each board of selection so far held there had always been one layman, and it was intended that there should always be a layman among those who interviewed candidates. At the end of the period the selectors met together and pooled their opinions about each individual and decided whether he should be recommended for training, or whether he should not be recommended, or whether his case should be postponed and he should go to another selection conference in, say, six months' time. It was intended that those centres should be mobile. The Bishop of Maidstone had been abroad to arrange for the setting up of such centres with the B.L.A. in the Middle East, and no doubt even further afield, even in India.

---

33 From a report by Leslie Owen on his visit to the area.

34 From a conversation with Preb. Donald Barnes of London Diocese, who attended a selection conference in Nairobi.

35 See correspondence between the Metropolitan of India and Fisher later in this chapter.

He would like to reassure any who felt that there was a caucus of officials at the centre determining who should and who should not be ordained. The panel of selectors included one member of the diocesan training committee, at least one member who had theological college experience, a parish priest and a layman. The cost so far had been very small, but it might be a good deal greater if this method was to be pursued. Of course, the ultimate responsibility lay with the bishop; the selection centres embodied the principle only of preliminary selection, but it was the hope of all those who had been employed in this work that the scheme would be permanent.[36]

Kenneth Carey, General Secretary of CACTM, wrote to the archbishop (Fisher) on 8 October 1945, enclosing a copy of the report on selection conferences circulated in the summer. He explained that 14 conferences had been held in England and that probably over 1,000 men had been through the centres both in England and overseas. CACTM had been permanently based at Cuddesdon but with the reopening of the college a new centre would be needed. Of the selection conference programme he reported: 'We are still learning from criticism and experiment, and while the programme still retains something of its original features, it would not be true to say that it has reached its final form.'[37]

Fisher continued to be very supportive of the development of CACTM's role and, in particular, of its new selection methods. On 11 October 1945 he gave his presidential address to the Church Assembly and his comments on CACTM are included in Appendix K. On the selection matters he said:

A method of Selection Boards was approved and has now been in operation for some time both at home and overseas. In a situation in which the Church is having to deal with four thousand or more candidates for ordination, these Boards have provided a method which not only has prevented a quite chaotic confusion, but, as I believe, has also proved itself sound in principle and of permanent benefit to the Church. Of course, under any system – and most certainly under the previous system – mistakes can be made, though it is to be remembered that not all those

---

36 CA proceedings 1945, Vol. XXV, p. 80f.
37 Fisher papers, Vol. 12, p. 34.

who think themselves the victims of a mistake are right in thinking so. There is certainly no justification whatever for thinking that the Selection Boards are applying too rigid standards of one kind or another or are anything but most careful and sympathetic in the consideration they give to each candidate. Two things especially should be noted. It is remarkable that in the Selection Boards the decisions reached on each candidate (and by now more than one thousand have passed through their hands) have been unanimous in all but about half-a-dozen cases. It is also remarkable that the Selection Boards here and overseas, composed of clergy and laity of different experiences, have independently arrived at a standard of balanced judgment approximately the same. The work will continue at very high pressure for a considerable time to come, and it throws an immense strain on CACTM in conducting it. Experience is leading day by day to improvements in detail, but I think I can say for the Diocesan Bishops of both Provinces that in this work CACTM has their full confidence and support.[38]

This was a ringing endorsement and CACTM was able to continue its procedures for selection with some measure of confidence.

Fisher did, however, make one change that irritated Owen. Kenneth Carey explains it in a brief tribute to Owen published after Owen's untimely death in 1947.

Temple realised that the job could not properly be done unless the Chairman of CACTM was invited to Bishops' Meetings as of right. Unfortunately, Geoffrey Fisher did not see things in this light and Leslie Owen had to wait until he became Bishop of Lincoln before he could pull his weight with the diocesan Bishops.[39]

In view of Fisher's comment to Temple about allowing Owen into Bishops' Meetings it does show something of the different style of leadership that Fisher was to give compared to Temple, although it may be that already Fisher was thinking of dioceses where Owen could become the diocesan bishop. But on the

---

38 CA proceedings 1945, Vol. XXV, pp. 175–8.

39 *Leslie Owen: A Man of Faith and Courage and Witness to the Things Unseen.* A collection of memories of Owen produced privately. In Lambeth Palace library, HS199.0909, p. 40.

essential matter of the new style of selection CACTM could not have had a stauncher advocate than the new archbishop.

The use of selection centres overseas, which were largely administered by military chaplains, also could create some difficulties when they were held in Anglican dioceses overseas. These were essentially missionary dioceses and would not necessarily have been sympathetic to the need of the Church of England to balance difference styles of churchmanship, and this was revealed in an extraordinary correspondence between the Bishop of Calcutta, George Clay Hubback,[40] Metropolitan of the Church in India, and the Archbishop of Canterbury. The essential question was whether worship at selection conferences held abroad should reflect local conditions or should reflect the need to balance different types of approach to the Eucharist by the use of surplice, stole and lights as opposed to more vestments. Hubback had kindly offered the use of his house as a base for a selection conference and for services to be held in his cathedral, but he was not pleased to be given instructions from CACTM on the use or otherwise of vestments in his own cathedral. Hence the correspondence, where Fisher consulted with CACTM and sent an emollient reply, which only partly satisfied Hubback. It could have been argued that giving servicemen an opportunity to experience the life of the local church would be a creative experience, but CACTM staff thought that balancing the arguments about churchmanship in the selection of candidates for the Church of England was more important. It was a moot point. (The full correspondence is in Appendix L.)

Not surprisingly, in February 1946 the directors of service ordination candidates (John Phillips and Launcelot Fleming) wrote about future overseas selection centres, reporting that the selection committee had decided that the need for overseas centres was now less acute and that normally men would attend in this country after returning.

It is noteworthy that the two men who had the biggest influence in CACTM during World War Two both had untimely deaths. Temple was Archbishop of Canterbury for only two and a half years, but in that time he completed the membership of the Services Ordinands Committee, oversaw a major change to CACTM's constitution, arranged almost single-handedly the raising of the

---

40 George Clay Hubback 1882–1955. Hubback was at University College, Liverpool, but went to work in Calcutta in 1906 and joined the Oxford Mission in 1908. He was a member of the community until 1924, being ordained in 1910 and coming back to England from 1910 to 1912 to work in a parish in Lambeth. He returned to India in 1912, and in 1924 was made Bishop of Assam, moving in 1945 to be Bishop of Calcutta and Metropolitan of India. He retired in 1950.

money to pay for a full-time chairman of CACTM, made the inspired selection of Leslie Owen for that, and created the position of Bishop to the Forces, which role continues today. It was a remarkable achievement.

Leslie Owen had the experience of his membership of the Archbishops' Commission on Training to prepare him for what turned out to be a critical role. He also had the vision, imagination and flexibility to recognize in the revised War Office selection boards a model of selection that could be used creatively by the Church. Sadly his contribution was cut short. In 1946 he was appointed Bishop of Lincoln, but earlier, in June 1944, he had been attending a service in the Guards Chapel in London when it was hit by a doodlebug. He was one of the survivors but according to Kenneth Carey 'he was never the same man again'.[41] In fact he had contracted cancer, and while it went into remission for a period it returned. Carey wrote: 'He knew he was dying and said characteristically, "I thought I was being sent to Lincoln to show the diocese how to live; now I realise I was sent to show it how to die".'[42] He died on 2 March 1947 aged 61. Central selection conferences were among his abiding legacy to the Church of England.

41 *Leslie Owen*, p. 40f.
42 *Leslie Owen*, p. 41.

8

The Fisher Years

Geoffrey Fisher's reputation as archbishop is that he was an excellent if at times headmasterly administrator, but he was weaker as a prophet about society or as an original theological thinker. From the perspective of CACTM in the post-war years arguably what was most needed was an effective administrator, who would ensure that the Council and its developing work in selection and training was well supported by the bishops and the Church Assembly as a whole. That Fisher certainly provided. He was also quite prepared to provide leadership over far broader matters concerning the institutional reform of the Church's administration and wished to see the Church modernized in its structures to enable it 'to inhabit the post-war world with credibility'.[1] Over his 15 years as archbishop it was often with his active support and sometimes direct intervention that CACTM's role in selection, in managing an effective grants system, and eventually vastly broadening its areas of responsibility was established. Of course he did not do that alone, often it was a corporate decision-making process that developed during the process of discussion, as shall be demonstrated. Also possibly towards the end of his time as archbishop there was something of a reaction to his managerial style, but CACTM could not have grown as it did, sometimes even against the wishes of its own leadership at the time, without the direction that Fisher provided. By the end of his period in office CACTM was a strong, effective and confident body.

Establishing the selection system

Fisher strongly supported the selection method, even when, as was inevitable with a system that resulted in some men being not recommended, criticism emerged. The *Church Times* carried a number of letters from disappointed

---

1 Andrew Chandler, 2006, *The Church of England in The Twentieth Century: The Church Commissioners and the Politics of Reform*, Woodbridge: The Boydell Press, pp. 148, 480.

candidates and clergy who questioned a central system of selection, although others wrote in its favour. The correspondence came to a head in the *Church Times* of 3 December 1948. The editor had requested an article from John Phillips, who from 1947 was General Secretary of CACTM having earlier been the director of service candidates, explaining the process.

Phillips defended the principle of selection being by representatives of the whole Church giving their advice to a bishop and said that it was simply that, advice to a bishop, who did not need to take it, and that it was given by selectors who were from a panel appointed by the bishops. To those who doubted whether it was possible to know a man at all well as a result of living with him for three days, he said it was a far more searching process than the short interview with a bishop or a theological college principal which men used to have. He also stressed that no decision was made until the references sent by the candidate's parish priest and by others who knew him well had been carefully read; full weight was given to the opinion of those who had known the candidate over a long period. Only then was the attempt made to see where the candidate's best contribution to the Church should be made. It might be in the ordained ministry, it might be in some full-time branch of Church lay work, it might be in the lay ministry doing his ordinary job as a Christian and to the glory of God. He said that in considering a man for training for ordination, the selectors had to bear in mind the responsibilities of incumbency. There were men whom all would agree would make efficient and hard-working curates, but whom none could visualize being equal to the demands of sole responsibility.

He also stressed that it was for training for the ministry in the Church of God that selectors had to recommend a man; it was not:

for this diocese, or for that province, or for this or that point of view. Therefore questions of a candidate's Churchmanship do not enter into their discussions at all. A candidate's devotion to our Lord, his sense of call, his love of souls, his ability to learn and think and his own character are the matters of real importance. The selectors' task is to ask: 'To what is God calling this man and with what gifts, actual and potential, has he endowed him?'

In an editorial of the same day the paper questioned whether bishops still retained any choice.

Several bishops have openly stated that there is an agreed Episcopal policy to respect CACTM's decisions. We only know of one English bishop since the war who has ordained an applicant rejected by CACTM ... We believe that, although post-war conditions may have justified the establishment of a centralised organisation for the selection and care of candidates, its permanent retention is definitely harmful.

It went on to note the figures. By May 1948 selection boards had recommended just over 2,000 candidates for training; 500 cases had been deferred to a subsequent board, while 1,200 had been rejected outright. The editorial asked 'Are there really so many cases of men who are fundamentally unsuitable for the priesthood, presenting themselves for ordination? It is hard to see what their motives can be; they cannot be worldly ones today.' The editorial also said that they were perturbed by the statement which implied that men who would 'make efficient and hardworking curates', but who would not appear to be 'equal to the demands of sole responsibility' should be rejected. They considered that selectors should be concerned with whether or not God had called a man to be a priest and should not be concerned with the details of his career after ordination. 'The point which CACTM seems to have forgotten is that ordination is a sacrament which confers not only character but grace.' Finally, they commented on the statement that 'questions of a candidate's Churchmanship do not enter into the selectors' discussions. If this is true it is deplorable.' The editorial said an investigation of what someone believed was essential, but the fear was that the selection boards only wanted central candidates and pushed candidates into that type of training; this appeared to be a particular concern of some on the definitely Catholic wing. The article believed responsibility should be given back to the bishops and the selection centre system abandoned.

The comment over the issue of churchmanship was journalistic distortion, reflecting no doubt the objections of some Catholic-minded correspondents to the paper who were upset that young men from their parishes had not been recommended. The Bishop of Gloucester (Woodward), who had succeeded Owen as chairman of CACTM, expressed his irritation about the whole editorial in a letter to Fisher. He had consulted Fisher on whether the article required an official reply and the archbishop had advised him to leave it to other correspondents. Woodward replied on 23 December 1948:

I am glad you feel it would be better not to attempt an official reply to the 'Church Times' attacks upon CACTM. As you really point out, the letters which appeared in the last number really do what is needed and are far more effective than any letter from the Chairman could be.

The really monstrous thing is that the Editor asked John Phillips to write an article explaining the policy of CACTM and describing the work of Selection Boards, and then made that article the text for a violent and quite unfair attack upon CACTM in the same issue.

I am constantly reminded of Gore's dictum that 'It is my profound belief that two-thirds of that paper are written by the devil in person'.[2]

In practice Fisher had certainly advised the bishops not to overrule CACTM's advice, so when Phillips said that it was advice a bishop could ignore he was being somewhat disingenuous. When the Bishop of Bath and Wells succeeded Woodward as chairman in 1950 he consulted Lambeth on what discretion a bishop had. Canon Waddams, acting as chaplain to the archbishop, replied in June 1950:

I can find no express agreement that a Bishop may accept a candidate in spite of his rejection by a selection board. The relevant agreement [June 1945] seems to be this:

The ultimate authority for deciding whether any man shall be ordained rests with the Bishop, but the Bishops of the Provinces of Canterbury and York have agreed, for an interim period, to observe the following Regulations for the selection, testing and training of all candidates, subject to any necessary qualifications in particular cases which might be agreed between the Bishop and CACTM.

The Regulations themselves do not state that no candidate who has not been recommended may be ordained. All they say is that they shall attend a selection board which is to 'decide whether they shall be recommended as candidates for testing and training'.[3]

Correspondence on the matter was not simply with bishops. The Principal of Ripon Hall, H. D. A. Major, objected to the suggested limitation on a Principal

---

2 Fisher papers, Vol. 40, p. 244.
3 Fisher papers, Vol. 68, p. 318.

implied by saying that a college should not take for ordination training someone who had not been recommended by a selection centre. He did this partly because he was not convinced that the system was perfect, but also because he believed the history of Ripon Hall encouraged freedom by the principal.

Fisher enquired of the Chairman of the Principals' Conference, and J. P. Thornton-Duesbury, Principal of Wycliffe Hall, responded on 16 January 1948. He told Fisher that at the Principals' Conference in Cuddesdon in 1946 there was a unanimous vote of approval of the method of selection centres. As the Archbishops of Canterbury, York and Wales had agreed not to accept any candidates under the age of 40 not recommended by a selection board it would prejudice the scheme and embarrass the episcopate if principals were to accept for training men whom bishops were not prepared to ordain. He advised that if a principal were to insist on accepting for training men who had not been recommended at a selection centre, the only course open to CACTM would be to advise the bishop to withdraw recognition of his college.

Fisher replied to Major on 2 April 1948:

You very naturally desire to retain for Ripon Hall liberty of action but I would remind you that the old system, by which both Principals and Bishops had complete liberty of action, gave rise to very great difficulties. I can state quite frankly that there were some Bishops who accepted for Ordination men who ought never to have been accepted. Equally, there were Principals who, out of goodness of heart and a desire to keep their college full, also admitted unsuitable men.

He went on to note that while it was easy to say that admission to a theological college should in no way guarantee ordination, in fact, when a man had paid his way through a theological college for four years, pressure to get him accepted for ordination was extreme and hard to resist. He concluded:

No system is perfect. I have no hesitation in saying that the system now adopted by the Bishops is a very great improvement on what went before. In a general view, it would be better that a few people should be wrongly rejected than that a much larger number of unsuitable men should be accepted. In fact, I believe the system has worked very satisfactorily. Under it, the right is reserved for a Bishop in a very exceptional case to back his own judgement against a Selection Board. It would obviously be possible only in the rarest cases since otherwise the whole system would break down. The confidence felt in the Selection Boards is shown by the fact that, so far as I know, no Bishop has desired to override them.[4]

Major still complained in two more letters, but to no effect. Finally the archbishop's chaplain simply wrote to say that the archbishop thanked him for his letter. Despite continued grumblings from disaffected candidates and clergy the majority of bishops and principals accepted the new system as a great improvement on what had gone before.

Recruitment

In 1938, 590 men had been ordained, in 1939, 589, and even in 1940, 562. Thereafter, the war had its effect and numbers dropped dramatically so that by 1945 it was 159 and in 1946 only 158. The service candidates then started emerging from training and by 1950, 419 were ordained, but through most of the 1950s numbers were only in the 400s each year when the Church thought they needed at least 600 a year to replace those who were leaving through death or retirement. A recruitment policy was clearly needed.

F. R. Barry, the former Principal of Knutsford, had become Bishop of Southwell and was Chairman of CACTM's Recruitment Committee. He had thought carefully about recruitment since his experience in World War One and was not afraid of using the word as he believed the Church should present the demands of the ministry frankly to people and asking for the best candidates. He wrote later:

> I never ceased from insisting to my colleagues that the prime considera-
> tion was quality. If any profession seems to be in low water, put up the
> requirements – the Army learnt that long ago. When recruitment was flag-
> ging in the first war, the War Office raised the chest measurement. The
> more you ask for, the more you will get.

He feared that if the Church gave the impression that it was prepared to accept men who could not make a living elsewhere, the more gifted would certainly

---

4 Fisher papers, Vol. 40, pp. 179–82.

look in another direction. He believed that to lower the standard in order to fill up the ranks was, for the Church, a policy of suicide.

> But for this I have found it hard to win more than lip service. I fear the Church has, on the whole, been too ready to think more of quantity than quality. I still believe that if we had been brave enough to require higher standards of qualification, we should have got more men as well as better men. And in the situation we are now in, a sub-standard Ministry may do positive harm.[5]

CACTM presented to the Church Assembly in February 1954 a report on recruitment for the ministry: *Supply of Fit Persons*. It stressed the need for the Church to attract able men; 'There can be no greater or more responsible task than the Christian leadership of a community, no richer opportunity of service than that of a parish priest in the Church of England. For this the Church needs not the second-best but the ablest and strongest of her sons.'[6] A detailed examination of the background of those who had enquired about training for the ministry showed that, of the 768 men who had attended selection centres in 1953, 226 were public schoolboys, 192 state schoolboys, 117 undergraduates and 191 national servicemen. Of the 768, 519 were recommended or conditionally recommended. There followed a series of practical suggestions for encouraging men to consider the ministry, building on an earlier policy of the Recruitment Committee of having with each public school a capable priest from the diocese in which they were situated with a brief 'to keep ordination on the map as boys considered their work in life',[7] but also making proposals for state schools, universities, dioceses and parishes. It seems by 'men of ability' Barry, who of course would have had the experience of Knutsford to call upon, was not talking about intellectual ability alone, but character more broadly and an ability to be an effective leader of others.

The report was received by the Church Assembly in the spring session of 1954 and it commended the facts set forth 'for prayer and earnest thought by the whole church and referred it to the dioceses for consideration and action as a matter of urgency', but the debate also provided an opportunity for some to

---

5 Frank Barry, 1970, *Period of my Life*, London: Hodder and Stoughton, p. 187.

6 *Supply of Fit Persons*, p. 5.

7 Fisher papers, Vol. 40, p. 197. The letter is undated but appears in the context of other letters sent around June 1947.

air other issues. A member from Ripon Diocese wanted the phrase 'fostering vocations' rather than recruitment, and the Dean of Chichester used the opportunity to attack heresy. The debate was ended by an emotionally appealing speech by the Bishop of Durham, Michael Ramsey, rather contrary to the report. He spoke of the call being from Christ as he called his disciples:

> Little as they knew about these matters, the call of men by Jesus Christ to His ministry today could not be so very different from His original call of His apostles. He did not show them a preview of the work that they were going to do, a picture in advance of its character, nature and conditions. A great deal of that work was in the dark for them. He did not give them what the Bishop of Southwell called 'more information about the scope of the task before them'. He did, on the other hand, call them and secure their allegiance to His ministry, by the overwhelming impression which He made upon their minds and consciences as being Himself the truth and the Life ... He felt a doubt about the dissemination of detailed pictures of the parish priest's work, partly for the reasons which he had mentioned and partly because the character of that work changed enormously and indeed somewhat rapidly, and was likely to be changing in the coming decades.

To the Dean of Chichester's comment about heresy he responded:

> What was needed, in order that the voice of the call might go home was that it should be more clear that the Church of England really did care for the things of the mind and not only in so far as those things assisted administrative or pastoral work.[8]

Barry had a good answer to that, as his books show, but he did not have the opportunity to reply in the debate as it was introduced and therefore responded to by the Chairman of CACTM. A member of the Assembly, clearly moved by the speech of the Bishop of Durham, suggested that no one else needed to speak further and that the question should be put. His motion was passed and the report simply accepted.

However, the report must have had some effect in the dioceses. Four years after its publication and the debate the number ordained passed the 500 mark

---

8 CA report of proceedings, Spring 1954, p. 71f.

for the first time since 1940 (508 in 1958). By 1960 it went up to 598 and for the following four years was over 600 a year, the figure the bishops had said was needed.

Training the non-matriculated candidate

For most of those years after the war about half of those ordained were graduates, and among the non-graduates the position and training of those who had not obtained the qualifications to enter university (matriculation) was a concern to CACTM. Immediately after the war it was possible to reopen the old Knutsford scheme for servicemen in the Old Rectory at Hawarden in North Wales, where they studied for the forces preliminary examination, which was accepted as the equivalent of matriculation. One hundred and seven candidates passed through the school, but delays in obtaining the results of the forces preliminary examination meant that CACTM declared it no longer a useful examination and the school was closed after a year, to become the home of the William Temple College for five years.[9] Other institutions, notably King's College, London and St Augustine's College, Canterbury had prepared men for matriculation, but by 1948 CACTM had changed its policy, describing the change in its annual report to the Church Assembly.

> The Council has carefully examined the question of pre-training as a normal part of the Church's work. Bearing in mind the recommendation of the Archbishops' Commission on Training for the Ministry it has been decided that in future all candidates, except for a few special cases, must have completed their preliminary examinations on their own responsibility and that it should not be part of CACTM's work to prepare men for matriculation or its equivalent.[10]

By 1950 that change of policy was being challenged, not least of all by a CACTM committee asked to examine the position of non-matriculated candidates and which reported in 1951. Underlying the report the conviction, strongly expressed by the secretaries, and reinforced by the evidence of selection boards, was that the Church was missing a certain number of valuable recruits for the ministry

---

9 T. W. Pritchard, 2002, *A History of the Old Parish of Hawarden*, Wrexham: Bridge Books, p. 133.
10 Annual report for 1948.

who, through no fault of their own, stood incapable of making effective use of the existing courses of training which the Church offered. These were men who had left school at 14 or 15, and had little opportunity of education subsequently. But along with a genuine sense of vocation they possessed what the report described as 'gifts of character, an alertness of mind, an interest in what is going on around them in the world', which suggested that they were educable, if the right method of testing, and then cultivating, that capacity could be found. They were probably not very numerous; the secretaries estimated that perhaps 30 or 40 would be available every year. In addition it was believed that more would be forthcoming, if it were known that an appropriate method of training was provided.[11]

An offer was considered by the Council from Revd D. Stewart-Smith, through whose generosity it had been possible to make the experiment envisaged in the report, at Brasted Place in Kent. The training was 'for the benefit of non-graduate candidates of special promise, who had not had sufficient educational opportunities to enable them to take a degree'. The courses would start from January 1953 for an experimental period of three years and this development was welcomed by the Council.

Brasted was in fact to last for some years and in the early 1960s there was a new venture for something similar in Durham through the agency of the Bernard Gilpin Society, in Farnham, Surrey through Moor Park, and in Cumbria through Greystoke. These developments were not in opposition to Barry's insistence on high standards, for they were all to produce some effective priests whose strength lay in their character rather than in their intellectual qualifications.

Pressure on staff and some devolution to dioceses

By 1950 concern was being expressed by some on the Council on pressures on the small staff of three clergymen with secretarial help to manage the work being placed upon them. Each of the clerical staff had to manage about 13 conferences a year, with all the paperwork that entailed. A group chaired by Canon J. McLeod Campbell, a Council member, examined the issue and reported to the Council in January 1952.[12] After looking at the workload they said,

---

11 CACTM minutes, 10–13 September 1951.

12 *The Administrative Policy of CACTM: A Report to the Council*, January 1952 (in archives file CACTM/COU/DD/1).

'The Committee was unanimous in concluding that this total load, however distributed, was heavier than any three men could carry without sacrifice of freshness and efficiency.' They then looked at various areas of the work, starting with the pre-conference stage. (At some stage between the late 1940s and 1950 the terminology in CACTM appears to have changed from reference to selection centres to first selection boards and then to selection conferences, but the process remained essentially the same.) The custom had survived from war days of centralizing the whole of this preliminary stage, with candidates applying directly to CACTM. Few dioceses had developed any local machinery for covering the work that needed to be done before men were registered by CACTM, preferring to leave it to the central office. The committee recommended that CACTM should no longer accept these responsibilities, and that the dioceses should be responsible for men up to the point where they could be recommended for selection conferences. This included the checking of references and medical certificates. They believed that if it were made clear that the Council could no longer relieve the dioceses of these responsibilities they would and could make provision. Men would then be told that they must secure the approval of the diocese in which they were brought up and confirmed before they could go any further. It was believed that establishing such a process as the normal one, always recognizing that there would be exceptions, would relieve pressure on the staff. It would also relieve what was then the practice of any candidate who wished to appeal doing so to CACTM's Selection Committee direct. The appeal procedure in the future would be through the diocese concerned, who could ask for a man to come to a further conference. The fear that different dioceses would have different standards could be counteracted partly by regular conferences with diocesan directors of training, but also by the results of selection conferences themselves. In practice the policy of using diocesan selection first was only partially successful, and the ending of some applicants applying direct to CACTM only happened finally with a decision of the House of Bishops in 1966.[13]

It was also noted that 40 to 50 per cent of those coming to selection conferences were not recommended, which indicated that some were coming who ought not to have been regarded as eligible. The staff view was that that applied to about 10 per cent of those who attended conferences. If that number could be sifted at the diocesan level it would also relieve the number of selection

---

13 Reported in the 1967 annual report of what by then had become ACCM (CA 1625).

conferences needed, it was estimated by three or four a year, which would also relieve the burden on staff.

Finance 1946–57

The fact that such matters were being discussed within CACTM explains the stance taken about managing financial questions, as inevitably one of the major issues to concern CACTM was the funding of training. There were three inter-related questions. How much money was needed? How would it be raised? Who would manage the funds? Prior to the war it was left to the individual, possibly in consultation with someone from his diocese, to work out what he could get from diocesan grants (which provided 66 per cent of the grants awarded in 1937), what he could find in the way of bursaries and awards from various societies, and what he could get from CACTM (which in 1937 only provided a total of 16 per cent of the grants awarded). While that might have appeared an unsatisfactory arrangement it had worked well enough for a reasonably large number of candidates to get through the training then required. Could or should that continue in the post-war period?

On the first question of how much money was needed there was a complication in that the government had declared that it wished to pay for the training of returning servicemen, but it was not clear how extensive those grants would be. Would it only cover the cost of completing training that had been started prior to the war or would it cover training for a new profession?

In presenting the Church Assembly budget for 1946 Sir Philip Williams of Salisbury Diocese, who had been the chairman of what he described as the 'hard-headed and hard hearted' committee which had to deal with the demands made on the Central Board of Finance, said 'the figure of £12,000 for training ex-Service ordinands had been inserted to let the diocese know that CACTM expected in 1946 to have a real rush of ordinands'.[14] The report of the Financial Commission, whose work had so irritated Woodward by delaying the possibility of an appeal, reported in 1945 and it defined three central needs, with the cost of training future ordinands for the ministry at the top of the list (the others were pensions and the training of teachers). The Financial Commission recommended the setting up of a central fund to pay for the returning candidates

---

14 CA report of proceedings, Summer 1945, p. 217f.

and after correspondence with Fisher it was agreed that the archbishops should launch an appeal in 1945 for the huge sum of £650,000 (£21 million in 2010 terms), which they estimated was the total cost the Church would have to raise for training all the returning servicemen over the next five years. The appeal was largely directed to the dioceses and was independent of the requests from the Church Assembly's budget. While it sounded a large figure if, as turned out to be the case, over 2,000 ordinands emerged from war service, it amounted to only about £300 an ordinand for their full training. Grants would be administered by a grants' committee representing CACTM, the CBF and the dioceses.

Nonetheless it was not long before there was criticism of the figure. In 1946 Fisher spoke in the Church Assembly of 'a whispering campaign ... that too much money was being asked for Service candidates, that the Government grants would go a very long way towards meeting the total cost'. That criticism was combined with comments about the cost of CACTM itself as an institution, which no longer had the army providing the accommodation in chaplaincy centres and whose selection policy was already drawing adverse criticism from some. Fisher defended the policy: 'in estimating the figure at £650,000 very careful consideration was given to all the relevant facts, including what might be expected from the Government scheme and what might be expected from the resources of the candidates themselves'.[15] He also pointed out that the cost of CACTM itself was included in a different budget and was very reasonable for what was being provided.

By 1947 the Ministry of Education had decided that grants for servicemen should cover all servicemen who had enlisted up to the end of September 1947, which provided a reason for the appeal target to be left at £650,000 to enable the Church to follow a similar policy. However, by 1948 it was acknowledged that the 'whispering campaign' had some truth in it as government grants turned out to be more generous than the Church was expecting, and the appeal target was revised down to £300,000, of which by then already £145,000 had been contributed. Nothing beyond the continuing appeal was requested in the 1948 Church Assembly budget for training but the Assembly was warned that there would be a considerable demand in the future.

By 1949 the situation had become critical again as only £10,000 was available in central funds for training civilian candidates, although it was recognized that other money was available in diocesan funds and for service candidates. It was

---

15 CA Report of Proceedings 1946, p. 214.

agreed by the Church Assembly to deal with that year with a special one-off request to the dioceses, recommending that it be partly met by a central fund raised by the Church as a whole and administered by CACTM, and partly by funds raised in individual dioceses and administered by diocesan training committees. It instructed the Central Board of Finance to open a central fund to receive contributions from dioceses and others in the hope of providing not less than £40,000 to be administered by CACTM in grants for the training of candidates to be adopted in 1949, and asked the budget committee to report as to how best the sums required could be provided in 1950 and onwards.

The matter came to a head in a debate in November 1949 initiated by a Central Board of Finance report, when the question of how much was needed was caught up with the other two questions of how it should be raised and by whom it should be administered. The Chairman of the CBF, Sir Richard Hopkins, introduced the report.[16] Explaining that government grants for servicemen were coming to an end he said that CACTM had advised that the financial arrangements for each candidate should be undertaken by the diocesan authorities, that this should partly be done by the collection in every church on Trinity Sunday (the normal day for ordinations) being taken for this purpose, that the sum provided in each diocese might be divided equally between a diocesan training fund and a central equalizing fund in dioceses in proportion to the declared needs of those dioceses. The Bishop of Bath and Wells (H. W. Bradfield), by then Chairman of CACTM, explained that at that stage 80 per cent of those in training were in receipt of government grants, which was a larger proportion than CACTM was expecting, but that the proportion was likely to diminish quickly. In 1947 CACTM grants totalled £2,611; by 1948 that was £5,300; and for the first ten months of 1949 it was £8,100. That figure would increase as government grants diminished. For the future he strongly supported a measure of delegation to the dioceses.

One weakness about the whole CACTM situation was that during this period of substantial Government grants it had worked in isolation from the diocesan training committees, with the lamentable result that in many cases the diocesan training committees had become little more than rubber stamps in relation to decisions taken elsewhere and by other people. At a recent conference of secretaries of diocesan training

---

16 CBF 223, *The Cost of Training for the Ministry.*

committees, the view was strongly and, he thought, unanimously expressed that there should be a close relationship between CACTM and the dioceses in the matter of responsibility for training men for the Ministry. It was recommended that a greater share of responsibility should devolve upon the dioceses and that responsibility should include arranging the finances of candidates.[17]

He supported the principle of the Trinity Sunday appeal as that was when many ordinations happened. However, the Bishop of Rochester (Chavasse) challenged delegation to the dioceses, describing the situation as he saw it after the war. 'It was then uncertain how many candidates were coming forward, how far Government grants would help, and there was no money in the till.' But he believed they surmounted that difficultly, because CACTM had made itself responsible for arranging the finance of these servicemen. It had told them how to get government grants, arranged for them to go to universities and colleges at a time of great difficulty, and administered grants that the Church provided to the tune of £300,000, and when the archbishops divided the burden over the dioceses in proportion to their quota, Chavasse did not suppose a single diocese defaulted and they had come through.

In 1949 he thought much the same position faced them. They were uncertain how many candidates would be coming forward and supposed it would be about 500 a year. They did not know how many would need grants and how far government grants would meet the needs of these candidates at universities and theological colleges. Again, there was the need for assessing the general burden and sharing it out among the dioceses. So he asked, 'Why, at this juncture, pass from a great agency of the Church which had seen them so successfully through a similar problem? Why not ask them to continue, with all their experience, instead of placing the whole responsibility of arranging finances upon the diocesan committees?'[18]

In his earlier speech the Bishop of Bath and Wells had noted that putting the burden on the dioceses where candidates lived, such as London with 313 candidates on CACTM's register, and Southwark with 203, was a major challenge for those dioceses and said, 'A possible modification would be that a diocese from which a candidate originated should be responsible unless a candidate

17 CA Proceedings, November 1949.
18 CA Proceedings, November 1949.

was in touch with another Bishop and another diocese.'[19] Chavasse thought that solution lacked appreciation of the situation. He asked how many boys of 18 at the beginning of their training for Holy Orders had decided or ought to decide to which diocese God had called them at the end of their training? Such an arrangement, he believed, would drive them back to the old wrong position where bishops, as it were, 'bribed ordination candidates with grants, with promises of work in their dioceses'. That had been ended during the war, with CACTM making financial arrangements and the Church sending up its money to CACTM to distribute: 'they were getting a body of men who were not pledged to any one diocese and were ready to go where they were most needed.'[20]

He therefore proposed that CACTM should continue to arrange the finances of candidates accepted for training for the time being. His amendment was put and carried, the chairman (Fisher) saying by a considerable majority.

This was a very significant change from the situation before the war, and it was the Church Assembly, encouraged by the Bishop of Rochester, which decided to continue the centralizing measure rather than CACTM or the CBF, which had encouraged greater delegation. It was agreed that 'before the end of 1952 a further report be submitted to the Assembly'. Meanwhile the results of the Trinity Sunday appeal enabled the grants situation to continue. The further report came to the Assembly in November 1951 when Preb. Eley, Chairman of the Grants' Committee, reported that the appeal 1951 had raised less than the previous year and it was essential that the 1952 appeal was successful. He said that some had asked, 'Supposing the result of the Trinity Sunday appeal next year is no more encouraging than the result so far this year, what will be the position when we meet next November? The answer was simple, the fund they administered on the Grants Committee would be bankrupt.' Not surprisingly the Assembly agreed to his resolution that a committee be appointed.

Fisher wrote to Sir Hugh Dow, a former Indian civil servant who had been Consul General in Jerusalem and was now living in England, inviting him to be chairman, which he accepted. The others included the Bishop of Bath and Wells, the Bishop of Carlisle, Preb. Eley and Sir Richard Hopkins (chairman of the CBF) with three other laymen. It reported at the 1952 summer session of the Church Assembly, by which time it was known that the Trinity Sunday appeal for 1951

---

19 CA proceedings, 1949, p. 414.
20 CA proceedings, 1949, pp. 418–20.

had raised only £42,124 compared to £48,785 the previous year. Clearly there was a problem.

The Dow Commission's report[21] started by an examination of the figures. The desire was for 600 candidates a year. The actual number of ordinations in 1949 was 362, in 1950, 419, in 1951, 411. The committee concluded that there needed to be a flexible scheme that could be adjusted annually, and CACTM should be authorized to take up to 600 a year, but the committee thought it was unlikely to be more than 500 a year.

CACTM's estimate of £300 a year for the training costs of an ordinand was the average figure. Five hundred candidates at £300 a year meant a total cost per year of one year's intake of £150,000 or, given that on average a course lasted four years, a total in any one year of £600,000. Ministry of Education and LEA grants contributed 28 per cent in 1949–50 and 22 per cent in 1950–1. 'Generally speaking, the better the educational qualifications of candidates, the more money can be obtained from L.E.A.s and the less demand on Church funds, and this is a matter that should be borne in mind by Selection Boards.'[22] Making a realistic assessment of grants, scholarships and private resources of candidates the committee estimated that 40 per cent of the costs must be found from Church funds – £240,000 a year for 500 candidates.

The Dow Commission thought it right to put the main responsibility for financing candidates squarely on the dioceses where the money was raised, and 'to make use of the central machinery only for the purpose of securing the necessary co-ordination'. It suggested an apportionment system between the dioceses, with the dioceses sending 40 per cent of the sum raised to a central fund. It suggested raising by this method £168,000 for the academic year 1952–3, and the figure to be reviewed each year in the Assembly budget reflecting the likely number of candidates in training. The apportionment scheme meant, for example, for London Diocese, £11,071; for Southwark, £7,039; for Chichester, £6,569; but for Rochester, £3,713; for Manchester, £6,658; and for Sheffield, £2,604.

Prior to the debate the Bishop of Chichester (George Bell) wrote to Fisher saying that he would be opposing the report's recommendations, and be producing an alternative amendment.[23] The stage was set for a decisive decision.

---

21 Ordination Funds Commission (CA 1038).
22 Ordination Funds Commission, p. 4.
23 Fisher papers, Vol. 106, pp. 142–51.

Finance in various areas was a major factor in the whole Church Assembly summer session of 1952, with debates on the diocesan stipends measure and a debate on the repair of churches (where it was agreed that a trust for the preservation of historic churches should make a national appeal to raise £4 million). The debate on the Ordination Funds' Commission's report had to be seen in that context and it was spread over three days. Preb. Eley presented the report to the Assembly, being aware of both the decision of the Assembly in 1949 to put the responsibility for financing on CACTM and of the amendment suggested by the Bishop of Chichester. He chose his words carefully.

> He was ... surprised in the amendment proposed by the Bishop of Chichester, (and supported by the Bishops of Norwich and Sheffield) that they regarded the Report as being 'a further advance in the concentration of control in the hands of a central authority' ... The purpose of this Report was to take away that responsibility from CACTM and, in the judgment of the Commission, restore it to where it properly belonged, upon the dioceses; and therefore they regarded this Report as being one designed to remove authority from the centre and to place it back upon the dioceses.[24]

However, the report did suggest that the raising of the funds should be by a mixture of an apportionment system and diocesan funds. The raising of the money rested on the whole Church, and thus upon dioceses, not in proportion to the number of candidates who happened to live in a diocese, but in proportion to the capacity of the diocese to contribute its share.

Speaking next, the Bishop of Chichester raised four issues.

First, when the report said it would 'make use of existing central machinery only for the purpose of securing necessary co-ordination' he asked who was to decide what was the necessary co-ordination? He accepted that there needed to be a central pool or fund which was available to supplement what the dioceses could produce, but 'the issue was whether the dioceses or CACTM were to be the really responsible authority. Was CACTM to be the tool or the controller?'

Second, he doubted the figure of £240,000. 'In the past there had been over-estimates of what was required, was it not possible that a similar over-estimate was now before them?'

---

24 CA proceedings, Summer 1952, p. 50f.

Third, there was a more fundamental concern. The argument in favour of the high figure was based on the assumption that, because the State had made large grants to service candidates at the cost of the taxpayer, when the State ceased to pay those grants the Church must pay them in exactly the same way. He feared that discouraged the principle of self-help. 'In the First World War, the Archbishops of Canterbury and York then gave a pledge that not a single Service candidate should be prevented from ordination by financial considerations. That pledge was met, but when the pledge had been made the matter went back to the dioceses and societies.' Bell was not asking that no aid should be given towards ordination candidates in need of help, but that it should take the form of scholarships, bursaries and grants in aid, instead of being governed by the general idea that everything must be found – and found at the cost of self-help. 'If they did not ask for sacrifice before a man was ordained, they would be creating a new class of clergy who would continually ask after ordination.' Bell believed the Church could not afford this large sum, and ought not to afford a sum based on what he thought was a false assumption.

Fourth, he was also concerned about academic standards. The report had suggested that the better the educational qualifications of candidates, the more money could be obtained from local educational authorities, and the less demand there was on Church funds. He noted that Preb. Eley had said that he thought most of them realized that they did not need only the highly intellectually trained candidates, but a number of men who might not be able to go through a university course. But, Bell commented:

The ordination statistics showed that the proportion of graduates to non-graduates was decreasing. When CACTM began, some thirty years ago, resolutions were passed to the effect that after an interval of, say, five years, every man ordained into the Ministry of the Church of England must be a graduate. That had now gone further and further away. He did not say that there were not excellent men who could not take a degree, but he did say that unless they kept the intellectual quality of ordination candidates well to the fore and saw that graduates were in the majority among the clergy, it would fare ill for the Church of England.[25]

---

25 CA proceedings, Summer 1952, pp. 56–9.

The Dean of Chichester supported his bishop and noted the problem of CACTM controlling the grants. What would happen if a bishop disagreed with a CACTM recommendation about a man's suitability for ordination, and nonetheless wanted him to go into training, would CACTM give him a grant? It seemed to him unfortunate that those who chose the candidate also paid for him. The dean believed the bishop ought to have the last say in the matter.[26]

The Bishop of Bath and Wells, speaking in a personal capacity and not as Chairman of CACTM, pointed out that the total amount asked for from the Church was only about 40 per cent of the total cost and so the policy was not at the expense of self-help.[27] But the Bishop of Norwich, supporting the Bishop of Chichester, thought the sums involved were quite impossible to raise so they had to think again. He believed the right line was to let candidates know that, beyond outside grants and comparatively small grants through or from dioceses, they were expected to finance their own training, probably by accepting for a few years other and secular employment.[28]

The following day (19 June 1952) the Assembly considered first the Bishop of Chichester's amendment.

The Bishop of Bradford, in supporting the amendment, said that he was suspicious of an attempt to magnify CACTM out of all recognition. He thought the combination of choosing men and giving them grants gave CACTM too much power.

> They were now coming to the stage when CACTM would be in charge of or largely in control of the finances required for the training of ordination candidates, and the theological colleges having been turned into tributaries. If the responsibility and power of the bishops in regard to these matters was to be put into the hands of a central London committee, which called itself advisory when it was really autocratic, they would be to a large extent jeopardizing their Episcopal character. Would the dioceses accept these inflated quotas, apparently under the obligation of loyalty to CACTM? He did not believe his diocese would raise it and that other ones would not either.[29]

---

26 CA proceedings, Summer 1952, p. 62.
27 CA proceedings, Summer 1952, p. 68.
28 CA proceedings, Summer 1952, p. 67.
29 CA proceedings, Summer 1952, p. 151.

The Bishop of London (Wand) was disturbed by some of the speeches, and 'although some were made by his own personal friends as well as colleagues, he thought they were lamentable'. The whole debate had been turned into an attack on CACTM but he believed wholeheartedly in CACTM. When he:

> came back from abroad after nine years and found the selection boards in full swing, he thought this was the greatest advance that the church had made in its administration and methods. Whilst he had been a diocesan bishop in this country and had had to rely upon CACTM, he had rejoiced because of the expert advice he had obtained from it ... Speaking personally he would have far more confidence in CACTM dealing with the whole question than he could have in it being dealt with by the individual dioceses.[30]

The Bishop of Chichester's amendment, which represented the last attempt to go back to the system that operated before the war, was lost. An amendment by the Bishop of Rochester, which put the responsibility for arranging the finances of all candidates for training on or after 1 October 1952 'with CACTM in collaboration with the diocese in which the candidate lived', was passed, as was the main motion and the request that the sum of £168,000 should be apportioned between the dioceses. The new structure was now firmly in place.

A letter from the Chairman of the Grants Committee (Eley) and the Secretary of the Central Board of Finance (Sawden) to all bishops explained how the scheme would work. Each diocese was given a figure for the apportionment from their diocese for the new central fund (£168,000 for 1952–3). If a diocese was going to seek to meet the costs of all its candidates it could retain 60 per cent of that sum, if it were in the habit of paying 50 per cent of the costs and looking to the centre for the other 50 per cent it should retain 30 per cent of the sum and send 70 per cent to the centre, and if a diocese wished the centre to pay all the costs it should send the full amount.[31]

The Dow Commission's solution also worked. By June 1954 in the annual report of the CBF for the previous year Sir Richard Hopkins said:

> 1953 was the first year in their history in which every diocese had succeeded in paying the whole of its apportioned quota ... This achievement was specially creditable to the dioceses that had the most difficulty in this

---

30 CA proceedings, Summer 1952, p. 154f.
31 Fisher papers, Vol. 106, p. 150.

matter, in view of the fact that 1953 was also the first year in which the dioceses were asked for a very large sum for the training of ordinands. The sum asked for was £168,000 and over £164,000 was received.

By 1957 the increase in the number of candidates in training and inflation meant that £250,000 was requested, and by 1958 £300,000. The recruitment policy advocated by the Bishop of Southwell had its financial implications, but Preb. Eley explained that in the year ending 30 September 1957, 36.1 per cent were either entirely dependent on local education authority grants or State grants or were self-supporting, and 37 per cent received some help from the Church, the remainder being found from those other sources. In 1956, 26 per cent received grants from Church sources, and in 1957, only 16 per cent. The combined effect of generous LEA and State grants and the 'co-ordinating role of CACTM' enabled the Church to ensure that its candidates for ordination were adequately supported for their ordination training.

Engagement and marriage 1946–85

One issue that was considered a number of times over the whole of this period was candidates in training wishing to get engaged and married. It was a complex matter, mixing financial, pastoral and theological questions. For training the most immediate issue was the financial one as there was no central church money to support a married candidate, while the pastoral problems included the provision of housing which extended into a man's curacy, with many parishes being only able to offer assistant clergy rooms in someone else's house. However, the matter also raised broader pastoral and theological questions about the appropriateness of the Church interfering in what was a highly personal matter for the ordinand and his future wife, the suitability of the woman the ordinand wished to marry, what her possible role as the wife of a parish priest might be and when might be the right time to have children.

It was that last matter that was mentioned in a confidential note to the archbishop from CACTM dated November 1946, where it was noted that most curacy housing would make having children difficult.

Most of the candidates will say openly that they will take steps to avoid a family during the time of training. This would not appear to be a circumstance allowed for by the Lambeth Conference statement on the use of contraceptives.[32] Apart from any doctrinal significance, medical opinion which has been taken is unanimous that physiologically and psychologically this may be injurious to the health of both the man and woman. To marry and then to seek to escape parenthood for what may be a period of 5–7 years would seem to cut across the purpose of Christian marriage. It therefore recommended that candidates under 25 should know that marriage before two years after ordination would be impossible and that an early engagement would not be encouraged.[33]

CACTM was told in January 1947 that the bishops had supported the CACTM approach and a resolution of the Council was:

With the approval of the Archbishops and Bishops CACTM wishes to make it known that all candidates under the age of 25 should accept the discipline of knowing (a) marriage will be strongly discouraged until at least two years after ordination, and (b) that the making of engagements before or during the period of training may lead to a reconsideration of the candidate's acceptance.[34]

However, at the following Council meeting in April 1947 the Principal of Wycliffe Hall, Oxford, spoke of the reaction of the students to the bishops' ruling. The rule about marriage was accepted, but the ruling about engagement had caused resentment.[35] It was agreed to report that to the bishops.

The matter continued to be debated over the next decade[36] with apparently different views on the details within CACTM between its selection committee

---

32 The Lambeth conference 1930 passed resolution 15 which stated: 'Where there is clearly felt moral obligation to limit or avoid parenthood, the method must be decided on Christian principles. The primary and obvious method is complete abstinence from intercourse (as far as may be necessary) in a life of discipline and self-control lived in the power of the Holy Spirit. Nevertheless in those cases where there is such a clearly felt moral obligation to limit or avoid parenthood, and where there is a morally sound reason for avoiding complete abstinence, the Conference agrees that other methods may be used, provided that this is done in the light of the same Christian principles. The Conference records its strong condemnation of the use of any methods of conception control from motives of selfishness, luxury, or mere convenience.'

33 Fisher papers, Vol. 12, p. 215.

34 Minutes of CACTM meeting, 16 January 1947.

35 Minutes of CACTM conference, 24 and 25 April 1947.

36 The subject is mentioned in Committee or Council minutes on November 1948, March 1951, October 1952, May and November 1953, July and September 1958, September and October 1961.

and the Council, and between CACTM and the bishops. The strictest statement came in a policy accepted by the selection committee and the Council dated January 1951, and which was put on the noticeboard of every selection centre.

1. The marriage of the clergy, though a matter for the individual conscience, cannot be disassociated from their vocation. Conscience must be instructed. Some experience of clerical life is normally desirable before a decision is made.
2. During the period of training, which includes post-ordination training, nothing should be allowed to hinder a man from giving himself wholly to his vocation.
3. A priest's wife may make or mar his ministry. His effectiveness depends largely upon her understanding, sympathy and co-operation with him in his calling. It is all the more important therefore that he should wait and discover from personal experience what the minister's life entails before deciding to share it with a helpmate. A priest's home should be one on which others can model their own.
4. Christian marriage implies a home and the possibility of a family, and this is normally impossible during the period of training and apprenticeship in the ministry. Ordination candidates cannot expect their wives to be supported by the Church during their training. Even after ordination the strained resources of the Church cannot usually provide houses and adequate stipends for married assistant curates.
5. Candidates should be warned that if they disregard the advice of those responsible for their training the whole question of their training and grants will have to be reconsidered.

The minute of this was accompanied by a note saying the Council would consider at the next meeting whether an addition should say that marriage or engagement of candidates under the age of 25 would be strongly discouraged.[37]

However by 1961, after consultation with bishops and principals of theological colleges, that had been replaced by a statement signed by both the archbishops that was only slightly less intimidating, although the threat to candidates' grants was removed and there was flexibility in the policy. The paper stated that a vocation to the ministry covered the whole of life and must,

37 In archives file CACTM/COU/DD/1.

therefore, for an ordinand be the determining influence for the ordering of his life. It recognized that the Church needed both married and unmarried clergy, but that some jobs, both at home and overseas, could probably only be done by unmarried men, so it asked every ordinand to weigh this call as one which could not be lightly dismissed. It said that provision could not be made from central Church funds for wives and families of men in training at a time when parishes were already being asked to contribute annually a large sum of money for the training of candidates themselves.

> For such reasons, we must ask ordinands to accept that the timing of engagement and marriage is not a matter for the decision of a student and his fiancée alone. He should neither marry nor become engaged to marry during his period of training without previous consultation with his Bishop and the Principal of his Theological College.[38]

That remained the policy for many years, although in practice dioceses and, from 1952, the *Church Times'* Train-a-Priest fund[39] did provide some grants to enable married candidates to support their families during training. Nonetheless the statement was interpreted differently by different bishops, sometimes to the irritation of college principals who found men in their colleges being given very different advice from different bishops.[40]

To complete the picture, by the mid-1980s the official statement was changed and a more open statement was included in a longer document sent to all candidates, which included broader advice on the whole matter of financing training. On engagement and marriage the archbishops drew the attention of single candidates for ministry to a number of matters which needed consideration when a single candidate contemplated engagement and marriage. The implications needed to be carefully thought through as they related to the way in which a future public ministry would involve each of them. There was no one

---

38 Ramsey papers, Vol. 4, p. 236.

39 Bernard Palmer, 1991, *Gadfly for God: A History of the Church Times*, London: Hodder and Stoughton. The Train-a-Priest fund was set up by Rosamund Essex (editor) in 1952, during Advent, as an appeal for Ember Pence. It was in response to a suggestion from an elderly spinster in Nelson, New Zealand, who gave £50 to start the ball rolling and appealed especially to the spinsters of England to help. The readers were asked to give 6d, and in the first year the appeal raised more than £2,000. In the second year, it was suggested that the readers should give at least 1s (p. 315). Chapter 14 describes the development of the fund. The appeal was later moved to Lent and given its present name.

40 Ordination Candidates Committee minutes, 25/26 September 1961.

pattern, and couples would be wise to talk with other married ministers, as well as discussing it with their principal and DDO or DLMA. It stressed that the bishop should be kept fully in the picture so that at an appropriate moment his consent and goodwill could be obtained. It also pointed out that while grants to the cost of training could be given, there was no central provision for families other than grants available from the *Church Times* Train-a-Priest fund and the archbishops' ordination funds. It concluded: 'This is a matter of arrangement between the candidate and the sponsoring diocese. It should not be assumed that financial help from the diocese will be available without prior consultation.'[41]

Of course by the 1980s many of the candidates at conferences were older and already married, but the requirement remained that a candidate who wished to get married was required to obtain 'the consent and goodwill' of his bishop, which provision continued until the end of the century.

Ancient languages, 1951

In the midst of all of these discussions one long-standing issue, the question of the study of ancient languages, was finally settled. No doubt there were many clergy who were grateful that they had been required to learn Greek and Latin and used their knowledge of those languages constructively. There were others, though, with less natural facility for languages, who had spent long periods of their study trying to get their knowledge of those languages up to the level required to pass the General Ordination Examination but who then, after ordination, rarely if at all used their knowledge of the language other than perhaps occasionally to recognize a Greek word in a commentary. In the debate on CACTM's annual report for 1951 there was a motion put on the agenda by a layman from St Albans Diocese, 'That this Assembly request the Standing Committee to make recommendations for the calling into being of a permanent body to encourage the study of Hebrew, Greek and Latin by younger candidates.' Before the motion was moved, one member, Canon A. F. Smethurst of Salisbury Diocese, said that he could not believe it to be a great advantage that people should be compelled to take a certain course merely because it happened to include Greek, Latin or Hebrew. When the vast majority of people had a scientific

---

41 From information given to the author by Dr Mark Hodge, Grants Secretary of the Ministry Division.

education or something other than a classical education, it was not vitally important that they should have knowledge of those languages. He hoped the new regulations which might be issued would be far less rigid and more elastic than the existing ones.

However, the mover of the motion said that ministry would involve a good deal of biblical exposition and teaching, and for that they needed access to the Bible in its original languages.

> The picture he had before him was of a Church of England clergyman going into his study, taking down his English Bible, with his Greek New Testament and Hebrew Old Testament, and for an hour or so each week before he prepared his sermon, ransacking the sacred texts, with such commentaries as were available. Without a knowledge of Greek and Hebrew, he could not understand the commentaries that were on his bookshelves.

The proceedings noted that several members asked 'Why?'[42]

The Bishop of Sodor and Man, as Chairman of the Examinations' Committee, reported that a sub-committee of three of its members, the Warden of Keble, the Regius Professor of Divinity at Cambridge, and the Dean of King's College, London had produced a weighty memorandum, which was summarized in the three sentences in the annual report.[43]

> If training at a Theological College was only for two years there was a need to lighten the burden of the syllabus. In the light of that demand how could they add to the curriculum a tremendous burden in requiring men to carry through the study of Hebrew and/or Latin to a point that was going to be of any real service to them afterwards, in addition to all the other subjects which they had to take? It would be quite beyond the bounds of reason.

The motion was then amended to read:

> That this Assembly draws the attention of theological colleges to the importance of encouraging the study of Hebrew, Greek and Latin by

---

42 CA proceedings 1951, p. 360.
43 Annual report of CACTM 1951 (CA 1009).

ordinands, particularly by those fitted to contribute to the scholarship of
the Church.

The amendment was put and carried by 190 votes to 182, and the motion, as
amended, was put and carried. An essentially vacuous amendment ended years
of debate.

Constitutional change, 1953–9

The biggest change to CACTM in this period came towards the end of Fisher's
time as archbishop, although the two developments that led to it started far
earlier in his archiepiscopate. He was closely involved in both. It involved a
whole series of complex debates in the Church Assembly, but it eventually
ended in a change to the title although not the acronym: the Central Advisory
Council of Training for the Ministry became the Central Advisory Council for the
Ministry. The process of getting to that change, particularly towards the end,
was tortuous.

The first development arose from concern about the capital needs of the
theological colleges. In 1946 the Report of the Financial Commission had recommended that the central administration of the Church should undertake
responsibility for the provision of theological colleges and their upkeep over
and above any income derived from special endowments and students' fees.
However, at the time opinions in the theological college world were divided.
CACTM reported that the proposal fell because of a view from the Principals'
Conference that the responsibility for the provision of theological colleges and
their upkeep by central fund was strongly to be deprecated. The colleges valued
their status as independent institutions and did not want to come under
any sort of central control, financial or otherwise. By the mid-1950s no
central money had been spent on capital projects in the theological colleges,
which contrasted with the £1.3 million spent on the Church training colleges
for teachers.

In June 1953 the chairman reported to the Council that, as a result of
discussion at the Bishops' Meeting, a small group of bishops had been appointed
to review CACTM and its work with special reference to the Final Report of the
Archbishops' Commission on Training published in 1944. The chairman of that
Commission, Alwyn Williams, who had moved from being Bishop of Durham

to Bishop of Winchester, chaired the group, which reported to the bishops by January 1954. As a result the archbishops appointed, in 1955, a commission to consider the capital needs of the theological colleges, known as the Turner Commission.[44] Its principal recommendations were that CACTM should be relieved of financial responsibility other than to decide on grants to individual students, that a Theological Grants' Commission should be established which would be the authority governing the fees chargeable to candidates applying for grants, that the commission should also be able to make capital grants, but that the commission should not seek to limit the autonomy of the colleges but it should require a full financial statement and forecast from a college before considering any claim to help whether by authorized increase of fees or by special grant for capital expenditure. In that way they believed the Assembly should take its proper measure of responsibility with regard to the theological colleges as indeed it had done in other fields. While that commission was doing its work there was also a suggestion from the college principals that CACTM should ask whether the Church Commissioners could meet the stipends of those teaching in theological colleges because their work was, essentially, 'the cure of souls'.

The second development was completely independent of that process and came through a direct intervention in a Church Assembly debate by Fisher, starting from an apparently distant point. At the autumn session of the Assembly in 1953 Canon F. Harford Cross (Lincoln) produced a motion arising out of a report of the Central Co-ordinating Council for Evangelism, which in effect encouraged its own suspension. The Bishop of Rochester (Chavasse), chairman of the existing council, which was provided with office accommodation by the Church Army but no more, said that 'they were asking an old man to try to make bricks without straw, living on the charity of the Church Army and politely tolerated as long as he did not come along asking for a penny'. He believed this was stupidity and also an insult to the ministry of evangelism which seemed to him 'to lie nearest to the heart of Jesus Christ'.[45]

The Bishop of Liverpool (Clifford Martin) responded by suggesting that if the setting up of a permanent council would forward the cause of evangelism, the expense ought not to stand in the way. But he was not convinced that it would

---

44 G. C. Turner, the chairman, was a former headmaster of Charterhouse School and chairman of the Headmasters' Conference in 1950.

45 CA proceedings 1953, p. 405.

do so. He feared that if they were to form a new organization at the centre it would have the effect of stifling the work of evangelism.

The Chairman (Fisher) said that he was conscious that there were a number of matters which might need money from the Assembly, and it was important to find a way of balancing the various needs. He therefore proposed 'that a Committee be appointed to consider, in relation to the budget, the proposal for a Central Council for Evangelism, together with other claims on central Church money'. Fisher's intervention led to a small matter being used to deal with a far larger issue. Canon Harford Cross was willing to withdraw his motion in favour of that one, and Fisher's proposal was passed.

The Committee on Central Funds had 14 members, including two diocesan bishops (Rochester and Sheffield), a provost (of Leicester), two archdeacons, two other clergy and seven lay members. Of the latter Commodore P. G. Agnew RN was first appointed chairman, but on his election to Parliament felt he had to resign as chairman while remaining a member of the committee and the deputy chairman, Mrs M. B. (Betty) Ridley, became chairman.

The committee looked at the present structure of the Assembly's organization and noted that there were 22 bodies which had achieved the status of separate mention in the Assembly's estimates of expenditure. Among them was CACTM. The report identified three defects in the present organization: the basis on which the existing councils were constituted was inappropriate to the present situation, the present organization was too inflexible and there was a lack of effective co-ordination and direction at all levels. They therefore recommended regrouping the various councils into four main departments dealing with education, social responsibility, external relations and the ministry. To these four departments should be added the Assembly's own secretariat and the Central Board of Finance.

On the ministry it noted that there were four Councils: CACTM, the Central Council for Women's Church Work (formed in 1930 from the amalgamation of three bodies), the Central Council for the Order of Deaconesses (formed in 1934 as a result of a merger of the two Provincial Councils), and the Central Readers' Board (which came into being in 1905). While CACTM was concerned with the selection and training of clergy the other bodies were also concerned with terms of service as much as with recruitment and training. The committee felt the time had come when there should be established a central council, not to usurp the inalienable duty of the diocesan bishops to decide whom to ordain, but to assist them by promoting unity of thought and action in relation to problems which are common to all.[46] Such a council would promote the most effective use of men and women in the service of the Church. It should be presided over by a bishop and have as secretary a man of real standing in the Church. Its work would be divided into appropriate divisions, each in charge of an assistant secretary. One of these divisions would take the place of CACTM, which should be dissolved, and would be concerned with methods of recruitment, selection and training of ordinands. It would provide, as part of its duties, such facilities for the selection of candidates as the bishops may from time to time require, and would be responsible, in co-operation with the Central Board of Finance and the dioceses, for the financial assistance of candidates.[47]

It went on to recommend that the other bodies could be dissolved and their work incorporated into the new council, which might in time also relate to the Hospital Chaplaincies Council and the Council for the Spiritual Care of the Deaf and Dumb.

The report recognized that this would be complex given the burden of work CACTM had, and that in order to facilitate this move a commission should be established to look at the details, preferably under the chairmanship of the Archbishop of York, and that while that commission was doing its work the present bodies should remain in being.

The report was introduced to the Assembly on 14 November 1956 by Betty Ridley. She pointed out that the first thing the committee was asked to do was to decide whether the Church needed a central council for evangelism. They did not believe that it did, but from that task there grew the need 'to consider what parts of the Church's whole work and responsibility should be done centrally and what ought properly to belong to the dioceses and parishes, and in that context what machinery ought to be provided to do the central work.'[48] The report argued for a standing committee that would have the oversight of policy for the Church as a whole, with four divisions, each with a chairman, which would cover education, social responsibility, Church relations and the ministry – ordained and lay.

On the latter Betty Ridley thought it was vitally important for the work of the Church that it should be thinking and planning in terms of its total ministry, ordained and lay. There were many problems in connection with recruitment

---

46 CA 1207 report of the committee on Central Funds, para. 123, p. 47.
47 CA 1207, para. 124.
48 CA proceedings 1956, p. 379.

and training and the right use of each of these which should not be considered in isolation. It was obvious that much remained that must be thought about and done separately, but within an overall plan. For that reason she regretted that they were not able to recommend the immediate establishment of one council for the ministry, with two divisions of work and a man of real standing in the Church as its secretary. But the difficulties of bringing this about were considerable – not least the special relationship of CACTM to the episcopate, and the fact that CACTM was not a council of the Assembly in the ordinary sense. So instead it was recommended that a small commission be appointed to consider how the creation of a single council could be effected and to make recommendations by the Spring session of 1958. They hoped it might be possible for the Archbishop of York to be chairman of that commission. In the meantime, the Central Readers' Board, the Central Council for Women's Church Work and the Deaconess' Council would hasten their negotiations and move towards closer co-operation, so that they were ready for forming one part of the larger whole in the future.[49]

The debate started at 10.30 on the first day of the November 1956 Assembly and ran for the whole day and the morning of the following day, and was adjourned at lunchtime until the Spring session of 1957. No action was taken (and the 'small commission under the Archbishop of York' never established) until the resumed debate in 1957, by which time a report[50] was available from the Standing Committee (the then existing one, not the new proposed one) which included a critical response from CACTM.

CACTM pointed out the constitutional agreement made in 1924 which expressed the position as it still was, though CACTM in its annual report to the Assembly included information which was not only financial, in the belief that the Assembly would be interested in questions concerning the recruitment, selection and training of ordinands. Constitutionally, since 1943 the Council had included in its membership the same number (15) of Church Assembly representatives as there were representatives nominated by the Archbishops of Canterbury and York.[51] It noted certain consequences of the Committee on Central Funds' report's proposal.

---

49 CA proceedings 1956, p. 386f.
50 CA 1200, *Comments by the Standing Committee and the Councils on the Proposals of the Committee on Central Funds. Made Pursuant to a Resolution of the Church Assembly of 16 November 1956.*
51 CA 1200, p. 19.

On the formulation of policy the main effect on CACTM of the Committee's proposals was likely to be to transfer decisions of policy relating to the selection and training of ordination candidates from the bishops to the standing committee of the Church Assembly, unless it was made clear that the division of authority between the bishops and the Assembly was to continue.

> We cannot ignore the fact that CACTM was set up to advise the Bishops and that this advice is mainly concerned with the task of selecting and preparing men for 'ordination' not simply as a function, but as an 'order' within the total life of the Body of Christ. We therefore urge that the present agreement should be explicitly reaffirmed.[52]

On the relation of ordained and lay ministries, while CACTM sympathized with the Committee's desire to consider the Church's ministry, ordained and lay, as a whole, and recognized the importance of co-ordinating the various problems in the whole field of this twofold ministry, the Council was not convinced that this end could be achieved by the establishment of one council for the ministry. The Council emphasized two points. First, that the considerations governing the selection and training and post-ordination position of ordination candidates were different from those that applied in women's church work and in the lay ministry generally. The bulk of the work of CACTM – as the committee itself recognized – would therefore have to continue to be done separately from the other departments of the Council for the Ministry. Second, they noted that the Committee stated that one of the main functions of the proposed council would be 'to promote the most effective use of men and women in the Church', but in the Council's view again the position differed between lay and ordained ministries. The lay ministry councils concerned themselves with the 'use' and terms of service of men and women after they had been commissioned, but 'unless the Bishops direct otherwise, we think that the "use" of ordained men should continue to be determined through consultation between the men themselves, their Bishops and, where applicable, Theological College Principals.'[53]

On the working of the proposed council it concluded that a diocesan bishop would not have the time to do justice to being chairman of a body dealing with such a wide range of issues, especially if it required him to be a key member of

---

52 CA 1200, p. 19.
53 CA 1200, p. 20.

the new Standing Committee. It also said that representing the Church in the dioceses and colleges on selection and training was so important as to demand the services of a chief executive officer who was not just the secretary of a division of an overall council: 'it requires one who can speak as General Secretary of a Council which preserves its independent relationship, not only to the Bishops, but also to the Church Assembly.'[54] CACTM therefore doubted whether any advantage of administration or economy would be secured by the proposals of the Committee on Central Funds.

It therefore came up with an alternative proposal. It suggested the appointment of a small consultative committee, with an episcopal chairman, which in the first place should review the whole field of ministry, ordained and lay, and give overall consideration to matters of policy on the training and use of men and women by the Church. It could give fuller consideration to how best the work of the bodies concerned might be drawn closer together and related both to the bishops and to the proposed new Standing Committee. 'Out of such a group might grow a permanent advisory body which could more constructively fulfil many of the purposes envisaged for the proposed new Council by the Committee on Central Funds.'[55]

In the same report the Central Council for Women's Church Work and the Council for the Order of Deaconesses broadly supported the proposal of the Committee on Central Funds. However, the Central Readers' Board opposed it. It pointed out that it was set up in 1921, was created by a constitution approved by the archbishops and bishops of the Provinces of Canterbury, York and Wales, and was essentially a voluntary council with limited costs. It feared that a more developed central council would be far more expensive and readers could not be expected to fund that. They also resented a proposal from the Committee that their annual grant of £500 should be discontinued, which they described as 'most unjust'.

In the light of the Church Assembly discussion it was agreed that the Committee on Central Funds should produce a final report.[56] It essentially reaffirmed its original decision while seeking to allay some of the fears that had been expressed, including about the possible power of the Standing Committee. It particularly stressed that the four boards would each be able to bring matters

---

54 CA 1200, p. 20.
55 CA 1200, p. 20f.
56 CA 1207, Committee on Central Funds final report.

direct to the General Assembly without requiring the approval of the Standing Committee to its proposals. On CACTM's comments it remained firm. The Committee on Central Funds continued to believe the time had come when there should be a central council, 'not to usurp the inalienable duty of the diocesan bishops to decide whom to ordain but to assist them by promoting unity of thought and action in relation to problems which are common to all'. It appreciated that it would be difficult for a diocesan bishop to carry this burden unless he was supported by a secretary of real standing and experience. 'A Board able to look at the whole picture and strong enough and wise enough to deal firmly with whatever problems arise is essential.'[57]

It proposed for the Church Assembly a Standing Committee of 32 members, chaired by the archbishops and including the chairmen of the four new boards including the Board for the Ministry. For the new Board of Ministry it suggested a chairman appointed by the Archbishops of Canterbury and York, the chairman and seven other members of the Central Advisory Council of Training for the Ministry, nominated by that Council, and 19 other people including some representing the other Councils involved in ministry and seven persons appointed by the Standing Committee of the Church Assembly. The function of the board 'shall be to promote the most effective use of men and women in the service of the Church'.

At this point on 5 June 1957 Fisher made a significant intervention[58] by writing to the secretary of the Council, Peter Curgenven, who had become general secretary in 1954, with three points, which brought together both the discussion about theological college funding and the proposals of the Central Funds Committee.

First there was the proposal for a Theological Colleges Grants' Commission to deal with all the material side of theological colleges. Fisher preferred that the word 'grants' be omitted; it would deal with the physical arrangements of theological colleges including the level of fees and the problem of some additional capital fund.

Second, Fisher noted that CACTM had originally opposed the setting up of a board for the ministry but he wondered whether that opposition was wise. He thought there were a number of matters relating to wider issues of ministry that were not CACTM's concern but which needed co-ordinated

---

57 CA 1207, p. 10.
58 Fisher papers, Vol. 184, p. 227f.

thinking: the ministry of women, the work of readers, the whole role of lay ministry, and:

> Quite apart from that, all over the Anglican Communion problems are arising about what I might almost call hybrid forms of ministry – clergy who are also in industry or in the national health service, or what not, on one side: and from the mission field, and perhaps here, a possibility of laymen performing a part-time ministry, whether as permanent deacons which they want in some part of the mission field, or as priests licensed for certain duties but not for others, such as preaching. Here is a very great range which is really outside CACTM's immediate business, but in the discussion of which CACTM certainly ought to take its part. Furthermore for my own part I should like to see brought into the Board for Ministry the Hospital Chaplains' Council and the Council for the Deaf and Dumb; it is absurd to leave them as appendages of the Standing Committee: they are obviously concerned with the Board for the Ministry ... Must we not have a Board, and must not CACTM be glad to co-operate with it? ... Personally I believe that a Board for the Ministry is a crying need. I simply do not know how these varied developments that I have indicated can be tackled in any other way. CACTM cannot tackle them: it seems to me very short sighted and introspective of CACTM to say that it does not want a Board.

Third, while Fisher thought it was worth raising with the Church Commissioners whether they could meet the cost of the staffs of theological colleges, 'I feel dangerously tempted to say that you cannot expect the Church Commissioners even to look at such a suggestion unless there is a Board for the Ministry to put it forward.'

In a postscript he added that he did not understand why the Committee on Central Funds insisted that bodies underneath a board should be called a department.

> It is, of course, quite unthinkable that CACTM should change its name and become a Department of the Board for the Ministry ... I believe if that one amendment were made the last reason for CACTM resisting would be removed. Could CACTM possibly reconcile itself to the existence of a Board and then present to the Church Assembly that as a condition it must claim

for the Boards, all of them, to dignify any of their subordinate committees with the title of Council.

In a supplementary letter dated 10 June Fisher added that he envisaged both CACTM and the Board for the Ministry having diocesan bishops as their chairmen. But he also envisaged the 1924 Assembly motion on CACTM being reaffirmed, which would mean that CACTM would retain its own separate identity and special relationship with the bishops. It would only report to the Assembly on the administration of funds entrusted to it by the Assembly.

Curvengen consulted all members of the Council, who were due to meet very shortly, and had a variety of responses. The Bishops of Winchester, Rochester and Manchester broadly supported Fisher's proposals, as did Revd R. H. Preston and Canon C. K. Sansbury. Three members were firmly opposed. The Archdeacon of Blackburn commented: 'The proposed field for the Ministry Board is much too wide to be ploughed over at all adequately. If there is confusion now, it is likely to be worse confounded by the proposed Board.' The Principal of Wells was also against the change: 'Although a new Board is not to usurp the Bishops' powers and duties, it would reduce CACTM in status and interpose another authority between us and either the Bishops or the Assembly.' The Principal of Cuddesdon wrote:

> The whole idea of a high-powered central secretariat should be opposed. It is the kind of thing which increases efficiency but at the price of the life of any institution. There is no particular need to lump together CACTM, the Central Council for Women's Church Work and the Readers' Board under one comprehensive organization, in spite of the fact that they are in some sense all concerned with training people for the Ministry. The people with whom they deal are so different and the work they do so varied, that there would seem to be neither advantage nor need to combine them.[59]

At the subsequent Council meeting of June 1957 the minutes record the decision:

> That while members of CACTM are divided in their attitude to the proposals of the Committee on Central Funds as a whole, CACTM would, if the Assembly

---

59 The responses of Council members and a further copy of Fisher's letter are in the C. of E. archives, file CACTM/COU/DD/4.

decides to set up a Board for the Ministry and subject to any directions from the Bishops, readily co-operate with the Board on the assumptions:-

(a) That the functions of CACTM as laid down by the Convocations in 1912 shall be maintained;

(b) That CACTM retains its title as a Council and does not become a department of the Ministry Board; and

(c) That CACTM's membership continues to represent the interests of all concerned.

The final report of the Committee for Central Funds was considered by the Assembly on 18 June 1957. In introducing it, Betty Ridley acknowledged that the selection and training of candidates for the ministry was primarily the responsibility of the bishops, and could not come under the control of the Assembly or a board of the Assembly; and the relationship of the body doing work delegated by the bishops, and the Ministry Board, had to be worked out carefully. But the Committee were convinced there was an immediate need for this board and for its chairman to be on the Standing Committee from the start. They believed also that the board itself was suitably constituted and could do the work of advising the bishops, the Convocations and the Assembly as to the right future pattern. She recognized that similar thinking had to be done about the relationship of the Ministry Board to the Central Readers' Board or its successor, and the Council of the Order of Deaconesses, who valued a link with the Convocations, which must be taken into account. So while these questions were being resolved, only the Central Council for Women's Church Work, which was the only one of those bodies at present a full Council of the Assembly, would come directly under the supervision of the board.[60]

She noted certain fears that had been expressed in the discussion of the proposals. The first bogey was centralization. She said the role of the boards was not to control the dioceses but to provide some corporate thinking from which the dioceses could benefit if they wished. Some centralization had already been conceded in the setting up of the Councils in the first place and she did not think the new proposals would lead to any greater centralization. The second peril was bureaucracy. She did not think bureaucracy was automatically bad, and it could help in providing some co-ordination over what

---

60 CA proceedings 1957, p. 220.

would otherwise be a series of disjointed actions. A third fear was that they were aping 'big business', but she asked why it was not appropriate to adopt suitable business methods.

The debate started in the afternoon of 18 June and continued to 4.40 pm on 19 June. The proposals for each board were considered and voted upon separately. The Board of Education and the Board for Social Responsibility were approved, but the Board for Church Relations was defeated in the House of Bishops (10 ayes, 23 noes) and the House of Clergy (92 ayes, 122 noes) but approved in the House of Laity (158 ayes, 71 noes). That motion was therefore defeated.

On the Board for the Ministry the chairman (the Archbishop of Canterbury) said that he thought the chairman of CACTM was much overworked so if a board for the ministry was established some of the work of CACTM could be transferred to that.

> If there was a Board, what could happen to CACTM? A certain amount of its work was not concerned with the spiritualities at all, and that could be given to the Board and the Secretary to deal with. He would have thought that CACTM would be relieved to be able to turn its mind more upon its own affairs.[61]

However, disquiet was expressed by the Archbishop of York (Ramsey) particularly of the new board's alleged role for thought. He believed that there was nothing, second only to prayer, that the Church of England desperately needed than more thought, but the way to get more thought was to leave people more leisure to pursue it in their own way. He was reminded of a remark by Asquith: 'The trouble is that some people can only think while they are talking, which to my mind is akin to not thinking at all.' He believed the essential deep and wide thought of the Church on either of these particular matters would not be forthcoming by the creation of a board. The case had been overwhelmingly made for the Board of Education and for something to which the Church could turn for knowledge and data on social and industrial problems, but as at present advised, he felt he could not vote for the other two boards.

He was also sceptical about the use of the word Ministry being applied to the clergy and laity together. 'One of the things that the English mind understood

---

61 CA proceedings 1957, p. 253.

was the clear-cut difference between a clergyman and a layman ... he did not think it helped to call these things "Ministry", lumping them together as if they all had a sort of quasi-clerical status.'[62]

The Bishop of Ripon (Chase), speaking on behalf of CACTM, reported CACTM being divided on the matter but that it had decided that, if the board were set up, it would co-operate with the board provided certain conditions were met (as in the CACTM minutes). He expressed no personal view on the wisdom of setting up a board.

The motion was defeated in the House of Bishops (10 ayes, 21 noes) and in the House of Clergy (83 ayes, 124 noes). Only the Laity voted for it (161 ayes, 73 noes). In view of Fisher's strong support for the proposal, the vote in the Bishops was an example of the mild revolution against Fisher's style that was beginning to be developed among the bishops.[63]

The matter therefore returned to the Standing Committee of the Church Assembly, still the existing one, not the new proposed one, and they produced a further report.[64] It proposed a smaller Standing Committee, which was accepted by the Assembly, together with a Standing Committee proposal:

> That a Commission be appointed to consider the problems raised by the Turner Report on Theological Colleges and the Warrington Report on the Training of Women Church Workers and after consultation with the Central Advisory Council of Training for the Ministry, the Church of England Council for Education and the Central Council for Women's Church Work to make recommendations as soon as possible as to the action which should be taken by the Assembly and the administrative machinery which may be necessary.

The two strands that had started this whole process now came together in a commission established by the Church Assembly.

The Commission was chaired by Kenneth Riches, who brought to it his experience as Secretary of the Service Candidates Committee at the end of the war, and then as Principal of Cuddesdon. By the time of the Commission he had

---

62 CA proceedings 1957, p. 264.

63 See Edward Carpenter, 1991, *Archbishop Fisher – His Life and Times*, Norwich: Canterbury Press, p. 213. The opposition was to Fisher's pushing ahead with the revision of Canon Law, but there was also concern at the centralizing of power in the Standing Committee of the Church Assembly.

64 CA 1220, *Central Funds: Report by the Standing Committee.*

become Bishop of Lincoln, and the report[65] was published in early 1959. They noted the Commission had been asked to consider generally the wider aspects of the two reports and should make proposals, including recommendations for the revision of the existing machinery, but 'obviously the Commission would have to proceed cautiously in view of the rights, interests and duties of others besides the Assembly'.

The financial problems of the theological colleges were considered, and although they were in one sense independent institutions they were heavily dependent on their students receiving grants from the Central Fund for Ordination Candidates. 'In 1959 the dioceses, or more accurately church people in the parishes, are being asked to fund the large sum of £300,000 towards the cost of training.' They noted with approval the recommendations of the Turner report and that the colleges were full, possibly as a result of the ending of National Service, but 'it is not yet possible to say whether this is a temporary "bulge", or whether a total of 1,440 places will be insufficient for many years to come.'

They asked four fundamental questions:

How can the claims of the Governing Bodies of the Theological Colleges to control their colleges be reconciled with the claims of subscribers to the Central Fund for Ordination candidates to see that their money is laid out in the best possible way?

Can the Church Assembly have ultimate control over capital expenditure by the Colleges without impinging to some extent on Episcopal responsibilities?

Can any plan be made for the Training Houses until the whole question of the use and function of women in the Church has been thought out?

To what extent must any plans for training men and women take account of the totally inadequate numbers of full-time workers in the Church of England today?[66]

They took two statements as expressing the situation, that CACTM was overloaded and could not take on any more than the recruitment, selection and training of ordinands and that, in the words of the Bishop of Ripon as a member

---

65 CA 1279, *The Theological Colleges and Training Houses Report.*
66 CA 1279, para. 19.

of CACTM in the Assembly's debate on the report on the Committee on Central Funds, 'CACTM is not a particularly suitable body for financial considerations.' They also examined the issue of whether it was possible to have different bodies, one dealing with spiritual matters and the other dealing with financial and practical matters regarding training. This was not generally accepted by the constituent bodies, 'chiefly because the practicability of separating spiritual and intellectual matters from fabric and housekeeping matters was doubted'.[67]

They came back to the conclusion of the Committee on Central Funds that a new Board of Ministry was needed, not for the sake of 'administrative tidiness' but for reasons of 'practical necessity'. They recommended that two new bodies needed to be brought into being with the least possible delay – the first dealing primarily with questions of policy, and the second, which would be a subordinate committee of the first, dealing with questions of finance. The second recommendation was that the chairman of both bodies should be the same person, preferably in episcopal orders, who would be devoted wholly to this work.[68]

They suggested that the new policy body should be called the Council for the Ordained and Lay Ministry, with a chairman appointed by the archbishops.[69] The new financial body should be called the Theological Colleges and Training Houses Committee.[70] CACTM would remain responsible for the recruitment, selection and training of clergy. On the matter of the Church Commissioners covering the costs of the staffs of theological colleges they noted that it was up to a diocesan bishop to declare that someone had 'the cure of souls' so they could assert that for the ordained staff of theological colleges in their dioceses. This would adversely affect those dioceses that had more than one theological college in the diocese (Oxford and Ely), but they also continued to think that the costs of staff should normally be included in the costs of the college and therefore be recovered through fees.

---

67 CA 1279, para. 22.

68 CA 1279, para. 29.

69 The membership would be three persons appointed by CACTM, one being the chairman who would be vice-chairman of the Council, one from the Council for Women's Work, one from the Council for Deaconesses, two from the Board for Social Responsibility concerned with the training of moral welfare workers, one from the Board of Education, one from the Central Readers' Board, one principal of a theological college appointed by the annual Conference of Principals, two members of the Church Assembly appointed by the CBF, seven appointed by the Standing Committee of the Church Assembly, and four persons to be co-opted, making a total of 24.

70 It was proposed this body should have 18 members representing essentially the same groups, but with three principals of theological colleges and four appointed by the Council for the Ministry. CA 1279, para. 34.

The Commission's report was debated on 5 February 1959, the Bishop of Lincoln introducing it. He pointed out that already £300,000 was spent on grants for ordinands, and he estimated a further £250,000 would be needed for capital grants for the colleges. He explained that while he knew that the Bishop of Manchester would be moving an amendment to say that CACTM should take on the responsibility as the policy body, that was not the conclusion of the report: 'In the end they came to the conclusion that to try to re-shape CACTM not only would not be effective in doing what needed to be done, but also would destroy the particular status which CACTM had gained and earned in the Church, the independence, even from the Assembly, in matters relating to ordination.' He therefore recommended what the report concluded.

The Bishop of Manchester (William Greer) proposed an amendment giving the wider responsibilities to a new reconstituted CACTM.

> He believed the proposal which the Commission made had arisen from a misunderstanding of the evidence given to the Commission by CACTM. The evidence by CACTM was that it could not cope with anything more. What CACTM meant by that was not that CACTM was overloaded, but that the staff as constituted was overloaded, and that nothing further could be put upon it effectively; but given more staff, enlarged in its scope, CACTM would be competent and able and willing to cope with the total question. So he would ask, why create another body when CACTM, the body which carried the experience, was ready to deal with the task?'[71]

In the debate concern was expressed about the existence of two or three bodies all dealing with overlapping matters, and it was thought that there would be grounds for great confusion. However, Betty Ridley continued to argue for a wholly new Council as did the Bishop of Lincoln in his summing up, although both noted that CACTM had changed its view on the whole matter. The Bishop of Manchester's amendment was accepted as was the further motion, 'That the Standing Committee be instructed to revise, in consultation with the Archbishops of Canterbury and York, the functions and membership of the Council and to consider its future name and to report to the next Session of the Assembly.' This was carried.

---

71 CA proceedings 1959, p. 102.

The report by the Standing Committee on the reconstitution of the Central Advisory Council of Training for the Ministry was signed by the chairman of the Standing Committee, the Archbishop of Canterbury, on 11 June 1959.[72] It recommended that, from 1 September 1959, the Council hitherto known as the Central Advisory Council of Training for the Ministry be known as the Central Advisory Council for the Ministry, that notwithstanding that the Council is a Council of the Assembly under Standing Order XVIII, a majority of its members need not be members of the Church Assembly and it proposed a membership and constitution detailed in Appendix C. There would essentially be a Council that would cover the major policy issues relating to ministry, with two subsidiary bodies, an Ordination Candidates Committee which would carry out essentially the same functions of the previous CACTM, and a Houses and Finance Committee which would deal with the capital needs of the colleges and grants to ordinands.

The report was debated on 15 July 1959, nearly six years after the decision to establish the Committee on Central Funds and over two and a half years after the debate on the first report of the Committee on Central Funds. It was accepted and the new CACTM came into being.

Under Fisher, CACTM had therefore developed remarkably. Its selection system was very firmly established, its financial role in the funding of training had become critical, despite the Council's own desire that the responsibility should remain primarily with the dioceses and, after a huge amount of the Church Assembly's time and effort, CACTM was given vastly increased responsibilities, even though they were never sought by the original Council.

It was also a significant move towards centralization, although that was always denied at the time. Of course once the selection conferences were well established an individual bishop could, and sometimes did, overrule a selection conference recommendation for an individual candidate, and he could well debate or even decide unilaterally on some matters relating to an individual candidate's training, provided a course did not require special funding from CACTM. A diocesan bishop in consultation with his diocese also still had ultimate responsibility for the organization of ministry in his diocese, but it would take a very courageous bishop to ignore completely the general policy of CACTM on issues relating to the ministry.

---

72 CA 1291.

9

The Pendulum Years, 1960–70

It was the journalist Bernard Levin who coined the phrase The Pendulum Years[1] for the 1960s, and it certainly summarized the experience of the Church of England over that decade. The swinging sixties certainly meant for many a period where conventions, including conventional morality, were challenged, old certainties questioned, and a new drive to personal freedom pursued. All of those factors had their influence on the Church of England. The publication of *Honest to God* in 1963 symbolized the opening up of a theological debate that made the decade for some Christians exciting and stimulating, although for others it induced despondency and gloom. Michael Ramsey, who became archbishop in 1961, was far more of a theologian than his predecessor and someone with strength in that area was clearly needed as the 1960s unfolded. Ramsey was aware that his initial negative response to *Honest to God* was a mistake, but he was possibly the right man at Canterbury for a period of theological radicalism. In terms of concern for the institutional life of the Church he was far less interventionist than his predecessor; he certainly provided little of the direction and drive that Fisher had given CACTM although, as will be seen, his support for non-stipendiary ministry was significant.

From the point of view of CACTM and its concerns, although numbers of men being ordained at the beginning of the decade seemed good, there were already concerns about recruitment to the ministry, but by the end of the decade the picture looked far worse. A reduction by over a third of men being ordained each year was a huge change. As a result the theological colleges faced a far more difficult situation and closure of theological colleges became a probability towards the end of the decade, made actual in the early years of the 1970s. But developments in ministry, first with non-stipendiary ministry, then later with the possibility of the ordination of women at least being

---

1 Bernard Levin, 1970, *The Pendulum Years,* London: Jonathan Cape.

discussed, indicated that significant change in the ministry was afoot, as was a far greater emphasis on the role of the laity. As with all major changes in an institution, while some saw the whole decade as a disaster, others saw it as a challenge and an opportunity.

After Bishop Leslie Owen's time as full-time chairman of CACTM the day-to-day administration of the Council's work was in the hands of its General Secretary. Prebendary Philip Wheeldon had succeeded John Phillips in 1949, and Wheeldon in turn became Bishop of Whitby in 1954 and was succeeded by Revd Peter Curvengen. Curvengen moved in November 1959 to become the incumbent of Goring-on-Sea, which gave the opportunity for the archbishops, with a new Council with wider responsibilities, to develop a different staffing structure, and with a senior figure working full-time for the Council. Ramsey strongly advised Fisher that there should be a full-time vice-chairman of the Council.[2] Fisher agreed but preferred the title Moderator. In the event the new post held both titles. Fisher, Ramsey and the Bishop of London (Montgomery Campbell) agreed that the best person for the post was Thomas Craske,[3] the Bishop of Gibraltar, then a suffragan bishop in London Diocese responsible for the episcopal care of chaplaincies in mainland Europe. While his new role was not identical to that of Owen's during the war years, there were obvious parallels in giving the Council's staff the active presence of a full-time episcopal member, although other names had been considered by the archbishops for the post who were not in episcopal orders, and the reasons for creating the new post were largely related to the wider responsibilities that were being remitted to the new Council. In Craske's first couple of years at the Council the post of Secretary of the Council (as opposed to General Secretary) was held by a layman, Geoffrey Heawood, a former headmaster of Cheltenham Grammar School, who had joined the staff in an assistant capacity in 1953. After his retirement in May 1962 a full-time General Secretary was appointed, William Saumarez-Smith, the only layman to have held that post in the twentieth century. Also in 1960 the Bishop of Bath and Wells, who had been Chairman of the Council since 1950, died in office and

---

2 Fisher papers, Vol. 215, pp. 272, 277.

3 Frederick William Thomas Craske 1901–71. He was educated at King's College, London and was ordained in 1927 as a curate in Manchester. From 1929 to 1932 he worked for the Student Christian Movement, but then went back to the north of England for two incumbencies. In 1939 he became Education Secretary of the Missionary Council of the Church Assembly until he moved in 1950 to be the representative of the British Council of Churches in Germany. In 1953 he became Bishop of Gibraltar until he moved to the role in CACTM. The details of his appointment are in the Fisher papers, Vol. 215, pp. 317, 318, 333.

he was succeeded as Council Chairman by the Bishop of Lincoln (Riches) who had been the chairman of the body that had proposed the wider responsibilities to the Council. With a new Chairman, a new post of Moderator and a new General Secretary all within two years, the leadership of the Council had changed dramatically.

The *Paul Report*

The Council's new responsibilities soon came to the fore with it being invited to handle a major task. In the 1960 July session of the Church Assembly a lay member from Winchester Diocese, Lieutenant-Colonel H. E. Madge, asked the Assembly to establish a Commission to review the stipends, pensions and deployment issues surrounding the clergy.[4] He described the whole system as 'chaotic, uneconomical, and wasteful of their existing financial resources', and it was also teeming with anomalies and even injustices'.[5] In the course of the debate his proposal was amended and rather than the setting up of a commission the matter was referred to the new Council, who were asked to consider 'in the light of changing circumstances, the system of the payment and deployment of the clergy, and to make recommendations'. The Council decided at its December 1961 meeting[6] that it would be better to appoint one person to review the whole area and Leslie Paul, who was known to CACTM as Director of Studies at Brasted preparing men to go on to theological colleges, and whose background was as a sociologist, was appointed to carry out the review.

The report,[7] widely known as the *Paul Report*, was published in 1964 and included the results of a survey of clergy and a mass of other statistics. Paul saw clear evidence of decline both in numbers and in the influence of the Church, and he identified a number of critical areas in ministerial life. Manpower was not evenly distributed, with some clergy, especially those in some urban areas, ministering to large populations, while others, often in rural areas, seeming to have far lighter demands placed upon them, although the divide in the size of

---

4 The history of the *Paul Report* and its successor, the *Morley Report*, is also told in Paul Welsby, 1984, *A History of the Church of England 1945–1980*, Oxford: OUP, pp. 131-9.

5 CA proceedings, Vol. XL, 1960, p. 236.

6 CACTM minutes, 19 December 1961.

7 Leslie Paul, 1964, *The Deployment and Payment of the Clergy*. Church Information Office.

the task was not simply an urban rural divide.[8] Stipends for incumbents also varied within dioceses, some incumbents receiving up to twice the stipends of other incumbents even within the same diocese, but the pay differentials were based on a whole variety of different factors including historic endowments to particular livings and did not necessarily relate to the size of the task facing different clergy. Expenses of office were unevenly paid as between different parishes, and there was no agreed retirement age. Inevitably for some clergy such disparities sapped morale, and the report, while recognizing the devoted and faithful service given by many parochial clergy, painted a gloomy picture of clerical despondency.

The report was warmly welcomed by some but was viewed with dismay by others. The 62 recommendations included some that caused major controversy. The most contentious for many clergy were that the parson's freehold of office should be replaced by leasehold for a fixed term, that a new system of a clergy staff board, answerable to the Church Assembly, should be established and that regional appointment bodies should replace the patronage system whereby individual patrons nominated clergy for many parochial posts.[9] Both of those proposals were seen by their critics as lessening the parish priest's independence, increasing the power of bishops and creating a new clerical bureaucracy. The proposal to pool all endowment income to establish a common stipends fund, with the possibility of increments for long service and increased pay for particularly heavy posts, was also seen by some to give too much power to central or diocesan bodies with whom such decisions would rest.

Other less contentious proposals included the setting up of major parishes staffed by a team or group of clergy and dealing in a more coherent way with the placing of junior clergy. CACTM's report *The Paul Report: The Next Steps*[10] recommended that progress could be made on these two more minor issues but that it would leave to one side the issues concerning the tenure of office,

---

8 Page 141 of *The Paul Report* gives some revealing statistics as between urban areas. Bournemouth and Bridlington, for example, had a ratio of about one clergyman to every 3,000 of the population, but in two deaneries in Chelmsford Diocese, Romford and Barking, there was one clergyman to every 10,000 of the population.

9 In *Issues Raised: A Further Report by CACTM on the Issues Raised in The Deployment and Payment of the Clergy* (CA 1527) the percentage of patronage bodies was noted: the Crown and its officers (6 per cent), diocesan bishops (32 per cent), deans and chapters (6 per cent), parochial clergy of a mother church (9 per cent), diocesan boards of patronage (3 per cent), colleges (7 per cent), religious trusts and societies (15 per cent), private patrons (22 per cent).

10 CA 1501, 1964.

retirement, the exercise of patronage and the place of any regional boards. It therefore established working parties under the Archdeacon of Lincoln to examine team and group ministries and another under the Bishop of Derby to look at the placing of junior clergy. Both reports were produced in 1965 and the proposals for team and group ministries were incorporated into a complex piece of legislation that took four years to get through the Assembly and finally formed the Pastoral Measure of 1968.

The report on the placing of junior clergy was completed in March 1965. It was asked to consider,

> in the light of the Paul report, the suggestion that during the first five years of a man's ministry, he should have less wide power of choice as to where he will serve than he has at present; and that in deciding an appointment, the need for training should be the governing principle for the first three years, with manpower demands as the governing principle for the remaining two years.

Because some hesitation had been expressed about any direction of candidates other than direction by the Holy Spirit in what was essentially a free market, it examined the very principle of direction by the Church for junior clergy. It concluded that the Holy Spirit's action worked in the same way that an ordination required the action by the bishop, the mind of the Church about the candidate and the decision of each individual. The Holy Spirit did not just act on the individual's mind and conscience, but through the whole decision of the Church.

> The Apostolic Church is a Church under commission and sent on a missionary task into the world. In the Apostolic Ministry of the Church, the deacon or priest should go to his work, conscious that he has been chosen and commissioned and sent for it, yet conscious too that he himself has used his own judgement and agrees that it is the right sphere of work for him.[11]

The report advocated the suggestion of the *Paul Report* about training being the need in a first post and the Church's needs of manpower in a second post. It also

---

11 *CACTM Report of Working Party on the Placing of Junior Clergy*, p. 3. The report is signed by the Bishop of Derby and dated March 1965, but it has no CA reference number. A copy is available in the Lambeth Palace library, ref. H5041.C4.

recognized that in the placing of deacons, principals of theological colleges had a significant role (often through relationships with particular parishes where previous curates from that college had gone) and that bishops had a role in taking account of the needs of his diocese compared to the needs of other dioceses. The report stopped short of endorsing a proposal from the Bishop of Birmingham for a quota system for each diocese. 'We prefer to rely on the knowledge and goodwill of all concerned in directing men towards the areas of greatest need',[12] but it did hope that the statistical unit of the Central Board of Finance would circulate information each summer on those dioceses where clergy were relatively scarce. The ethos of the report was well summarized in its final paragraph: 'Much that we have said both in our report and in the two codes of procedure simply puts in writing proper courtesies within our present Church of England order. Yet these courtesies are often not known and often not observed.'[13] Time would show that courtesy and goodwill were not enough in deciding on the fair deployment of the clergy.

In February 1965 CACTM presented to the Church Assembly a further document relating to the more contentious proposals[14] and the Assembly committed their consideration to a commission, which was chaired by Canon Fenton Morley, Vicar of Leeds. The Commission's report, *Partners in Ministry*,[15] was not a CACTM document, and it broadly accepted Leslie Paul's view and made in more detailed form many of Paul's proposals regarding transferring patronage to diocesan ministry commissions, the replacement of freehold by tenure for a term of years, and moves towards the centralizing of stipends. It also recommended that what by then was called ACCM should be a constituent part of a central ministry commission, which would be an executive and not an advisory body. Its proposals suffered the same fate as the major Paul proposals and nothing happened apart from some modification to, but not replacement of, the patronage system.

The supply of candidates

The Paul proposals assumed that recruitment for the ministry would at least continue at the then current rate and, if possible, should increase. At the

---

12 *Report*, p. 4.
13 *Report*, p. 9.
14 *Issues Raised*, CA 1527, CIO 1964.
15 *Partners In Ministry*, CA 1640, 1967.

beginning of the decade there were grounds for modest optimism. In 1960, 598 men were ordained, and that rose to 633 in 1963 but fell to 605 in 1964. There is always a three- to four-year gap between selection and ordination and the 1964 decline in numbers of ordinations was already evident in numbers being recommended some years earlier. The 1962 Annual Report said it would concentrate on recruitment issues, which led to the appointment of a recruitment officer to the CACTM staff (Revd John Neale) and a report *The Men He Wants.*[16] It spoke in terms of all Christians having a vocation 'to be caught up in the divine work of the world' but it also spoke of the particular commitment to the ordained priesthood. 'This, in turn, is as distinct from the vocation of a layman as Christ's call to his Apostles was distinct from his call to others. The distinction stands in the will of Christ, who gave and gives the ordained ministry to his Church.'[17] The Church Assembly debated the report in February 1962 and agreed to ask CACTM, the Board of Education, the Board of Social Responsibility and the Council for Women's Ministry to appoint a joint working party to consider what advice and assistance could be given concerning the issues raised. In introducing the debate on *The Men He Wants* the Dean of Westminster, Abbott, Chairman of the Ordination Candidates' Committee, said:

> the ministerial vocation was in a special degree addressed to the whole Church, and that in the present crisis of man-power – that man-power which was often badly distributed, but with patience might be remedied – the burden must be shared not merely for expediency and for efficiency, but was also a matter of doctrine and practical theology.[18]

Others in the debate also talked about the need to develop the ministry of women. The practical outcome was that by 1963 a brochure entitled *You?* was produced by CACTM as a supplement to *Church Illustrated,* and over 130,000 copies were sold, with free copies issued to all dioceses so that each incumbent could have one. A poster had also been produced saying 'Pray more for your clergy. Pray for more clergy.'

The result was scarcely an obvious success. The year 1964 was the last year in which the number of ordinations was over 600, by 1970 it had dropped to

---

16 *The Men He Wants,* CA 1396.

17 *The Men He Wants,* p. 10f.

18 Report of Proceedings, Spring 1962, p. 95.

437 and the following year to 393 and the annual figure for ordinations remained below 400 for most of the following decade until 1979, when 417 were ordained, of which 114 were for non-stipendiary ministry. A 1966 report on ordination statistics[19] (by which time CACTM had become ACCM) suggested various reasons for the decline. The first they described as 'intellectual uncertainty', by which they meant the very public debate which followed some controversial books in the early 1960s: *Soundings, Objections to Christian Belief,* and perhaps above all the publication in 1963 of *Honest to God* by John Robinson, Bishop of Woolwich, which was by far the best-selling theological book of the whole decade and which opened up a very public debate about the nature of God. Its thesis that the Church's way of thinking about God needed to recognize some of the wartime and post-war theologians' challenge to traditional concepts, particularly those of Dietrich Bonhoeffer, Rudolph Bultmann and Paul Tillich, had certainly been a liberation for many but it was also a source of dismay for others. The ACCM report also noted increased secularism, and a more general reluctance towards a life-long and irreversible commitment on the part of many in society at the time. But they also noted more narrowly church reasons such as an increased emphasis on lay ministry and certain features of the then church life, including confusion about the role of the parish priest, a questioning about the effectiveness of the parochial system and a general impression that the clergy were over-burdened and that there was little hope of speedy reform. This latter point no doubt reflected the debate about the *Paul Report,* which had received very wide publicity. What the ACCM report wisely did not attempt was to make any assessment of the relative strength of each of those reasons.

The decade was also the start in a change in the age of candidates recommended or conditionally recommended for training. In 1960, 463, or 65 per cent, of the candidates recommended or conditionally recommended at selection conferences were below 25, and 157, or 22 per cent, were under 20. Of the just under 1,000 candidates that attended a selection conference in that year, 74 per cent were recommended or conditionally recommended for training. In 1960 candidates for ordination over the age of 40 did not normally attend selection conferences but were chosen more locally. Of those ordained that year, 107, or 17 per cent, were over 40.

---

19 CA 1591.

By 1970 all candidates for ordination, including those over the age of 40, normally attended a selection conference and 218, or 55 per cent, of candidates recommended or conditionally recommended were under 25 but only 28, or 7 per cent, were under the age of 20. Sixty-four per cent of those who attended conferences were recommended or conditionally recommended and 95, or 22 per cent, of those ordained, were over 40. It was still the case in 1970 that the majority of those accepted appeared to have made ordination in effect their first career choice, but it was a significantly smaller proportion than at the beginning of the decade.

One other practical change in the arrangements for the selection process that had already started some years before was brought to completion by the ending of National Service. While some candidates for ministry were sponsored for a selection conference by a bishop, men in military service had always been able to apply direct to CACTM for selection, but with the ending of National Service the decision was taken in 1966 that in future no one could attend a conference unless they were sponsored by a diocesan bishop.[20] Some dioceses had the role of Diocesan Director of Ordinands prior to that change; the *Church of England Year Book* for 1964 identified two, Guildford and Sheffield, and many others simply had an Ordination Candidates Committee or Fund. The decision about sponsorship was greatly to strengthen the pressure to create such an office in each diocese and by 1970 well over half the dioceses recorded someone with that title in the Year Book of that year, while other people with different titles effectively fulfilled that role in the other dioceses.

Concern about the educational standard of those coming forward was also expressed in the period. In the November 1962 session of the Church Assembly the Chairman of CACTM was asked what steps were being taken to change the development that while 60 per cent of those ordained in 1932 were graduates, by 1962 that had fallen to below 40 per cent. In fact that percentage was not quite that low; in 1962, 270, or 43 per cent of the 628 men ordained that year were graduates, but nonetheless the decline from the 60 per cent of 1932 was evident. The chairman replied that the solution was not to ordain fewer non-graduates but to ordain more graduates, and that CACTM's policy was to encourage young ordinands to obtain a degree. That too did not turn out to be particularly effective. In 1970, of the 437 who were ordained that year, 175, or 40 per cent, were graduates, a slightly lower proportion than in 1962.

---

20 A decision reported in the 1967 Annual Report (CA 1625).

The Council for Women's Ministry in the Church

The relationship between CACTM and the Council for Women's Ministry in the Church was an issue throughout the 1960s. The Council had been given an interim constitution pending its work being fully integrated into CACTM, and the two bodies shared offices in 9 Tufton Street, Westminster. But as the 1965 *Report by the Council for Women's Ministry as its Interim Constitution*[21] noted, the pressure on CACTM, not least of all in dealing with some of the matters relating to the *Paul Report*, had meant there had been no opportunity for integration. Bishop Craske chaired a working party that produced in 1962 *Gender and Ministry*,[22] which was debated in the Church Assembly in November of that year. It advocated a more developed policy for women's ministry as deaconesses and licensed lay workers, but it stopped short of calling for the ordination of women. In the November debate there was an additional motion that a committee should be appointed 'to make a thorough examination of the various reasons for withholding of the ordained and representative priesthood from women'. That request was approved by the Assembly.

In response the archbishops appointed a commission under the chairmanship of Gerald Ellison, Bishop of Chester, which reported in 1967 with *Women and Holy Orders*.[23] The Introduction explained:

> Had the Commission been called upon to advise whether women should be ordained to the priesthood or not, its members would have found themselves divided, and they would have had to present majority and minority reports or at least statements of reservation on particular points. But this was not, in fact, the Commission's task. We are able, therefore, to present a unanimous Report in which we set out the principal matters of fact and interpretation as we see them.[24]

The main recommendation of the report was that the next Lambeth Conference should be asked to reconsider its previous pronouncements on the subject (possibly in the context of a wider consideration of the relevance of the

---

21 CA 1548.

22 *Gender and Ministry,* CA 1430.

23 *Women and Holy Orders*: being the report of a commission appointed by the Archbishops of Canterbury and York, CA 1617.

24 CA 1617, p. 8.

Christian ministry), and to state positively what was the status of a deaconess. It made a number of specific recommendations about the role of deaconesses, including suggesting that it should be firmly decided whether they may, by virtue of their office, administer the chalice and read the epistle. It also provided an extensive bibliography, notes of official publications and reports, including from other churches, and there were six major appendices by members of the Commission including, 'Why the Christian priesthood is male' by Revd Professor V. A. Demant and, 'The case for the ordination of women to the priesthood' by Kay M. Baxter.

The report was debated in the Church Assembly in February 1967 and it was received and commended to consideration by the Church. A following motion proposed by Professor Geoffrey Lampe of Cambridge University was:

> that this Assembly, believing that there are no conclusive reasons why women should not be ordained to the priesthood, but recognizing that it would not be wise to take unilateral action at this time, would welcome further consideration of this matter by representatives of the Church of England and the Methodist Church.

The debate was adjourned and resumed in July 1967, when Professor Lampe's motion was defeated in all three Houses. More modest moves were happening elsewhere. In October 1966 as reported in the ACCM Annual Report for that year the Council of St John's College, Durham, had requested permission that women could train for lay ministry alongside men training for ordained ministry in the college, which request was accepted by both ACCM and the Council for Women's Ministry.[25] However, the battlelines had been set for a debate that was to continue in the Church for much of the rest of the century.

The Council for Women's Ministry was finally integrated with what by then had become ACCM in 1971.

Constitutional reform again

While the Council of CACTM was preoccupied with discussions about the *Paul Report* the Ordination Candidates Committee, which was the body that retained

---

25 Reported in the 1966 Annual Report of CACTM, CA 1578.

the responsibilities of the old CACTM, including the matters relating to theological colleges and courses, also oversaw some more significant developments in theological education. In 1960 it introduced an essay scheme to replace the General Ordination Examination for candidates over 30, and in 1962 it established a Theological Education Committee, which became an important forum for 'exploring all aspects of theological education', as its terms of reference required. But the preoccupation of the Council with wider ministry issues had led to some delay in the Council finally approving some recommendations of the Ordination Candidates Committee and this frustration fuelled the review of the new CACTM's constitution asked for at the end of its first period in office in its original establishment in 1959.

After surveying the history, the review body made some recommendations.[26] It suggested the Council should be renamed the Council for the Ministry of the Church with the function 'To promote the most effective ministry, both of men and women, in the service of the Church and to make appropriate recommendations for this purpose to the Bishops and to the Church Assembly.' It also suggested a new composition and constitution for the Council, which would have an overarching view of all matters relating to ministry, but with two major subordinate bodies. The first, to be called the Training Committee, was essentially a continuation of the Ordination Candidates Committee with slightly enlarged responsibilities relating to buildings and finance, and the other a new Ministry Committee, whose functions would be:

(i) To keep under review different forms of ministry by men and women, ordained and lay, to enable the Council to give appropriate advice to the Church Assembly

(ii) To promote discussion within the Church, so far as this may be practical, about the adaption of the ministry to meet the changing pastoral situation.

(iii) To keep in close touch with the other central Church bodies concerned with different forms of ministry, in particular (a) the Council for Women's Ministry in the Church; (b) The Central Readers' Board: (c) M.E.C.C.A. (d) The Board of Education's Adult Committee and the Advisory Committee on Chaplaincies in Modern Universities; (e) The Industrial Committee of the Board for

---

26 CA 1569.

Social Responsibility; (f) The Hospital Chaplaincies' Council; (g) The Prison Chaplaincies' Council.

The report was debated in the Assembly on 11 November 1965. In introducing it the Chairman of CACTM (the Bishop of Lincoln) said of the existing structure that while anything relating to the training and selection of men for the ordained ministry automatically went to the OCC, there was no preliminary body to deal with ministry issues. The Council believed:

that these matters would be given proper attention only if there was a complementary body to the Ordination Candidates Committee, and they proposed the creation of a new Committee, which would be responsible, in the same way as the Training Committee, directly to the Council.[27]

On the matter of the Council's title:

They were of the opinion that there was a case for changing the existing title, which in the minds of many was perhaps not wholly free from either suspicion or dislike. If, however, the Assembly wished the word 'Advisory' to be retained, they would accept such an amendment.[28]

It was also noted that this review was being done in the context of the retirement of Bishop Craske and the move of Mr Saumarez-Smith, Chief Secretary of CACTM, to be the Appointments' Secretary to the Archbishops. In future the new Secretary would combine the two posts of General Secretary and Moderator and Canon Basil Moss had been appointed to take up the duties in April 1966. Less publicly it was also known to the archbishop and to other senior members of the House of Bishops that Kenneth Riches wished to give up as Chairman of CACTM, although he was willing to leave the timing of that to the archbishop.[29]

The revised constitution was not warmly welcomed by all. B. J. Stanley (Portsmouth) wanted more representation on the Church Assembly and particularly by lay people both on the Council and its main committees. The Archbishop of York regretted any suggestion of losing the name CACTM. He also

---

27 CA Report of Proceedings, Autumn 1965, p. 617.

28 *Report*, p. 617.

29 Ramsey papers, Vol. 73, p. 204.

wondered whether the Church needed the expense of a Council of 26 members, a Ministry Committee of 24 members and a Training Committee of 31 members, making 81 in all. Concern was also expressed by other speakers about extending the new proposed Council's responsibilities to include lay training which was already dealt with by the Board of Education. More generally there was unease about a Board of Ministry assuming some sort of say over all forms of lay work in the Church.

The Bishop of Bedford (John Trillo), who had succeeded Eric Abbott as Chairman of the Ordination Candidates Committee in 1964, and whom Ramsey and others had identified as a possible successor to Riches as Chairman of the Council, defended the proposals.

> They should be seen against the background of the way in which the constitution of CACTM had been worked during the last five years, a great deal of success had been achieved. But it was an open secret that there had been difficulties, not least because as far as the Ordination Candidates' Committee was concerned time had been wasted and frustrating decisions taken because the Council had mulled over things.

In terms of lay representation and the constitution he said:

> The Assembly was represented, on the Council of 26 members, by eight of its own members. When it came to terms of reference, the function of CACTM had been laid down for years and the Assembly had given consideration to it many times. Such consideration was given on the Report of the Committee on Central Funds, and the Commission which reported in 1959, before the setting up of the present constitution, made the matter quite plain. They were attacked on both sides. On one side it was said that the laity were not given sufficient consideration and that such consideration was not given to the whole concept of lay ministry. In the mind of CACTM at the moment, the fullest possible concern existed about the lay ministry in every sense. They were in touch with every board of the Assembly. They did not want to take over the whole business of the laity – it must be dealt with piecemeal and co-ordinated, and CACTM would have a function in overseeing this important part of their work, which had been neglected in the past. What advantage was there in delay? When CACTM died, and they had not a constitution fit to start, it would

cause difficulties of administration. This Assembly would be turning down proposals carefully worked out by the Council and which had been presented by the Standing Committee of the Assembly. This was a delicate matter. It might be necessary to increase the number of theological college principals, and the balance would be destroyed. He asked the Assembly to assent to these proposals and give the new General Secretary a good start with the new constitution.[30]

This speech, which undoubtedly expressed some of the frustration and irritation members of CACTM had at the concerns expressed in the Assembly, did not go down well. Michael Nott, Chaplain to the Archbishop of Canterbury, in a file note to Ramsey, said 'the tone of the speech was arrogant and patronising, and John Trillo completely misread the tone of the Assembly. As a result the Bishop of London, (Robert Stopford) feels his appointment as Chairman of CACTM cannot now be entertained.'[31]

The report was received by the Assembly, but the following motions seeking to implement the new constitution were changed. The proposal to change the name was subject to an amendment to leave the existing body in existence for six months while further work be done. That amendment was carried in the House of Laity but lost in the Houses of Bishops and the Clergy and so was rejected. The Bishop of Lincoln's motion to implement the proposals was then voted on by Houses. The Bishops approved it (12 ayes, 0 noes), the Clergy narrowly agreed it (37 ayes, 33 noes), but it was lost by one vote in the House of Laity (59 ayes, 60 noes). Eventually the motion was amended, 'That in the light of this debate the Standing Committee and CACTM be instructed to lay before the Assembly proposals for the reconstitution of the Council and its subordinate bodies.' Canon Smith of Rochester asked whether the effect was that CACTM, in which many of them had great confidence, and the Standing Committee would be able to think again about the whole matter, and CACTM would continue with its present constitution. The chairman said that was precisely the situation, and the motion was approved.

A revised constitution was presented to the following meeting of the Assembly.[32] It decreased the size of the Council to 21, changed the size of the

---

30 Report of Proceedings, p. 625f.
31 Ramsey papers, Vol. 73, p. 198.
32 CA 1569A.

Training Committee by adding one more (to 32) and decreased the size of the Ministry Committees (from 24 to 22). It also suggested a change in name to the Advisory Council for the Church's Ministry. It was hoped that the new title would make clear that the body now had a broader responsibility for ministry as a whole than the old CACTM, but that it was responsible to both the bishops and the Assembly as a whole. The essential functions of both the Council and the two main subordinate committees remained the same as in the earlier suggested constitution.

The revised constitution was debated in February 1966, and immediately prior to the debate it was reported that the Bishop of Lincoln had resigned as chairman. The report was received, and the change in name agreed. Concerns in the debate included whether a Methodist representative should be a voting member of the Training Committee, what the role of women should be on the key bodies, what the role of laity in each body should be and, more fundamentally, whether there should be two bodies answerable to the Assembly, the Ministry Committee and the Training Committee, and no overarching body. It was asked whether any one body could be responsible for the whole ministry of the Church and hence the limits of the new body's responsibilities. A proposal to adjourn the whole matter for a period was defeated and the motion on the subordinate bodies was modified by amendments. The final motion was:

That the proposals for the Council with regard to its subordinate bodies be generally approved, provided that:

(a) The minimum number of lay members of the Ministry Committee be increased from 5 to 8

(b) At least 2 members of the Training and Ministry Committees shall be women

(c) No member of any committee shall have a vote unless he is a communicant member of the Church of England or of a Church in communion with the Church of England, and

(d) No provision is made in the membership of the Training Committee for a representative of the Methodist Church.

It was scarcely a warm endorsement of the proposals, but enough had been given to permit the new body to come into being. CACTM ceased and ACCM replaced it, the new acronym remaining in force for nearly 25 years. Laurence

Brown, Bishop of Warrington and later Bishop of Birmingham, became the first chairman.

Five years after ACCM came into being there was a review of its structures, as had been agreed at the beginning of its life. This was now implemented by the General Synod, which replaced the Church Assembly in 1970. A report, the *Future Boards and Council Structure of the General Synod*,[33] suggested the immediate integration of the Council for Women's Ministry into ACCM and a new structure for ACCM, where it was said 'The Council shall have power to appoint such committees or sub-committees (as the case may be) as they shall from time to time think fit.' The result was a new committee structure which involved a reduction in committee members of the various bodies from 220 to 80[34] and the demise of the Ministry Committee, the responsibility in future being held by the Council itself.

The theological colleges

While that was all being debated, the change in the numbers of candidates coming forward for ordination had an effect on the position of the theological colleges. Given the good numbers at the beginning of the decade it is not surprising that it provoked proposals to increase the number of theological colleges and increase spending on the existing colleges. In 1960 a CACTM report, *The Interim Report on the Capital Needs of Theological Colleges and Women's Training Houses*[35] said that £140,000 had been already set aside for various colleges and a further capital sum of £100,000 would be presented in the future. It also noted that there was a proposal for a new graduate college for 120 students, set in a modern university with a theology faculty. By 1962 that sum had been increased, including £20,000 to purchase a site in Nottingham, and in November of that year the Church Commissioners requested a Measure that would enable them to grant a loan of up to £1 million for these grants. It was accepted without debate.[36] This was to result in the redevelopment of an existing college, Queen's College, Birmingham, which was to become an ecumenical college shared with the Methodist Church. By 1965 a further report

---

33 GS 42.
34 Noted in the Annual Report of ACCM for 1972 in GS 152.
35 CA 1346.
36 *Report on the Capital Needs of the Theological Colleges and Training Houses for Women*, CA 1419.

on capital expenditure[37] showed that just under £1.2 million had been spent on the colleges either for the restoration of an existing asset or the possible creation of a new one, and that 60 per cent of that (£716,000 in total, which in 2010 figures would be approximately £10 million[38]) had come from central grants. While the colleges were content collectively to see money being spent on existing institutions there was an understandable reluctance to see the creation of new, potentially rival institutions, and in the event the Nottingham site was granted to the London College of Divinity, who were able to move there from Northwood to become St John's College, Nottingham in 1970.[39]

In the first part of the decade the Southwark Ordination Course, which provided part-time training for men still in employment, had been started. In the 1963 CACTM Annual Report it was noted that the bishops' inspectors 'commend the Course strongly and hope that this courageous experiment will receive every encouragement'. By 1964 the Annual Report was able to say that the first 14 men from the course had been ordained, of whom four would continue in their secular work, two were giving part-time help in their parishes which would become full-time when they retired, and the remainder were serving normal full-time curacies in the Diocese of Southwark. Its official recognition by the bishops as a part-time course was the precursor of future developments in ordination training that would eventually become a major change in the pattern of theological education for many ordinands, although that broader change was still some years off.

By the mid-1960s the number of recommended candidates was declining and that inevitably had an effect on the theological colleges.[40] There were 20 per cent fewer ordinands than places at the colleges towards the end of the decade[41] and this provoked a financial crisis. The Church Assembly, which met about half

---

37 CA 1563.

38 According to the Historical UK Inflation website http://safalra.com/other/historical-uk-inflation-price-conversion

39 The London College of Divinity was the subtitle of St John, Highbury, the principal of whom had the correspondence with Randall Davidson, then Bishop of Rochester, mentioned in Chapter 2. The students from that college had been evacuated at the beginning of World War Two and the college had a peripatetic existence until it moved to Northwood in 1957. (From information supplied by Bishop Colin Buchanan, a former Principal of St John's, Nottingham.)

40 Paul Welsby, 1984, *The History of the Church of England 1945–1980*, Oxford: OUP, pp.143–6 covers the whole issue.

41 The figures given in the de Bunsen report were that in 1937 there were 24 theological college which could accommodate 1,125 ordinands. By the time of the report in 1968 there were 25 residential theological colleges in England, training 1,060 ordinands, but with accommodation for 1,369.

the cost of training and with LEAs meeting the other half, could not be expected to subsidize empty places.

At the same time there was some criticism of the style of training offered in most colleges. It had changed little from earlier in the century and in the atmosphere of the 1960s it was being seen as too narrowly academic and not adequately preparing clergy for the parochial task. The House of Bishops in June 1965 accepted a proposal from the Chairman of CACTM, the Bishop of Lincoln, that an existing theological college should be encouraged to 'start a new form of training, which makes planned practical experience the starting point of theological education'. They were also sympathetic to a proposal for a final year of training 'in which the study of theology is constantly related to ministerial training and the needs of the church in the contemporary world', although understandably the bishops were concerned at any increase in the length of training.[42]

College councils and their principals, some of whom were also aware of the challenge posed by the non-residential training method adopted by the Southwark Ordination Course, were inevitably concerned about their future. The principals therefore asked the bishops for an independent review. At first the bishops were uncertain about the Commission and Ramsey wrote to Canon Basil Moss, the recently appointed new General Secretary of ACCM asking for a clearer brief on what was intended.[43] Moss said he would refer the matter to a meeting of the Council at which the Chairman of the Principals' Conference would be present (Alan Webster, Principal of Lincoln Theological College, later Dean of Norwich, then of St Paul's). The Council supported the proposal of a 'fairly independent Commission' by a two-thirds majority.[44]

ACCM also produced a brief for the Commission. They believed that the traditional comprehensiveness of the theological outlook of the Church of England must be respected, and that among the questions which the Commission should examine should be the size of colleges, their relationship to faculties of theology, whether there should be specialized colleges for older men and auxiliary ministries, and whether new experiments were needed, including relationships with colleges of other denominations.

---

42 Ramsey papers, Vol. 73, p. 144.
43 Ramsey papers, Vol. 90, p. 234.
44 Ramsey papers, Vol. 90, p. 252.

Ramsey accepted that there was a need for a commission and, on the suggestion of the ACCM Council, Sir Bernard de Bunsen, Principal of Chester College of Education, was appointed chairman. Kenneth Haworth, Dean of Salisbury and Henry Chadwick, Regius Professor of Divinity in Oxford were the other two members and Basil Moss, the General Secretary of ACCM, was Secretary. The Report was published in 1968[45] and it made four main recommendations: that most colleges should be in or near universities with faculties of theology, that they should be larger than had been traditionally the case on both educational and financial grounds (they recommended an ideal size of 120 students per college), that older and younger ordinands should train together and that ecumenical training should be developed. In order to achieve these recommendations they made a number of specific suggestions of possible unions of colleges, none of which in the event came about other than the amalgamation of Clifton Theological College and Tyndale Hall, both of which were in Bristol, and in the evangelical tradition, to form Trinity College, Bristol.

The archbishops in consultation with ACCM appointed a Joint Planning Group to work on the details of the proposals. The group included the Chairman of ACCM, the Chairman of the Training Committee (the Bishop of St Edmundsbury and Ipswich) and three college principals, one of whom was Principal of Cuddesdon, Robert Runcie.[46] They were not convinced by the arguments for amalgamations in all cases but favoured the possibility of clusters of colleges working together when near universities with faculties of theology, but they also believed that some colleges should be self-contained and separate from universities. They also hoped that the colleges themselves should be left to come up with proposals and that there should be no control from 'the centre'.

At a debate in the Church Assembly in November 1968 it was acknowledged that there was a reluctance on the part of some colleges to face the issues raised by the de Bunsen report and a motion was passed:

---

45 *Theological Colleges for Tomorrow*, Church Information Office, 1968. Published for the Archbishops of Canterbury and York and for the Advisory Council for the Church's Ministry.

46 One of the proposals of the de Bunsen Report was that Cuddesdon and St Stephen's Oxford should amalgamate. A. N. Wilson, who had been a student at St Stephen's, wrote a book about the college in 1978 called *Unguarded Hours* (Secker and Warburg), in which he suggested that the College had become a hot-bed of homosexuality. That fact was well known even in the 1960s and Runcie was widely reported among theological college students at the time to have said that he had not become Principal of Cuddesdon 'to see it go co-ed'.

That if constructive proposals are not submitted by the colleges by 1st March 1969, ACCM be instructed to ask the Joint Planning Group to make proposals to the colleges, and to report the colleges' answers to the Assembly in November 1969, or at the subsequent session together with its own recommendations made after consultation with the Bishops.[47]

By 1970 the Church Assembly, in almost its final act, received a report from ACCM[48] which gave the Assembly two choices: Policy A, which was that no attempt should be made to interfere with the freedom of the colleges to determine their own future; or Policy B, which recognized that reorganization must happen and that the House of Bishops had the power to withdraw recognition from any college refusing to co-operate. The Church Assembly voted by a majority for Policy B. When it became clear that the colleges would not be able to resolve all the issues by themselves ACCM asked the archbishops to appoint another commission to prepare a scheme for the regrouping of theological colleges. It was chaired by Runcie, by then Bishop of St Albans, and included the Principal of Edinburgh Theological College, Canon Kenneth Woollcombe, later Bishop of Oxford, and D. R. Wingram, a former headmaster of Monkton Combe School. The report, at first strictly confidential, made a series of recommendations designed to ensure that there were training places for 850 residential students, which would include women candidates for lay ministry, and with an upper limit for the number of ordinands in each college. It also sought to ensure that there was a reasonable balance of churchmanship between the colleges, with about 300 places in 'Evangelical' colleges, 220 in 'Tractarian' colleges and 325 in 'other' colleges.[49] The report was sent to college councils asking them to respond to the House of Bishops. The House then came up with some final proposals which largely followed the advice of the Runcie Commission and which resulted in the almost immediate closure of some colleges.

For the others there followed a period of negotiations, horse trading, arguments and special pleading, and eventually by the middle of the 1970s

---

47 The resolution and history of the whole discussion is contained in *Report by the House of Bishops on the Reorganisation of the Theological Colleges*, GS 20.

48 CA 1766.

49 A first draft of the report is in Ramsey papers, Vol. 192, pp. 307–26, 3 September 1970. It went into details about some proposed college amalgamations and closures and formed the basis for some discussions with various colleges.

the number of colleges had been reduced from 25 to 14. Ripon Hall and Cuddesdon, both colleges just outside Oxford, were amalgamated to become Ripon College, Cuddesdon. Wells and Salisbury Theological Colleges were amalgamated on the Salisbury site. At Cambridge, Westcott House and Ridley Hall formed a 'cluster' with Wesley College, the Methodist training college in Cambridge and Westminster College then of the Presbyterian Church of England and later of the United Reformed Church. Tyndale Hall and Clifton Theological Colleges combined in Bristol to form Trinity College, Bristol. Ordination training for theology graduates from King's College, London, which took place originally at Warminster but then moved to Canterbury, was finally ended in 1976. The two colleges for older men at Rochester and Worcester were closed, as were St Chad's, Durham, Lichfield Theological College, the 'seminary'-type college of Kelham and the two pre-training colleges of Brasted and the Bernard Gilpin Society in Durham, to be replaced first by Ian Ramsey College on the Brasted site but eventually, in 1977, by a new non-residential pre-theological course known as the Aston Training Scheme. All the surviving colleges and the newly united colleges formed links with universities with faculties of theology, and many of them also had women alongside men training together for ministry, although not yet ordained ministry for the women. By then, more courses on the style of the Southwark Ordination Course had also been established, although only the Southwark course and the Northern Ordination Course based at Manchester were recognized for training for stipendiary ministry.

Non-stipendiary ministry

Discussion about the possibility of men being ordained while remaining in their secular employment was talked about long before the 1960s. Throughout the nineteenth century there had been severe disincentives for ordained men to continue in gainful employment outside the parochial system other than as ordained schoolmasters or ordained dons,[50] but Thomas Arnold had argued for the ordination as deacons of working men in 1841[51] and in 1887 the 'Deacons (Church of England) bill attempted to change the law, but it was defeated in

---

50 Mark Hodge, 1983, *Non-Stipendiary Ministry in the Church of England*, London: CIO (GS 583A) contained a 'Historical Background' by Patrick H. Vaughan, from which some of this information is obtained.

51 Vaughan in Hodge, p. 9.

Convocation largely because of the strength of feeling that ordination admitted a man to a professional occupation.[52] In 1900 the Secretary of the Additional Curates Society, Paul Petit, asked in a letter in *the Church Times*:

> Why cannot the rule which forbids clergymen to engage in secular occupations be withdrawn in the case of deacons? Why cannot the diaconate be thrown open to those many hundreds of devout Churchmen who are earning their own livings, and even now are spending their whole Sundays and all their spare time in helping on the Church's work?[53]

Nothing happened as a result of that letter, presumably because it was felt that the Convocation decision of 13 years before would not change.

Pressure for change did not go away, especially with the work of Roland Allen, who in 1923 wrote *Voluntary Clergy* and whose arguments were accepted by some bishops, including Headlam and Burrows, Chairman of CACTM at the time.[54] However, the Lambeth Conference of 1930 took a different view: 'The Conference ... cannot recommend a widespread adoption of this proposal', but it did allow a bishop to ordain voluntary clergy 'provided he had the approval of all the bishops of his Province'.[55] Within the Church of England the Commission on the Staffing of Parishes[56] had called attention to three arguments for voluntary clergy: that it was 'apostolic' and primitive; that some clergy thus occupied will be better able to understand the problems of the laity in ordinary occupations; and that it would help in the provision of ministry.[57] In the Convocation discussions on the matter in 1932 some supported such a view but the Convocation was clearly divided and was disinclined to follow the path of change.[58] F. R. Barry supported the idea of voluntary clergy in *The Relevance of the Church*,[59] and the experience of the worker priest movement in France after the war revived discussion on the matter again in the 1950s. In 1960 the whole

---

52 Vaughan in Hodge, p. 10.

53 *Church Times,* 20 July 1900.

54 Vaughan in Hodge, p. 11.

55 Vaughan in Hodge, p. 11.

56 *Report of the Commission on Staffing of Parishes,* 1930, CA 334, Church Assembly and SPCK.

57 *Report of the Commission on Staffing of Parishes,* p. 35: pp. 34–9 deal with the matter, the later part dealing with their rejection of the notion of men being ministers of the sacrament only.

58 *York Journal of Convocation,* January 1932, pp. 20–5, 55–72. *Chronicle of Convocation,* Vol XLIV, pp. 262–96 (for Canterbury Convocation).

59 F. R. Barry, 1935, *The Relevance of the Church,* London: Nisbet, pp. 188–218.

matter was discussed by a variety of contributors in *Part-Time Priests* edited by Robin Denniston.[60]

Meanwhile the revision of Canon Law instituted by Archbishop Fisher had produced some change. When the draft Canon 83 'of the Manner of Life of Ministers' was considered by the convocations a Joint Committee was set up to examine 'what changes are desirable and practicable in law relating to the pursuit by a clergyman of a gainful secular occupation'. The committee reported in 1955 and was sympathetic to clergy earning money through other occupations. Among the members of that committee was Mervyn Stockwood, soon to become Bishop of Southwark, who was influential both in the development of the Southwark Ordination Course and in implementing change to allow non-stipendiary ministry. What became in 1959 Canon C28, allowed a priest to pursue a secular occupation with a licence from the bishop.

> The Bishop of the Diocese shall have power to grant such a licence after consultation with the PCC of the parish in which the Minister holds office, or to refuse such a licence after consultation with that Council.

Any such priest who was refused had the right of appeal to the Archbishop of the Province. In the 1958 Convocation discussions that preceded that change the Archbishop of York (Ramsey) in a presidential address did not think that the road to 'part-time' priests should be barred, but that we should not tolerate 'mass priests'. 'There can be no division between the ministry of the Sacrament and ministry of the Word.'[61] That became a key concept in later discussions about what eventually became known as Non-Stipendiary Ministry, but with Ramsey's contribution the balance of argument was clearly moving in the direction of allowing such ministries.

That shift was further affected by the 1958 Lambeth Conference, where the bishops concluded 'there is no theological principle which forbids a suitable man from being ordained priest while continuing in his lay occupation' and it encouraged Provinces to make provision along such lines.[62] Ramsey, who became Archbishop of Canterbury in 1961, initiated the next development by asking CACTM to set up a Working Party to examine the issue of 'supplementary

---

60 Robin Denniston (ed.), 1960, *Part-Time Priests*, London: Skeffington.
61 *York Journal of Convocation* 1958–59, pp. 24, 25.
62 Lambeth Conference 1958, Resolution 89, 'Supplementary Ministry'.

ministries'. It was chaired by John Robinson, Chairman of the Southwark Ordination Course who was Bishop of Woolwich in the Diocese of Southwark, where Stockwood was the Diocesan Bishop. The Working Party's report was produced in 1961, but was never formally published.[63] It urged 'active experiment', but did not like the phrase 'part-time priests' so much as priests

> truly called to a full-time ministry, much of whose time is, and should be, occupied in matters very different from those which are the concerns of the parish priest. It is by tapping that source that we believe a fuller ministry should now be provided.[64]

Stockwood and Robinson then exercised the freedom given to them by the change in Canon Law to ordain six non-stipendiary ministers in Southwark Cathedral in 1963. That was followed by the Clergy (Ordinations and Miscellaneous Provisions) Measure of 1964, which removed the final legal constraints. The measure was permissive, not proscriptive, so any development depended on how a bishop saw the issue in his diocese, but the possibility of the development of such ministry was then firmly established.

In 1968 ACCM published a working party report, *A Supporting Ministry*,[65] which discussed 'the theological and practical questions involved and made recommendations about the selection, training and supervision of these men',[66] and in the following year produced *Selection and Training for the Auxiliary Parochial Ministry* (CA 1923) which preferred the title *Auxiliary Priests* and went into greater detail on selection.[67] On the matter of standards it noted that *A Supporting Ministry* had said: 'We reject the idea that auxiliary priests should be regarded as "second-best" and we emphasise that standards of selection and testing should be as careful as for full-time ministry.'

The second report fully agreed and,

> we conclude that it would be right to set the sights high, even if only a few men were involved. If, however, it should turn out that auxiliary ministries

---

63 A copy is in Ramsey Papers, Vol. 12, pp. 65–78.

64 Page 14 of the report in the Ramsey Papers.

65 *A Supporting Ministry*, 1968, Church Information Office.

66 Welsby, *History*, p. 142. In fact the working party that produced this report for ACCM's Ministry Committee was chaired by Paul Welsby, who modestly made no reference to that fact in his book on the history of the Church of England.

67 That working party, set up by ACCM's Training Committee, was also chaired by Paul Welsby.

multiply and become a norm in the Church of England, then insistence, from the outset, upon the best will be a source of strength to the whole life of the Church.[68]

It set some age requirements, believing that no one should be ordained to this ministry until he was well established in his secular occupation, which meant that no one should commence training until he was at least 30, but they also had an upper age limit of 50 as they believed any sort of retirement ministry should be clearly distinguished from this type of ministry. In terms of the training for this ministry they recommended that it should not last less than three years and that there should be at least 21 residential weekends over the three years and a summer school of at least two weeks each year.

The report was debated on five separate sessions during the three days of the Spring 1969 Assembly. The most fundamental objection came from a layman from Southwell Diocese, D. E. Stocker, who thought it required men to be dishonest with their employers.

> In my opinion a Christian has a primary duty to do the job for which his employers pay him. That is the first thing. What does the report say? . . . 'He must be primarily a priest whose secular work brings him sufficient reward to enable him to attend to his priestly functions: he must not be primarily a layman who is prepared to devote some of his leisure hours to being a part-time priest. If these general principles are borne in mind, we think the answer will be clear in many cases.' I would think 'If these general principles are borne in mind' should more truly read 'If this general lack of principle was borne in mind' because the two lines before are, in my opinion, a plain declaration of dishonest intent . . . I am told I am speaking against a scriptural principle. I suggest it is not a scriptural principle, but a scriptural practice and these are not the same, and that what was true and applied properly in the days of self-employed craftsmen cannot necessarily apply in terms of employees in the complex modern situation.[69]

In the course of the debate the Chairman of ACCM, the Bishop of Warrington, responded to Mr Stocker's apprehensions, which he described as 'only natural'

---

68 CA 1723, p. 6.
69 CA proceedings, Vol. XLIX, 1969, p. 125f.

but 'it is my conviction that we must prove the validity of this conception in practice',[70] while Welsby, who had chaired the group that produced the report, said:

> it is only right that the employer should be brought into this. I do not think it is fair to an employer if one of his men goes off to be trained and ordained to the ministry of the Church without his knowing it.[71]

Various amendments were suggested but all were rejected and the original proposals accepted. It was then left to ACCM to decide the practicalities of selection conferences. To start with, there was a suggestion that special conferences should be held at weekends for candidates for auxiliary parochial ministry, but in the event that was modified and candidates for such ministries:

> were being invited to certain of the regular Bishops' Selection conferences, so as to form about 50 per cent of the candidates at a conference. By using the same conferences for the different types of ministry a common standard should be maintained. At the same time care would be taken to ensure that the selectors at such conferences fully understood what was required in candidates for auxiliary ministries.[72]

It was left to the selectors in each case to decide whether the demands of a man's secular job could be held satisfactorily in conjunction with a priestly role.

There was also some discussion in the Church Assembly debate on the distinction between auxiliary parochial ministry and what some referred to as retirement ministries, although that term was disliked by the bishops who preferred post-retirement ministries. These referred to men usually over the age of 58 who had taken early retirement, enabling them to devote most of their time to parochial ministry in the parishes to which they were licensed. At the beginning of the decade candidates for retirement ministry and, indeed, all candidates over the age of 40 did not go to selection conferences but were selected within their dioceses, but that was changed in 1966, so although there was some debate about the upper age limit, in practice the decision on such

---

70 CA proceedings, p. 137.

71 CA proceedings, p. 131.

72 ACCM Candidates Committee minutes, 24 October 1969.

candidates was left to individual bishops. It was left to the selectors in each case to decide whether the demands of a man's secular job could be held satisfactorily in conjunction with a priestly role.

Arguments continued, and still continue, about the most appropriate title. Auxiliary parochial ministry was replaced by auxiliary pastoral ministry,[73] but then non-stipendiary ministry became the approved one by the bishops, but some objected to the emphasis being put on how a clergyman is paid. The earlier title of self-supporting ministry was considered unacceptable because personal piety would suggest that no ministry can be sustained without the support of God. Auxiliary ministry was considered at one time, as was supplementary ministry and supporting ministry, but were rejected as implying it was somehow a second-class ministry. Priests in secular employment did not cover those who were retired but exercising a parochial ministry, while an honorary ministry implied a question about the nature of stipendiary ministry.

But by the end of the decade the Church had changed substantially. It had definitely decided to have a more structurally diverse ministry with recognition of non-stipendiary ministry as a category. There was by the end of the period the possibility of men training for ordination non-residentially. There was a growing debate about the possibility of women being ordained. But there was continuing concern about how many stipendiary clergy the Church would have in the future, given the sharp decline in the number of candidates over the decade. The consequences of that and alternative forms of training then available also heralded profound changes for the theological colleges: a reduction from 25 to 14 institutions over a few years after the decade would be a shock for any educational enterprise. What was certain was that by 1970 the Church of England would never be quite the same as it had been ten years earlier.

---

73 Reported in the 1970 Annual Report, GS 11.

10

Keeping Up to Date: Revisions to the Selection Procedures, 1945–98

The Church of England was fortunate to be in the right place at the right time when selection conferences were started. The War Office selection boards were widely considered to be a great advance in selection methods, and were adopted by many other organizations, including the Civil Service. If the Church was to remain in touch with the best thinking about selection it needed advice from others, and at various critical stages in the second half of the twentieth century it sought that advice.

As the century progressed, in many areas of life, not merely selection, there was often more attention given to the process of any activity than to the content of the activity itself. Was the process designed in a fair and reasonable way to get the best results? The revisions to the Church's selection system could be seen as a response to that trend, although they often emerged in practice more from a sense that circumstances were changing and that something that was reasonable could, by a process of change, be made even better.

From 1945 to 1978

The Selection Committee of CACTM from 1945 and then the Candidates' Committee of ACCM from 1966 kept the selection conference programme under review. From the outset there was a policy that selectors should continue to talk about candidates until they came to a common view. If that proved impossible then they could record 'no decision', which in practice was very rare. Candidates could attend three selection conferences in all, normally with at least a two-year gap between each, when on each occasion they would encounter a different set of selectors. The committees believed that was sufficient protection against wrong decisions against any particular candidate, since by then a candidate would have seen 15 different selectors all of whom thought he should not proceed to training.

One issue that came up from time to time was the group observation, which was the new, and key, element in the selection process devised by the War Office selection boards. In late 1949 the Chairman of the Selection Committee (Canon D. Armytage) observed a Civil Service selection board, which, like CACTM, had adopted a system based on the War Office selection boards. As a result of his visit some more detailed arrangements were made for the observation of discussion groups.[1] But by 1953 a member of the committee was questioning the value of these exercises.[2] Nonetheless they were retained and in 1956 another committee member strongly advocated closer observation of them.

> He suggested that the men should be divided into groups and set problems, which they could then discuss thoroughly, with the selectors in the background. A parish priest could be perfectly competent in dealing with individuals, and very bad at dealing with groups of people.[3]

Group observation had always been part of the process and the committee member's insistence resulted in it being maintained.

The 1960s saw three major issues considered. First, in 1963 following some experiments over the previous year, it was recommended to the bishops that women should be included among the selectors, either for the layman's role or as educational selectors, which recommendation the bishops implemented. Second, in 1966 it was agreed to hold panel interviews during some experimental selection conferences, but following negative reports on them by members of the committee that experiment was effectively abandoned in 1967.[4] Third, there were a number of discussions in the committee regarding psychological profiling of candidates, with advice being taken from various specialists in the field.[5] The matter was finally resolved in 1967, by which time CACTM had become ACCM, and its Candidates Committee reported to the new ACCM Training Committee.

---

1 CACTM Selection Committee minutes, 1 December 1949.

2 Selection Committee minutes, 6 February 1953.

3 Selection Committee minutes, 28 May 1956.

4 Selection Committee minutes, 28 July 1967.

5 Selection Committee minutes, 22 July, 28 October, 2 December 1965, 20 May and 16 September 1966.

It was the Training Committee that effectively decided not to use such tests at selection conferences, largely as a result of comments from two members. Canon Kenneth Woollcombe, later Bishop of Oxford, had experienced the use of such tests in the church in America and believed they were potentially damaging for emotionally disturbed candidates. Another member, L. Roberts, who worked for British Rail, had seen them used regularly there and reported that British Rail had decided to discontinue them largely for the reasons that Canon Woollcombe had reported. While that decision ended the discussion in the Candidates Committee the matter returned to the Training Committee at its following meeting. The Bishop of Manchester had reported that

> The Bishop of East Carolina [T. H. Wright] had told him that in his diocese a psychological test was used which involved a detailed questionnaire to be completed by the candidate who then saw the psychiatrist for about an hour. The result was that 50 per cent of the men coming forward were turned down. The subsequent history of these men had confirmed these recommendations as correct.

The ACCM staff members were asked to make further enquiries of the American Episcopalian Church and to report in writing to the Training Committee, but the matter was dropped, largely it appears because of the cost of using professional psychologists.[6] They were not introduced.[7]

Despite those various discussions and occasional experiments the selection procedure essentially remained unchanged until towards the end of the 1970s. When criticisms were offered as in a detailed article in *the Church Times* on 30 August 1974 from a lay member of the General Synod, Tim Belbin, the response within ACCM was that any selection system that said no to some people was bound to come in for criticism from time to time; the decision was taken not to reply to the article.[8] The essential defence was that a system that had been in continued use for over 30 years and which was trusted by most bishops need not be changed. When the Candidates' Committee reviewed its procedures at a residential meeting in September 1978 it decided to make no fundamental change to the conferences programme.

---

6 Training Committee, 1–2 October 1968.

7 ACCM Council minutes, 20 September 1968.

8 Church of England archives ACCM/CAND/SEL/POL/23.

A time of review 1978–83

Three factors brought about a different approach. The first was changes in personnel. The Candidates' Committee was the key body in overseeing the selection process. It was chaired by a bishop and had 12–14 members, with a slight majority of clergy but with at least five laity. Inevitably the Chairman and the Senior Selection Secretary, who was Secretary of the Committee, were critical people in the process.

In the review of its procedures in September 1978 the Bishop of Aston, Mark Green, was chairman. As an army chaplain during World War Two he had been involved in helping establish the early selection conferences, running a church house in Germany where some of the early conferences took place. He had a distinguished war record, was mentioned in dispatches in 1945, and from 1947 to 1948 had been Director of Service Candidates in CACTM. He had served on the Candidates' Committee for many years and had become chairman in 1976. Given his involvement in the creating of the selection process it was not surprising that he was committed to maintaining and, if necessary, defending the existing procedures.

The Secretary was Arthur Mawson. He had joined the ACCM staff in 1973 after being Vicar of a parish in Sheffield for seven years, and had become Senior Selection Secretary in September 1976. He was acting Chief Secretary when Canon Hugh Melinsky left in early 1978 until Canon John Tiller arrived in September 1978, and had already been extended in his post beyond the normal five-year contract of ACCM staff by the time of the September 1978 meeting. Perhaps inevitably he was not looking for major change towards the end of his time.

In 1979 Mawson was appointed to Exeter Cathedral and was succeeded by John Cox, who had joined the staff in April 1978 having already served on the Candidates Committee. In December 1979 Bishop Green resigned as Chairman of the Candidates Committee having been asked by the Bishop of Birmingham to be Diocesan Director of Ordinands as well as Bishop of Aston; he thought that it was impossible to be Chairman of the Committee as well as a DDO. He was succeeded by the Bishop of Bedford, Alec Graham, who had been Warden of Lincoln Theological College before becoming Bishop of Bedford. On leaving Lincoln he had written to the Chairman of ACCM, the Bishop of Portsmouth, expressing some criticisms of the selection process. Those two changes were undoubtedly critical in bringing about a major review of the selection procedures, for without them the review would probably never have happened.

The second factor was a working party on the psychological assessment of candidates. Ten years had passed since the matter was considered in 1967 and it arose again as a result of the letter Alec Graham had written to the Chairman in May 1977:

Too many students are recommended for training who are either of rather low calibre and personality or who have defects of personality which will gravely impair their ministerial usefulness ... Too much time has been wasted here in dealing with students of cantankerous and bloody-minded dispositions, and to others who are spineless and feeble, failing to do justice to life here in a way which would have satisfied any fair-minded employer. These observations apply to both men and women ... there has been too high an incidence of disorders of personality, some of which were apparent even at the time of their medical examination and selection ... More attention should be given to assessment of personality and to psychiatrist/psychologist evaluation at the time of selection, and this should be obligatory for both husbands and wives. Of course, this will be more expensive than the present method of selection, but just think how much money will be saved and how much anguish saved by weeding unsuitable people out in good time.[9]

That had been considered in the September 1978 residential meeting, but no major changes were agreed at that time. However, by late 1978 Alec Graham had been appointed Chairman of the Lay Candidates Committee and was asked to chair a working party to look into the whole question of the psychological assessment of all candidates.

The working group first tested the extent of any problem with the current procedures. Through a questionnaire to college and course principals they asked how many candidates had been ordained about whom the staff had considerable doubts, to which the answer was 5.6 per cent. This was out of a total of 1,480 ordinands at the college and courses whose principals replied. One in 20 of those being ordained did indicate a significant problem, made the more acute by the fact that once a man was ordained it was quite difficult to force him to leave the ministry.

---

9 Church of England archives ACCM/CAND/SEL/POL/42, printed as an Appendix to the report on *The Psychological Assessment of Candidates for Ordination.*

The working party made a number of recommendations. On the core question of psychological tests it recommended not to introduce them into ACCM's central procedures.

> Many of the advantages that some advocates of psychological testing see in tests ... may be able to be gained from those in the church who have assimilated the lessons that the study of psychology may bring without using its language. It may well be more appropriate to use the skills of that growing body of people ... rather than introducing an element into the selection procedures that some would consider alien.[10]

It recommended that the place for that use should be the dioceses.

The report also suggested five broad changes to the procedure which they believed should allow selectors to obtain a fuller picture of candidates: longer interviews with each candidate, from 30 to 40 minutes, increased opportunities for assessing a candidate's behaviour in group settings, a written exercise to test pastoral approaches, ending the rule that there should be no discussion between selectors of candidates until the final assessment session; and, possibly most significantly, having joint selection conferences for both men candidates for ordination and women candidates for lay ministry. The recommendations were accepted at a joint meeting of the Lay and Ordination Candidates Committee in September 1979 to be tried for an experimental year.

The third major strand leading to change was the appointment of an external consultant. Shortly after the Candidates' Committee accepted the psychological assessment report, Cox made contact with a former head of the Civil Service selection boards, Kenneth Murray. Murray had served as a young army officer on the group that developed the War Office selection board proposals, and had also been used by the Church of Scotland to assist them as a psychologist on their selection boards for ministers. The Candidates Committee, who had accepted the principle that thinking about the best methods of selection had developed since the first WOSBs, agreed in March 1980 that for a year he should be a consultant for the period of experiment. During that year staff also observed a wide range of other selection methods in industry, the military and other churches, which experience was fed into the review process.

---

10 *The Psychological Assessment of Candidates for Ordination*, para. 24.

Murray presented his final report to a joint meeting of the Ordination Candidates Committee and the Lay Candidates Committee in December 1980, by which time Graham had become chairman of both Committees. Murray noted that 16 experimental conferences had been held in 1980, three of which had been joint conferences for lay candidates and ordination candidates.

The most major change he proposed was to divide candidates into two groups of eight, each with some selectors specifically allocated to each group. Murray observed of the old system of each selector interviewing 18 candidates, 'No other selection system investigated expected selectors to interview so many candidates as part of a selection procedure.'[11] The proposed two-group structure would also allow far greater opportunities for candidates to be observed in how they reacted within three group exercises. At a later stage, when a draft report on the review was presented to the House of Bishops, the Bishop of Liverpool (David Sheppard), supported by some other urban bishops, suggested that these exercises might be non-verbal ones to test candidates' abilities at working in teams. This was investigated by the staff but it was concluded that the level of training for selectors this would entail would be difficult to achieve.[12] Nonetheless the amount of observed group work was substantially increased.

Murray also suggested that the experiment of a written exercise should continue and that there should be a mid-conference meeting of selectors. It was stressed that this was not to start making any provisional assessment but to compare notes on responses to exercises and to identify what needed to be looked at in subsequent interviews. He also recommended that references, which had hitherto been seen only by the Selection Secretary, who gave a summary to the selectors at the final assessment session, should be given to the selectors before the conference. He recognized this was a sensitive issue, changing the practice of over 30 years, but commented:

far more is to be gained from free access to referees' reports beforehand than might be lost ... It is not 'provable', but the philosophy of telling assessors as much as possible and trusting them as much as possible to keep their independence is to me, as to many others, much the sounder.

---

11 *The Time of Review* report, para. 4.2.

12 From personal conversation with the Venerable John Cox who, as Senior Selection Secretary at the time, attended the House of Bishops discussions on these matters.

There has not been in my experience any lessening of the independence of judgement of assessors, only an increase in confidence and sensitivity.[13]

The Committee accepted Murray's report and agreed to a further period to try out some of what he had recommended.

At an earlier stage of the review process the whole thing had nearly been derailed by a recommendation from the General Synod's Joint Budget Committee, who wanted as a cost-cutting exercise to increase the numbers of candidates at conferences from 18 to 20.[14] This would have presented a major problem for the experimental conferences with longer interviews, as it was envisaged that a conference might have fewer rather than more candidates. At the 1978 Candidates Committee Conference it had already been noted that the total annual cost to the Church of selecting was less than the cost of training three candidates, and the *Psychological Assessment of Candidates for Ordination* report had said on the financial implications:

> The Church at present gets its selection procedures very cheaply. If a man is selected at 23 and is active in full time ministry until retirement the Church will have spent something in excess of £1/4 million on him during his ministry. The consequences of wrong selection, not only in terms of financial waste but also for the man himself in facing a life of often growing frustration and unhappiness, and for the parishes in which he serves are very considerable. It is well worth taking a good deal of time and, if necessary, spending a good deal of money to ensure the best possible method of selection.[15]

Although it took time to contest the Joint Budget Committee's suggestion it was finally accepted that the way of organizing selection conferences must be determined by the committee responsible for it and not by a financial body.

During the experimental period, reactions from both selectors and candidates were collected and reactions to the changes were positive.[16] The major changes had all been well received. Of the longer interviews in the experimental conferences it was observed that 98 per cent of the selectors and 77 per cent of the candidates had felt that the new length of interviews was about right.

---

13 *The Time of Review* report, para. 5.3.
14 Candidates Committee minutes, for 7 December 1979, 23 May 1980 and 18 July 1980.
15 *Psychological Assessment*, para. 22.
16 Candidates Committee minutes, 21 October 1981.

This compared to the traditional conferences where 45 per cent of the candidates and 80 per cent of the selectors felt that the 25-minute interviews were too short. For the increased number of group observation exercises guidelines had been drawn up to assist selectors in observing groups. Selectors were asked to observe how candidates related to the group as a whole, or whether they just related to the same few with similar backgrounds; whether they sought to dominate, withdraw into silence, always wanted to pair off with someone else, and whether they took the discussion further forwards or merely repeated the views of others. They were also asked to observe whether candidates were able to defend their viewpoints or quickly submit, whether they always followed the majority, or were willing to defend a minority view, whether they were supportive of the less able, or took the opportunity to prove their superiority, and whether they listened to what others were saying and were able to accept disagreement and criticism, and offer it in a way that did not alienate others. They were also asked to note how they related to others' leadership and, if at mixed conferences, whether they related to the opposite sex without manipulation or patronizing attitudes. Of the new pattern of group discussions 42 per cent felt they provided a great deal of additional information, 42 per cent felt they provided a reasonable amount and only 5 per cent felt they provided nothing at all. This contrasted to, at traditional conferences, 12 per cent thinking that group exercises provided a great deal of additional information and 32 per cent feeling they provided little or nothing at all.

> At some conferences the information gleaned from the group exercises has proved very significant in the final recommendations. Some articulate and intellectually able candidates, who appeared good in interview, were seen to be domineering and grossly insensitive to others in the group situation. Other candidates who have appeared shy and lacking in confidence in interview have been seen to have considerable ability in gently leading a discussion along thoughtful lines. Properly conducted the group exercises provide a valuable supplement, and at times a corrective to the evidence of the interviews.[17]

A variety of written exercises had been tried at the conferences. The vast majority of the selectors felt they were a useful addition, 81 per cent felt it was

---

17 *Time of Review* report, para. 7.8.

quite helpful. It was agreed that the primary purpose should be to check pastoral understanding and sensitivity.

Seeing the references in advance was also reaffirmed by the experience of the experimental conferences; 78 per cent of those selectors who had attended the experiments thought it had been helpful. 'A number of selectors, including some chairmen, said that initially they were hostile to the idea of seeing references in advance, but that their experience on the Conferences caused them to change their views.'[18] It was recognized that this would also lessen the influence of the secretary. The experience of having an opportunity in the conference for the selectors to compare notes and identify issues that needed to be explored with individual candidates was also affirmed. Twenty-eight per cent of selectors at traditional conferences felt this would be unhelpful, but none of those on experimental conferences found that to be so. Thirty-two per cent of selectors at traditional conferences thought such meetings would be helpful, but 95 per cent of selectors at the experimental conferences found them to be so. A staff written report on the experiment commented:

> All the selectors agreed that this was helpful beyond what any of us had anticipated. Subsequent interviews were sharpened up as a result and the sense of teamwork among the selectors was greatly increased ... We carefully avoided any element of provisional assessment and concentrated entirely on identifying areas which required closer investigation in the case of each individual.[19]

Because at that time there were many more men candidates for ordination than women candidates for lay ministry it would have been impossible to have every conference mixed if there were to be a reasonable number of lay candidates at a conference. However, the advantages of observing candidates relating to members of the opposite sex were obvious, but a technical question was whether the distinction between ordained and lay ministry would be blurred. The evidence of the experimental conferences was that this was not the case; indeed one selector felt that it sharpened the process. The report recommended that all candidates for lay ministry should in future attend joint conferences, but that at mixed conferences there should always be at least a third of the candidates for lay ministry.

---

18 *Time of Review* report, para. 5.13.
19 *Time of Review* report, para. 6.5.

ACCM forwarded the report to the House of Bishops,[20] who considered it at two meetings in 1982 and approved the recommendations. The new scheme became effective from January 1983. One suggestion from the review process was, however, rejected by the bishops. It had been suggested that selection might be better achieved if there were a smaller number of selectors used more regularly; a group of about 80 used a few times each year was one suggestion. The bishops were reluctant to see selection in the hands of a small cadre of 'professional' selectors, preferring to have representatives of the wider Church involved in the process.[21]

A further element dealt with in the review was the writing of reports. After each conference the secretary produced the final report that was sent to the sponsoring bishop, but from time to time the question was raised whether it was appropriate for there to be some monitoring of the reports. At the July 1983 meeting of the Candidates Committee the chairman reported that the bishops had requested the committee to think how the chairmen of conferences could be involved in the reports. The practical difficulties of this seemed considerable and the committee was reluctant to accept the proposal. Eventually it was agreed that there could be an experimental period when the reports drafted by the secretaries would be sent to the chairmen of those conferences for their comments before they were sent to the bishops. That was accepted by the bishops and it was carried out for the first 12 conferences of 1984. In March the committee received a report on the monitoring experiment. It was noted that changes were made by the chairmen in only 15 out of the 142 reports written in that period and that only five of the changes involved more than a single word. The committee thought that this did not justify the cost, time and potential for delay and recommended that the original practice should be resumed. 'Whenever an especially difficult and sensitive report had to be written the secretary and chairman should be free to confer in whatever way they deemed appropriate.'[22]

In May 1984 it was reported that the ACCM council had accepted and even strengthened the committee's advice and on 8 June it was reported that the House of Bishops had accepted it.[23]

---

20 ACCM Council minutes, 24 November 1981.
21 From personal conversation with the Venerable John Cox (see footnote 12).
22 Candidates Committee minutes, 9 March 1984.
23 Candidates Committee minutes, 18 May, 8 June 1984.

Murray had also suggested that it was far easier to judge a candidate's suitability for a job if there were clear criteria against which they should be measured, so it was suggested also that there should be a report on criteria for selection. Four members of the Candidates Committee were asked to produce a draft. The Revd Richard Buck had been a residentiary Canon of Truro Cathedral until he moved in 1976 to be Vicar of St Mary's, Primrose Hill in London Diocese. Mrs Ann Cameron had joined the committee in 1973 while still a tutor with the National Marriage Guidance Council. She represented Oxford Diocese on General Synod. Fred East was a reader in Rochester Diocese and had been deputy secretary of the Ministry of Defence until he retired in 1980, and had joined the Candidates Committee shortly after his retirement. Cox was secretary.

While the suggestion of a report on criteria was understandable there is a variety of jobs that clergymen could do and the qualities needed for one clerical role might be very different for those needed for another. It was, perhaps, reasons like that, but also possibly a notion that all selectors instinctively knew what was needed in an effective ordained person, which had meant that very little had been produced on the subject since the 1942 joint memorandum of the Archbishops of Canterbury and York to the Forces Chaplains (Appendix I). The 1972 Handbook for Selectors stated:

> Selectors are appointed by the Bishops and are thus representatives of the whole Church; it would clearly be wrong for us to lay down absolute standards for selection. We rely on the Selectors' discretion in deciding where the line should be drawn.

The 1972 handbook went on to give some comments from the Candidates Committee: 'high standards should be maintained; there should be definite positive reasons on why a man should be ordained – not enough to say there are no reasons why not!'[24]

The difficulty of producing clearly defined criteria was recognized. 'Those who expect such a report as this to produce a neatly defined list of criteria with objective standards and a blueprint model of the ideal candidate will be disappointed.'[25] But having recognized that clergy should minister to the whole community and not just those who are regular churchgoers, the authors went

---

24 Church of England archives ACCM/CAND/SEL/POL/7.
25 *Selection for Ministry: A Report on Criteria*, para. 1.4.

on to comment on such matters as assessing spirituality, character, integrity, personality, and the quality of a candidate's mind.

> To pose the extremes: it is as possible for a person to have a first in theology or religious studies and yet not to have the quality of mind needed for the professional ministry of the church, as it is for a person to have the right quality of mind and no educational qualifications.[26]

There were three areas in the report that were later to occasion some debate, not least of all when the report was revised some years later. The first was the matter of vocation. The authors recognized that all Christians, whether ordained or not, are called to ministry, but for some there is the opportunity to exercise a particular leadership and authority role such as ordination confers. The question is from where such a call arises.

> No simple answer can be given to this question since the Holy Spirit works on the material that is available. For some the call begins with an inner recognition of the need, indeed the demand, to serve God in a particular way... This inner urge will be present in all who have a vocation to the professional ministry. But this should be complemented by the Church's confirmation that he has the necessary gifts, the right personality and attitude of mind, and the level of Christian commitment which would fit him for ministry within the Church. In all vocations the interior and exterior influences will vary in their precise proportions. But in the end for the sense of vocation to become an actual vocation they will both need to be present.[27]

That certainly represented the view of vocation current within ACCM at that time, but it was to be challenged, partly by the development of local ordained ministry, where candidates were often put forward by the congregation, but also by the more detailed examination of the nature of vocation in the 1989 report *Call to Order* mentioned in Chapter 1.

The second area related to a candidate's faith. They recognized that faith covered both the substance of what is believed and the commitment to living according to that faith. They said:

---

26 *Report on Criteria*, para. 9.10.
27 *Report on Criteria*, para. 4.4–5.

it is not enough for the candidate simply to reiterate his faith in Jesus Christ as 'Lord' and 'Saviour' as many do. He must go on to say what he means, coherently, in relation to his own experience, using language current in everyday life.[28]

They also believed that the candidate's faith needed to be tested over a period of time, 'in order to make sure that, as one whom we consulted put it, "the fire in the belly is not a flash in the pan".[29] They also argued for a candidate being open to growth and change. 'A glib and watertight faith that acknowledges no doubt becomes a tool of the devil than of God, for it does harm both to the gospel we proclaim and to the person proclaiming it.[30] However, they went on to say that they were very aware of the special difficulty experienced by those who represent the Church as members of its professional ministries.

Many feel that they are letting the side down if they admit to any doubts about any of the traditional teaching of the Church, and pretend that they believe it all, all the time. Yet the relief experienced by some of the most thoughtful Church members (and would-be members) when clergy or other professional representatives honestly acknowledge their own difficulties can be enormous. Naturally this must be done with discretion and pastoral consideration and for that reason is probably more appropriate to discussion in small groups or in a one-to-one situation than to proclamation from the pulpit.[31]

But they went on:

In order to be able to live with uncertainties and be open to fresh experience, knowledge, insights and ideas, a candidate's basic conviction needs to be all the stronger, and to be deeply rooted: to be strong but not rigid. Rigidity should not be mistaken for strength in faith any more than in steel. But firmness and strength there must be. The firmness is to be found, we suggest, not so much in commitment to creedal statements as

---

28 *Report on Criteria*, para. 5.3.
29 *Report on Criteria*, para. 5.4.
30 *Report on Criteria*, para. 5.8.
31 *Report on Criteria*, para. 5.12.

in the strength of the candidate's personal commitment to God in Christ and the effect of this upon his life so far, the strength and restlessness of his yearning for God, and the strength of his conviction that God is the truth. This will hold him firm in the exploration of his faith.[32]

Some years later that approach too was to be challenged.

The third matter, which they described under 'sensitive areas', was the delicate one of homosexuality. They recognized that the difficulty is increased because the Church as a whole has not come to an agreed mind on some of these issues, yet they are significant in ministry and cannot be ignored by selectors. Where the Church had not declared itself, they believed that it was particularly important for the sponsoring diocese to state its view on the matter. 'Two such matters are homosexuality and, in the case of candidates for lay ministry, divorce and re-marriage.'[33] They then suggested the concept of 'pastoral effectiveness'. If a diocese openly sponsored such a candidate the selectors should note that 'and look for evidence that the generally accepted level of pastoral effectiveness will not be critically diminished'.[34]

The bishops accepted the report in January 1983 but said that 'ordinands should not be questioned about their sexuality unless there were external reasons for the subject to be reviewed'. The committee were emphatic that no area of personality should be forbidden to selectors' scrutiny; especially not one so relevant to the maturity of the candidate and the stability of his family life and it was asked that this should be made clear in the report.[35] The committee were told in May 1983 that the bishops and the council had then agreed to the publication of the report.

This concluded a major review of the process that took almost five years. It represented the most major change to the conference programme since the selection was started at the end of World War Two. But having once let the genie of change out of the bottle, it would not then easily be put back.

The introduction of the new style of conferences from January 1983 made a difference. The recommendation rates for one year and five years either side of the new system were:

---

32 *Report on Criteria*, paras. 5.15–5.16.
33 *Report on Criteria*, para. 12.25.
34 *Report on Criteria*, para.12.28.
35 Candidates Committee minutes, 4 February 1983.

Year(s)	1982	1983	1978–82	1983–7
For all candidates (priesthood, diaconate and accredited lay ministry)	64.3%	55.7%	65.4%	59.1%
For candidates for priesthood	63.0%	55.0%	65.0%	58.6%

The total numbers of candidates for those two five-year periods were not vastly different, 4,359 in 1978–82 and 4,535 for 1983–7, but if the recommendation rate for the first five years had applied to the second five years, then it would have produced just over 300 more people entering training over the period 1983–7.[36]

The evidence from the experimental conferences implied that some were recommended who may not have been under the old system, but clearly there were far more who were not recommended who might otherwise have been so. The evidence of the conferences was that this happened because the selectors now had a far more rounded and thorough picture of the candidates.

Later reviews 1993–7

The new system was in operation for nearly 12 years before it was decided to initiate a further review. This was partly occasioned by a fall in the recommendation rate from 53 per cent to 47 per cent in 1993 and a flurry of correspondence in *the Church Times* about non-recommended candidates at the end of that year. That had led some to suggest that the reports should be open to the candidates concerned rather than simply be confidential reports to bishops. The establishment of local non-stipendiary ministry had raised questions about the relationship of the local to the national, which in turn was part of a larger concern about how to integrate the work of dioceses and the national body, by now renamed the Advisory Board of Ministry (ABM) with the Candidates Committee of ACCM now renamed the Recruitment and Selection Committee. There remained a continuing debate about the possible use of psychometric tests in national selection, and whether the then system discriminated unfairly against those coming from socio-economic classes 4 to 6. More fundamentally, there was also among some a feeling that the Church was now facing a

---

36 Figures from ABM ministry paper No. 13, *The Report of the Recruitment Strategy Working Party*, p. 51f.

considerably changed situation in the nation as a whole, and that this might require some revision of the qualities needed in potential clergy.

The review process started in 1993 with a consideration of the criteria for selection. Two changes in the Church since the publication of the original 1983 report had resulted in 1990 in minor modifications to the criteria, the first being the admission of women to the diaconate and the second being the discussions on sexuality that had resulted in the 1991 bishops' report *Issues in Human Sexuality.* At the time of those modifications it was suggested that the whole criteria should be considered afresh. 'The aim was to produce a document reflecting fully the changes in Church and Society since the original publication.'[37] *The Report of a Working Party on Criteria for Selection for Ministry in the Church of England* was published in October 1993.

Exactly what those changes were in society were spelled out in the report, where it was noted that patterns of employment and unemployment were changing, that in some areas communities were multi-faith and multicultural, and 'there is evidence that English society is becoming more divided and this poses a particular challenge to ministers of a Church which is represented in all parts of England'.[38]

As for changes within the Church the most obvious one was the decision in 1992 to ordain women to the priesthood but that had been preceded by a large number of women entering Holy Orders as deacons. By 1993 there were over 1,000 women in such positions and women were 29 per cent of candidates for ordained ministry in 1991.[39] Other changes within the Church were incremental rather than dramatic, but there was a greater recognition that ministry by lay people was an important part of the Church's life and that clergy had to be able to work collaboratively with others, both lay Anglicans and also in ecumenical relationships as evidenced by the creation in 1990 of Churches Together in England. In 1988 the Lambeth Conference had suggested that there needed to be a major shift to a mission orientation, with the Decade of Evangelism starting in 1989. While it was obvious that a general knowledge and understanding of the Christian faith was less evident in the nation as a whole, there were some in the Church who were cautious about this shift; but significantly in the 1990s the two archbishops changed. In 1983 Robert Runcie was Archbishop of

---

37 From the preface to ABM policy paper 3A, *The Report of a Working Party on Criteria for Selection for Ministry in the Church of England,* October 1993.

38 *Criteria for Selection,* 2. 26.

39 *Criteria for Selection,* 2. 17.

Canterbury, and in his final presidential address in 1990 to General Synod said that 'our tradition is to cast evangelism in the mould of pastoral care'.[40] John Habgood was Archbishop of York, and both Runcie and Habgood were essentially in the liberal Catholic tradition of the Church. By 1993 George Carey was at Canterbury, someone more definitely from the Evangelical wing and, from 1995, David Hope was at York, from the more definitely Catholic wing. Both were theologically more conservative than their predecessors, and the Evangelical element in the Church was probably more prominent than in the earlier decade. That had partially influenced the Church's understanding of itself, although it was far from clear that was reflected in the wider society or that it had affected all elements within the Church. But not all was change. In its response to the 1992 report *The Ordained Ministry: Numbers, Cost, Recruitment and Deployment* the House of Bishops had 'affirmed the parochial system as a basis for mission and for providing access to pastoral care and worship for the whole nation',[41] although they also referred to 'the need to give radical consideration to developing and using imaginative and varied patterns of lay and ordained ministry'.[42]

Against such a background the working party on criteria, chaired by David Connor, then Vicar of the University Church in Cambridge,[43] broadly reaffirmed the 1983 criteria but noted areas where they needed to be developed. They wanted an emphasis on mission to sit alongside the provision of pastoral care,[44] a far greater emphasis on the need to lead and work collaboratively,[45] and they restated the House of Bishop's policy on human sexuality.[46] On vocation they noted the report *Call to Order*, with its greater emphasis on 'the place of the Church's decision to call the individual as opposed to the conviction of the individual which derives from an inner certainty', and they noted the experience of those who 'seek a local non-stipendiary ministry to which others may have called them initially before they themselves had even considered it',[47] but they

---

40 General Synod proceedings 1990, Vol. XXI, p. 1042.

41 Quoted in ABM policy paper 3A, p. 31.

42 Quoted in ABM policy paper 3A, p. 32.

43 David Connor was a member of the Recruitment and Selection Committee of ABM, which body had incorporated the work of ACCM's Candidates' Committee. Later he was to become Bishop of Lynn and then Dean of Windsor. There were six other members of the working party, including the senior selection secretary of ABM.

44 *Criteria for Selection*, p. 39.

45 *Criteria for Selection*, p. 40.

46 *Criteria for Selection*, p. 46 and p. 92.

47 *Criteria for Selection*, p. 82.

also spoke of 'a balance of the inner and outer aspects of calling ... to allow for the variety of different ways in which candidates apprehend their calling'.[48] Regarding what both reports had described as 'quality of mind' they stressed that the Bishops' regulations for training only laid down formal requirements for candidates under the age of 25 and were anxious to distinguish between educational achievement and educational potential and not to penalize those who did not have the former. However, they thought that all candidates at the end of their training would need to achieve a level 'which is roughly equivalent to the level of a pass in Honours Degree Finals'.[49] Possibly their most major difference with the 1983 report lay in the area of faith; they noted that the 1983 report

> rightly stresses the individual search for authentic faith and meaning but seems to neglect the community and the traditional nature of the Christian faith. This imbalance should be readdressed to make it clear that, as ministers who will be representatives of the Church, candidates should be in a position to identify themselves with the faith of the community and not merely seek to pursue their own notions and interests and to treat faith as a matter only of personal belief.

They summarized their recommendations under eight criteria: ministry in the Church of England; vocation; faith; spirituality; personality and character; relationships; leadership and collaboration; quality of mind. It was recommended that it should be made available for 'wider distribution as a separate publication intended for a general audience'.[50] (Reproduced in Appendix M.)

While that report was being prepared it was also agreed that there should be a further review of the selection procedures. This reflected the recommendation in 1983 that they should be subject to regular review, but it was also noted that with the new clarity on criteria the selection system should be designed to enable those criteria to be properly assessed. A working party was established under the chairmanship of Canon Michael Whitehead, who was both an experienced selector as a chairman of conferences and a member of the Recruitment and Selection Committee of ABM. In addition to those with

---

48 *Criteria for Selection*, p. 42f.
49 *Criteria for Selection*, p. 47.
50 *Criteria for Selection*, p. 9.

specialist experience of selection in dioceses and in selection conferences it also included the Prime Minister's Appointments' Secretary, John Holroyd, a former Civil Service Commissioner and a former Bishops' Selector, and Julian Moore, also a former Civil Service Commissioner and Director of the Civil Service selection boards. Their report *A Review of Selection Procedures in the Church of England* (ABM Policy Paper No. 6) was published in September 1995.

It reaffirmed the value of central selection for all candidates and rejected one suggestion that had been made to them that conferences should only be used for marginal candidates, with the top 25 per cent as identified by dioceses being fast tracked. Apart from the problems of identifying the top 25 per cent and creating a two-tier view of ministry they believed it would make providing and upholding national standards very difficult, particularly for dioceses that produce only a fairly small number of candidates.[51]

It also recognized that some candidates for non-stipendiary ministry later transferred to stipendiary ministry (and vice versa) and therefore recommended that candidates for ordained ministry should be sponsored under three categories: ordained ministry (stipendiary and non-stipendiary ministry), ordained ministry (permanent NSM), and ordained ministry (local non-stipendiary ministry), believing that the last category should be subject to its own later review.[52] Those wishing to transfer at a later stage from permanent non-stipendiary ministry or local non-stipendiary ministry would have to be reviewed by the Selection and Recruitment Committee.

The report repeated the recommendation of the 1983 changes that the number of selectors should be reduced so that selectors should be called upon once every 9 to 12 months instead of the practice of once in every 18 to 24 months, and they recommended a rolling pattern of the appointment of selectors so that there was not a large number of inexperienced selectors appointed every five years.

On psychological testing they believed that while personality tests might be a useful tool in the overall selection process they agreed with the diocesan directors of ordinands, who had said in 1992 that such tests were more usefully used at earlier points than national selection conferences. However, the report did recommend the introduction of specially designed cognitive exercises to be

---

51 ABM Policy paper 6, paras 53–5.

52 This review of LNSM was published in 1998 as *Stranger in the Wings*, and is considered in the section on local non-stipendiary ministry on page 267.

administered at the conferences by the secretaries, who would need specialist training in administering them. It also recommended the introduction of a personal inventory, which would be a specially designed form completed by each candidate at the conference and which would 'elicit the type of information which candidates and Selectors could usefully explore in interview in order to make an assessment based on the national Criteria of the Church'.[53]

The report further recommended a number of other far-reaching changes to the conference structure itself. It developed further the use of dividing the candidates into two groups, but giving each group a senior selector as well as the pastoral and educational selector, each of whom would have a 50-minute interview with each candidate in their group. The conference secretary would no longer interview candidates or be a selector, but they would be there to manage the process of the conference, including administering the cognitive exercises and to be present as a moderator at the final assessment sessions. It did, however, recommend that secretaries should, from time to time, act as selectors in their own right at conferences, with other staff members acting as the secretaries of those conferences. In practice it seemed that their role as moderator did prove critical, both in maintaining a constant standard between the two groups in the conference and across the conferences as a whole.[54]

It also recommended that the reports on individual candidates should be written by the selectors themselves before they left the conference, with the secretary simply maintaining their monitoring role in the process. The reports would be closely related to the criteria identified in the Criteria Report, with each selector being asked to report on specific areas in the criteria; the senior selector commenting on ministry within the Church of England, vocation and spirituality; the educational selector on faith and quality of mind; and the pastoral selector on personality and character, relationships, and leadership and collaboration.

The report also considered the matter of open reporting, which the authors believed related to what they described as the mythology and fantasy surrounding the central selection process. It recommended more openness about the process, including the producing of a leaflet for candidates due to attend a conference that explained the conference procedure, but they continued to

---

53 ABM policy paper 6, para. 105.
54 Confirmed by the author during observation of a new-style conference in 2010.

advocate reports that were to be confidential to the bishops as the people who had to make the final decision in the light of the report on whether someone should go forward for training for ministry.

The recommendations of the report were accepted both by ABM and the House of Bishops and became operative from the beginning of 1997.

Unlike the 1983 change in procedures these recommendations did not result in a significant reduction in the overall recommendation rate. Prior to the changes, after the low point of 47 per cent in 1993 it rose to 55 per cent in 1994, 71 per cent in 1995 and back to 64 per cent in 1996. In the first year in which the changes were introduced it rose to 76 per cent, in 1998 it was 70 per cent, and in 1999, 71 per cent. In the belief of the staff at the time the experience of previous years of working more closely with dioceses meant that diocesan procedures had become more thorough, and that some who might have been sent to conferences were now halted, or at least delayed, through the pre-selection processes at diocesan level.[55]

Towards the end of the century there was one further change that came about as a direct result of government policy. The Data Protection Act of 1998 was designed to ensure that individuals had access to information held about them and this resulted in the pressure to move towards open reporting becoming irresistible. The bishops accepted that fact and agreed that in future selection conference reports should be open to the candidates reported on. One consequence was that selectors were required by the selection secretaries in their capacity as moderators to be sure that they did not simply give their conclusions about whether a candidate matched the criteria, but gave their evidence for coming to that conclusion. That, and the fact that each selector now had to write their own reports on the areas they were investigating, inevitably led to far longer reports. It represented a significant change.

Throughout the period of selection conferences, while the Church had certainly taken responsibility for its own selection procedures it was open to receiving advice from those who were experienced in other fields of selection. The original War Office selection board model of World War Two was the most advanced system of selection of its time and for that reason was adopted by other bodies including the Civil Service, but it was also wholly appropriate for selecting candidates from the forces for ministry. Later changes in selection

---

55 From personal conversations of the author with the senior selection secretaries of the time and later.

methods from non-military areas were more relevant for the Church as candidates came from a wider variety of backgrounds than simply the military ones of World War Two. In both the 1983 and 1995 reviews experience from a wide variety of other bodies was obtained, but the experience of the Civil Service selection boards, provided by individuals who had held key positions in the Civil Service but who were known to be sympathetic to the Church, was very significant.

Similar considerations applied to the two major reviews on the Criteria for Selection. Any serious churchperson, lay or ordained, is both a provider and a recipient of ministry. The groups that produced the two reports on Criteria for Selection contained both clergy and laity who worked together in deciding what was needed in an ordained person. The ordained ministry had, however, developed from that envisaged by the Service Candidates Committee in World War Two as outlined in the paper in Appendix I. Although the majority of clergy throughout the period when the reviews were taking place were working within the parochial ministry there was a far wider range of ways in which they might be used. Developing clarity about the core criteria that were needed in any candidate was therefore an important task, partly for potential candidates themselves to make some more personal judgement of their own suitability but equally for those involved in the selection of candidates.

By the end of the century there was far greater clarity on both criteria and the process of selection. The decision on what was finally done was always taken ultimately by the bishops, but in coming to their decisions they could know they were receiving well-judged advice from well-informed people. It was a good example of what is considered in the next chapter: shared ministry.

11

The Search for a Strategy 1970–2000

The decision to authorize non-stipendiary ministry as a recognized category was essentially a strategic decision about ordained ministry, and it was the precursor of three more major decisions over the next 30 years. First was the development of what to start with was known as local non-stipendiary ministry from the early 1980s, the second was the ordination of women as deacons which took effect from 1987, and the third was the ordination of women to the priesthood in 1994. None of those changes were presented as part of a coherent strategy, although they may have been seen as such in the dioceses where local non-stipendiary ministry was being developed. But they were all to have a significant effect on the availability of clergy, and in 2000 a total of 562 men and women were ordained, the first time the number had gone over 500 since 1966, mainly because of the addition of women and what by then had become known as local ordained ministers.

But talk about the need for a strategic approach to ministry happened at various other stages during the 30 years, and were normally about attempting fundamental change to the way clergy were deployed and even to changing their role. Some of that was in the context of what was variously described as 'shared ministry' or 'every-member ministry'.

That the exercise of ministry had to be shared in some way with the laity was obvious; the parish priest as a one-man band was an almost impossible model when clergy had to respond to the needs of parishes with populations of many thousands. The Church of England in the parishes was not lacking in lay people of ability who were perfectly competent to take responsibility for aspects of a local church's life, and in some cases could probably do it far more effectively than their clergy. In addition many parish clergy would also find themselves in situations in local institutions, as governors of a local school for example, where they could easily make common cause with other people who might not have much connection with any church or even call themselves Christians. Such 'shared ministry' long pre-dated the 1970s, but it was talked about far more openly from then as a way of dealing with parochial needs.

Every-member ministry was a slightly different matter as here it was thought that every member of a congregation had some sort of contribution to the church's life to which was often attached the word 'ministry'. While in principle that may be the case, any parish priest would also be well aware that there were some in his or her congregation who might want to exercise some authority in the local community, but whose judgement was deeply suspect to the priest and quite possibly, although less obviously, to many in the congregation as well. If every-member ministry was to be pursued it raised all the questions of selection and training that those responsible for ordained ministry over the century had grappled with. Fortunately from ACCM's point of view it was only concerned with ministers authorized by Canon, that is approved by a bishop, but those wider issues were never far away from its concerns.

Responding to declining numbers 1970–9

In 1971, 393 men were ordained, the first time the figure had fallen below 400 since 1949, and for the first time the number of men retiring on pensions exceeded the number ordained.[1] Numbers being recommended or conditionally recommended for training were also in decline. In 1970 the total for candidates for stipendiary ministry was 403, but for the rest of the decade it was below 400, dropping to fewer than 300 in 1973 and 1977 and only going above the 400 figure again in 1980. The challenge facing the Church was to find ways of managing a decline in active clergy numbers while maintaining an effective ministry.

The first issue was to ensure that there was a fair distribution of those who were ordained. On 7 July 1972 the General Synod asked the bishops to appoint a working party 'to assist them in the formulation of a scheme for a fairer distribution of clergy manpower and to report their proposals to the Synod'. A group under the chairmanship of the Bishop of Sheffield[2] reported in 1973.[3] They concluded that four factors, population, physical area, number of churches,

---

1 From the 1971 Annual Report, p. 3, GS 91. See also the statistical tables in Appendix N.

2 The Rt Revd Gordon Fallows (1913–79) Principal of Ripon Hall, Oxford, 1959–68; Bishop of Pontefract 1968–71; Bishop of Sheffield from 1971.

3 *Deployment of the Clergy: The Report of the House of Bishops' Working Group*, GS 205.

and number on electoral rolls should be taken into account, with each factor given a different weighting. Population had the highest weighting, the number of churches and the size of electoral rolls were given an equal weighting in the middle, and physical area the least. On the basis of a simple mathematical calculation each diocese was given its 'Sheffield allocation', which was the number of stipendiary clergy it should aim to have. Over a few years the system was to prove effective and the wide discrepancies that were evident when the report was first published were gradually diminished. By 1980 17 dioceses were within 5 per cent of their Sheffield target, 13 had over 5 per cent more, all in the Southern Province, and 13 over 5 per cent under, all in the Northern Province. By 1984 the imbalance between Canterbury and York Provinces was at its lowest: Canterbury 1.1 per cent over and York 2.6 per cent under, and there were then only four dioceses with 5 per cent or more above their allocation, all of which were in the Southern Province, and seven dioceses with 5 per cent or more below their Sheffield allocation, of which five were in the Northern Province and two were in the Southern Province (Lincoln and Hereford).[4] By 1990 only eight dioceses were more than 5 per cent over or under their allocation, which meant that 35 dioceses were therefore within 5 per cent of their figure.[5] Thereafter financial pressures meant that some dioceses decided they could not afford their full Sheffield allocation, which enabled other dioceses to move above their allocation, but nonetheless overall the Sheffield scheme represented a remarkable rebalancing of clerical resources.

The second issue was to make some attempt to plan for the future in the face of concern among the theological colleges at what the declining number of candidates might mean. In 1978 the House of Bishops carried 13 resolutions on the future of the ministry,[6] which resolutions were endorsed by the General Synod in July 1978.[7] They recommended that the future of colleges and courses should be ensured for the following three years as long as there were 350 candidates recommended for full-time ordained ministry and they set a target of 400 to 450 candidates a year for the future. In 1977 there were 349 candidates recommended, but that rose to 365 for the year of the resolutions and in 1980

---

4 *Deployment of Stipendiary Clergy* was produced each year, the one for 1983 being GS Misc. 186.

5 *Deployment of Stipendiary Clergy* 1990, GS Misc. 368.

6 *The Future of the Ministry*. A Report Containing Thirteen Resolutions of the House of Bishops, GS 374.

7 Report of Proceedings 1978, p. 638.

hit the target range with 404 candidates recommended, and it remained above the 350 figure for two more years which, with the three-years roll-on assurance, gave some breathing space to the colleges.

A strategy for ministry? 1979–2000

Shortly after the 13 resolutions were passed there was discussion in ACCM about the need for some form of longer-term strategy for ministry. The Annual Report of 1979 noted the start of developing such a process, with ACCM at first considering the contribution of accredited lay ministry. By the following year a strategy for ministry was promised for 1983 and the Council had agreed that it would be left to the relatively recently appointed General Secretary, Canon John Tiller, to produce the report with the possibility of consultation with some members of the Council. It was published in September 1983[8] and it set out a review of the Church of England's ministry from 1963 and proposed a strategy for the next 40 years.

At its core the report advocated a 'shared ministry' between clergy and laity, which went beyond the notion of the laity co-operating with or assisting the clergy but rather the laity being the Church in the community, assisted by the clergy. Tiller noted that the Church of England had at the time fewer than 11,000 full-time diocesan clergy, while the Jehovah's Witnesses claimed to have 88,000 ministers in England because every Jehovah's Witness was considered to be a minister. It was such an emphasis on lay ministry that he wished to encourage.[9] He therefore thought that each local church should assume responsibility for its own ministry, which he readily acknowledged would in time have major consequences for the ordained ministry including the end of clerical freehold, the end of clergy as office holders, the end of patronage, and with clergy on the diocesan staff as employees, available to assist local churches where the bishop thought such assistance was needed and not as incumbents of benefices with 'the cure of souls'.

The report clearly presented the Council of ACCM with a problem. Some members accepted neither the analysis nor the proposed solution, but on the other hand they had invited the chief secretary to produce the report and they

---

8 John Tiller, 1983, *A Strategy for the Church's Ministry*, CIO.
9 Tiller, *Strategy*, p. 65.

could not disown a project they had commissioned. The ACCM paper that went to General Synod to accompany the report[10] therefore stated:

> The Council notes that Canon Tiller's report presents his own personal view of the problem and his vision for the future, and while the Council welcomes the report as a coherent strategy for the future it is not the only practicable way forward.

The paper noted that two other possibilities were a strong affirmation of full-time parochial ministry, with all the financial implications that would involve in terms of a recruitment strategy and the cost of training, or the development of a traditionally based ministry with something like the present number of full-time clergy working in a collaborative way with strong local ministry teams.

The report was debated in General Synod in November 1983 where it received a mixed response, and some follow-up resolutions were further debated in February 1984, which essentially asked for the report to be studied in the dioceses, and which advocated the notion of shared ministry with the laity. Dioceses were asked to respond to the report, and these were summarized in a paper in 1986 which included the statement:

> detailed work is at present under consideration that affects many of the implications of the Tiller report: the dioceses are also pursuing their own plans. ACCM therefore judges that the time is not ripe for it to initiate a further debate in General Synod, until the outcome of these developments can be taken into account. It will, however, monitor the situation carefully.[11]

By then Tiller had moved to be a canon of Hereford, and in practice the traditional pattern of ministry continued but with encouragement for some measure of collaboration. None of the radical elements of his proposals were adopted.

The 1978 13 resolutions also recommended that there should be a new body, to be known as the Ministry Co-ordinating Group, which would bring together under the chairmanship of an independent member of the House of Bishops some of the ACCM bishops, the Church Commissioners, the Pensions Board and

---

10 *Strategy for the Church's Ministry*, GS 589, to accompany the Tiller report.
11 *Diocesan Responses to the Tiller Report*, GS Misc. 262, para. 47.

the Central Board of Finance; its role was to keep under review the outworking of the Sheffield scheme, the numbers of clergy and future requirements. It was there as much as anything to assemble information, but in one practical move in 1981[12] it recommended that in future there should be a modification to the five-year-old system for the allocation of deacons between the dioceses which would assist in dioceses reaching their Sheffield targets. Thereafter each diocese had not only its allocation of Sheffield numbers overall, but within that number an allocation of deacons for ordination each year.

In 1980 the Ministry Co-ordinating Group produced a survey of the Church's ministry[13] which showed that the combination of retirements and deaths in service substantially outnumbered new ordinations and in a discussion paper produced in 1988[14] it gave the figures of the decline in the number of full-time stipendiary clergy, from 23,670 in 1901, to 18,196 in 1951, 10,882 in 1981, and 10,480 in 1991. An accompanying paper to the dioceses asked for responses to ten questions and the responses were compiled by the new secretary-general of General Synod, Philip Mawer.[15] He reported that to the question 'Does the Church need radically to reconsider the shape of its ministry in the light of changing society and an increase in ecumenical ventures, or should it seek to maintain a nationwide parochial ministry on broadly the same lines as now?' the responses indicated an overwhelming affirmation of the nationwide parochial system, but there was also expressed a feeling that the existing clergy were overstretched, that other types of ministry were required to support the parochial clergy, but that all candidates who were accepted for training should be enabled to train. Those responses were turned into resolutions of the House of Bishops passed in January 1992[16] affirming the parochial system, the Sheffield scheme for allocating clergy, and the commitment to support the training of all 'whose call to ordained and accredited ministry had been successfully tested'. Without saying so in as many words it effectively buried the Tiller report nine years after its publication.

In 1991 the new Advisory Board for Ministry replaced ACCM and took on some of the functions of the Ministry Co-ordinating Group, which ceased

---

12 *The Deployment of Stipendiary Clergy*, GS 511. A Report of the Ministry Co-ordinating Group.

13 *The Church's Ministry – A Survey*, GS 459.

14 *The Ordained Ministry: Numbers, Cost and Deployment*, GS 858, 1988, 1991.

15 Diocesan responses to GS 858, GS Misc. 370, 1990.

16 The resolutions of the bishops were reported in the first annual report of the Advisory Board for Ministry 1991, GS 1002.

with the creation of ABM. In 1992 ABM produced *Order and Diversity*[17] which said:

> This paper ... sets out to map the present state of ordained ministry in the Church of England and to point to some of the opportunities and challenges that are presented ... This will be based in part on the call from the Lambeth Conference for 1988 for a 'shift to a dynamic missionary emphasis going beyond care and nurture to proclamation and service.

It then surveyed many aspects of ministry with a mass of statistics, and ended with a number of statements which revealed a level of financial unease that led to a profound uncertainty about the future. In terms of a future strategy it noted that in the financial circumstances of 1993, when the difficulties surrounding some investment decisions by the Church Commissioners were being widely reported, some dioceses were feeling that they must reduce clergy.

> In these circumstances it is difficult for ABM to draw together any coherent indication of the numbers of clergy that dioceses will be seeking to deploy in ten or even five years time, but it is important that the Church should continue to develop resources appropriate for the mission that it has been given by Christ.[18]

Such gloomy assessments were reinforced by the statement that there is no upper limit to the numbers who could be selected but 'The reality of the Church's present situation suggests that ordinands cannot assume that there will always be a paid stipendiary post, with housing, for them.'[19]

It therefore suggested that candidates should be open as to whether it should be for stipendiary or non-stipendiary ministry they were offering, as while there was no limit on the number of ordinations, there might need to be a limit on the numbers ordained for stipendiary ministry.[20] The report also recommended to the bishops that candidates for stipendiary ministry should not be aged above 45 years at the time of sponsorship[21] and it also asserted that:

---

17 *Order and Diversity*, GS 1084, ABM policy paper No. 5, 1993.
18 *Order and Diversity*, para. 5.12, p. 53.
19 *Order and Diversity*, para. 5.22, p. 55.
20 *Order and Diversity*, paras. 5.27–9, p. 56f.
21 *Order and Diversity*, para. 5.29, p. 57.

because of the need to find posts for younger candidates ABM had also encouraged those aged 65 and who had worked for the 37 years that would give them a full pension should consider retirement.[22]

The response of the General Synod in a debate on the report in November 1993 was not entirely surprising:

That this Synod commends the report 'Order and Diversity' to the Church for bishops and dioceses to use as a resource in their ministry planning, but deplores the lack of a coherent strategy for the Church's ministry revealed in GS 1084 and calls upon the House of Bishops urgently to address this.[23]

The call for a coherent strategy raises the question of whether such a strategy is ever possible or even desirable for a body such as the Church of England. *Order and Diversity* had suggested that this was primarily a diocesan responsibility, but even within a single diocese individual diocesan bishops might strive to produce in discussion with their synods and its boards and councils a coherent strategy for their dioceses, and even the strongest willed of bishops might find it difficult to achieve what he wanted given the presence of freehold, independent patronage and the general independence of the clergy. It was not entirely clear what the General Synod was asking for in its motion.

What it did get, though, was a decision regarding the proposal about sponsorship, which proposal was in the 1995 report on selection procedures and which was put into effect from 1997 onwards when candidates were either sponsored for permanent non-stipendiary ministry or for a single category that was both for stipendiary or non-stipendiary ministry. That did have the effect of ensuring that the standard for that whole category was the same at selection conferences. What also happened in the remaining years of the century were two very strategic matters: the ordination of women to the priesthood and some working out of the implication of an earlier decision to allow the category of local non-stipendiary ministry, which are discussed below. They were the two main factors in bringing about by the end of the century some positive news in terms of the number of candidates and ordinations.

---

22 *Order and Diversity*, para. 5.37, p. 59.
23 Report of Proceedings, November 1993, p. 1076.

In 1996 the Recruitment Strategy Working Party produced *Recovering Confidence*[24] which encouraged the development of a culture of recruitment at every level, and it explicitly reversed a tradition of telling young people to 'go away and get some experience of the world' and rather encouraged the Church to look for younger people. In 1997, for the first time in six years the total number of candidates recommended for various forms of ordination was over 500, the increase coming with the arrival of significant numbers of women candidates for priesthood and a burst of candidates, both men and women, for what had been called local non-stipendiary ministry but by then was called ordained local ministry. The number of ordinations went over 400 in 1998 for the first time since 1994 and in 2000 to 569, the first time it was over 500 since 1966.

The developing role of women in ministry 1971–96

In 1971 ACCM was asked to present to the Synod a consultative document on the ordination of women to the priesthood, which was largely prepared by Miss Christian Howard, but in consultation with those who took different points of view.[25] After a full debate in November 1972 the General Synod took note of the report, and in July 1973 referred it to the dioceses. The matter was brought back to General Synod by the Standing Committee in July 1975,[26] with a report on the diocesan voting on two questions: whether there were fundamental objections to the ordination of women and whether the Church should then start a process to remove the barriers to it. A majority of dioceses (30) voted in favour of the former, but only 15 for the latter, and that was reflected in the General Synod vote, which was narrowly in favour of the first proposition, but clearly not by sufficient majorities to make the second proposition practicable at that stage. The issue came back in November 1978 when the Bishop of Birmingham proposed a motion inviting the Standing Committee 'to prepare and bring forward legislation to remove the barriers to the ordination of women to the priesthood and their consecration to the episcopate'.[27] It was approved by

---

24 *Recovering Confidence*, ABM Paper No. 13.

25 *The Ordination of Women to the Priesthood*, GS 104.

26 *The Ordination of Women: Report of the Standing Committee on the References to the Dioceses*, GS 252. The debate took place on 3 July 1975.

27 GS Report of Proceedings, 8 November 1978, p. 996.

65 per cent in the bishops and by 53 per cent in the clergy, but 61 per cent of the laity voted against. The motion was therefore lost.

An ACCM report on the ministry of deacons and deaconesses was produced in 1976[28] and debated in November 1977. It noted that there were three possible ways forward: simply maintaining the diaconate as a preliminary year to ordination to the priesthood, abandoning it altogether, or expanding it to include a permanent diaconate. The Synod was only asked to 'take note of the report', which it did, but there was no enthusiasm for the total abandonment of the diaconate and very little for creating a permanent diaconate.[29] Thereafter, while the ordination of women both as deacons and then as priests had implications for ACCM, it was never a direct ACCM responsibility and there is no indication in the minutes of either ACCM or ABM that there was ever a formal discussion on the question. However, the Annual Report of 1978 noted that the House of Bishops had decided that the length of training for deaconesses and lay workers should be the same as for ordinands, which had the consequence of the older examination for lay workers and deaconesses known as the Inter-Diocesan Certificate becoming identical to the General Ordination Examination, and the bishops decided that GOE should henceforth be known as the General Ministerial Examination.[30] Joint selection conferences for candidates for ordination and for women seeking to become either deaconesses or accredited lay workers were agreed in 1979, so in both selection and training ACCM was ready for the decisions taken by the General Synod, first in 1985 that women could be ordained as deacons, which decision was implemented from 1987, and second the decision taken in 1992 that women could be ordained as priests, which was implemented in 1994. Otherwise, while individual members of the Council and of the staff no doubt had strong views on the matter, the ordination of women both as deacons and as priests effectively passed ACCM and ABM by.

In 1996, when ACCM had become ABM and taken on the responsibilities previously belonging to the Ministry Co-ordinating Group, its annual report did give the statistics relating to resignations and returns of those who left because of the ordination of women, which were later updated in the *Statistics of Licensed*

28 *Report on the Ministry of Deacons and Deaconesses*, GS 344.

29 The debate took place on 11 November 1977 and is recorded in the report of proceedings for that year, pp.1094–128.

30 1978 Annual Report, GS 406.

Ministers[31] produced annually. It showed that by 2000, 480 priests had left the Anglican ministry, of whom 395 were stipendiary ministers, 26 non-stipendiary and 59 retired, but that 61 had subsequently returned, 29 to stipendiary posts, 18 to non-stipendiary and 14 as retired priests. Over that same period the annual statistics showed over 1,000 women had been ordained, 496 to stipendiary ministry and 582 to non-stipendiary ministry or ordained local ministry.

Local non-stipendiary ministry (later called ordained local ministry) 1970–2000

The notion that some clergy should emerge from their congregations, be selected locally and trained to go back to the congregations from where they came has been around for some time.[32] In the early 1970s the Bishop of Stepney, Trevor Huddleston, and the incumbent of Bethnal Green, Ted Roberts, both agreed that the East End needed to develop an indigenous ministry and in the parish of Bethnal Green four men were identified as possible candidates. Once the four were accepted by the local congregation they went to a national selection conference, where they were accepted as non-stipendiary clergy, and after local training were ordained deacon in 1972 and priest in 1974. What was perceived essential about the scheme was that it was a team of four rather than solitary ministers, they were called by the local church and were settled rather than itinerant. They were given seven-year licences after which they could resign. The experiment led to 'Local Ministry' ACCM Occasional Paper No. 1, produced by an ad hoc working party chaired by David Sheppard, Bishop of Woolwich, which identified three areas where local ministry might be suitable: the remote rural team or group, the inner city, and what was described as the 'divided parish' by which was meant a parish that had a large council estate in what was otherwise an owner-occupied area and where a special local ministry in the council estate might be appropriate. The matter was reviewed in a report of an ACCM working party on auxiliary ministry[33] chaired by the Bishop of Southwell

---

31 Figures taken from *Statistics of Licensed Ministers: Some Facts and Figures as at 31 December 2000*, GS Misc. 638.

32 The story is well told by Malcolm Torry and Jeffrey Heskins (eds), 2006, *Ordained Local Ministry*, Norwich: Canterbury Press.

33 *The Place of Auxiliary Ministry, Ordained and Lay*, 1973, published for the Advisory Council for the Church's Ministry by CIO.

(Wakeling), which went wider than simply local ministry. While it noted in some places there was sympathy for developing the notion of a more local style of ministry, the authors of the second report were not convinced. 'Our view after careful study of these proposals was that they had not sufficiently answered the theological, sociological and practical difficulties here set out.'[34] The Church as a whole was divided on the issue.

In the early 1980s a similar scheme was developed in the Brandon experiment in Southwark Diocese. The Brandon estate covered four parishes in Walworth and the incumbents there agreed to work together although not all in a formal team or group ministry. With the encouragement of the Bishop of Southwark (Stockwood) who was about to retire, the local parishes identified five candidates from the churches who were made deacon during their local, specially devised training in 1981 and priest in 1983.[35] At about that time Roberts moved to Bermondsey in Southwark Diocese and two candidates there were ordained in late 1982 for such an indigenous ministry.[36]

In the case of the Brandon experiment there was no involvement by ACCM, where it was known some were undoubtedly cautious about such a development; part of the rationale of ACCM was to preserve the academic standard and credibility of the ordained ministry and to them such developments seemed to threaten that. However, in 1978 a formal request from Lincoln Diocese to establish a scheme in that more rural diocese was received by ACCM. Some thought it could be incorporated as simply a variant of NSM, but others believed that it needed to be a new category in its own right, named then as local non-stipendiary ministry (LNSM). At a Council meeting three methods of selection were considered: ACCM representation on some locally organized form of selection; candidates for LNSMs attending national selection conferences, although with some method of the local situation being described to the selectors, possibly by a representative of the diocese coming to meet the selectors at the conference; or ACCM setting up special national conferences for candidates for LNSM.[37] All three methods were tried at various times in the next few years, although the ACCM special conferences were never completely national but did sometimes involve two or three dioceses working together.

---

34 *Place of Auxiliary Ministry*, p. 17.
35 Torry and Heskins, Chapter 3, written by Graham Shaw.
36 Torry and Heskins, Chapter 2, written by Ted Roberts.
37 ACCM Council minutes, 28 November 1978.

ACCM produced a report entitled *Local Ordained Ministry*[38] which included the House of Bishops' resolutions cautiously permitting the development and saying that candidates should go to normal selection conferences but with a diocesan nominee being allowed to tell the selectors about the local situation. It was debated in July 1980,[39] when there was both enthusiasm and caution about the notion of local ministry in the debate, but the Synod 'took note' of the report and individual diocesan bishops were allowed to pursue the possibility in their dioceses. Four dioceses established LNSM, with diocesan training schemes recognized by the House of Bishops.

In 1991 ABM's policy paper No. 1[40] gave some suggested regulations and guidelines for LNSM which were accepted by the House of Bishops and thereafter there was a rapid increase in dioceses asking for such schemes. By 1998 16 diocesan schemes had been approved. A further report was requested by the bishops on the whole development and a working party under the chairmanship of the Bishop of Truro (Bill Ind) was appointed. Its report, *Stranger in the Wings*, was published in 1998.[41]

It included a chapter on vocation and selection,[42] quoted the 1991 report 'It is a mark of Local Non-Stipendiary Ministers that they should have been invited by the local church to set out on the path towards ordination', and noted that a further ABM ministry paper in 1992,[43] *Developments of Models of Ministry and Training in Recent Diocesan Proposals for LNSM*, identified three models of vocation operating in local schemes. First, the local church might identify a group of lay people whom they believed should be a 'ministry team' and from whom they might subsequently identify some they considered suitable for ordination. Second, the local church directly identified someone whom they believed should be ordained and the candidates should be expected to demonstrate some sense of an inward call to ministry. Third, candidates would be called to ordained ministry by the local church, but nothing was said about any 'personal or inward call' to ministry. The 1998 working party initiated a survey of LNSMs and asked where their sense of vocation came from. Out of 62 responses the most

---

38 *Local Ordained Ministry*, 1979, GS 442.

39 Report of Proceedings, 1980 pp. 448–69.

40 *The Report of a Church of England Working Party Concerned with Local Non-Stipendiary Ministry* 1991, ABM policy paper No. 1.

41 *Stranger in the Wings: A Report on Local Non-Stipendiary Ministry*, GS Misc. 532, 1998.

42 GS Misc. 532, pp. 65–76.

43 *Developments of Models of Ministry and Training in Recent Diocesan Proposals for LNSM*, ABM ministry paper No. 4, 1992.

significant theme for 30 was the personal, for 27 the congregation and for five the incumbent. The report commented:

> It is important to be pragmatic and sensible about the variety of ways in which vocation to ministry may emerge. However, when the call is initiated by the individual, the local church must have the opportunity to endorse that sense of vocation or not, otherwise it would be totally inappropriate for the particular candidate to be a candidate for local non-stipendiary ministry rather than non-stipendiary or stipendiary.[44]

Wherever the sense of vocation came from, the report was clear that it also needed to be endorsed by the bishop who would need the advice of a wider grouping than just the local parish. It recognized that some dioceses or groups of dioceses organized selection conferences locally with ABM representation, while others chose to send their LNSM candidates to national selection conferences. While the report was being produced the new national selection procedures described in Chapter 10 were being introduced, which included the use of cognitive tests, and the report suggested that these should be used in diocesan conferences or where groups of dioceses worked together locally to ensure that the process of selection was essentially the same whatever category of ministry was being pursued.

The report, which also made some financial suggestions about contributions from central church funds towards the costs of local courses and which recommended for the future the name Ordained Local Ministry (OLM) was accepted and implemented. Up to 1997 the numbers ordained to that type of ministry were included in the statistics for non-stipendiary ministry, but from the 1988 figures onwards they were separately recorded. From 1998 to 2000, 92 men and 110 women were ordained as OLMs, which was just under 70 a year. Statistically as well as theologically and ministerially it was a significant development.

Theological colleges and courses 1972–2000

After the major cull of theological colleges in the early 1970s described in Chapter 9, attention was turned to wider issues of training including a

---

44 *Stranger*, GS Misc. 532, p. 66.

developing number of non-residential courses that provided part-time training while ordinands continued in their secular paid employment. In 1972 a committee was appointed to look at those broader aspects and the 1972 Annual Report of ACCM freely acknowledged that it was partly set up as a result of the increased cost of training. The committee's report entitled *Alternative Patterns of Training*,[45] published in 1975, recommended among other things establishing ten regional theological centres all with full- and part-time training preparing men for stipendiary and non-stipendiary ministry. It believed the existing colleges and courses could be grouped in such a way. A further report by the House of Bishops[46] questioned some other aspects of the report, but they were sympathetic to the notion of ten regional centres. They recognized that progress towards that 'will depend upon the willing and patient co-operation between all the agencies involved',[47] by which they meant theological colleges, courses, universities, polytechnics, colleges of education, synods, bishops, dioceses and ACCM. They also asserted that the Church must accept realistically the cost of training ordinands, which they noted was far less than the cost of training other professions.

> The average annual cost *to the Church* in 1975 of training men residentially and non-residentially was £815 per ordinand. Comparative figures for other professions are difficult to come by, but the cost of training a teacher in 1975 was running at roughly £2,200 p.a., a social worker about £1,500 p.a. An undergraduate medical student is costing around £5,000 p.a. and an RAF pilot to wings standard costs something like £100,000 in the first year.[48]

Four years later a further report on courses,[49] chaired by Bishop Oliver Tomkins, who had recently retired as Bishop of Bristol, made a number of detailed proposals regarding training and one major policy recommendation, that ACCM should encourage the formation of a national network for non-residential training for stipendiary ministry. In fact a national network of courses was already well on the way to being developed and in the following year the 1977

---

45 *Alternative Patterns of Training*, GS 265, 1975.
46 *Theological Training: A Policy for the Future. A Report by the House of Bishops,* 1975, GS 303.
47 *Training*, para. 14 (b), p. 6.
48 *Training*, para. 14 (a), p. 6.
49 *The Second Report of the Working Party on Courses*, GS 359, 1976.

ACCM Annual Report[50] noted that at the beginning of that year there were nine non-residential courses and in that year three more were recognized and others were planned. The recommendation that they should be recognized for training for stipendiary ministry as well as non-stipendiary ministry was put into effect by a decision of the House of Bishops in 1978, by which time there were 14 courses in existence and one more planned, which would make such a pattern of training available nationwide for all candidates over the age of 30. The check on standards of training was provided by two factors, that all the courses had to prepare candidates for the GOE essay scheme (or GME as it was to become in that same year) or one of the recognized equivalents, each of which required some monitoring by external examiners, and that all the non-residential courses were subject to the same regular inspection regime that applied to the colleges.

The archbishops invited three bishops under the chairmanship of the Bishop of Guildford to advise how to take forward the proposals in *Alternative Patterns of Training*, and their report was published in 1977 and was known as the Guildford Report.[51] It spoke of regional institutes rather than centres as the authors thought they should be places of active co-operation between different bodies. They suggested a regional council for each region, with an academic board representing the staffs of the various bodies in the region, with a regional director. Rather than the ten regions suggested by the *Alternative Patterns of Training* proposals they recommended 12 regional institutes. On the issue of churchmanship the report stated:

> As far as non-stipendiary training is concerned the Bishops require that every course shall cater for the whole range of traditions found in the Church of England. If the principle is sound should it not apply to stipendiary training? ... We believe the governing bodies of the colleges should be invited to re-examine the traditions of their foundation in the light of present needs and future developments.[52]

It was an imaginative but essentially naive suggestion. Financially the cost of 12 full-time regional directors would have been a problem, as could the

---

50 1977 ACCM Annual Report, GS 366.

51 *Theological Training: A Policy for the Future*, The Guildford Report, GS Misc. 57.

52 *Training*, para. 20, p. 9.

relationship of them, any regional council and any regional academic board to independent principals of theological colleges and courses in each region. But the far more fundamental problems were the three that beset any of the attempts at regionalization of theological education in the last quarter of the twentieth century. First, while theological courses clearly related to their region, residential theological colleges did not. They took candidates from across the nation and sometimes even from overseas and sent them back to parishes all over England. That was far more significant for their corporate life than the region in which they happened to be physically situated. Second, if they were in any close relationship with one of the major academic universities they would have absorbed the national or even international outlook of those universities. To describe Oxford or Cambridge or any of the other major universities of England as regional bodies is fundamentally to misunderstand their nature and their self-understanding. Third, some of the governing bodies of the colleges would certainly not abandon the churchmanship traditions which were enshrined in their foundation documents. They were often established to affirm the Evangelical, Catholic or liberal tradition which gave them their foundation and as long as those traditions remained active elements of the Church of England the college councils would not abandon their birthright. In its 1970 Annual Report ACCM had noted that there was a Standing Conference of Theological Colleges, where each college was represented by its principal and one member of the governing body, and each college council also had by then an ACCM staff member as a non-voting consultant. From the comments of many of those involved, that led to some measure of mutual understanding and respect across traditions, and certainly some of the principals were enthusiastic about broadening the range of churchmanship represented in their colleges, but to move from that to an abandonment of their whole foundation tradition was unrealistic. The Guildford Report led to no changes.

Those issues which encouraged a measure of independence by the theological colleges were to some extent re-enforced by one major change in theological education that was introduced in 1987 through *Education for the Church's Ministry: The Report of the Working Party on Assessment* (ACCM occasional paper 22), which was normally referred to subsequently as ACCM 22.

The General Ordination Examination, or General Ministerial Examination from 1978, had been since 1921 the normal examination which the bishops had agreed should be completed satisfactorily before someone was ordained. This involved examinations in Holy Scripture, Doctrine, Church History and Worship, with Ethics reintroduced in 1963[53] and, from 1978, a formal assessment of Pastoral Studies. It was open to a theological college principal to give exemption from some papers to those who had a degree in theology, and for candidates over 30 an assessment could be provided by way of the essay scheme. From 1972 it was possible for candidates under 30 to be assessed by a long essay rather than an examination in some subjects.

However, since the mid-1960s colleges (and subsequently courses) could submit their own schemes for recognition, some of which were validated by a local university or by the Council for National Academic Awards (CNAA). According to the report this arose from a general dissatisfaction with the standard of GOE and a desire to offer a qualification that was believed to have a wider validity. Subsequent revisions to GOE increased the academic rigour of the training required for that examination, but not its standing, and the changes had been introduced piecemeal, largely adding to the work that had to be done without taking anything away. By 1984 far more ordinands were following alternatives to GME than were doing it; of the 554 ACCM students in the colleges in that year only 61 were doing GME, and of the 669 training on the non-residential courses only 320 were doing GME via the essay scheme.[54]

The report outlined three possible ways forward. First, the authors could have simply recommended a tidying up of the pattern of assessment for that minority of ordinands doing GME, but that would have left untouched the situation with all the other ordinands. Second, they could have recommended a return to a centrally regulated syllabus to be used by all candidates, but that would entail dismantling potentially creative relationships with universities or with CNAA by many of the colleges and some of the courses. Third, they could recommend a scheme which would rationalize the present system and encourage a partnership between the colleges and courses, the validating bodies and ACCM and which would be designed to bring about the ending of GME as a single centrally organized examination. The report recommended this third option, in effect devolving responsibility to the colleges and courses for the training they provided, but without abandoning ultimate responsibility. Each training institution would be asked to provide answers to three fundamental questions:

53 From the minutes of the Ordination Candidates Committee, September 1962.
54 Appendix 1 of ACCM 22, p. 57.

(i) What ordained ministry does the Church of England require?

(ii) What is the shape of the educational programme best suited to equipping people to exercise this ministry?

(iii) What are the appropriate means of assessing suitability for the exercise of this ministry?

The report itself suggested some outline responses to those questions, and in the case of the second question suggested three parameters: interpretation of the Christian tradition for today; the formation of church life; addressing situations in the world. The authors maintained that those parameters could not simply be met by studying in the traditional subject areas of theology, Biblical Studies, Doctrine, Church History, Liturgy, etc., but required more co-ordination between subject areas than normally happened.

To some at the time it seemed that to invite the theological colleges and courses to decide what ordained ministry the Church of England required was to put the cart before the horse. The bishops had earlier agreed the criteria for selection and some thought the bishops collectively rather than individual colleges and courses should decide what ministry was needed.[55] However, ACCM 22 did require the colleges and courses to submit their proposals to the Committee for Theological Education and it was hoped through that to produce an agreed statement that would provide the rationale for the educational programme and method of assessment the institution was proposing. Each educational programme would be subject to the scrutiny of the Courses and Examinations Sub-Committee of the Committee for Theological Education, and it was proposed a GME board of examiners would be set up to approve the assessment procedures suggested by each institution and to appoint external examiners to moderate and monitor standards.

The report was first put to the ACCM Council and given general approval. It was then discussed at a meeting with college and course principals, who also gave their general assent and agreement to work with the procedures.[56] It was put to the House of Bishops and also accepted there. The result was the ending

---

55 Graham James was senior selection secretary at the time and expressed that in personal conversation with the author. He is now Bishop of Norwich and Chairman of the Ministry Division, and in a Ministry Council meeting with course and college principals on 10 November 2010 he said: 'The application of ACCM 22 was on individual institutions rather than the Church itself. It was a catholic concept implemented in a protestant way.'

56 Appendix II to ACCM 22, pp. 59–64, is the paper that went to the House of Bishops.

of GME, an examination that had served the Church since 1921 and it was now left to the training institutions to agree with ACCM what it was preparing candidates for, how preparation should be provided and how it should be tested. It represented a decisive break from the past, albeit one that had been in the making for many years.

The position of the colleges and courses remained essentially unchanged for nearly 20 years until a combination of questions about the structure of training involving the balance between the provision by courses and colleges and financial concerns led to a further report. The wider financial concerns in the early 1990s were partly generated by a much-publicized concern over the Church Commissioners' investment decisions in commercial property at that time but also because the proportion of the total cost of training met by LEA awards was dropping fast. In 1991 LEAs provided about 14 per cent of the cost of clergy training, by 2000 that had dropped to just over 1 per cent.[57] But it was primarily the over-provision of places in theological colleges that led to the Bishop of Lincoln, Robert Hardy, who had earlier been the Chairman of the Candidates Committee of ACCM, being asked to chair a group that produced a report *Theological Training – A Way Ahead*[58] published in 1992. The group had ecumenical representation as many of the courses and some of the colleges either had students from other churches training with Anglicans or were in partnership with training institutions of other churches. The group carefully examined each of the courses and the colleges and came up with proposals. On the future of the courses it strongly recommended that the nationwide network of courses should offer high quality ordination training which should be acceptable not just to Anglican bishops but to the Methodist and United Reformed Churches as well. It made a number of recommendations on amalgamations of existing courses so that they could serve a wider area and be in a closer partnership with some of the training provisions of other churches in their area. What proved far more controversial were the proposals for colleges. They believed that if colleges were in a federation with other colleges, as applied to the theological colleges in both Oxford and Cambridge, then that partnership was potentially creative and should not be ended, but that for non-federated colleges 60 students was the absolute minimum number for a college and that

---

57 David Morris and Mark Hodge, 'The Financing of Training', in Gordon Kuhrt (ed), 2001, *Ministry Issues for the Church of England,* London: Church House Publishing, p. 152.

58 *Theological Training – A Way Ahead,* GS Misc. 401, 1992.

ideally they should have between 100 and 120 students. The report also invited the bishops to: 'endorse the view that an institution which does not train women alongside men, in an integrated manner, is not preparing men adequately for the ministry they will be exercising after ordination', and they were also asked to: 'endorse the view that it is not practicable at present for ordinands to be trained in Church Colleges of Higher Education or for CCHE's to take over responsibility for providing part of theological training for ordinands'.[59]

Applying those principles led them to recommend that three colleges should be closed. Mirfield in Yorkshire was a college in the Catholic tradition associated with the Community of the Resurrection, and was the only college to retain a formal link with a religious community. It had a maximum capacity of 38 students but at the time of the visit by the group it had only 28 students, and the college limited itself to taking men only. Oak Hill was a college in the Evangelical tradition in north London, and the group was concerned by one aspect of its Trust deed, that 'no one may give religious teaching unless prepared to sign a declaration that "he is a Protestant and Evangelical in the strictest sense of those terms"'. The group also thought that Oak Hill had an inadequate response to the training requirements for women. Salisbury/Wells College in Salisbury had only a small number of students, most of whom were over 30; many could not use the teaching resources of the School of Theology at Southampton University, and it had an insecure financial position. While recommending that those three colleges should close, the group did, however, recommend that the possibility of forming a new ecumenical college in Manchester should be investigated.

The report was discussed on two occasions in the House of Bishops and was then published and debated in General Synod in November 1992. It undoubtedly suffered from the fact that the debate took place the day after General Synod had voted to approve the legislation for the ordination of women to the priesthood, and many in Synod who were supportive of the ordination of women were nonetheless concerned at a proposal that would have led to the closure of two colleges, Mirfield and Oak Hill, that would each have had many who were strongly opposed to the ordination of women. Very unusually Synod declined even to 'take note' of the report.

The House of Bishops therefore appointed an 'assessment group' under the chairmanship of the Bishop of Hereford, who would subsequently become Chairman of the Advisory Board for Ministry, to produce a new report for the

---

59 GS Misc. 401, p. 84.

House of Bishops within six months on the future pattern of training in the light of the House's concern that 'training in both Colleges and Courses should be considered together'. The report, *Theological Colleges – The Next Steps*[60] recommended that training for the ordained ministry should be focused on eight centres, Birmingham, Bristol, Cambridge, Durham, Leeds/Mirfield, London, Nottingham/Lincoln and Oxford, where the existing colleges should be invited to work in close partnership with each other and with other agencies offering training, including the courses, the colleges of other churches and university faculties and departments of theology. They therefore recommended that two colleges should be closed, Salisbury/Wells, as the earlier report had also recommended, and Chichester Theological College, which was a college in the Catholic tradition. That recommendation was accepted and implemented.

There was, however, one sequel to this process. After the closure of Salisbury/Wells, Lincoln Theological College was one of two colleges outside Oxford and Cambridge in the broad central tradition and which, like the other non-Oxbridge college broadly in that tradition, Queen's College, Birmingham, trained Methodist and Anglican students together. Lincoln's college council had been giving some thought to its future and it believed that there was a case for a different style of training which would not necessarily be residential in the traditional sense, but it would be full-time with students living at home and pursuing their studies. The college council thought this was an imaginative way of proceeding and believed it could best be achieved by moving to Sheffield to a Church Army establishment there. The *Way Ahead* report and *The Next Steps* report had both recommended that Lincoln should establish closer links with Nottingham, and although the college had pointed out that the journey from Sheffield to Nottingham was easier than the journey from Lincoln to Nottingham, the bishops nonetheless decided in 1995 to close Lincoln.[61] The subsequent General Synod debate[62] revealed the extent of the anger this had caused both locally and to the Methodists, but General Synod nonetheless endorsed the decision.

This meant that by the end of the century there were 11 theological colleges still training candidates for ordination. Two were definitely Catholic in outlook: St Stephen's House, Oxford, and Mirfield. Six were largely Evangelical in outlook: Oak Hill in London; Ridley Hall, Cambridge; Cranmer Hall, Durham; St John's

---

60 *Theological Colleges – The Next Steps*, GS 1070.

61 *Lincoln Theological College. Report by the House of Bishops*, GS 1170, July 1995.

62 *Report of Proceedings July 1995*, pp. 351–69.

College, Nottingham; Trinity College, Bristol; Wycliffe Hall, Oxford. Three were more central: Queen's College, Birmingham; Ripon College, Cuddesdon, Oxford; Westcott House, Cambridge. At the end of 2000, 618 ordinands were training at those colleges and four were at Llandaff College in the Church in Wales. Alongside those residential colleges there was a national network of 12 courses training on a part-time basis for both stipendiary and non-stipendiary ministry where there were 578 ordinands in training. There were also 18 dioceses that had 209 ordinands training on local courses for ordained local ministry.

Constitutional change again 1988–2000

In the last decade of the twentieth century there were two constitutional changes each of which added to the responsibilities of the previous body. The *Infrastructure Review*[63] published in 1988 was preparation for the new General Synod that would be elected for 1990. It examined whether central selection of ordination candidates was necessary and concluded that it was, with the bishops strongly in favour of it. It recommended adding the responsibilities of the Ministry Co-ordinating Group to the responsibilities of ACCM, and incorporating within the structures of the new board the work of the Ministry to the Deaf and the Hospital Chaplaincy Council. It also suggested that the new name should be the Board for Ministry. ACCM's response,[64] while accepting the additional responsibilities, noted that the work of the Ministry to the Deaf and the Hospital Chaplaincy Council could be marginalized in a larger body, and it also thought that the word 'advisory' should remain in its title. It also pointed out that responsibility for any lay ministry regulated by Canon should be its responsibility. In effect that was given to it in its new Constitution (Appendix C), and which the board reported in its Annual Report of 1990 to give it 'a broad remit to advise on all matters concerning the ministry of the Church and to investigate and evaluate new patterns of ministry'.

In 1995 *Working as One Body: The Report of the Archbishops' Commission on the Organisation of the Church of England* was published.[65] The Commission was

---

63 *Infrastructure Review*, GS 827, 1988.

64 *Response from ACCM to the Infrastructure Review*, GS 302. (Undated, but it must have been 1988 or 1989.)

65 *Working as One Body: The Report of the Archbishops' Commission on the Organisation of the Church of England*, 1995, London: Church House Publishing.

chaired by the Bishop of Durham, Michael Turnbull. It recommended the creation of a new national council to which all the bodies then answerable to General Synod would in future be answerable, and it would be chaired by the Archbishop of Canterbury with the Archbishop of York as vice-chairman. In the subsequent discussions the name of the council was changed to the Archbishops' Council, and there followed a lengthy series of debates that modified the Turnbull proposals in detail but not fundamentally. It recommended the establishment of a Ministry Division which would have three areas of work:

- Vocation, recruitment and selection.
- Theological education and training.
- Deployment strategy, remuneration and conditions of service.

The first two of those had, since World War Two, been the responsibility of first CACTM, then ACCM and then ABM, and ABM also had responsibility for monitoring deployment, but the third area of responsibility was far enhanced from anything that ABM had dealt with and represented a major extension of work. It was agreed that those with the day-to-day management of the division would have the title of director, replacing the title general secretary. (The detailed supporting committee structure is in Appendix C.)

The concept of a strategy

In the last 30 years of the twentieth century the ministry had developed, most notably with the increasing presence of women in the ordained ministry, but also with the development of ordained local ministry. Most people in the Church of England saw those developments as building on something that was already in place rather than destroying root and branch an older system, although a small minority did view the ordination of women in that more destructive light. A certain amount of structural change occurred, both in the creation of, first, the Advisory Board of Ministry followed by the Ministry Division, and the considerable changes in the pattern of training begun in the 1960s had been confirmed and deepened. Did that all amount to a comprehensive strategy?

A strategy can either build on what you already have, or attempt to destroy something you have to replace it by something better. It was clear that, with the possible exception of the ordination of women as viewed by those most passionately opposed, the Church of England had followed the first type of strategy. The basic structure of the ordained ministry remained the same, most stipendiary clergy were incumbents of parishes, patronage remained in place for their appointment, and in 2000 freehold was still the normal form of appointing parish priests. Tiller's strategy hoped to change all those things, but to attempt that by a single report was a hopeless task and proposals like his would have had to emerge from a far more detailed period of consultation with the whole Church if they were to have any chance of being implemented. That consultation did happen much later on the far narrower question of freehold and led to its gradual abolition, but that only came through a very long process and a whole series of debates in General Synod and Diocesan Synods. Common tenure as the present method of employing the clergy is far less radical than anything Tiller proposed.

Nonetheless major developments have happened, but they were also not part of any self-conscious declared national strategy. Rather they were decisions taken by some sort of combination of principle and pragmatism. Perhaps that is all that can be expected of a national Church.

12

In Retrospect

This book has shown some of the major changes that happened in the central management of clergy in the Church of England over the twentieth century. When the bishops agreed to the establishing of the Central Advisory Council of Training for the Ministry in 1912, few if any of them or of those who attended its first meetings in 1913 could have foreseen the development from a body that brought together some key people for meetings in London with a part-time secretary to what by the end of the century had become the Ministry Division, with a permanent base in Church House, Westminster and a significant number of full-time staff. At every stage when the organization changed its name and its fundamental constitution additional responsibilities were given, all of which were approved either initially by the bishops or later by the Church Assembly or General Synod. Apart from the comments in the 1922 Church Assembly debate about 'an ultra-montane institution in the south-east of England', initial debates over the introduction of selection conferences and then the complex debates over the changed responsibilities given in 1959, the additional responsibilities all eventually became uncontroversial and widely accepted. That represented a fundamental vote of confidence over many years in the organization.

External factors led to some of the noteworthy changes over the years, of which the two World Wars were perhaps the most obvious. Finance was a major but not the only factor. Archbishops Davidson's and Lang's letter to all servicemen in World War One inviting them to consider the possibility of ordination after the war and making the promise that the Church would find the cost of their training if necessary led to a striking widening of the social background from which many of the clergy came. The willingness of the Central Board of Finance and through them the rest of the Church to meet that cost was deeply impressive. Although the debates over Knutsford after the first war might have indicated a certain rowing back from the commitment to enable anyone to train who wished to, in fact the Church through the dioceses and from various societies associated with particular churchmanship traditions did respond in the inter-war years and enabled many to receive at least some financial assistance. After World War Two it was the British Government that made the difference, first with grants to returning servicemen to enable them to train, and then by encouraging the development of Local Education Authority awards from which many ordinands benefited. By the end of the twentieth century that financial support for ordination training apart from for initial degrees had significantly tailed off, but by then a Church grants system had been developed and payment to it from the dioceses was widely accepted. It enabled the Church to support anyone who was accepted for training.

Other wider social changes also had their influence. The changes in educational policy that flowed from the 1944 Butler Act with the desire to provide a fuller education for all fostered the notion that education should be available irrespective of social background. The developing welfare state in the years after World War Two, with the State providing what had hitherto been provided by charities, was part of the general social background against which the centralization and other changes of the Fisher years must be viewed. When the Church of England developed a fund to enable ordination candidates to obtain grants for training it was pushing at a door that had already been partially opened by government initiatives. Both the development of non-stipendiary ministry and the ordination of women happened against the background of changing patterns of employment and far greater opportunities for women in many other areas of society. A national church swims in a national pool, and it cannot expect to be unaffected by what is happening elsewhere.

Those changes also had a direct effect on the Church's ministry. The widening of categories of ministry first by the development of non-stipendiary ministry, then by ordained local ministry and by the ordination of women first to the diaconate and then to priesthood, had a profound effect, not just in maintaining parochial ministry but extending ministry to areas where it might not otherwise have reached. Of course numbers have declined over the century: in 1900 there were just over 25,000 stipendiary clergy, by 2000 there were just under 11,000 stipendiary clergy including those in chaplaincies and other forms of stipendiary ministry which would have been included in the 1900 figures. But by 2000 there were also nearly 2,000 non-stipendiary or ordained local ministers and in addition there were 6,000 retired clergy, many of whom would have still been active in ministry. That was a very different situation from the one in 1900, when there would have been relatively few retired clergy. One of the major changes of the century was the introduction of pensions for clergy wishing to retire, the Pensions Board being founded in 1926; but that has not been discussed in this book as it was never a responsibility of CACTM or its successor bodies.[1]

Training for the ministry has changed over the century, with it being compulsory in 2000 in a way that it was not in 1900, and with the range of ways in which someone can train for ordination having been widely developed. Non-residential training for both stipendiary and non-stipendiary ministry provided training for slightly over half of all those in training at the end of the century, but residential theological colleges, although reduced in number since 1900, still provide substantial training opportunities for those seeking ordination and many of those in training both residentially and non-residentially do so in ecumenical settings.

What had changed in training was the balance between churchmanship traditions. From World War Two onwards there was normally a very rough parity in training provision between Evangelical colleges, Anglo-Catholic colleges and so-called 'central' colleges. Many ordinands might have been unwilling to identify too strongly with any one of those traditions and the presence of a particular ordinand in a college did not mean they necessarily identified wholly with the college's perceived public stance; certainly there were some ordinands who very definitely rebelled against the prevailing tradition of their college. But the balance between churchmanship in the residential colleges was changed by the final decisions in the 1990s, and a far higher proportion of colleges are more clearly in the Evangelical tradition than was the case in the 1960s or even in the 1980s. Some would say that was a result of market forces and simply acknowledged a broader growth of that grouping within the Church, but the decision to decide which colleges were to be closed was not taken on the basis of purely market forces, but neither was it taken by those with churchmanship axes to grind.

One other major change documented at various stages throughout this book has been the development of a far more rigorous system of selection. It started in a partial, but for those going through it, a very thorough way with Knutsford, which was known as a test school. Subsequently it happened in a slightly more haphazard way through those seeking a grant being interviewed by those

---

1 The figure of 6,000 in 2000 comes from the Church of England Pensions Board. Interestingly enough in 2001 the number went up to 7,703 of whom 4,647 were deemed as active retired based on the number of permission to officiate, licence to officiate and posts held. The figure for active retired clergy is not available for 2000.

awarding the grant, although that did not apply to all candidates. It was only in World War Two that selection became compulsory for everyone. In one sense it was by accident that the Church of England happened to latch on to the War Office selection boards as the way to select returning servicemen, but it was a fortunate accident. The army's concern at the inadequacies of its earlier selection systems had led to an extensive examination of the best selection methods, and the WOSB model was undoubtedly at the forefront of best practice in the 1940s. It was subsequently used by the Civil Service, and at every stage when major reform of the selection system has happened the Church has sought advice from a wide range of expertise in those concerned with selection in other fields, but with key figures from the Civil Service selection boards having a significant role. The Church of England has not been afraid of seeking advice in many areas of selection and training from some of the best informed in the country at the time. But since the first selection boards for potential ordinands in the 1940s dioceses have also developed more thorough approaches to assessing candidates prior to sending them to a national selection board. No selection system is perfect, and selection itself is not an exact science; mistakes are bound to be made, but the Church of England can be proud of its system, which it delivers at remarkably low cost. When the financial consequences of making a wrong selection are taken into account, to say nothing of the human consequences, the modest cost of the selection system means that the Church is getting excellent value for money. One other factor should also be noted about selection: it has no churchmanship bias. John Phillips' comments to the *Church Times* in 1948 mentioned in Chapter 8 remained as true at the end of the century as when he wrote them.

This change has undoubtedly had an effect on how episcopacy is exercised. The almost casual dismissal of a proposal from the Lower House of Canterbury in 1901 that a central council should be established, apparently on the grounds that the bishops knew best, mentioned in Chapter 2, would not have happened in quite the same way towards the end of the century. Bishops remained, rightfully, the ultimate guardians of the process, and the various attempts to wrest control of episcopal functions from any central council for ministry have rightly failed, but episcopacy by the end of the century was exercised in a far more consultative and even synodical way. To chart the change in how episcopacy was exercised over the century would be a large and complex investigation, but the changing pattern of selection would be a significant factor in such a study.

But where does this all leave vocation? Mary Tanner, now European President of the World Council of Churches, in a lecture given in 1986 entitled *Towards a Theology of Vocation*, spoke of the notion of vocation to an individual always being related to the wider vocation of the corporate. 'It is within this primary call of Israel as the chosen people that we hear of individual Israelites being called'[2] she said of the Old Testament picture. 'As in the Old Testament, so in the New Testament, the notion of the calling of the individual is always within this primary sense of the calling of the baptised community to fulfil the purpose of God.'[3] The Church is called to be the Body of Christ in the world of today, and in that it should be thoughtful, effective and even efficient in the use of its resources.

It is not entirely fanciful to see the developments recorded in this book as being aspects of the Church of England responding to its corporate vocation. When in 1912 the bishops agreed to the setting up of CACTM they were reacting to a proposal from a commission in an essentially pragmatic and practical way. They presumably thought this was a wise and sensible way of dealing with what were at the time complex and potentially divisive questions. But in pursuing that programme, although they may not have used the language at the time, were they not also through that responding to the Church's vocation? This, they thought, would lead to a better way of dealing with matters which might lead to a more effective training programme for the clergy of the future, so that those clergy could make their contribution to the fundamental charge given to the Church of England to respond more effectively to the nation's need for ministry. And the same thing could have been said of all the developments recorded in this book: producing an effective and well-trained ministry and, when appropriate, finding new ways of exercising that ministry is part of the Church's corporate vocation. It could be argued that all the developments discussed here were part of the process of testing that vocation, not least of all against a background where the general population's knowledge of the Christian faith was probably becoming weaker. Whether the Church as a whole has been faithful to its vocation is a more complex question. For example, has it ever responded thoroughly to the theological and historical questions raised in the Archbishops' Commission and summarized in Appendix H? The 1938 Archbishops' Commission on Christian Doctrine report went some way towards addressing that, but while a variety of individual clergy, including some bishops, have

---

2 *Towards a Theology of Vocation*, p. 2. Unfortunately this paper has never been published.
3 *Vocation*, p. 3.

undoubtedly addressed those matters, was there at the end of the twentieth century a widespread understanding among the laity of the issues discussed there? Has the Church, or has it not, failed in its vocation to meet the intellectual concerns of those whom Raven described as 'certain outstanding young men' in this matter?

But as this book shows, the pursuit of the Church's corporate vocation in a wider sphere than doctrine has often been done in discussion with those outside the Church, whether that be government ministers and officials as in Temple's correspondence with them in Chapter 7, or with the post-war government in funding returning servicemen, or in continued discussions with those knowledgeable in other spheres of national life in matters of selection and training. Following vocation for a national church involves engaging creatively with the wider society. Clearly it needs ministers who are still able to do that effectively.

But what about vocation in the more personal sphere? Any Christian should remember that the primary call is to follow Jesus Christ by loving God and loving your neighbour, which can be done in almost any sphere of life. No one needs to be ordained to do that. That primary vocation takes precedence over anything else. How a Christian man or woman lives his or her life is every bit as important as what their occupation is. But what of vocation in that more personal sphere of an individual deciding what to do for their occupation, particularly for those seeking ordination? In practice it seems that men and women offer for ordained ministry for a whole variety of reasons, but they can probably be categorized into three broad divisions.

There undoubtedly remain some who believe they are responding to some inner call from God to offer. Much of what has been said in the Church about vocation over many years encourages that view; Griffith Thomas wrote of it in the early part of the twentieth century but many other clergy have expressed it in similar terms since then. It should, of course, be respected. But Philip Larkin has an arresting phrase in his poem 'Church Going':

> A serious house on serious earth it is,
> In whose blent air all our compulsions meet,
> Are recognised, and robed as destinies.

Robing as our destinies something that has apparently been decided from compulsions we may have recognized, but equally may not have fully understood, is a dangerous business. So those who approach ordination from that notion of a strong inner call would be wise to seek the advice of others. In two interesting sermons on vocation in *Open to Judgement*[4] Rowan Williams suggests of vocation that, 'God's call is the call to *be*: the *vocation* of creatures is to exist. And ... the vocation of creatures is to exist *as themselves* ... answering to the word that gives each its distinctive identity.'[5] Yet truly to know who we are nearly always requires the perceptions of other people, and possibly even more we need their advice in knowing what we will have to deny in ourselves to pursue a particular course. That is why relying purely on some sort of 'inward call' is so risky; the cautions of Moberly, Barry, Baelz and others mentioned here should be heeded. But whatever reasons someone may give for offering for ministry, it is just that, an offer, which may or may not be accepted. The external judgement of the Church and its confirmation that ordination for an individual might be the right way forward is critical. If God calls, he also calls through the judgement of the Church.

That will also apply to those who might offer on a slightly different basis. Those contemplating leaving full-time education have to decide what they are going to do with the rest of their lives, just as anyone may decide at any stage of their life that they are unfulfilled in what they are doing and want to change. If they are at all sensible they will examine what really interests them and excites passion, and they may also ask themself where there are areas of real need: if I do that job can I make a difference? In that context they may then ask what their strengths and weaknesses are, and what gifts they have been given, where for those contemplating ordination the list of qualities looked for in the selection process will help. On the basis of that sort of self-examination a Christian man or woman may well consider the possibility of ministry in the Church, but it will not be through a fundamentally different process from someone who wants to offer as a doctor, a teacher, a lawyer or any of the other roles that are often described as vocations. It should be perfectly possible for someone to offer for ordination saying that they had thought this was a role for which they might be suited, they think it would be a context in which they can genuinely be themselves, not least of all because they could see that the role was a significant way of helping other people and because it was a matter that excited passion in them; no one will be able to survive the rigours of ordained ministry over many years unless that degree of passion is there. In assessing someone approaching ordination in such a way, the Church would have to point

---

4 Rowan Williams, 1994, *Open to Judgement,* London: Darton, Longman, Todd, pp. 171–84.

5 Williams, *Judgement,* p. 173.

out that ministry is not primarily about self-fulfilment but about fulfilling others, and it is essentially a call to serve as the ordinal makes clear. The candidate may or may not dress his or her offer up in the language of an inner call, but a real examination of the motives for offering is part of the critical purpose of selection and the motivation to be of service is central. Again it would then be for the Church to decide, and through that decision the call is given and confirmed at ordination.

The third broad category is one that has been recognized through the development of ordained local ministry but it may well be of wider significance. The 'call' may come through the request of the Church to someone who had not beforehand ever thought of the possibility. When a local church invites one or more of its members to consider being a priest in their congregation it is only doing what in a far earlier period of the life of the Church was common. Mary Tanner points out:

> In two cases, Ambrose of Milan and Martin of Tours, they were ordained deacon, priest, and consecrated bishop all at once and against their own will and desire. Those called by the community were expected to obey the community's call at once. The responsibility of the congregation in the choice of ministry was held to be the choice by the Holy Spirit. According to Cyprian, God, with whom the real decision lies, speaks through the voice of the community. Recognition of the candidate by the Church and sending by the Church is the really decisive thing about the ordination service.[6]

It is very doubtful today whether any bishop would agree to ordain someone against their own will. The *Criteria for Selection* report said that the candidate has to make the sense of calling their own. But there are undoubtedly candidates coming to selection conferences who do so because others have asked and then encouraged them to consider the possibility. Possibly that should happen more widely.

Call to Order suggested that the Church needed vigorous recruitment and rigorous selection, and that policy should continue to apply for the twenty-first century. But to do that also requires a coherent concept of what it means by vocation. Whether this book provides it, like the decision on whether someone should be ordained, is for the Church to decide.

---

6 *Vocation*, p. 5.

Appendix A
Correspondence between Randall Davidson, Bishop of Rochester, and C. H. Waller, Principal St John's, Highbury

The correspondence followed an application to the bishop from Humphrey Hirst, a student at St John's, Highbury, to be allowed to sit the bishop's examination for the diocese. Hirst was the son of a retired grocer from Yorkshire, who had left school when he was 14, but then served an apprenticeship to an elementary schoolmaster, and had become a schoolmaster himself. The bishop's chaplain wrote to Hirst on 7 March 1895.

> I am, however, to point out to you that the ordinary rule of this diocese is to accept for Ordination those only who are graduates. The Bishop makes an exception, as you will see in the paper of Instructions herewith sent, in favour of those who have passed through Highbury <u>with marked success.</u> I do not quite gather that the success in your case has been conspicuous, although I gather you have passed the necessary examinations. In these circumstances the Bishop does not think he ought to encourage you to come forward in this Diocese. There are many other dioceses in which the conditions are less stringent. Should you desire to present yourself, the Bishop does not prohibit you from doing so, but it would be necessary that you should, to justify your acceptance, pass a really good examination in every respect. You will realise that in the event of your failing thus to reach a really high standard, the Bishop would decline to accept you, and you would have seriously prejudiced your position in the event of your becoming a candidate in another Diocese. In these circumstances you will probably think it best to apply to some other Bishop, but I shall be grateful if you will let me hear from you what is your decision.

The principal, C. H. Waller, wrote to the chaplain, comparing Hirst to a Cambridge graduate (Ridsdale), also at the college, who had been allowed to sit the examination but who had failed. Hirst had done rather better in the college examinations than the Cambridge graduate.

> It strikes the student members of this College (who know all this) that the Rochester standard is framed on somewhat curious principles, accepting without question the <u>ignorant graduates,</u> and warning off the trained student who leaves him helplessly behind in our College examination ... Now letters such as yours to Mr Hirst, however kindly meant, elicit from our men a style of remark which I do not like to hear, and which does not indicate that respect for Diocesan authorities which it is desirable to preserve. It is not possible in the present day to draw such a line of demarcation between the average graduate and the trained Theological student as your letter indicates.

Davidson himself wrote to Hirst on 9 March saying that he could sit the examination if he wished, but that he would only consider a mark over 75 per cent as indicating a 'really good examination'. He wrote the same day to Waller:

> I am sorry you should think my general action respecting Ordination Candidates so unreasonable. I do not know that I quite follow your arguments, especially as regards its allusion to Mr Ridsdale, who as you remind me, twice <u>failed</u> to pass our examination. The whole question of the Bishop's responsibility for the acceptance or rejection of candidates for Holy Orders is at present to my mind full of difficulty. If you think a Bishop is not justified in forming a general opinion as to prima facie qualifications of a candidate – taking into consideration the character of his education from childhood, his social surroundings, the fact that he has not had the advantage of residence in a University, and the probable character of his influence quite apart from his intellectual attainments – I fear I should not agree with you. Of course in such a case as Mr Hirst's I can only judge of these matters in the most superficial manner while my illness prevents me from seeing him; but I thought it kinder to direct my Chaplain in the first instance to warn Mr Hirst that I had seen so far no grounds for assurance that he would show himself in all respects qualified for ordination in this Diocese. It would be quite easy for me in such cases to allow an applicant to become a candidate without question and thus afterwards to reject him

if he failed to meet all the conditions I think it necessary. I can only say that the other course appeared to me the kindlier one, and I cannot help it if your students misunderstand or misinterpret my advice in such matters. You will be aware that I do not accept, as many Bishops do, an ordinary Theological College *per se* as qualifying a man to be accepted as a candidate. I have wished if possible to make an exception in the case of Highbury. If you feel however that my action in the matter is so unreasonable as to cause misunderstandings and difficulties, it may perhaps be wiser that I should place Highbury in the same category as other Theological Colleges and accept only those who were graduates before entering on their Theological College course. I really do not wish to have a series of protests as to my exercise of what seems to me the Bishop's proper discrimination in this most responsible matter, and I gather from what you say that you think I am doing harm by causing misunderstandings on the part of the students.

The principal, who was clearly surprised to have received a reply from the bishop himself, responded:

I am obliged by your letter. Mine was written, not to a Bishop, but in reply to a letter that was written in the handwriting of a clerk, signed by a chaplain.

I thought it well to tell <u>him</u> the feeling with which our men regard the withdrawing of the recognition accorded to us in the Diocese of Rochester from the first days of this College.

On both sides of the Thames one sees, when standing on one of the bridges, the same teeming population, with the same wants; the very wants which our men are especially trained to supply. I readily admit that they are not so well qualified for wealthy and cultured congregations as to preach and carry the gospel to the poor.

On the north side of the river we are a Diocesan College. On the south we have been so regarded until a few years ago. This very moment I have been reading a paper of instructions from the present Bishop of Winchester in which he recognises this College side by side with King's College, London. When St John's College had been recognised throughout the whole of greater London for years, and that recognition is withdrawn by the Bishop on the poorer side of the river, when it is assumed that our students <u>as a</u>

<u>body</u> were unfit for Holy Orders in South London, unless some one or two of them may perchance rise to a higher level intellectually than the rest, is there room for surprise that the colleges should think less of the favour shown to one or two, than to the stigma (I can call it nothing less) affixed to the body by withdrawing the recognition hitherto accorded to them in South London by shutting the Diocese of Rochester against them in all but exceptional cases.

A College like this is not established in the metropolis except at the cost of great labour and large outlay. If the Bishops of the metropolis by constant recognition for some time encourage men to spend their money and their lives upon it, a great responsibility must needs attach to any Bishop who withdraws the countenance already given to the undertaking. Supposing a generation of Bishops to arise who did this, the foundations may be lost to the church entirely. It could be withdrawn if our students as a body were unfit for the ministry, no injustice would be done.

But when the Bishops in their corporate capacity have guarded an exit by one public examination (in 1874) and our entrance by another (in 1893) the recognition awarded to us upon the whole is manifest; so I venture to say it binds them morally to receive and examine our candidates on a level with other candidates. The entrance examination more especially does so; for it interferes with the right of admission to our College course.

Personal fitness or unfitness for Holy Orders is entirely a matter for a Bishop's discretion. But the letter to which I replied assumed the unfitness of Highbury men as a body and laid the burden of proving the fitness of every individual candidate upon the college and the candidate himself.

Unless my memory is strangely at fault, every applicant of ours for Holy Orders at Rochester since the See was last vacated has been met by a challenge to shew that he was fit for the Diocese at all.

Personally your Lordship heartened me with the greatest courtesy and kindness at all times. This very fact brings out all the more forcibly the entire change in the policy of the diocese. When I began my work here, my father's old friend, T. L. Claughton, whom I remember fifty years ago, held the See of Rochester. My first pupil here, Dr Lonsdell, was gospeller at his Ordination. He never forgot it, and always received our men most kindly. The next Bishop I had served as curate at Curzon Chapel. He also has always received our men. It is a fact, then, that from the very first days of the College, we have been recognised by Rochester: even before we were recognised as a Diocesan College in London. Under the present regime, for no charge made against us, the recognition is withdrawn, and our position in half London seriously imperilled. Should we be human, if we refunded the withdrawal of confidence, the entire change of position, with silence, with equanimity, may I not add – without strongly protesting against it, as the affixing of a stigma and rebuke which it has never been shewn (or attempted to be shewn) that we have done anything to deserve? Again I say, far be it from me to attempt to fetter the discretion of a Bishop in any individual case. But the relations of a Metropolitan Bishop to Metropolitan institutions are surely not other than covenant relations binding in equity upon the Diocesan, unless the very gravest reason can be shewn why they should be altered? While all Theological College men were treated as literates, there was something to be said for isolated and separate action by individual Bishops. But I respectfully submit, that the formal recognition of all non-graduate Theological Colleges, implied by the establishment of a central and episcopal list of entrance to them, a matter which seriously affects their income, teaching and independence, deprives the Bishops in a measure of their liberty to treat these colleges one by one as having no formal right to recognition as places of clerical training. I think that if the Bishops in their corporate capacity take upon themselves the government of our Colleges – and this they have now done –, we can claim from them as a body that they should receive our candidates just as they receive graduates, when the general conditions are fulfilled. Is not this both just and reasonable?

As to Mr Hirst, if he be personally unfit, I have no more to say. All I ask is that he shall not be pronounced unfit simply because he is a Highbury man – and that the burden of proving the fitness of every [...] student of this College to be examined by a Bishop for ordination be no longer added to the list of my labours and responsibilities after thirty years of tested labour as a teacher of students for the ministry.

I am sorry to be troublesome or pertinacious, when your Lordship has been so kind to me personally, and the more so when you are unwell. Pray let this matter rest until you feel able to deal with it; and do not take the trouble to reply. And let me make one more suggestion in the last place; that your Lordship should take the opportunity of visiting this College and inquiring into its manners, customs, rules of appliances, with a view to this question: whether a place of training equipped as this is, within four miles of Charing Cross, is really so inferior to a College of Cambridge – or even at Oxford – as to necessitate the use of a pair of – shall I say 'selecting tongs' before a candidate for Holy Orders is taken from it. We shall be most happy to see you and to give every facility for looking into the question.

Despite his illness Davidson replied the following day on 11 March 1895:

... The issue you raise seems to me a yet graver one than I had supposed. You contend, as I understand, that all Bishops are now bound to regard any and every Theological College which satisfies the rule drawn up respecting entrance examinations as *ipso facto* placing its students in a position to claim acceptance as candidates in any Diocese, whether they be graduates or not. I am quite certain that this is not the view of the Bishops generally, but if you desire it, I will enquire, say, from the Archbishop of Canterbury, the Bishop of London, the Bishop of Oxford and others among the leading Bishops, as to whether they now consider themselves bound to accept a non-graduate candidate say from Chichester, or Lincoln, or Lichfield Theological Colleges. It is obviously right that if they are understood to have so pledged themselves, the matter should be immediately made clear.

Waller received the letter the same day and immediately replied, referring again to the central entrance examination.

My best thanks are due for your Lordships' kind letter: and for the offer to bring this point I raised before other Bishops. I do not know that the matter is quite ripe for that. I should be only too glad if their Lordships would seriously consider the position. That it is really and substantially altered by the new examination is, to me, undeniable. Much more than it was in 1874 by the establishment of the Universities Preliminary Examination for Holy Orders. That the Bishops recognised rather than established. Some of them make no use of it to this day. The entrance examination has been enacted universally. The enactment came from the Primate himself to me and others, through the Principal of King's College, London. Nothing that has happened in the last 30 years has so seriously affected the freedom of the Colleges as this. We cannot admit a single student to our three year's course, without carefully considering his classical position. We cannot compel any man to commence his course at any particular time of year, the moment he can pass the new standard, he is entitled to begin a two years' training: we cannot force him to stay longer or we lose him. The work of our tutors is changed; our course is altered, to what precise extent we hardly know; it will take several years to settle into regular ways. Now such interference as this, such closely controlling legislation is recognition. To what extent remains to be proved.

Before long some formal representation or petition is likely to come to the Bishops, not perhaps to remove the fresh test they have imposed upon us, but to come to some distinct understandings in regard to it.

Our own governing body and our own staff are seriously exercised. So are the persons in charge of other Colleges. We are all forced upon level ground at a certain point of a course: whether it be levelling up, or levelling down. I am not sure which. But I think it is somewhat hard on men like myself, who have given their lives to the training of men for Holy Orders whom the Bishops cannot do without, men who cannot afford University training, but whose business-training and knowledge of men and things goes far beyond that of a graduate of 23; – I say it is hard upon us, to be always liable to an earthquake, and to have our own foundations shaken under us, every time a new Bishop takes his seat on the bench. Every fresh Prelate seems to think himself at liberty – or shall I say bound in conscience –, to reopen the question of our right to exist at all, de novo. No matter what service we have done, say in Ripon, in Rochester, in York, in Norwich Diocese, I speak purposely of these in view of actual change, a new Bishop comes to the throne and the first man who applies to him can be met as it were by the questions 'Who are you?' 'What's Highbury?' I know nothing of St John's Hall. 'What right have you to ask ordination at my hands?' The 'new king' never knows Joseph; though his predecessor may have been saved by him from a famine. Now I do think it time that some sort of fixity [. . .] should be given to our relations with the Bench; and that the time has come when, with an Episcopal gate at our entrance and another at our exit, and a most vigilant set of examiners at both of them, people who pass should be allowed to present themselves as candidates for Holy Orders; and should be received at least as lawful candidates.

Other questions present themselves, which exercise me seriously: this among them. What right a bishop has to require honours (i.e. a 1st or 2nd class) in an examination called the 'Universities Preliminary Examination for Holy Orders.' Surely an Examination for that Holy Office is a pass Examination. Are we right to state marks and places, and introduce competition at all? I doubt it seriously.

Now if the Bishops would debate these things from the bottom, as they debate our right to exist, regularly every time a new man puts on a mitre, there would be some hope. As it is, we find labour and sorrow and uncertainty and anxiety, but our condition is for ever expressed by St Paul's 'One blessing I have to be thankful for: I know where to put my trust and it is here. I know thy works, behold I have set before thee an open door, and no man can shut it, for thou hast little strength, and hast kept my word, and hast not denied My Name.' But I have learnt another lesson too. 'Put not your trust in princes, nor in the son of man in whom there is no help. His breath goeth forth, he returneth to the earth: in that very day his thoughts perish.' The Bishop dies or is translated. His field passes to another, and our men may no longer enter that vineyard as before.

If this view of the matter should present itself to your Lordship's mind as worthy of consideration, I can vouch for its genuineness. I use no figures; I speak the literal truth – I began this work [under?] 24 – I continue it at 54, and I am not good for many more years of it. Naturally I should like to feel things a little more settled under my feet, after 30 years. I shall soon be too old to begin again. I don't want to put anything crude before the Bishops. I should like to see them earnestly and seriously consider these matters: and I should like one case, I mean my own and that of others who are labouring at the same sort of work, fairly and ably put before them. And with sincerely thanks for your Lordship's kind forebearance with my prolixity. I remain

Your very faithful servant

Mr Hirst is so far impressed with the great things required of him, that he will not attempt the diocese of Rochester if he can find a title in London, where he is already accepted by the Bishop.

Davidson replied on 13 March 1895:

I thank you for your letter received today. You will not expect me to answer it in detail. If I understand it right it practically says this: No Bishop ought to be at liberty to insist in his Diocese upon a higher standard of qualification than the minimum standard required in any other Diocese. But I do not want now to argue the point, as I gather that you propose to arrange for a formal statement to the Bishops collectively upon the subject. You are aware that the present changes with regard to the admission of non-graduates as candidates for Holy Orders (in those Dioceses which accept non-graduates) were the result of mature deliberations by the Bishops who have the most ample experience in the training of ordinands. Clearly I cannot lightly reject or depart from rules laid down upon such authority. I quite agree that your wisest plan is that which you propose, namely, to lay a formal statement before the Bishops collectively.

Waller replied the same day:

I do not wish to be understood as holding that any restriction is to be laid on a Bishop in his private examination. If Bishops will examine our men, it is all we ask. The rest of your Lordship's letter refers to matters of which I have no knowledge.

He asked that the bishops as a whole should consider the matter, which Davidson took as a suggestion that the principals should produce a proper submission to the bishops.

There is no evidence that any statement was forthcoming from the principals.

It is perhaps interesting to note that Humphrey Hirst was ordained in 1895, but in the Diocese of London, where St John's Highbury was recognized as a diocesan college. He served in London, Bristol, Norwich and was chaplain of Bath Union before becoming incumbent of a parish in Oxford in 1917. After serving in two parishes in Oxford he was licensed as a public preacher in Derby Diocese after 40 years of active ministry.[1]

---

1 The whole correspondence between Waller and Davidson is in the Davidson papers, Vol. 41, pp. 21–67. Humphrey Hirst still appeared in *Crockford's* in 1941, from which this information is obtained.

Appendix B
Chairmen and Secretaries of
CACTM/ACCM/ABM/Ministry Division

Information for these biographies has been obtained from *Crockford's*, *Who's Who*, the *Dictionary of National Biography*, and *Some Biographical Information about the Bishops*, by John Smallwood in Lambeth Palace Library.

Chairmen

Archibald Robertson (1853–1931) Chairman 1913–16

Robertson was 59 at the time of the first meeting of CACTM. He had a distinguished career in education, having graduated with first class honours in *literae humaniores* from Trinity College, Oxford, where he was subsequently made lecturer, fellow and then dean. From there he moved to Durham University as Principal of Bishop Hatfield's Hall and was then appointed Principal of King's College, London. Apart from his experience as an educational administrator his main academic contributions were made in the area of patristic and historical studies, particularly a major work on Athanasius. He was appointed Bishop of Exeter in 1903 and had served on the earlier Committee of Bishops dealing with ordination training. The *Dictionary of National Biography* says of him, 'His charge of 1905 summarised his approach to the Church of England, *English Churchmanship, an invitation to brotherly union on the basis of the Book of Common Prayer*.' Ill-health forced him to resign his See and hence the chairmanship in 1916.

Winfrid Burrows (1858–1929) Chairman 1916–27

Burrows was educated at Eton and Corpus Christi College, Oxford, where he obtained firsts in classics and mathematics, and rowed at bow in all four years at the college as an undergraduate. He then moved to Christ Church, Oxford, where he was senior student (i.e. fellow) and was ordained in 1886. Within five years of ordination he moved to be Principal of the Leeds Clergy School until Charles Gore invited him to become Vicar of St Augustine's, Edgbaston and then appointed him in 1904 to be Archdeacon of Birmingham. He became Bishop of Truro in 1912, and was translated to Chichester in 1919, mainly to be closer to London to work on the revision of the Prayer Book. He became Chairman of CACTM in 1916 at the age of 58 following the resignation of Archibald Robertson. He resigned as Chairman because of ill health in 1927. He died in office while staying in Lambeth Palace in 1929 aged 70.

Guy Warman (1872–1953) Chairman 1928–43

Warman was educated at Merchant Taylors' School and Pembroke College, Oxford, where he obtained a second class honours in classics and then theology. He was curate of Leyton from 1895, Vice-Principal of St Aidan's, Birkenhead from 1901 to 1902, Vicar of Birkenhead, 1902–8, and Principal of St Aidan's 1907–16. While there he was elected as one of the first principals on CACTM. From Birkenhead he moved in 1916 to be Vicar of Bradford, and in 1919 succeeded Winfrid Burrows as Bishop of Truro, moving to Chelmsford in 1923, then to Manchester (in succession to William Temple) in 1929. An Evangelical by conviction he was tolerant of other views. He was a very effective chairman and respected by the business community. He resigned as Chairman to make way for Leslie Owen as full-time Chairman of CACTM, but remained Bishop of Manchester until he retired in 1947.

Leslie Owen (1886–1947) Chairman 1944–6

Owen was educated at Merchant Taylors' School and St John's College, Oxford. After curacies he served as a temporary chaplain to the forces 1916–19, then became a lecturer and Vice-Principal of Bishops' College, Cheshunt from 1919 to 1922, overlapping briefly with Nugent Hicks. He became Secretary of the Candidates Committee from 1922 to 1924 dealing with the question of returning servicemen after World War One and then briefly succeeded Hicks as General Secretary of CACTM in 1924. Later that year he moved to be Chaplain to the Duke of Portland at Welbeck from 1924 to 1928, then moved to be Warden of Lincoln Theological College, where he remained until 1936. He stated, 'The purpose of a theological college is to teach men to pray theologically.' In 1936 he moved to Durham as Archdeacon of Auckland and in 1939 Hensley Henson appointed him Bishop of Jarrow. From there his appointment as Bishop of Maidstone and Chairman of CACTM is described in Chapter 7. In July 1946 he moved back to Lincoln as Bishop, but he died within a year.

Clifford Woodward (1887–1959) Chairman 1946–50

Woodward was educated at Marlborough and Jesus College, Oxford, where he obtained second class honours in classic mods and lit. hum. From there he went to Wycliffe Hall and was ordained in 1902 as Curate of Bermondsey. In 1905 he was appointed Secretary of the South London Church Fund, and in 1909 moved back to Oxford to be tutor at Wycliffe Hall and Chaplain of Wadham College. In 1913 he moved to Southwark as a canon of Southwark Cathedral while also serving as a Chaplain to the Forces, and in 1916 was awarded the MC. In 1918 he was made Vicar of St Peter's, Cranleigh Gardens and Rural Dean of Kensington, and in 1926 became a Canon of Westminster and Rector of St John's, Smith Square. He was appointed Bishop of Bristol in 1933 and in 1946 moved to be Bishop of Gloucester. His doctrinal views were moderate; his earlier liberalism moved more towards a Tractarian stance. Politically he described himself as left of centre. Smallwood wrote of him, 'He was neither a great scholar nor a noted preacher, and he laid no claim to being a leader in public thought. But he was warmly remembered by his clergy for his high character, kindly sympathy and wide parochial experience.' He retired as Bishop of Gloucester in 1953.

Harold William Bradfield (1898–1960) Chairman 1950–60

Bradfield was educated at Alleyn's School, Dulwich and King's College, London. After seeing active service in France during World War One he was ordained in 1922 and served a curacy and then incumbency in Lancashire. He was persuaded by Lang to become Secretary of Canterbury Diocesan Board of Finance 1934–44. Lang made him also Archdeacon of Croydon from 1942 until he became Bishop of Bath and Wells in 1946, where he devoted himself to visiting the clergy in their homes. In addition to being Chairman of CACTM he was also Chairman of SPG. He died in office in 1960.

Kenneth Riches (1908–99) Chairman 1960–6

Riches was educated at the Royal Grammar School, Colchester and Corpus Christi College, Cambridge. After two curacies he moved in 1936 to be chaplain and librarian of Sidney Sussex College, Cambridge. He was a member of the Archbishops' Commission on Training. In 1942 he moved to be an incumbent in Suffolk while also being Director of Service Ordination Candidates from 1943 to 1945. He was then Principal of Cuddesdon Theological College from 1945 until appointed Archdeacon of Oxford and Suffragan Bishop of Dorchester in 1952. He became Bishop of Lincoln in 1956 and retired in 1974.

Laurence Brown (1907–94) Chairman 1966–71

Brown was educated at Luton Grammar School, Queens' College, Cambridge and Cuddesdon Theological College. After two curacies he became Vicar of Hatfield Hyde in Welwyn Garden City in 1940 until, in 1946, he became Secretary of the Southwark Diocesan Reorganisation Committee and remained in that role until 1960, but from 1952 was also secretary of the South London Church Fund and Southwark Diocesan Board of Finance. In addition, in 1950 he was appointed a residentiary Canon of Southwark Cathedral and in 1955 he was also Archdeacon of Lewisham and Vice-Provost of Southwark. In 1960 he was appointed Suffragan Bishop of Warrington, and in 1969 Bishop of Birmingham from where he retired in 1977.

Leslie Brown (1912–99) Chairman 1972–6

Brown was educated at Enfield Grammar School and the London College of Divinity and after a curacy went with the Church Missionary Society to Travancore in South India as a missionary. In 1943 he returned to England as Fellow and Chaplain of Downing College, Cambridge, but returned to India after a year to Kerala United Theological College in Trivandum, first as tutor and then, from 1946, as Principal. He returned to England in 1950 to be Chaplain of Jesus College, Cambridge, but only stayed a year before returning to Kerala as Principal again. In 1953 he was appointed Bishop of Uganda, which diocese subsequently changed its name to Namirembe, and in 1960 was appointed Archbishop of

Uganda, Rwanda and Burundi. In 1966 he returned to England as Bishop of St Edmundsbury and Ipswich from where he retired in 1978.

Ronald Gordon (1927–) Chairman 1976–83

Born in 1927, Gordon was educated at Rugby School, Balliol College, Oxford and Cuddesdon Theological College and after a curacy in Stepney went back to Cuddesdon as chaplain in 1955. In 1959 he went to be an incumbent in Birmingham and in 1967 became a residentiary Canon of Birmingham Cathedral. In 1971 he was appointed Vicar of the University Church in Oxford and then, in 1975, was appointed Bishop of Portsmouth. In 1984 he became Bishop at Lambeth as head of the Archbishop of Canterbury's staff and remained there until 1991. From 1985 to 1990 he was also Bishop to the Forces. From 1991 to 1996 he was Canon and Sub-Dean of Christ Church, Oxford.

Alexander Graham (1929–) Chairman 1983–7

Born in 1929, Graham was educated at Tonbridge School, St John's College, Oxford and Ely Theological College. After a curacy in Hove he became chaplain and lecturer in theology at Worcester College, Oxford in 1958, becoming also a fellow in 1960. In 1970 he became Warden of Lincoln Theological College until, in 1977, he was appointed Bishop of Bedford and then in 1981 Bishop of Newcastle. In 1987 he was also Chairman of the Doctrine Commission, retiring from that in 1995 and from Newcastle in 1997.

Barry Rogerson (1936–) Chairman 1987–93 (during which period ACCM became ABM)

Born in 1936, Rogerson was educated at Magnus Grammar School and Leeds University. After two curacies he became in 1967 lecturer at Lichfield Theological College, and was vice-principal from 1971 until the college was closed in 1972, when he moved to be a lecturer at Salisbury and Wells Theological College. In 1975 he moved to be Vicar of St Thomas in Wednesfield and became Team Rector of the Wednesfield team ministry in 1979, but moving that same year to become Suffragan Bishop of Wolverhampton. In 1985 he was appointed Bishop of Bristol. He retired in 2002.

John Oliver (1935–) Chairman 1993–8

Born in 1935, Oliver was educated at Westminster School, Gonville and Caius College, Cambridge and Westcott House. After a curacy he went to be chaplain and assistant master at Eton College, and in 1973 became first team rector of a group of parishes in Devon, and then of the parish of Central Exeter in 1982. In 1985 he was appointed Archdeacon of Sherbourne, and then Bishop of Hereford in 1990. He retired in 2003.

John Gladwin (1942–) Chairman from 1998 (during which time ABM became the Ministry Division)

Born in 1942, Gladwin was educated at Hertford Grammar School, Churchill College, Cambridge and St John's College, Durham. After a curacy he went back to St John's College in Durham as a tutor, and in 1977 was appointed Director of the Shaftesbury Project on Christian Involvement in Society. In 1982 he became secretary of the General Synod's Board of Social Responsibility, leaving in 1988 to become Provost of Sheffield. In 1994 he was appointed Bishop of Guildford and was translated to be Bishop of Chelmsford in 2003. He retired in 2009.

Secretaries

(Frederick Cyril) Nugent Hicks (1872–1942) General Secretary 1913–24

Hicks was educated at Harrow, Balliol College, Oxford and Cuddesdon Theological College. In 1896 he became a lecturer at Keble College, Oxford and after ordination in 1897 became Dean of Keble from 1901 to 1909. He moved to be the first Principal of Bishops' College, Cheshunt in 1909 and remained there until 1920 and held that post in combination with being secretary of CACTM until he resigned the principalship in 1920 to be full-time secretary of CACTM. In 1924 he became Vicar and Rural Dean of Brighton, in 1927 Bishop of Gibraltar and in 1933 Bishop of Lincoln.

Leslie Owen, General Secretary 1924, later Chairman 1944–6

See page 300.

Dr Sydney Lawrence Brown (1880–1947) General Secretary 1924–7

Brown was ordained in 1904. After being assistant chaplain and lecturer at Ripon College, Oxford, he became Vice-Principal of Bishop's Hostel, Newcastle in 1905, and in 1910 Warden of St Asaph and Bangor Clergy Education. In 1915 he moved to the Diocese of Chelmsford, being Rector of Fryerning and, from 1920, Rural Dean of Barstable, holding those posts while also being secretary of CACTM from 1924. In 1927 he became Vicar of Brentwood until, in 1935, he was appointed Professor of Hebrew and the Old Testament at King's College, London where he remained until he retired in 1944. He continued as Honorary Secretary of CACTM until 1944.

Frank Woolnough (1886–1973) General Secretary 1927–34.

Woolnough was educated at Christ's College, Cambridge after serving in the army during World War One. After a curacy in Gloucester Diocese he became Chaplain of Christ's College, Cambridge in 1923 and remained in that post while also being General Secretary of CACTM from 1927. In 1934 he became a residentiary Canon of Manchester Cathedral and from 1937 was domestic chaplain to the Bishop of Manchester. He retired in 1960.

Irven David Edwards (1907–73) General Secretary 1935–44

Ordained in 1931. After a curacy, Edwards succeeded Woolnough both as Chaplain of Christ's College, Cambridge and as General Secretary of CACTM. In 1940 he became Rector of Milton, Diocese of Winchester while remaining General Secretary, and in 1947 he moved to Durham as Vicar of Norton, Diocese of Durham. He was Archdeacon of Leicester from 1956 to 1963, and from 1963 was Dean of Wells Cathedral.

Kenneth Carey (1908–79) General Secretary 1944–7

Carey was educated at Marlborough, Exeter College, Oxford and Westcott House. He was Chaplain of Oxford House, Bethnal Green from 1932 to 1936, then became curate of Handsworth, Birmingham in 1936, then Vicar of Whitworth with Spennymoor in 1939 until he moved to CACTM. In 1947 he became Principal of Westcott House, staying there until 1961, when he became Bishop of Edinburgh. He retired in 1975.

John Phillips (1910–85) General Secretary 1947–9

Educated at Weymouth College and Trinity Hall, Cambridge, Phillips was ordained in 1934. After two curacies he became Rector of Farnley in Leeds in 1938 and was then Chaplain RNVR from 1942 to 1945. He was Director of Service Candidates from 1945 to 1947. On leaving CACTM in 1949 he became Vicar of Radcliffe-on-Trent and Shelford and Archdeacon of Nottingham. He was appointed Bishop of Portsmouth in 1960 and retired in 1975.

Philip Wheeldon (1913–92) General Secretary 1949–54

Wheeldon was educated at Clifton College, Bristol, Downing College, Cambridge and Westcott House. He was Curate of Farnham, Guildford Diocese from 1937 and then Chaplain to the Forces from 1939 to 1946. He was Chaplain to the Archbishop of York (Garbett) from 1946 to 1949, when he moved to CACTM. He was appointed Bishop of Whitby in 1954, translated to Kimberley in 1961. He resigned in 1965 to be an assistant bishop in Worcester, but then returned to Kimberley as Bishop in 1968, leaving in 1976.

Peter Curgenven (1910–2002) General Secretary 1954–9

Curgenven was Chaplain of Cuddesdon from 1951 to 1953 and became Recruitment Secretary to CACTM in 1953 and General Secretary from 1954. He resigned in November 1959 to become incumbent of Goring-by-Sea (where he had been curate). In 1970 he moved to be incumbent of Rotherfield in Chichester Diocese. He retired in 1979.

After Peter Curgenven's resignation the Rt Revd Thomas Craske, formerly Bishop of Gibraltar, was appointed Vice-Chairman and Moderator. Geoffrey Heawood, a layman who had been Headmaster of Cheltenham Grammar School until he joined the staff of CACTM in 1953, was Secretary of the Council from 1959 to 1963, when he retired, but he was not General Secretary. Bishop Craske resigned in 1966 and he died in 1971.

William Saumarez-Smith, General Secretary 1963–7

Saumarez-Smith was the only layman to hold that office in the twentieth century. He moved to be Archbishops' Appointments Secretary in 1967, retiring in 1974.

Basil Moss (1918–2006) Chief Secretary 1967–72

Moss was educated at Canon Slade Grammar School, Bolton, Queen's College, Oxford and Lincoln Theological College. After a curacy he became Sub-Warden of Lincoln Theological College in 1946 and then Senior Tutor at St Catherine's Cumberland Lodge, Windsor Great Park in 1951. In 1953 he became an incumbent in Bristol Diocese adding to that three years later also being Director of Ordination Training. He retained the latter role when he became a residentiary Canon of Bristol Cathedral in 1960 until he moved to CACTM. In 1973 he was appointed Provost of Birmingham, retiring in 1985.

Hugh Melinsky (1924–) Chief Secretary 1973–7

Melinsky was born in 1924 and educated at Whitgift School, Christ's College, Cambridge, London University's Institute of Education and Ripon Hall, Oxford. After serving with the intelligence services during World War Two he became a schoolmaster and was then ordained in 1957. After a curacy he became an incumbent in Norwich and then Canon Missioner of Norwich from 1968 until he was appointed to ACCM. In 1977 he became Principal of the Northern Ordination Course and remained there until he retired in 1988.

John Tiller (1938–) Chief Secretary 1978–84

Tiller was born in 1938 and educated at St Albans School, Christ Church, Oxford and Bristol University. After two curacies he went to be chaplain and tutor at Tyndale Hall, Bristol in 1967, and after the union with Clifton Theological College to form Trinity College, Bristol, in 1971 stayed as lecturer in church history and worship. In 1973 he moved to an incumbency in St Albans Diocese until he was appointed Chief Secretary. In 1984 he moved to be Chancellor and residentiary Canon at Hereford Cathedral and was also Director of Training for the Diocese of Hereford from 1991 until 2000. He was appointed Archdeacon of Hereford in 2002 and retired in 2004.

Tim Tyndall (1925–) Chief Secretary 1985–90

Tyndall was born in 1925 and educated at Jesus College, Cambridge. After incumbencies in Newark, Nottingham and Sunderland he became Chief Secretary and retired in 1990.

Hugh Marshall (1934–) Chief Secretary 1990–6

Marshall was born in 1934 and educated at Marlborough, Sidney Sussex College, Cambridge and Lincoln Theological College. After a curacy and three incumbencies he was appointed Chief Secretary and in 1996 became Vicar of Wendover. He retired in 2001.

Gordon Kuhrt (1941–) Chief Secretary 1996–8, Director of the Ministry Division 1999–2006

Kuhrt was born in 1941 and educated at Colfe's Grammar School, London University, Oak Hill Theological College and Middlesex University. After two curacies and two incumbencies he became Archdeacon of Lewisham in 1989 until he moved to what was then ABM in 1996. He retired in 2006.

Appendix C
Constitution of CACTM/ACCM/ABM/ Ministry Division

The Constitution of the Central Advisory Council of Training for the Ministry

The first suggestion of anything looking like terms of reference for this body came from the 1900 *Report on the Supply and Training of Candidates for Holy Orders* from the Lower House of Canterbury.[1] They proposed the following terms of reference for the new Council:

1. To watch the supply of candidates for holy orders, and its sources;
2. To obtain financial support for the various forms of educational machinery needed for the general and special training of candidates for holy orders;
3. To make suggestions from time to time in regard to teaching and subjects of teaching having reference to holy orders;
4. To endeavour in some degree to co-ordinate and unify examinations for holy orders;
5. To advise as to the formation and supply of new theological colleges, if needed, for specific purposes;
6. Generally, to promote unity of action between University professors and diocesan authorities concerning the training of candidates for holy orders, and to be ready to collect information and make suggestions at the desire of their Lordships the Bishops.

The Bishops' Meeting on 22 and 23 October 1912 considered a draft constitution produced by its Standing Committee. In discussion it was slightly modified and the agreed final version was:[2]

---

1 No. 343 in Chronicle of Convocation, Vol. XVII, 1900, p. 231.
2 From the minutes of the Bishops' Meetings for 22, 23 October 1912.

Initial constitution and composition of CACTM

I. Functions

1. To watch the supply of candidates for Holy Orders, and its sources.
2. To consider the best methods of training and testing candidates.
3. To draw up, and from time to time to revise, a list of Theological Colleges the recognition of which by the Bishops the Council advises.
4. To provide for the inspection of existing Theological Colleges; and to advise as to the formation and supply of new Theological Colleges.
5. Generally to promote unity of action between all those concerned in the training of candidates for Holy Orders, and to collect information and make suggestions for the guidance of the Bishops.

II. Composition

The Council should be constituted as follows:

a. Six Bishops (Exeter, Ely, Gloucester, Lichfield, Oxford, St David's) of the Province of Canterbury, and two (Durham, Carlisle) of the Province of York, vacancies to be filled by election by and from the members of the respective Upper Houses of Convocation, but no selection shall be made which shall increase the number beyond seven (five from Canterbury, and two from the York Upper House).
b. One representative each from the Theological faculties of Oxford, Cambridge, and Durham (being members of the Church of England) and from the Theological faculty of King's College, London and from St David's College, Lampeter.
c. Seven representatives, elected by the Principals, of recognised Theological Colleges. For the first selection the Principals of colleges which were directly represented at the ninth Conference on the Training of Candidates for Holy Orders shall be the Principals qualified as Electors under this sub-section.
d. Seven persons elected by the Lower Houses of Canterbury (four) and York (three) Convocations.
e. Seven persons elected in like proportions by the Houses of Laymen.
f. Not more than seven members co-opted by the Council.

III. Meetings

The council to meet not less than twice in each year.

First Amendment – to allow CBF representation on the Council.

On 26 October 1916 a resolution was passed asking the Convocations to increase the numbers on the Council to allow the Central Board of Finance to appoint not more than three members to sit on the Council. Convocations accepted this proposal.

Second Amendment – to allow the Council to have a financial responsibility to distribute funds to candidates.

On 3 May 1917 the Bishop of Truro proposed to the Upper House of Canterbury Convocation that an addition should be made to the functions of the Council, and this was reported in the 1918 Yearbook as a new fifth function:

5. To receive money in order to make grants in aid of Diocesan Ordination Candidates' Funds, Theological Colleges, and other bodies engaged in the work of preparing candidates for Ordination.

Third Amendment – reflecting the new relationship with the Church Assembly. The words italicised in point 4 reflect the need to have authorization to inspect Knutsford.

From the 1924 Year Book

The Council's functions were provided by its constitution:

1. To watch the supply of candidates for Holy Orders, and its sources.
2. To consider the best methods of training and testing candidates.
3. To draw up, and from time to time to review the list of Theological Colleges the recognition of which by the Bishops the Council advises.
4. To provide for the inspection of existing Theological Colleges *and any other institutions offering similar preparation to candidates for Holy*

        Orders which are not of an exclusively Diocesan character; and to advise
        as to the formation and supply of new Theological Colleges.

5.   To receive money in order to make grants in aid of Diocesan Ordination
        Candidates funds, Theological Colleges, and other bodies engaged in
        the work of preparing Candidates for Ordination.

6.   Generally to promote unity of action between all those concerned in
        the training of candidates for Holy Orders, and to collect information
        and make suggestions for the guidance of Bishops.

In 1925 the functions remained the same, but the membership was changed
to: (a) ordinary members: 21 members to be appointed by the Church
Assembly (seven by the House of Bishops, seven by the House of Clergy,
and seven by the House of Laity). (b) Representative members: five members
representing theological faculties at universities, and seven members representing the principals of theological colleges. (c) Co-opted members: not more
than seven members to be co-opted by the Ordinary and Representative
Members: it being understood that all questions involving the expenditure of
funds provided by the Church Assembly shall be decided by the votes of the
Ordinary members.

In the Church Assembly reports for the spring session of 1924 the Bishop of
Chichester moved this change, but with a third clause: 'That as the Council is an
Advisory Council of the Bishops and deals with many matters concerning
Ordination, in which the decisions must rest with the Bishops, it should not be
asked to report to the Church Assembly except on matters that concern the
administration of funds entrusted to it by that Assembly.' (Report of Proceedings,
Vol V. No. 1, p. 45)

On 1 March 1943 the Church Assembly approved a new constitution of
CACTM reflecting the discussions explained in Chapter 6. It was proposed by
the Bishop of Manchester and seconded by the Bishop of Bristol as chairman
of the Service Candidates' Committee. The terms of reference were maintained
but the constitution changed. A few voices sought to change the proposals
but all substantial amendments were defeated, apart from two, those
saying that appointments should be for a three-year period with members
eligible for re-election and those changing the theological faculties to be
represented.

The constitution approved then was:

That the Central Advisory Council of Training for the Ministry be re-constituted as follows:

15 members nominated by the Standing Committee of the Church Assembly, such members shall retire triennially, but be eligible for reappointment;
15 members appointed by the Archbishops of Canterbury and York; such members to retire triennially, but be eligible for reappointment;
6 members appointed by the Conference of Principals of Theological Colleges;
1 member each representing the theological faculties of Oxford, Cambridge, Durham, London, Manchester, Leeds, and St David's College, Lampeter.

In 1959 a new constitution for the new Central Advisory Council for the Ministry was produced following the extensive discussions in the Church Assembly described in Chapter 8.[3]

The Council shall consist of:

A Diocesan Bishop appointed by the Archbishops as Chairman;
A (full-time) Moderator appointed by the Archbishops, who would have access to all Committees;
Ten members appointed by the Standing Committee, who need not be members of the Church Assembly;
Eight members nominated by the Archbishops of Canterbury and York;
Two members of the Church Assembly nominated by the Central Board of Finance;
Not more than four members to be co-opted who shall generally be Chairmen of Committees of the Council. This would make a Council of 26 members in all.

The functions of the Council would be:

(a) To keep under review the needs and opportunities of the Church for the ordained ministry, for Deaconesses and for the various forms of lay

---

3 From the Report of the Standing Committee on the reconstitution of the Central Advisory Council of Training for the Ministry (CA I1291) and the Church of England Year Book 1960.

service, to make recommendations to the Bishops and the Church Assembly, and to serve those needs as and when directed to do so.

(b) To make recommendations as to the disbursement of monies received from the Church Assembly or elsewhere with which to finance the training of candidates for Holy Orders in conjunction with Diocesan Ordination Candidates Funds and other bodies engaged in the work of preparing candidates for Holy Orders; and similarly in regard to training of Deaconesses and for recognised forms of lay ministry.

(c) To approve places and courses of training for the ordained and lay ministry, and to advise upon all questions concerning their provision, maintenance, fees and economic management.

(d) To formulate in conjunction with the Central Board of Finance a policy of finance with regard to the capital needs of the Theological Colleges and Training Houses for Women.

The work of the Council is at present organised into two main sections, pending clarification of the full scope of the Council's responsibilities.

I. THE ORDINATION CANDIDATES COMMITTEE

The main duties of this committee are:

(i) To watch the supply of candidates for Holy Orders, and its sources.

(ii) To consider the best methods of training and testing candidates, and to control the General Ordination Examination.

(iii) To provide for the Inspection of Theological Colleges and any other institutions offering similar preparation to candidates for Holy Orders, and to advise as to the formation and supply of new Theological Colleges.

(iv) Generally to promote unity of action between all those concerned in the training of candidates for Holy Orders, and to collect information and make suggestions for the guidance of Bishops.

The Ordination Candidates' Committee has also taken over the selection work which was formerly done by the Central Advisory Council of Training for the Ministry. It would have three sub-committees: a Selection Committee; an Inspections' Committee; an Examinations' Committee.

II. THE HOUSES AND FINANCE COMMITTEE
[This body looked at the capital needs of colleges and dealt with grants to ordinands]

From 1 April 1966

The Advisory Council for the Church's Ministry

The Council, formerly known as the Central Advisory Council for the Ministry, was established by the Church Assembly, with a revised constitution on 1 April 1966.

A Chairman appointed by the Archbishops who shall be a member of the Assembly	1
The Chairman and Vice-Chairman of the Training Committee	2
The Chairman and Vice-Chairman of the Ministry Committee	2
Five members appointed by the Standing Committee who need not be members of the Assembly	5
Five members appointed by the Archbishops of Canterbury and York	5
Two members of the Assembly appointed by the Central Board of Finance	2
The Chairman of the Principal's Conference	1
Not more than three members to be co-opted	3
Total	21

At least two members of the Council shall be members of the House of Bishops, at least four shall be members of the House of Clergy, and at least four shall be members of the House of Laity.

The Council shall elect its own Vice-Chairman.

Terms of reference:
To promote the most effective ministry, both of men and women, in the service of the Church and to make appropriate recommendations for this purpose to the

Bishops and to the Church Assembly. The work of the Council will be carried out by two main Committees: with the help of a Training Committee and a Ministry Committee.

The Training Committee

Terms of reference:

(i) To keep under review different forms of training for the ministry, ordained and lay, and to work together with all those concerned with such training.

(ii) To encourage the supply of candidates for Holy Orders.

(iii) To arrange and control Selection Conferences, and to report their advice to Bishops.

(iv) To consider the best methods of training and testing candidates for Holy Orders, and to control the General Ordination Examination.

(v) (a) to advise on policy concerning the location, establishment, inspection and continuing support of Theological Colleges and other places of training for the ordained ministry.

(b) To advise on training for other forms of ministry, where appropriate.

(vi) In conjunction with the Central Board of Finance to formulate a policy of finance with regard to the capital needs of Theological Colleges and Training Houses for Women and to make grants in aid of individual candidates.

(vii) To advise and assist in the development of Post-Ordination Training, in consultation with the Ministry Committee.

Constitution

- A Chairman appointed by the Council in consultation with the Archbishops.
- Six members appointed by the Council who need not necessarily be members of the Council, one of whom must be a member of the Central Board of Finance.
- Four members appointed by the Archbishops.
- The Chairman of the Conference of Principals of Theological Colleges, and four other Principals nominated by that Conference.

- Five representatives of Theological Faculties appointed by the Council.
- One representative of Missionary and Ecumenical Council.
- Representatives of theological education from the Church in Wales and the Episcopal Church in Scotland.
- Four co-opted members.
- The secretaries of the Inspections, Examinations and Post-Ordination Training Committees *ex officio.*

Total 32

In an amendment accepted by the Church Assembly it was agreed that at least two members should be women.

The Ministry Committee

Terms of reference:

(i) To keep under review different forms of ministry by men and women, ordained and lay, to enable the Council to give appropriate advice to the Bishops and to the Church Assembly.

(ii) To promote discussion within the Church, so far as this may be practical, about the adaption of its ministry to meet the changing pastoral situation.

(iii) With these two aims in mind, to keep in close touch with other central Church bodies concerned with different forms of ministry, in particular (a) the Council for Women's Ministry in the Church; (b) The Central Readers Board; (c) M.E.C.C.A.; (d) The Board of Education's Adult Committee and the Advisory Committee on Chaplaincies in Modern Universities; (e) The Industrial Committee of the Board for Social Responsibility; (f) The Hospital Chaplaincies Council; (g) The Prison Chaplaincies Council.

Constitution

- A Chairman appointed by the Council in consultation with the Standing Committee of the Church Assembly.
- Four members appointed by the Archbishops.

- Fourteen members appointed by the Council, of whom one shall be a member of the Central Board of Finance, at least three shall hold a parochial benefice in the Province of Canterbury and at least two shall hold a parochial benefice in the Province of York.
- Three co-opted members.

In an amendment accepted by the Church Assembly it was agreed that eight members of the Ministry Committee should be lay, and at least two should be women.

Total 22

Under the motions to be moved the final one was 'that notwithstanding that the Council is a Council of the Assembly under Standing Order XVIII a majority of its members need not be members of the Church Assembly'.

In 1970

It was agreed that the Council shall have power to appoint such committees or sub-committees (as the case may be) as they shall from time to time think fit. That led to the demise of the Ministry Committee.

In 1991

The Annual Report for 1990 noted that the Advisory Board for Ministry will come into being on 1 April 1991. The additional work will be:

(i)   The work of the Council for the Deaf.
(ii) The areas of work previously within the purview of the Ministry Co-ordinating Group.
(iii) The work carried out at Lambeth on the deployment of deacons.
(iv) Taking the lead in co-ordinating advice on the terms and conditions of stipendiary ministers.
(v)   Broad remit to advise on all matters concerning the ministry of the Church and to investigate and evaluate new patterns of ministry.

ACCM advised the ABM that it will need five main committees:

(i) Recruitment and Selection (with sub-committees on Vocations Advisory Work and to manage the Aston Training Scheme).

(ii) Initial Ministerial Education (with a Further Degrees Panel and a sub-committee to carry out Educational Validation for Theological Colleges and Courses).

(iii) Ministry Development and Deployment (with a sub-committee for CME).

(iv) Ministry among Deaf People (with a sub-committee for Training and Ministry).

(v) Finance.

The structure was agreed with the Policy Committee in December 1990.

The Advisory Board of Ministry

1. Title and status

   (a) The name of the Board shall be 'The Advisory Board of Ministry of the General Synod of the Church of England', hereinafter referred to in this constitution as 'the Board'.

   (b) The short title of the Board shall be 'The Advisory Board of Ministry'

   (c) The Board shall be an advisory committee of the General Synod constituted in accordance with the Standing Orders of the General Synod.

2. Functions

The functions of the Board shall be:

   (a) To advise the bishops and the General Synod on all matters concerning the ministry of the Church, to make recommendations as required, and to take such action as may be authorised.

   (b) To consult with the Doctrine Commission and the Faith and Order Advisory Group as necessary on theological issues relating to the ministry of the Church.

(c) In conjunction with the Standing Committee (through the Policy Committee) to promote ministry concerns in the work of all Boards and Councils of the General Synod.

(d) To work in close collaboration with the Church Commissioners, the Church of England Pensions Board, the Central Board of Finance, the Clergy Appointments Adviser, the Secretary-General and any other persons or bodies with responsibilities for the terms and conditions, remuneration, housing and pensions of stipendiary ministers, and, as appropriate, to take the lead in the preparation by these persons and bodies of co-ordinated advice to the House of Bishops and to the General Synod.

(e) To encourage and advise dioceses in working out a ministerial deployment policy which takes account of the variety of forms of ministerial resources available to the Church, and to co-ordinate and facilitate the work of those with responsibility for all aspects of ministry in the dioceses.

(f) To investigate new patterns of ministry.

(g) To encourage dioceses and those in education and careers work in the provision of sustained programmes of vocational development and recruitment for accredited ministry, ordained and lay.

(h) To advise on policy for the selection of candidates for accredited ministry, ordained and lay, to arrange and participate in selection conferences and promote the training of bishops' selectors.

(i) To scrutinise and validate programmes for those training under the Bishops' Regulations, and to keep under review alternative forms of training for candidates for accredited ministry, ordained and lay.

(j) To advise on policy concerning the location, establishment, inspection and financial support of theological colleges and courses.

(k) To advise and support dioceses in the provision and development of continuing education for and review of accredited ministries, ordained and lay, and to monitor standards of this provision; and to advise on facilities for re-training.

(l) To provide the necessary arrangements for the allocation between dioceses of those in accredited ministry, ordained and lay, and for those being ordained deacon each year.

(m) To monitor and advise on the progress of sector and chaplaincy ministries within the total ministry of the Church, in consultation with those responsible for specific areas.

(n) To encourage and strengthen the participation of deaf people in the life and witness of the Church, to represent the views of deaf people to the Church and of the Church to deaf people, and to support the work of their chaplains.

(o) To have oversight of the work of Readers, and to have responsibility for validating and monitoring programmes of their training.

(p) To prepare and administer the Training Budget, and to advise on the support for married candidates.

3. Membership

The Board shall consist of a Chairman and twenty-three other members.

(a) The Chairman shall be a member of the House of Bishops appointed by the Presidents after consultation with the Standing Committee of the General Synod.

(b) The other members of the Board shall consist of:

    (i) Three members of the House of Bishops appointed by the House.

    (ii) Three members of the General Synod appointed by the House of Bishops.

    (iii) Seven members elected by the General Synod.

    (iv) Two members appointed by the Standing Committee of the General Synod.

    (v) One member appointed by the Standing Committee on the nomination of the Church Commissioners.

    (vi) One member appointed by the Standing Committee on the nomination of the Pensions Board.

    (vii) One member appointed by the Standing Committee on the nomination of the Central Readers Conference.

    (viii) Two members appointed by the Standing Committee on the nomination of the Principals Conference.

> (ix) Two members appointed by the Standing Committee on the nomination of the Association of Ordinands and Candidates for Ministry.
>
> (x) Two members appointed by the Standing Committee on the nomination of the Board.

It shall be open to the Board to invite a third member of the Principals' Conference to be present at meetings of the Board as an observer.

4. Term of Office

Members shall hold office for a fixed term of five years terminating on the last day of March in the year after the dissolution of the General Synod and the bringing into being of the new Synod. No member shall serve for more than two successive terms.

5. Business and Procedure

The Board shall have power to regulate its own business and procedure subject to the Standing Orders and the directions of the General Synod. In the absence of such regulation the provisions of Standing Order 157 shall apply.

6. Committees of the Board

The Board shall appoint a committee for ministry among the deaf and such other committees as circumstances may require, as may be agreed in consultation with the Policy Committee.

From January 1999

Ministry Division

A Ministry Division Co-ordinating Group oversees the work of the Division. The Group consists of the Chairman of the Division, the Chairmen of the main committees, together with a representative of the Archbishops' Council.

Archbishops' Council: Supporting Committee Structure[4]

Ministry Division: Vocation, Recruitment and Selection Committee

Membership

The Committee shall consist of a Chairman and thirteen other members.

The Chairman shall normally be a member of the House of Bishops Committee on Ministry (other than the Chairman of the Ministry Division) appointed jointly by the Archbishops after consultation with the Appointments Committee.

(a)   The other members of the Committee shall consist of:

   (i)   Eight members appointed by the Archbishops' Council to include at least two clergy persons and two lay persons.
   (ii)   Four members elected from the General Synod from among its members, to include at least one clergy person and one lay person.
   (iii) Two members appointed by the Central Readers Council.

Terms of Reference

Functions

The Committee shall be a Committee of the Archbishops' Council and in discharging its functions shall seek to assist the Council to co-ordinate, promote, aid and further the work and mission of the Church of England.

The functions of the Committee shall be:

(a)   To advise the Archbishops' Council and the House of Bishops on a strategy for the development of vocation to ministry.
(b)   To encourage those in education and careers work throughout the Church in the provision of sustained programmes of vocational development and recruitment for accredited ministry, ordained and lay.

---

4 From GS 1303.

(c) To advise the House of Bishops on policy for the selection of candidates for accredited ministry, ordained and lay.

(d) To oversee and advise the work of staff in the arrangement of and participation in selection conferences.

(e) To oversee the training of bishops' selectors.

(f) To report regularly through the Ministry Co-ordinating Group of the Archbishops' Council on the work of the Committee.

(g) To work in collaboration with Diocesan Directors of Ordinands and others as appropriate on policy and practice related to the selection and care of candidates for ministry.

(h) To work in collaboration with ecumenical partners on matters within the Committee's terms of reference.

Ministry Division: Theological Education and Training Committee

Membership

The Committee shall consist of a Chairman and thirteen other members and an ecumenical representative.

(a) The Chairman shall be appointed jointly by the Archbishops after consultation with the Appointments Committee (and shall not be the Chairman of the Ministry Division).

(b) The other members of the Committee shall consist of:

    (i) Six members appointed by the Archbishops' Council, of whom at least one shall be an ecumenical representative.

    (ii) Four members elected by the General Synod, to include at least one clergy and one lay person.

    (iii) Three members representing the training institutions, including one person particularly concerned with the training of Readers.

(c) The ecumenical representative shall be appointed by the Archbishops' Council.

Functions

The Committee shall be a Committee of the Archbishops' Council and in discharging its functions shall seek to assist the Council to co-ordinate, promote, aid and further the work and mission of the Church of England.

The functions of the Committee shall be:

(a) To advise the House of Bishops and the Archbishops' Council on a strategy for theological education and training.

(b) To scrutinise and validate programmes for those training under the Bishops' Regulations, and to keep under review all forms of training for authorised ministry, ordained and lay, including Reader training.

(c) To advise the House of Bishops and the Archbishops' Council on policy concerning theological colleges and courses.

(d) To advise the Archbishops' Council and the House of Bishops on the financial aspects of theological education and training.

(e) To work in collaboration with ecumenical partners on matters within the Committee's terms of reference.

Ministry Division: Deployment, Remuneration and Conditions of Service Committee

Membership

The Committee shall consist of a Chairman and sixteen other members.

(a) The Chairman shall normally be a member of the House of Bishops Committee on Ministry (other than the Chairman of the Ministry Division) and shall be appointed jointly by the Archbishops after consultation with the Appointments Committee.

(b) The other members of the Committee shall consist of:

(i) Seven members appointed by the Archbishops' Council (to include at least two parochial clergy persons and two lay persons), including two members of its Finance Committee and one member on the nomination of the Central Readers Council.

(ii)   Four members elected by the General Synod from among its members, to include two clergy persons and two lay persons.

(iii) Three members elected by diocesan representatives who attend meetings of the Diocesan Finance Forum.

(iv)   One member appointed by the Archbishops' Council on the nomination of the Church of England Pensions Board.

(v)   One member appointed by the Archbishops' Council on the nomination of the Church Commissioners from among the members of its Pastoral Committee.

Functions

The Committee shall be a Committee of the Archbishops' Council and in discharging its functions shall seek to assist the Council to co-ordinate, promote, aid and further the work and mission of the Church of England.

The functions of the Committee shall be:

(a) To advise the House of Bishops and the Archbishops' Council on a strategy for ministry, with particular reference to the deployment, remuneration and conditions of service of those in authorised ministry, working in collaboration with dioceses, the Church Commissioners and the Church of England Pensions Board, and with ecumenical partners.

(b) To produce, in partnership with dioceses, a framework of national policy for stipends and other related matters, and to advise dioceses as appropriate on such matters.

(c) To produce, in partnership with dioceses a framework of national policy for the deployment of resources, ordained and lay, available to the Church.

(d) To monitor and advise in consultation with interested parties on sector chaplaincies within the total ministry of the Church.

(e) To work in collaboration with dioceses and, as far as possible, with ecumenical partners in the provision of continuing ministerial education for and review of accredited ministers, ordained and lay.

Appendix D
Working-class Candidates

Report of a Committee appointed at the Fourth Ordinary Meeting, 13 and 14 February 1914, to organize a conference on the testing and training for ordination of those who had little early education. The conference was held in May 1915 under the chairmanship of the Bishop of Exeter. From paper 41 of CACTM papers from 1915.

The Committee concluded:

1. There is abundant evidence that there is a considerable number of vigorous, intelligent and earnest lads, between fourteen and eighteen years of age, at work in dockyards, factories, collieries, and other industrial works, who believe themselves to be called for Holy Orders, and clergymen and others likely to be judges of vocation think that they are so called.
2. In all probability many of these lads would eventually, for one reason or another, be found unsuitable.
3. But a noteworthy remainder of men of sterling qualities would be left, and these, if properly trained, would be of great value to the ministry of the Church.
4. In order to secure this remainder, it is necessary to have a well-thought-out plan for dealing with the whole class of these men with apparent vocations.
5. Before any of them are encouraged to give up their present occupations with a view to more direct preparation for Ordination, great care should be taken to test, as rigidly as is possible at so early a stage, the reality of their vocation. This should be done by parochial clergy, in communication with a clergyman especially appointed for this work by the Bishop of the diocese in consultation with the Diocesan Training Committee.
6. Should there be good reason to think that a lad has a true call, every assistance should be provided to give him the best education that can be

suggested for him. The utmost use should be made of the Workers' Educational Association; but only a small portion of training can be given conveniently with other employment.

7. From the first the following facts should be made clear to the candidate:

   (i) In all probability he is seeking a life of greater poverty than that of a skilled artisan.

   (ii) Even after he has given up his present prospects in the hope of being ordained, he may quite possibly be rejected as unfit for Ordination. The greatest care would be taken not to allow such a sacrifice in a doubtful case, but at such an early stage mistakes cannot be avoided.

   (iii) Since as a rule no candidate would be accepted if he were engaged to be married, it would be considered a serious argument against the continuance of financial help if one of the candidates became engaged during the course of training.

8. The course of training must be longer and more supervised than that of candidates for whom Non-graduate Colleges were founded. This is necessary because of the lack of early education and the need of doing all that is possible to make up for it. It is not intended that these men should form a special ministry, to minister only to the class from which they came. Any idea of a class ministry must be entirely excluded; and these lads must be given the best education that they can use.

9. Very possibly it will be found advisable not to require both Latin and Greek from these candidates.

10. To deal with this class of candidates it is advisable to have a Central Committee, as distinct from the Training Committee in each diocese, because the work needs the combined deliberation of those who in many different parts of the country have been trying to deal with these lads. And considerable funds will be needed, for they will have to be trained and supported for five or six years, and it may be necessary to found a special college for their education in the first two or three years before they begin their distinctly theological work.

The resolution that followed was:

The Advisory Council submits to the Archbishops the report of its Committee on the recent Conference, and heartily commends for their consideration and acceptance the following resolution passed at the Conference:

The Conference urges that the Central Advisory Council for Training should represent to the Archbishops the great need for:

(i) A permanent committee to deal with and advise upon the search for, and the selection, education, and training of, these candidates.

(ii) The abundant provision of the necessary funds through the Central Board of Finance, assisted by a sub-committee within this special department.

Appendix E
Earl Grey's Letter to *The Times*, 4 June 1927, on the Sponsorship Scheme

Too few clergy: Lack of means, not of men.
A Scheme of 'Sponsors'.

The Times has always been so generous in helping the Church to make known its wants that no apology is needed for asking you to call attention to the great dearth of clergy in the Church of England and to a new scheme for helping to supply a remedy.

A working force of about 21,000 men in 1914 is represented by 16,500 today, and by far the greater part of the wastage has occurred among the assistant clergy in industrial districts, where the need for service is greatest. What this means in terms of overwork and anxiety to those who are struggling to carry on can hardly be exaggerated. If no result can be given, the result will be disastrous.

Fortunately, however, a careful investigation has shown the dearth of men desirous of entering the ministry is very much less than generally supposed. There are many young men who feel a real vocation to take holy orders, but who are at their wits' end to find the sum (often amounting to £1,000) required to pay for their keep and education between the ages of 19 and 24, by which latter age they are usually ordained. Some of them are helped by diocesan and other organizations, but the existing facilities for the purpose are quite inadequate.

For example, at this moment in the offices of the Church Assembly there is a waiting list of 150 men of the very best quality who may be lost to the ministry of the Church simply for lack of means to complete their education. In this list are included men from nearly all the leading public schools, ex-Servicemen, bank clerks, farmers, school teachers, sons of artisans, 'double firsts', University 'Blues', and many sons of clergy. Every one of them is a picked man. In some cases sums varying between £25 and £150 for one or two years are needed for post-graduate training, and in others sums varying from £20 to £220 per annum for four or five years, to aid the necessary process of education. The scheme is that individual Church men and women should make themselves responsible in whole or in part for the education of one of these men. Full information will be sent to anyone writing to 'Sponsors', Church House, Westminster.

Whoever helps one of these men to dedicate his life to the service of God and his neighbours will be doing far more than an individual act of personal kindness. The work of the Church is crippled by want of them.

Yours faithfully,
Grey

The following examples are taken from the full list of candidates for assistance under the scheme for sponsors. The amount required is stated at the end of each example:

A.B. – Widowed mother unable to help. Scholar of his college (Cambridge). Double first in classical Tripos; now reading Theology (Philosophy and Ethics). Has supported himself entirely by scholarships. Wishes to work in the diocese of Manchester. For one year's special training at Oxford needs – £80.

B.J. – Winchester. Eldest of three sons of clergyman, who are being educated at Oxford. First in Honours Mods. Taking Final Honours Schools this year. Running 'Blue' and member of OTC. Needs £50 more for post-graduate study of Theology – £50

C.N. – Railway worker, who has passed London Matriculation by private study. Wants to go to a Theological College to work for L.Th., and take Durham B.A. afterwards. A Yorkshireman; wishes to work in the north. Asks for £40 per annum for four years – £160.

Part of the leader, *The Times*, 4 June 1927

We are assured that there is available a considerable number of entirely suitable candidates for holy orders, whose only hindrance to the achievement of their purpose is lack of money for the long and expensive training required at a university or theological college. Practically all other Christian bodies are ready to train their candidates for the ministry for nothing, but until quite recently the Church of England has obtained the majority of its clergy from those classes in the community who are able to provide the cost of their sons' education. It is largely because the professional classes of this country are no longer able to incur the increased costs of educating their sons, over so long a period as is required before ordination at the age of twenty-three, that the decline in ordination candidates is so great.

After noting the total numbers it continues:

If nothing more is done than maintain the present number, the Church must ordain at least 470 men a year; but in 1924 only 436 were admitted to the ministry, in 1925 the number dropped to 370, and last year to 363. The decline shows no sign of being arrested. There is ample justification for the statement in this year's *Crockford's* that:

The backbone of the Church is being slowly broken by the fact that men to do the work are not forthcoming ... We doubt whether the importance and urgency of the question has yet been realized by the laity – even by the House of Laity. It is not too much to say that if the history of the last ten years is continued for another ten the effective maintenance of the parochial system will become impossible in all but a few favoured localities.

The leader concludes:

Here is an opportunity of helping at least one man to devote himself to the working staff of the Church at a time when the depletion in the ranks of the clergy is causing great anxiety, and, if allowed to continue, must soon have disastrous consequences to the whole religious life of the nation.

Appendix F
Sources of Grants for Candidates for Ordination 1918–37

The complete table is available in Appendix II of the evidence provided by the Central Board of Finance to the Archbishops' Commission on Training in 1937, Church of England archives AC/TM/10/2 CTM 88.

Year	CBF	DBF	Anglo-Catholic	CPAS Cand.	Evangelical Churchmans Fund	Ord. Cand. Exhib. Fund	Total
1918		7,778		260			8,038
1919	53,281	9,349		288			62,918
1920	70,813	12,467		416			83,696
1921	83,065	17,729		447			101,241
1922	82,758	19,253		686			102,697
1923	68,742	20,253		683			90,068
1924	2,896	20,883		886			64,665
1925	21,295	21,879		776		2,072	46,022
1926	9,735	23,701		1,163		2,430	37,029
1927	36,365	24,610	13,479	1,547		2,536	78,664
1928	28,385	28,092	8,422	2,188	3,457	2,218	73,664*
1929	25,847	33,979	8,422	2,689	4,657	2,218	78,999
1930	24,832	36,441	8,877	2,688	4,384	2,185	80,705
1931	16,565	38,847	6,729	2,398	3,774	3,774	72,307
1932	8,001	37,651	6,868	2,331	3,209	2,760	62,301
1933	8,552	35,252	4,582	2,239	2,801	2,971	57,644
1934	12,636	33,076	3,205	2,195	2,151	2,735	56,800

(continued)

Year	CBF	DBF	Anglo-Catholic	CPAS Cand.	Evangelical Churchmans Fund	Ord. Cand. Exhib. Fund	Total
1935	8,351	30,407	2,282	1,980	1,863	1,727	47,478
1936	6,614	28,188	2,694	1,657	1,598	1,268	42,196
1937	6,706	28,179	3,114	1,366	1,779	1,269	42,725
Total	615,449	508,404	69,224	28,820	29,678	29,055	1,289,739

*Also from that year there was a body known as the National Church League Ordination Candidates' Fund, which in that year produced grants of £970, and which for the following five years had grants of just over £1,000 a year until 1934, when it reduced to £801 and declined to £312 in 1937. The total amount from that body to 1937 was £9,107.

Appendix G
The Awarding of Grants from 1933

CACTM minutes 11 January 1933

The following resolutions were received from the joint meeting of CACTM and CBF representatives on 9 December 1932.

(i)   That it be a recommendation to CACTM in voting grants for training from monies provided by the Central Board of Finance –

(a)   To arrange candidates in two sections (1) central and (2) diocesan, and each section in three grades, A, B, & C, and to give priority in this order: (1) A, (2) A, (1) B, (2) B, (1) C, (2) C; central candidates to accept CACTM's direction as to the place in which they are to serve for three years after ordination.

(b)   To arrange that each central candidate, before acceptance, shall be interviewed by not less than two interviewers, one of whom shall be a layman.

(c)   To make, and to urge dioceses to make, save where exceptional conditions forbid, some part of the provision for every candidate by grant, and the remainder by loan without interest [subject to various conditions].

(ii) That it be a recommendation to the dioceses (a) that when a candidate's references are being taken up by the dioceses a note of inquiry should be sent to CACTM, and (b) that after each meeting of the Diocesan Training Committees a copy of the Minutes should be sent in confidence to CACTM.

(iii)   That it be a recommendation to CACTM –

(a)   That diocesan committees should be asked to send to CACTM every year a statement on (1) the sum of money allocated in the diocesan budget for the purpose of training candidates for Holy Orders in and for that year, and money from other sources, and (2) the number of candidates whom it is proposed to adopt and the probable date of their ordination.

(b)   That this statement should be sent to CACTM every year in such time as the information may be available before CACTM presents its estimates to the Church Assembly.

(c)   That when a diocesan committee in only proposing to provide part of the cost of training a candidate and requests CACTM to consider the candidate for central assistance, the diocesan committee should give full information about the candidate's qualifications, the course of training proposed, and his need, when sending in its annual statement.

(d)   That diocesan committees, in considering the claims of candidates for adoption, shall be asked to observe the following as minimum requirements:

(1)   No candidate shall be eligible for adoption unless he presented a certificate of having passed some recognised examination of matriculation standard or its equivalent.

(2)   No candidate shall be eligible for adoption if he is over the age of 25 at the time when he begins his post matriculation training.

(3)   Candidates shall be encouraged in the giving of grants to undertake a period of training for the five years, three years to be spent in obtaining a degree at a university, and two years in special training at a theological college (or, in certain circumstances, four years at University and one at a Theological College).

Appendix H
From the Papers of the Archbishops'
Commission on Training

'On Attitudes Towards Ordination of Certain Outstanding Young Men'[1]:
A paper by Canon Charles Raven, Regius Professor of Divinity at
Cambridge, 1937

- They do not like clerics as a class. The few they revere are as a rule the rebels . . .
- They distrust dogmatism. Life is so bewildering and the scope of knowledge so vast that the claims of the Church to possess a unique revelation seem both arrogant in themselves and incompatible with the puerilities about which ecclesiastics are vocal and enthusiastic.
- They find healthy exercise and good comradeship more enjoyable and more beneficial than attendance at public worship, especially if they are working hard in the week.
- They think the Church a soft, ineffective and obstructionist institution, strangely unlike the tragic, challenging revolutionary whose name it bears.
- Public worship seems to them bewildering, unreal in itself and irrelevant to the world of today . . .
- The Church's moral witness often disgusts them. They are deeply concerned with the new problems that centre in the words property, sex and war. They do *not* want the Church to be a partisan or political controversialist, but what they hear and read of its utterances on these subjects convinces them that its attitude towards property is inhuman and reactionary, towards sex ignorant and degraded, towards war time-serving and contemptible. A parson justifying battle, denouncing

---

1 The papers for the Archbishops' Commission are held in the Church of England Records Centre. This is CTM paper 32.

birth-control, or attacking Communism almost invariably shocks them to the core of their being.

- The Church's Creed and formularies seem to them hardly compatible with common honesty ... this is, I think, specially true of the doctrine of the Eucharist: this is the one service whose form they do not criticise or dislike; but its doctrine and the conflicts over minutiae of dogma and ceremonial alienate them. We are not winning them back by replacing Matins by the Mass.

- The Church's organisation, the misuse of men and money; poverty and overwork at one end, luxury and laziness at the other; the perversities and intrigues of preferment; the inequalities of stipends and status; the tolerance of admitted scandals; the impossibility of getting traditional machinery overhauled; these all create the impression that the instrument is out of date and that its officers are more concerned to preserve their own vested interests in it than to reform it for the proper discharge of its functions.

- Added to all these they find men whose fruit in love, joy and peace, and whose quality calls out their reverence, in secular settings more readily than in the clergy ... Those who want to make the fullest use of their lives for the service of God and of their generation, however much they may admire particular clergy, feel that they cannot consider a vocation which so evidently involves handicaps fatal to its proper discharge.

A paper in the Commission files over the initials of the Chairman, Alwyn Williams, dated December 1937

Science and historical criticism have disproved so much of religious teaching of the past, and what still remains unchallenged is thereby placed under suspicion. Modern psychology has not eased the situation.

Thus it is asked whether the Virgin Birth, the Resurrection, the Ascension and other episodes in the Gospels are really credible, since as events in the physical sphere, in which in such matters uniformity seems to be unbroken, they would be absolutely unique.

Again it is noted that the earliest narratives of the life of Jesus are some 30 years later than the events, and that this gives plenty of time for the growth of legend and the distortion of the actual facts into implausible forms ... and further, that it is now held by many theologians that the gospels were written in part not as history but rather as interpretations (i.e. for edification or to support or to exclude particular views), and the narratives or language changed or coloured accordingly.

The answer from a personal spiritual experience too certain to be shaken, whatever the historical difficulties, which was open to those brought up from infancy in Christian habits, is not acceptable to those not so brought up; and it is objected that the conviction of the super-physical order so induced does not necessarily correspond to truth, and that subjective certainty of many things that are false can be produced by the appropriate methods.[2]

A much modified version appeared in the Final Report of the Commission, 1944.

The Church would appeal to many vigorous minds with more force if those minds were convinced that a real effort had been made by the Church to present its doctrinal basis authoritatively and intelligibly with due regard both to the essentials of the Faith and to the statement of it in language which should as far as possible be simple and unambiguous. If it can be said that the Creeds, the Thirty-nine Articles and the Prayer Book are a sufficient and adequate statement and explication of the Church's Faith, it is strongly argued that the Articles need revision: that the Prayer Book needs both revision and a large measure of supplementation, as well as far more explanation at the hands of the clergy than it commonly receives; that the historical explanations commonly given are not necessarily a justification for present acceptance and use; that the Creeds would be better understood, and some at least of their difficulties more sympathetically grasped, if an authoritative doctrinal statement were made available, making use of, but not confined to, the results of the work of the Doctrinal Commission. We believe that it is commonly felt that the better understanding of Biblical theology and of the faith of the Bible which has been brought within our reach by the labours of many generations has not yet been used as it might in the revision and explanation of forms of worship which nevertheless ultimately depend upon the Bible. As regards the Bible itself, although the difficulty of thirty years ago may not be the difficulties of today, yet for the present generation there are

---

2 Folder AC/TM/10/1, Note in CTM 25, Draft C Note: p. 3.

problems about the historicity of the New Testament which cannot be overlooked. No doubt many minds will continue to find stumbling blocks in creeds and formularies, whatever help be given for their understanding. We certainly do not hold that the acceptance of Christian doctrine can be or should be made a smooth and easy process or accommodated to the intellectual fashion of each generation. But when there are removable difficulties, whether of language or thought, they should be removed, and where there is legitimate room for difference of view it should be acknowledged. To leave things as they are would be to acquiesce needlessly in conditions which may well repel thoughtful men.[3]

---

3 Final report of the Commission para. 24 (p. 16f).

Appendix I
Memorandum (1942) from the Service Candidates Committee to the Archbishop of Canterbury (Temple) for Him and the Archbishop of York to Send to all Service Chaplains towards the End of World War Two[1]

One of the most urgent problems before the Church today is the recruiting of men for the Ministry. If its work is to be efficiently carried on and if it is to exert an effective influence upon the post-War reconstruction of national life, it is essential that an adequate supply of men duly qualified to serve God and his fellows in the Ministry of the Church should be forthcoming. At the present time the number of men being ordained is inevitably decreasing; should the War continue for any length of time the supply of Ordinands will almost entirely cease; it is of the utmost importance that it should begin to flow again at the earliest possible moment after the cessation of hostilities.

But of even greater importance than the number of Ordinands is their quality. It cannot be denied that the vitality of the Church and the effectiveness of its work depend to a very large extent upon the sincerity, the devotion and the capacity of its Clergy. It is, therefore, essential that those ordained after the War should be at least of such a standard as would fit them to play a responsible part in any other calling. Such men as fall below that standard should not be admitted to the Ministry.

We need to recruit the best type of men and we can confidently appeal to them because the Ministry is almost the only vocation in which a man is free to employ all his gifts to the full in service of God and his fellowmen. We believe that there are in the forces today many men of real ability who, if they

---

1 Temple papers, Vol. 3, pp. 104–6.

had a vision of the opportunity for service and leadership which the Ministry provides, would offer themselves for Ordination. It is hoped that between now and the end of the War it will be possible to build up from among them a body of carefully selected men who will be ready to proceed to Test Schools and Theological Colleges, having in the meantime undertaken such preliminary studies as may be possible under Service conditions.

The responsibility for finding the right men and encouraging them to consider whether God may not be calling them to the Ministry, as well as discouraging the obviously unsuitable, rests very largely upon those who are serving as Chaplains or Officiating Chaplains of the Forces. For their guidance we suggest that the following points should be borne in mind in this very responsible task of helping a man to discover whether he has a true vocation or not:

In considering a man as a possible candidate for Ordination we should look first for evidence of the reality of his own Faith in God. His convictions, if sincere, will find expression in (a) worship (b) in a serious regard for God's law in the ordering of his own moral life. No man who fails to bear witness to God in either of these respects should be seriously considered. Generally speaking, the man should be known and respected as a practising Christian by the better sort of his fellows, while he is known and valued by his superiors for faithfulness in the way he does his job. 'A bad soldier' should be at once disqualified, however 'devout'; the opinion of his superiors on this point should be obtained and weighed. It is just here that the 'layman's opinion' is really valuable.[2]

Not every enthusiastic communicant and good-living man, however, is a suitable candidate for Holy Orders. That vocation normally pre-supposes certain special aptitudes. These may perhaps be listed under the following headings.

(a) Intelligence. It should be recognised that the service of the church today requires for her ministry an average of intellectual ability above, rather than below, that of e.g. doctors or solicitors. Intelligence, however, is essentially the power of understanding: it involves capacity for reasoning, clearly and consecutively, but it is neither exclusively nor invariably to be found in unusually 'clever' or learned persons. A rough estimate can usually be formed by noting a man's interests, tastes in reading, topics of conversation, etc.

---

2 Presumably by this is meant the man's superior officer, by definition a layman.

(b) Promise of pastoral capacity and power of leadership. Normally, the ordinand should possess a manifest interest in men as men, and some real ability to get on with people of varying types. The parson's job is concerned with persons, not things. This pastoral capacity may be apparent in ordinary ways of true friendship – always a good sign – as well as in the more noticeable signs of real leadership.

(c) Devotion, readiness for sacrifice. What is in question here is not a matter of the man's natural endowment or constitution, but of the surrender of his own will in Love. Life in the Services will normally provide its own tests of practical unselfishness. Devotion is no substitute for intelligence, or force of character: but these things without devotion are, in a priest, ultimately useless or harmful (cf. 1 Cor. xiii).

Therefore a man's motives in seeking ordination should be carefully studied, remembering always that he may be largely unconscious of them himself. Why does he want to be ordained? Weigh his reply well, noting any unconscious indications he may give of e.g. Ambition, Self-importance, or mere Escapism. On the other hand, some of the best men are often diffident about themselves, and where there is a strong reason to suppose from knowledge of the man concerned that he has in him great gifts which could be used in the ministry of the Church it may be quite legitimate to say to him 'Is there any reason why you should not be ordained?', leaving him to answer the question in that form rather than the other.

In all this regard should be had to potentiality rather than to actuality. The Chaplain's recollection of his own state of mind and soul before he went to his University or Theological College will probably prepare him to find that a candidate's ideas and desires at this stage are often largely unformulated. Too much weight, therefore, must not be attached to a crude, or even an unsatisfactory, reply to a particular question: it is more important to discover whether the man can really see the point put to him. Similarly with regard to intellectual ability. Less importance should be attached to the examinations that a man has already passed, than to the use he has made of whatever opportunities he has enjoyed, regarded as a guide to his potentiality; and, above all, to evidence (or the absence of it) of a serious interest in the real meaning of things.

There followed details of how to contact Kenneth Riches as the new Director of Service Ordination Candidates and the procedures to be followed. As this was written before the selection boards were established the procedures are of interest.

> When a chaplain has reason to believe that a man has a vocation to the Ministry and is possessed of the necessary gifts and qualifications for the work, he should, wherever possible, arrange for him to be interviewed by the Bishop of the diocese in which his unit is stationed. After such an interview he should send the man's name and Service address to the Director of Service Ordination Candidates, to whom the Bishop will send his report upon the candidate. The D.S.O.C. will then supply the candidate with a form which will contain questions to be answered and a request for the names of three referees. The D.S.O.C. will be responsible for taking up the man's references and, if he seems suitable, advising him as to the steps he should take, immediately, and after demobilisation, towards realising his vocation. Before any candidate is definitely accepted as an ordinand he will be interviewed by a small selection committee; in some cases it may be possible to arrange this before the war is ended, but in most cases it will have to take place afterwards. Chaplains who have recommended men will naturally keep in close touch with them and will be careful, when they are transferred to other units, to commend them to the Chaplain into whose care they will come.

Appendix J
War Office Selection Boards

The development of War Office selection boards is described by Henry Harris in *The Group Approach to Leadership Testing*. In a foreword General Sir Ronald Adam, Adjutant-General of the Forces 1941–6, explains that the earlier interview boards that were used for testing officers were not successful, in that candidates who 'passed' did not all succeed in getting through officer training. General Adam knew of one course when 50 per cent of the course failed to pass out. He wrote, 'This was a waste of time and had unfortunate effects even on good candidates, for the knowledge of a high failure rate did not give confidence to those attending.' The decision to change the old methods was taken after a trial board, when groups of presidents interviewed candidates and recorded their opinions separately. This showed so marked a difference of opinions expressed on the same candidate that a new method had to be found.

Early experiments were based on the tests which the German Army had employed from 1923 onwards. Even though the UK was involved in a war with Germany it was evident that the British Army were prepared to investigate the officer selection methods of the enemy, which they realized at that stage of the war was a highly effective military machine. However, it was concluded that the German methods were not a success in the British context.

Dr Harris wrote, 'The British Army developed ... a technique during 1942–1945 and in doing so made what one considers to be the major psychological contribution to the war ... Developed in crisis – soon after Dunkirk – their prime purpose was to select junior leaders in a military field.'[1] The essential element in the technique involved not merely individual interviews with all the members of the panel but evidence of observing candidates in a group as well.

If one can control under experimental conditions the stresses to which a small group is submitted, one may hope to provide its members both with opportunities for action and leadership and with conditions that limit

---

1 Henry Harris, 1949, *The Group Approach to Leadership Testing,* London: Routledge and Kegan Paul, p. 1.

these opportunities. From their use of these opportunities and their adjustment to those limiting conditions, one may draw tentative estimates of their effectiveness in the group: and these may be related to estimates from other observations and sources.[2]

> WOSBs were scattered all over the country, usually in country houses: and there, candidates lived under officer conditions for 3 days while being observed and tested on leadership – not aptitude-level. The emphasis was not on a man's aptitudes or primarily on his technical capacity – though that would be considered – but on the quality of his personality in a social field and on his ability to manage men in the field of activity for which he was being considered.[3]

The conclusion of the WOSB process involved the 17-point psychological profile, each item being graded on a five-point scale of good, satisfactory, borderline, weak and very weak. The items were:[4]

1. Leadership experience.
2. Unit report, i.e. on behaviour and performance while in the army.
3. Officer intelligence rating (OIR) based on tests done to show where a candidate stood in terms of levels of the general population. OIR 0 was considered to be the lowest 50 per cent of the population. OIR 1, 2 and 3 were approximately between the 51st and 70th percentile – the lowest OIR with which a candidate could be passed for OCTU without special permission from the War Office. OIR 4 and 5 were between the 71st and 90th percentile. OIRs 6–10 were in the top 10 per cent of the population. OIR 10 was the highest score in this scale: its incidence in the population one in 700 or 800.
4. Educational suitability.
5. Planning ability.
6. Practical ability.
7. Athletic ability.
8. Level of aims i.e. type of job and level of responsibility sought in life.

---

2 Harris, *Testing*, p. 8.
3 Harris, *Testing*, p. 9.
4 Harris, *Testing*, p. 220f.

9. Effectiveness in pursuit of aims. This is partly an estimate of the success already achieved in relation to his opportunities; partly a predictive grading of the likelihood of his succeeding in his future aims.
10. Military compatibility
    a   his identification with the Army
    b   his suitability for the Army *on officer level*
11. Sense of responsibility.
12. Social interest.
13. Quality of personal relations.
14. Range of personal relations.
15. Dominance.
16. Liveliness.
17. Stability of health.

The early CACTM conferences did not include all of these items and certainly not the detailed scoring on each of these 17 personality profile qualities, some of which required skilled and experienced psychologists or educationalists. They did include, in addition to interviews with all the panel members individually, some group discussions which were observed by the selectors to see the interaction of candidates one with another. By such methods it was possible to detect qualities such as domineering or weak personalities, men who were prepared to take an unpopular stand and those who always sided with the lowest common denominator in a group, those who would be gracious in disagreement and those who became unduly angry or reticent, as well as to make a judgement on the general intelligence they showed in the group work. The selectors then met together to note the references, to discuss each candidate and come to a common mind on their suitability for undergoing ordination training.

Appendix K
Extract from Archbishop Fisher's Presidential Address to the Church Assembly on CACTM, 11 October 1945

In May 1944 the Upper House discussed the Report of the Archbishops' Commission on Training for the Ministry and referred it to CACTM with a request for comment and advice about the lines upon which the Diocesan Bishops might take action. The Lower House did not complete its discussion of the Report until May 1945, by which time a good deal had already been done to deal with the problem of post-war ordinands and particularly ex-Service ordinands. In the debate in the Lower House the desire was rightly expressed that the Lower House should know what action had been taken, and that desire I now wish to satisfy. CACTM, reconstituted, as you may remember on the recommendation of the Commission, has tackled a very large task with most commendable promptitude and ability. It first decided which of the Commission's proposals called for early consideration and action, so that the Church might be in a position to meet the immediate requirement and, after commending it to the careful consideration of the Church, referring it to CACTM ... and which of them must be and indeed could with advantage be left for consideration later. The questions requiring rapid settlement were four: the general scheme of training for ordination, the method of selection of men for training, the content of the General Ordination Examination and the restarting of Theological Colleges. On all these matters CACTM, after close consultation with the Principals of Theological Colleges, put recommendations before the Diocesan Bishops of both Provinces. These were considered by the Bishops and sometimes amended or referred back. Finally, they gave their directions and upon these CACTM is now acting. With regard to the general scheme of training, interim regulations were adopted, and copies of these will be provided for the Lower House. With regard to selection, a method of Selection Boards was approved and has now been in operation for some time both at home and overseas. In a situation in which the Church is having to deal with four thousand or more candidates for ordination, these

Boards have provided a method which not only has prevented a quite chaotic confusion, but, as I believe, has also proved itself sound in principle and of permanent benefit to the Church. Of course, under any system – and most certainly under the previous system – mistakes can be made, though it is to be remembered that not all those who think themselves the victims of a mistake are right in thinking so. There is certainly no justification whatever for thinking that the Selection Boards are applying too rigid standards of one kind or another or are anything but most careful and sympathetic in the consideration they give to each candidate. Two things especially should be noted. It is remarkable that in the Selection Boards the decisions reached on each candidate (and by now more than one thousand have passed through their hands) have been unanimous in all but about half-a-dozen cases. It is also remarkable that the Selection Boards here and overseas, composed of clergy and laity of different experiences, have independently arrived at a standard of balanced judgment approximately the same. The work will continue at very high pressure for a considerable time to come, and it throws an immense strain on CACTM in conducting it. Experience is leading day by day to improvements in detail, but I think I can say for the Diocesan Bishops of both Provinces that in this work CACTM has their full confidence and support.

The recommendations of CACTM for the revision of the General Ordination Examination have very recently been approved by the Bishops and will be put into operation in due course. Meanwhile, CACTM deals with an endless succession of administrative problems ... The more I see of the way in which CACTM is threading its way through a maze of problems, the more do I wonder at the amount of work achieved, the more do I admire the spirit in which it is done and the combination of firm principle in policy with infinite care and patience for every one of the thousands of men who pass through its hands. For that the Council and the Church owe more than a great deal to the Bishop of Maidstone above all, but also to his colleagues, Mr K. M. Carey, Mr W. L. S. Fleming and now Mr J. H. L. Phillips. The Church should know what a great burden they are carrying and should be grateful indeed that a task of such immense importance for the Church's well being is being met so effectively.[1]

---

1 CA Proceedings, Vol. XXV, 1945, pp. 175–8.

Appendix L
Correspondence Between George Clay Hubback, Bishop of Calcutta and Metropolitan of India, and the Archbishop of Canterbury Regarding Worship at Selection Centres

This correspondence began with a letter from Hubback to Fisher dated 25 January 1946. He quoted an extract from a letter of 6 December 1945 from the directors of service candidates signed by Launcelot Fleming.

> <u>Vestments. Silence after Compline, etc</u>. On these matters we must be quite firm. A selection board, even when it is Overseas, is run under the authority of the English Bishops for men in the Forces who are members of the Church of England. It would add tremendously to a Selection Centre to have the help of the Indian Church and clearly this is particularly valuable in regard to the missionary side of vocation, but they must understand that the responsibility for a Selection Centre comes from CACTM and it is for the English and not the Indian Bishops to say how each centre will work.
>
> I think you ought to make all this clear before arranging a particular centre, i.e. that you will have the 1662 Prayer Book, Surplice, Stole etc.

The Bishop commented:

> I do not propose to comment on the discourtesy of Fleming's remarks but I am quite clear that neither you nor any of the Bishops in England would dream of endorsing his statement that the Indian Bishops have nothing to do with the working of one of these selection Centres. I refer of course to the worship side of the Centre's work.
>
> Such a centre was recently in operation here. The men all stayed in this house and as a matter of course attended the daily Celebration at the Cathedral. I myself celebrated the Holy Communion on two of the mornings

and presided at the meetings of the Selectors. According to Mr Fleming's contention he would have the Local R.A.F. Chaplain instruct me to use only the 1662 Office and to refrain from using vestments. In this cathedral the Communion Office used has the express sanction of the Episcopal Synod and the Diocesan Bishop. Vestments have been used for years.

I should be grateful if Your Grace would inform Mr. Fleming that no Committee in England has any authority whatsoever to lay down what services shall, or shall not, be used in this Province. We are more than glad to do anything that we can to help the Selection Boards when they meet, but men who attend them will be provided with the normal worship of the Church which they use during the time that the Board is in session.[1]

The Archbishop consulted CACTM and Launcelot Fleming replied.

The history of the matter is as follows:- the pattern of Selection Centres began to emerge very clearly as soon as they were held in this country. It included a specified time, a programme of lectures, discussion and interviews, and times of worship which together created an environment in which all the candidates seemed to be at ease. With the very diverse Churchmanship of candidates it seemed right that in our liturgical services we should keep strictly to the Book of Common Prayer and use surplice and stole and lights at the Holy Communion. This point may seem minor, but in fact it has never produced any comment from either pole except that it has been acceptable and appreciated in the circumstances.

Naturally we have never wanted to over-emphasize what are relatively small points of detail, but we all felt it right to issue clear directions to Ordination Secretaries abroad about matters which had been found by experience in this country to induce an environment in which men could find a common unity in their diversity.

Consequently when I heard from our Ordination Secretary in India that he was finding it very difficult to get these rules kept in the Selection Centres for which he was responsible I wrote a strong letter to him pointing out the importance of retaining the original pattern of Selection Centres. It was this letter of mine which the Bishop of Calcutta quotes and to which he takes exception.

---

1 Fisher papers, Vol. 12, p. 100.

When Phillips, Carey and I met Shearburn [the Deputy Chaplain General of India back in the UK on furlough] he explained very fully that the Indian bishops are extremely sensitive about points of this kind, and that in so far as this particular centre was held in the Bishop's House in Calcutta and the men attended Services in the Cathedral it was both natural and proper that the Bishop should celebrate the Holy Communion according to the rite of India, Burma and Ceylon and wear vestments. With all of this we certainly agreed, and I am very sorry that the Bishop of Calcutta should have felt that CACTM was criticising this generous hospitality which he had given to Ordination Candidates. I can only say that of course my letter was never intended as a criticism of the Bishop or indeed of the rite which he uses in his Cathedral.

The mistake however seems to me to have arisen when the Ordination Secretary allowed a Selection Centre to be arranged in circumstances when it would have been discourteous, if not impossible to observe the CACTM directions.

We have recently discussed the question of the proper rite and ceremonial at Selection Centres at a meeting of the CACTM Selection Committee, and the members were unanimous in agreeing that the only possible way of being fair to all 'schools of thought' was to keep strictly to the Book of Common Prayer, and to use surplice, stole and lights.

I have also made enquiries from the Chaplain General's Office, and I find that although the Indian Bishops do issue some form of licence to Service chaplains to adopt the manners and customs of the church of Indian, Burma and Ceylon, it is perfectly possible for a Chaplain to use the rite and ceremonial which CACTM believes best for Selection Centres.[2]

The Archbishop thanked Fleming and replied to the Bishop of Calcutta on 16 February 1946.

My dear Metropolitan

When I got your letter of January 25th I was quite sure there was a misunderstanding somewhere as I knew that Fleming and the others concerned with Selection Centres would never wittingly be guilty of any discourtesy. The misunderstanding I now see arose from the fact that a

---

2 Fisher papers, Vol. 12, pp. 111–13.

Selection Centre which is by its very nature completely under the control of CACTM and the Directors of Service Ordination Candidates was by local arrangement and by your generosity held in your own house and in connection with the Cathedral where of course your authority is supreme. Thus there was a conflict of two jurisdictions. It was certainly never in the minds of CACTM to question in any kind of way your jurisdiction. The fault lay with the Service Chaplain who arranged for the Selection Board to be held in your house without explaining to you the instructions under which he worked. It is of course most natural that the local Service Chaplain should have wished to avail himself of your generous hospitality. If, as he ought to have done, he had explained the conditions under which he worked it would then have been for you to decide whether on those conditions you could have the Selection Board in your house, or alternatively he could have asked permission from CACTM in this case to get the conditions varied.

I do not know whether it is necessary for me to justify the conditions themselves. Selection Centres began in this country. They included a speci-fied time, a programme of lectures, discussion and interviews, and times of worship designed to create an environment in which all candidates might be at ease. The conditions were made so as to secure the least possible disturbance amongst candidates coming to the centres with very diverse traditions of churchmanship. The arrangements have excited no comment from either wing of the Church and have in fact been acceptable and appreciated. When Selection Centres abroad were started it was felt, and I think absolutely rightly, that the conditions which by experience had worked well in this country should also be observed overseas so that men might find a common unity in diversity. The Indian Ordination Secretary reported that he found it difficult to get these conditions observed. Fleming's letter was a reply. It was put strongly because the matter was of great importance. After all, these candidates are Service candidates whose domicile is in England and who are accepted and trained for Ordination in England. CACTM which acts for the English Bishops has every right to prescribe the conditions. In these circumstances I do not think exception could be taken to what Fleming said to the Ordination Secretary. He was simply telling him quite clearly what the situation was.

Let me emphasise again that this was no discourtesy to you or to the Indian Bishops. It was in no kind of way meant to suggest that CACTM had

353

any pretensions to say what Services should or should not be used in your Province. It was simply saying what rules should be observed in Selection Centres. By a mischance your own generosity led to a situation in which two jurisdictions conflicted. I am extremely sorry that this situation arose, but there is full appreciation here of the help which you gave.[3]

The Bishop of Calcutta replied on 21 March 1946. After thanking the Archbishop for his letter he went on:

The fact of the Service Ordination Candidates Selection Board meeting in my house did not really make any difference to the principles underlying the request of CACTM. I made it clear to the Chaplain concerned that if he wished special services for the candidates in the Cathedral, I was perfectly willing to consider his request. I am not, however, prepared to sanction in any Church in my diocese the alteration of the normal daily worship in order to meet the desires of a purely temporary organisation in India.

I entirely dissent from the assumption that because the Ordination candidates are going to be trained in England, therefore the English Bishops have the right to prescribe the conditions under which such men are to worship in our Churches in India. When we meet in May, I want to discuss with you the whole question of the Royal Army Chaplains' Department in its relation to Bishops of our Communion who are not subject to the jurisdiction of either of the English Provinces. Quite frankly I have been amazed at the assumption made by some of the senior men of the department that they are entirely independent of the local Episcopate.[4]

There appears to be no written account of what transpired when they met in May.

---

3 Fisher papers, Vol. 12, pp. 116–18.
4 Fisher papers, Vol. 12, p. 128.

Appendix M
From ABM Policy Paper 3A, Report of a Working Party on Criteria for Selection for Ministry in the Church of England, October 1993

Summary of the eight criteria looked for in candidates for ordination training

- Ministry within the Church of England. Candidates should be familiar with the tradition and practice of the Church of England and be ready to work within them.
- Vocation. Candidates should be able to speak of their own sense of vocation to ministry and mission, referring both to their own conviction and to the extent to which others have confirmed it. Their sense of vocation should be obedient, realistic and informed.
- Faith. Candidates should show an understanding of the Christian faith and a desire to deepen their understanding. They should demonstrate personal commitment to Christ and a capacity to communicate the Gospel.
- Spirituality. Candidates should show evidence of a commitment to a spiritual discipline, involving individual and corporate prayer and worship. Their spiritual practice should be such as to sustain and energise them in their daily lives.
- Personality and Character. Candidates should be sufficiently mature and stable to show that they are able to sustain the demanding role of a minister and to face change and pressure in a flexible and balanced way. They should be seen to be people of integrity.

- Relationships. Candidates should demonstrate self-awareness and self-acceptance as a basis for developing open and healthy professional, personal and pastoral relationships as ministers. They should respect the will of the Church in matters of sexual morality.
- Leadership and Collaboration. Candidates should show ability to offer leadership in the Church community and to some extent in the wider community. This ability includes the capacity to offer an example of faith and discipleship, to collaborate effectively with others, as well as to guide and shape the life of the Church community in its mission to the world.
- Quality of Mind. Candidates should have the necessary intellectual capacity and quality of mind to undertake satisfactorily a course of theological study and ministerial preparation and to cope with the intellectual demands of ministry.

Appendix N (i)
Numbers Ordained

Figures are from Haig, Church of England Year Books, Annual Reports and Statistics of licensed ministers.

1883	781	1912	686
1884	759	1913	670
1885	783	1914	685
1886	814	1915	526
1887	771	1916	387
1888	739	1917	210
1889	777	1918	119
1890	746	1919	192
1891	745	1920	280
1892	737	1921	379
1893	747	1922	458
1894	684	1923	463 (from now on
1895	720	excludes ordinations in the Church in	
1896	704	Wales)	
1897	652	1924	436
1898	638	1925	371
1899	661	1926	363
1900	650	1927	393
1901	569	1928	384
1902	576	1929	439
1903	594	1930	503
1904	569	1931	498
1905	624	1932	585
1906	580	1933	565
1907	587	1934	556
1908	670	1935	585
1909	649	1936	564
1910	672	1937	558
1911	711	1938	590

1939	589		1956	481
1940	562		1957	480 (according to
1941	418		the calendar from now on)	
1942	345		1958	508
1943	300		1959	534
1944	244		1960	599
1945	159		1961	604
1946	158		1962	628
1947	208		1963	633
1948	297		1964	602
1949	362		1965	592
1950	419		1966	576
1951	411		1967	496
1952	479		1968	478
1953	472		1969	436
1954	444		1970	437
1955	446			

	Total	SM	NSM	Deacons	
1971	393				
1972	361	340	21		
1973	373	350	23		
1974	389	345	44		
1975	373	321	52		
1976	362	281	81		
1977	383	301	82		
1978	391	309	82		
1979	417	303	114		
1980	428	310	118		
1981	440	311	129		
1982	425	313	112		
1983	460	341	119		
1984	432	313	119 (10 LNSM)		
1985	416	304	112 (10 LNSM)		
1986	413	326	87	SM	NSM
1987	394	299	95 (3 LNSM)	64	39
1988	451	373	71 (7 LNSM)	67	43 (2 LNSM)
1989	385	309	76 (5 LNSM)	61	42

	Total	SM	NSM		
1990	359	282	74 (3 LNSM)	79	40 (2 LNSM)
1991	314	246	63 (5 LNSM)	75	49
1992	320	271	59 (inc. LNSM)	59	74
1993	353	290	63	48	51

	Total	SM men	SM women	NSM men	NSM women	OLM men	OLM women
1992	473	273	67	59	63		◦
1993	455	285	56	63	51	For these 6 years OLMs	
1994	405	244	72	55	34	were included in the NSM	
1995	382	245	65	30	42	numbers ordained	
1996	373	201	67	46	59		
1997	379	186	57	69	67		
1998	468	174	67	73	87	27	40
1999	481	199	78	61	76	40	27
2000	569	223	90	81	107	25	43

Appendix N (ii)
Selection Conference Statistics

From Annual Reports and Annual Statistics of Licensed Ministers.

Selection Centre Statistics for 1949–54

	1949	1950	1951	1952	1953	1954
Number of centres	37	37	34	32	38	39
Number of attendances	724	710	665	699	768	785
Recommended	404	365	297	251	368	403
Conditionally recommended (CR)	30	95	111	176	151	194
Not recommended (NR)	246	188	167	179	130	127
Deferred	19	1	2	–	1	56
No decision	14	15	12	17	7	4
Special cases	6	2	–	–	–	–
Withdrawn at Board	5	9	1	4	3	1

Selection Centre Statistics for 1955–74

	1955	1956	1957	1958	1959	1960	1961	1962	1963	1964
No. of centres	43	43	43	44	45	46	44	46	49	49
Attendances	891	893	893	922	964	954	873	899	988	912
Recommended	505	479	491	531	565	541	488	519	586	508
CR	187	162	181	183	192	167	158	154	151	148
NR	114	153	142	133	118	150	140	143	141	143
NR at present	79	92	75	66	85	94	79	75	102	110
No decision	–	–	–	1	–	–	8	7	8	3
Withdrawn at Board	–	5	3	8	–	1	1	1	–	–

Note that from 1968 all candidates over the age of 40 were sent to selection conferences

	1965	1966	1967	1968	1969	1970	1971	1972	1973	1974
No. of centres	41	41	43	42	35	39	38	39	38	39
Attendances	655	625	754	660	602	640	606	627	606	639
Recommended	351	324	303	239	178	178	169	154	146	162
CR	121	146	212	192	210	225	197	180	131	178
NR	110	101	150	152	160	188	148	154	166	138
NR at present	69	50	86	72	52	46	32	20	36	29
No decision	4	3	3	5	2	3	1	1	–	–
Withdrawn at Board	1	–	–	–	–	–	–	–	–	–

Auxiliary Pastoral Ministry (the original name for Non-Stipendiary Ministry)

	1970	1971	1972	1973	1974
Attendances	27	59	118	127	131
Recommended	2	7	20	2	7
CR	15	24	55	61	63
NYR	–	1	4	1	4
NR	10	27	39	59	56

Selection Conference Statistics for 1975–94

	1975	1976	1977	1978	1979	1980	1981	1982	1983	1984
No. of centres	41	37	41	45	47	50	49	53	60	59
Attendances	685	594	673	726	767	806	754	730	709	688
SM attendances	536	417	488	525	567	605	566	541	537	506
Recommended	348	254	349	376	375	404	361	350	303	306
NR & NYR	186	163	137	149	192	200	205	191	232	199
No decision	2	–	2	–	–	1	–	–	2	1

Was Auxiliary Pastoral Ministry, now Non-Stipendiary Ministry

	1975	1976	1977	1978	1979	1980	1981	1982	1983	1984
Attendances	149	177	185	201	200	201	188	188	162	173
Recommended	90	102	109	126	121	121	115	109	80	86
NR	59	75	76	75	77	80	73	79	80	85
No decision									2	2

Local Non-Stipendiary Ministry

	1975	1976	1977	1978	1979	1980	1981	1982	1983	1984
Attendances								1	10	9
Recommended								1	7	6
NR									3	3
No decision										

Deaconess and Lay Workers (included in main conferences from 1982)

	1975	1976	1977	1978	1979	1980	1981	1982	1983	1984
Attendances				70	87	111	159	149	175	177
Recommended				44	52	173	73	105	102	117
NR				26	35	38	24	44	73	60

NSM

	1975	1976	1977	1978	1979	1980	1981	1982	1983	1984
Attendances							62	65	68	78
Recommended							43	45	41	49
Recommended (LNSM)										
NR							19	20	27	29
Total							62	65	68	78

	1985	1986	1987	1988	1989	1990	1991	1992	1992	1994
No. of centres	59	61	61	55	52	53	54	54	50	51
Total attendances now include all categories on ministry, including lay workers										
Total	692	727	698	818	753	774	820	792	759	734
Attendances (SM)	514	558	557	435	403	417	460	436	378	349
Recommended	347	363	320	252	239	264	275	239	190	182
NR	164	194	236	183	164	153	186	197	188	167
Attendances (NSM)	155	160	132	119	127	128	115	126	145	126
Recommended	63	76	69	48	61	46	59	51	46	57
R LNSM	20	8	4	2	2	2	1	12	7	21
NR	90	84	55	66	64	72	64	75	88	58
NR LNSM	1	1	4	3	0	8	0	1	4	7
Deaconess Candidates										
Total attendance	214	220	225	259	215	218	240	227	228	257
SM Rec	80	87	77	80	67	68	85	72	59	79
SM NR	49	43	60	63	46	52	64	48	59	54
NSM Rec	48	49	49	49	63	53	38	59	53	58
R LNSM	4	0	2	1	1	0	0	6	3	–
NSM NR	32	41	38	64	38	44	51	48	52	61
NR LNSM	–	–	1	0	0	2	0	1	2	0
Total R for Ordained Ministry	561	583	523	433	431	434	449	433	361	400

Selection Conference Statistics 1995–2000

(Note that from 1997 the distinction was between those who could be either stipendiary or non-stipendiary and those who would be permanently non-stipendiary.)

	1995	1996	1997		1998	1999	2000
Stipendiary Men				Stipendiary or Non-Stipendiary			
Recommended	147	178	227		212	212	224
Not recommended	101	74	67		95	79	78
Total	248	252	294		307	291	302
NSM men				Permanent Non-Stipendiary			
Recommended	65	63	40		61	58	42
Recommended OLM	26	42	32		50	40	31
Not recommended	63	56	48		29	41	23
NR OLM	7	15	7		13	7	10
Total	161	176	127		153	146	106
Stipendiary women				Stipendiary or Non-Stipendiary			
Recommended	68	66	95		130	141	129
Not recommended	41	41	47		56	53	48
Total	109	107	142		186	194	177
NSM Women				Permanent Non-Stipendiary			
Recommended	90	72	72		74	73	69
Recommended OLM	24	30	36		54	24	42
Not recommended	82	58	59		33	35	37
NR OLM	6	7	8		14	8	7
Total	202	167	175		175	140	153
Total R for Ordained Ministry	420	451	502		581	548	537
Percentage recommended							
SM	60%	68%	74%	SM & NSM	69%	73%	74%
NSM	52%	54%	51%	Perm NSM	69%	63%	65%
OLM	79%	77%	82%	OLM	79%	81%	81%

Acknowledgements

I first thought of writing something like this when I was on the staff of what was then called the Advisory Council for the Church's Ministry in the late 1970s and early 1980s, but it has taken a long time to get to this point. It could not have been achieved without the assistance of many other people.

Former colleagues of mine from ACCM days, particularly Archdeacon John Cox, Archdeacon Dr Bill Jacob and Bishop Graham James were very helpful at various stages. Dr Andrew Chandler, my supervisor for this work as a PhD, was unfailingly encouraging and constructive in his comments. The staff at Lambeth Palace Library and the Church of England Records Centre all responded to my various requests with friendly courtesy and efficiency. The present Ministry Division staff kindly allowed me to invade the privacy of their offices to work on some of the more recent minute books of committees and the council, and both Chris Lowson, Director of the Ministry Division when I started this work and his successor Julian Hubbard were hugely supportive, as was Revd Hilary Ison, who was the Selection Secretary of the new-style selection conference I was allowed to observe. I am particularly grateful to Chris Lowson, now Bishop of Lincoln, for writing the Foreword for this book.

An old friend, Lt-Colonel Jonathan Howard, kindly arranged for me to observe a selection board for military chaplains at the Army's Selection Centre at Westbury, which also made possible discovering more of the history of the army selection boards which were so influential on the Church of England's subsequent practice.

I am grateful to the Dean and Chapter at Westminster for the support they have given me in the five years of doing this research. My colleagues have been very tolerant of the time I have had to spend away from the Abbey and I am particularly grateful to the Canons' PA, Catherine Butler, who has been indefatigable in preparing the work for publication, and to my brother-in-law, David Nichols, for preparing the index. However, if there are errors in this book they are mine alone.

Finally I must record my thanks to the Society of the Faith for agreeing to sponsor this publication and to Thomas Allain-Chapman, the Publishing

Manager at Church House Publishing, for all his help and encouragement. I can only hope that all their assistance has resulted in a book that will be of service to the wider Church.

Robert Reiss
Westminster Abbey

This book is published in association with
THE SOCIETY OF THE FAITH

The Society of the Faith is a small charity founded in 1905 by two high-churchmen, the Revd Canon J. A. Douglas, Vicar of St Luke's, Camberwell, and his brother, the Revd C. E. Douglas.

The Douglas brothers were deeply committed to the Catholic tradition within the Church of England. The Society they founded was to be 'an Association of Christians in communion with the See of Canterbury for mutual assistance in the work of Christ's Church and for the furtherance of such charitable undertakings as may from time to time be decided upon, more especially for the popularisation of Catholic faith.'

The Society's first work was the printing of Sunday school stamps, which proved immensely popular. This success inspired the foundation of Faith Press, publishing books both scholarly and popular, as well as church music.

In 1916 the Society also founded Faith-Craft to produce high quality vestments and church furnishings. Their biggest single commission was the complete refurbishment of St Mary le Bow in London after World War Two.

The Douglas brothers lived on into the 1950s. Times (and tastes) were beginning to change, and this eventually led to the closure of both Faith Press and Faith-Craft in 1973. However, the Society of the Faith remains committed to its original objects: seeking to promote good standards in publishing and church furnishing, and in theological education. Recent co-publications with Canterbury Press include Michael Yelton's *Anglican Papalism* (2005), Paula Gooder's *The Meaning is in the Waiting* (2008), and John Gunstone's *Lift High the Cross: Anglo-Catholics and the Congress Movement* (2010).

Since 1935 the Society has held the lease of Faith House, 7 Tufton Street, Westminster. Faith House is currently home to the church furnishers Watts & Company, and to Restless Development (formerly Student Partnership Worldwide), 'the global leader in supporting young people to address the urgent health, education, and environmental issues which affect their lives, communities, and countries'.

The Society of the Faith – Faith House, 7 Tufton Street, London SW1P 3QB

Registered in England as a Limited Company number 214216
Registered with the Charity Commission number 232821

Bibliography

Allen, Roland, 1923, *Voluntary Clergy*, London: SPCK

Badcock, Gary, 1998, *The Way of Life: A Theology of Christian Vocation*, Michigan/ Cambridge UK: Eerdmans

Baelz, Peter and Jacob, William (eds), 1985, *Ministers of the Kingdom: Exploration in Non-Stipendiary Ministry*, London: CIO Publishing

Balthasar, Hans Urs von, 1983, *The Christian State of Life*, San Francisco: Ignatius Press

Barry, Frank Russell, 1931, *The Relevance of Christianity: An Approach to Christian Ethics*, London: Nisbet

Barry, Frank Russell, 1935, *The Relevance of the Church*, London: Nisbet

Barry, Frank Russell, 1958, *Vocation and Ministry*, Welwyn: James Nisbet

Barry, Frank Russell, 1964, *Mervyn Haigh*, London: SPCK

Barry, Frank Russell, 1970, *Period of my Life*, London: Hodder and Stoughton

Barth, Karl, 1958, *Church Dogmatics*, Vol. 4, *The Doctrine of Reconciliation*, Edinburgh: T & T Clark

Bell, G. K. A., 1952, *Randall Davidson*, 3rd edn, London: OUP

Bradshaw, Paul, 1971, *The Anglican Ordinal*, London: SPCK

Brown, Kenneth D., 1988, *A Social History of the Nonconformist Ministry in England and Wales 1800–1930*, Oxford: Clarendon Press

Bullock F. W. B., 1976, *A History of Training for the Ministry 1875–1974*, London: Home Words Printing and Publishing

Bundock, Edward, 2006, *Study in a Stable: The Tatterford Test School 1924–1949*, published privately by the author

Burne, R. V. H., 1960, *Knutsford: The Story of the Ordination Test School*, London: SPCK

Burns, Arthur, 1999, *The Diocesan Revival in the Church of England*, Oxford: Clarendon Press

Carpenter, Edward, 1991, *Archbishop Fisher – His Life and Times*, Norwich: Canterbury Press

Chadwick, Owen, 1970, *The Victorian Church Part II*, London: SCM Press

Chadwick, Owen, 1983, *Hensley Henson*, Oxford: Clarendon Press

Chandler, Andrew, 2006, *The Church of England in the Twentieth Century: The Church Commissioners and the Politics of Reform 1948–1998*, Woodbridge: Boydell Press

Denniston, Robin (ed.), 1960, *Part-Time Priests: A Discussion*, London: Skeffington

Dewar, Francis, 1991, revd 2000, *Called or Collared: An Alternative Approach to Vocation*, London: SPCK

Doctrine in the Church of England (1938): The Report of the Commission on Christian Doctrine Appointed by the Archbishops of Canterbury and York, 1982, London: SPCK

Dowland, David, 1997, *Nineteenth Century Anglican Theological Training*, Oxford: Clarendon Press

Ducdame, Magazine of the Knutsford Test School

Ensor, Robert, 1936, *The Oxford History of England 1870–1914*, Oxford: Clarendon Press

Goudge, Henry Leighton, 1938, *The Church of England and Reunion*, London: SPCK

Haig, Alan, 1984, *The Victorian Clergy*, London: Croom Helm

Harris, Henry, 1949, *The Group Approach to Leadership Testing*, London: Routledge and Kegan Paul

Heeney, Brian, 1976, *A Different Kind of Gentleman* (Studies in British History and Culture, 5), Archon Books

Henson, Henry Hensley, 1942, *Retrospect of an Unimportant Life 1863–1939*, London: OUP

Hodge, Mark, 1983, *Non-Stipendiary Ministry in the Church of England*, London: CIO Publishing

Hyde, Matthew, 2005, *A Window on Knutsford*, Hale: Silk Press

Jones, Henry, 1898, *An Entrance Guide to Professions and Business* (Methuen's Commercial Series), London: Methuen & Co

Knox, Edmund Arbuthnott, 1934, *Reminiscences of an Octogenarian 1847–1934*, London: Hutchinson

Kuhrt Gordon (ed.), 2001, *Ministry Issues for the Church of England*, London: Church House Publishing

Lambeth Conference 1908 Encyclical Letter from the Bishops with the Resolutions and Reports, London: SPCK

Leach, Joan, 2007, *Knutsford: A History*, Chichester: Phillimore & Co

Levin, Bernard, 1970, *The Pendulum Years*, London: Jonathan Cape

Lloyd, Roger, 1966, *The Church of England 1900–1965*, London: SCM

Lockhart, J. G., 1949, *Cosmo Gordon Lang*, London: Hodder and Stoughton

MacKinnon, D. M., Williams, H. A., Vidler A. R., Bezzant, J. S., 1965, *Objections to Christian Belief*, London: Penguin Books

Moberly, R. C., 1897, *Ministerial Priesthood*, London: John Murray, reprinted 1969, London: SPCK

Moorman, John R. H., 1947, *B. K. Cunningham*, London: SCM

Owen, Leslie, *Leslie Owen: A Man of Faith and Courage and Witness to the Things Unseen*. A collection of memories of Owen produced privately. Lambeth Palace Library, HS199.0909

Palmer, Bernard, 1991, *Gadfly for God: A History of the Church Times*, London: Hodder and Stoughton

Paul, Leslie, 1964, *The Deployment and Payment of the Clergy*, London: CIO

Platcher, William C., 2005, *Callings: Twenty Centuries of Christian Wisdom on Vocation*, Grand Rapids: Eerdmans

The Place of Auxiliary Ministry, Ordained and Lay, 1973, published for ACCM by CIO

Pritchard, T. W., 2000, *A History of the Old Parish of Hawarden,* Wrexham: Bridge Books

Ramsey, Michael, 1972, *Christian Priesthood Today,* London: SPCK

Robinson, John, 1963, *Honest to God,* London: SCM

Ryle, J. C., 1884, *Principles for Churchmen,* London: W. Hunt and Co

Smallwood, John, 2003, 2007, *Some Biographical Information about the Bishops,* 66 volumes collected for each See, some of which have two volumes. They are kept at Lambeth Palace Library.

Snape, Michael, 2008, *The Royal Army Chaplains' Department, 1796–1953,* Woodbridge: Boydell Press

Soria, Jose Luis, 1975, *Vocation,* London: Tamezin Publications

Studdert-Kennedy, Geoffrey A., 1927, *The Unutterable Beauty,* London: Hodder and Stoughton

The Supply and Training of Candidates for Holy Orders. Report, with notes, appendices and recommendations presented to the Archbishop of Canterbury by a Committee appointed by his Grace at the request of the Bishops of the Provinces of Canterbury and York, to consider the question of the Supply and Training of Candidates for the Sacred Ministry 1908 (reprinted 1910) London: SPCK

The Supply of Candidates for Holy Orders. Report of a Committee appointed by the Archbishops of Canterbury and York, 1925, Press and Publication Board of the Church Assembly, London: SPCK

Supply of Fit Persons, report by CACTM to the Church Assembly, February 1954, reprinted 1958 with updated statistics

Taylor, A. J. P., 1965, *English History 1914–1945,* Oxford: Clarendon Press (Book Club Associates edition 1977)

Theological Colleges for Tomorrow, 1968, London: CIO

Thomas, William Henry Griffith, 1911, *The Work of the Ministry,* London: Hodder and Stoughton

Thomson, H. Byerley, 1857, *The Choice of a Profession,* London: Chapman and Hall

Tiller, John, 1983, *A Strategy for the Church's Ministry,* London: CIO

Torry, Malcolm and Heskins, Jeffrey (eds), 2006, *Ordained Local Ministry,* Norwich: Canterbury Press

Training for the Ministry: Final Report of the Archbishops' Commission. As presented to the Archbishops of Canterbury and York, February 1944, Press and Publications Board of the Church Assembly

Troeltsch, Ernst, 1931 (and 1950), *The Social Teaching of the Christian Churches Vols 1 & 2,* London: George Allen and Unwin

Vidler, A. R. (ed.), 1963, *Soundings,* Cambridge: Cambridge University Press

Welsby, Paul, 1984, *The History of the Church of England 1945–1980,* Oxford: OUP

West, Frank H., 1980, *FRB: A Portrait of Bishop Russell Barry,* Bramcote: Grove Books

Wilkinson, Alan, 1978, *The Church of England and the First World War,* London: SPCK

Williams, Rowan, 1994, *Open to Judgement,* London: Darton, Longman and Todd

Wilson, A. N., 1978, *Unguarded Hours,* London: Secker and Warburg

Wingren, Gustav, 1958, *The Christian's Calling*, trans Carl C. Rasmussen, Edinburgh: Oliver and Boyd

Working as One Body: The Report of the Archbishops' Commission on the Organisation of the Church of England, 1995, London: Church House Publishing

Advisory Board for Ministry (ABM) publications all had numbers, which are given in the footnotes

Advisory Council for the Church's Ministry (ACCM) publications. Where they have numbers they are given in the footnotes. Unnumbered ones include:

1983 *Criteria for Selection*

1989 *Call to Order: Vocation and Ministry in the Church of England*

Central Advisory Council of Training for the Ministry (CACTM) publications all have numbers and are given in the footnotes

Central Advisory Council for the Ministry (CACTM) publications all have numbers and are given in the footnotes

Church of England publications

Books published by the Church Information Office are included in the main section of this bibliography

The Church of England Year Book, published every year from 1883. The title and imprint have varied, from 1883 it was known as the official year book of the Church of England, then from the creation of the National Assembly as 'The official year book of the National Assembly of the Church of England', but later as simply *The Church of England Year Book*

The Chronicle of Convocation: Being a Record of the Proceedings of the Convocation of Canterbury, published each year from 1858

York Journal of Convocation, published each year from 1859

Church Assembly Report of Proceedings, published every year from 1920 until its replacement by the General Synod in 1970

Church Assembly Papers are numbered with a CA reference number and are in Lambeth Palace Library in bound volumes for each year. All references to any of these papers have the relevant number attached

General Synod: Report of Proceedings, published every year from 1970

General Synod Papers. Published in one of two categories. Papers to be considered by the Synod all have a GS reference number and are in Lambeth Palace Library in bound volumes for each year. There are also GS Miscellaneous papers, also numbered and bound, in Lambeth Palace Library. All references to any of these papers has the relevant number attached

Lambeth Palace library

Archbishops' papers are in various numbered volumes for each archbishop. The records for Davidson, Lang, Temple, Fisher, Ramsey and Coggan were all consulted. There is a 30-year rule on looking at them and the Runcie papers are therefore not yet available in full

The minutes of Bishops' Meetings, the private and confidential meetings of bishops, are available but with a 50-year rule

Church of England Records Centre.

References given in footnotes are those used by CERC. CACTM files are CERC/CACTM/ and then whatever follows in the reference. When CACTM stood for the Central Advisory Council for the Ministry from 1959 the files CERC/CACM/ and then whatever follows. Papers relating to the Archbishops' Commission on Training have the preface CTM. Similarly for ACCM and ABM (although ABM papers are not yet available).

Index

Index